The Fourth Regional Plan

The Fourth Regional Plan was created under the leadership of
Scott Rechler, Chair, Regional Plan Association
Rohit T. Aggarwala, Chair, Committee on the Fourth Regional Plan
Thomas Wright, President & CEO, Regional Plan Association

The development of the fourth plan was overseen by
Christopher Jones, Senior Vice President and Chief Planner, Regional Plan Association
Juliette Michaelson, Executive Vice President, Regional Plan Association

Analysis and policy development for the fourth plan was undertaken by RPA's research team.

Values
Pierina Ana Sanchez, Mandu Sen, Robert Freudenberg

Fix the institutions that are failing us
Lead researchers: Christopher Jones and Juliette Michaelson
With contributions from: Richard Barone, Ellis Calvin, Robert Freudenberg, Moses Gates, Melissa Kaplan-Macey, Sarabrent McCoy, Pierina Ana Sanchez, Mandu Sen, Sarah Serpas, Kate Slevin and Julia Vitullo-Martin

Create a dynamic, customer-oriented transportation system
Lead researchers: Richard Barone, Vice President for Transportation, and Jeffrey M. Zupan, Peter W. Herman Chair for Transportation
With contributions from: Allison Henry, Robert Lane, Alyssa Pichardo, Emily Roach, Kate Slevin, and Jackson Whitmore

Rise to the challenge of climate change
Lead researcher: Robert Freudenberg, Vice President for Energy & Environment
With contributions from: Ellis Calvin, Emily Korman, Lucrecia Montemayor, and Sarabrent McCoy

Make the region affordable for everyone
Lead researcher: Moses Gates, Director of Community Planning & Design
With contributions from: Vanessa Barrios, Melissa Kaplan-Macey, Robert Lane, Pierina Ana Sanchez, Mandu Sen, Sarah Serpas, Kate Slevin, and Renae Widdison

Places
Lead designer: Robert Lane, Senior Fellow for Community Design
Lead researcher: Kate Slevin, Vice President for State Programs & Advocacy
With contributions from: Richard Barone, Robert Freudenberg, Moses Gates, Melissa Kaplan-Macey, and Pierina Ana Sanchez

This book and the accompanying website were designed by Ben Oldenburg, Jenny Volvovski, and Hyperakt. Cover Illustration by Matt Lamothe.

Creating the fourth plan also involved help from: Tess Andrew, Kellen Cantrell, Chasity Cooper, Christine Hsu, Christina Kata, Wendy Pollack, Dani Simons, Emily Thenhaus, and the entire RPA team.

Recommended citation
Regional Plan Association, "The Fourth Regional Plan: Making the Region Work for All of Us," 2017.

The Fourth Regional Plan

for the New York-
New Jersey-Connecticut
Metropolitan Area

MAKING THE REGION
WORK FOR ALL OF US

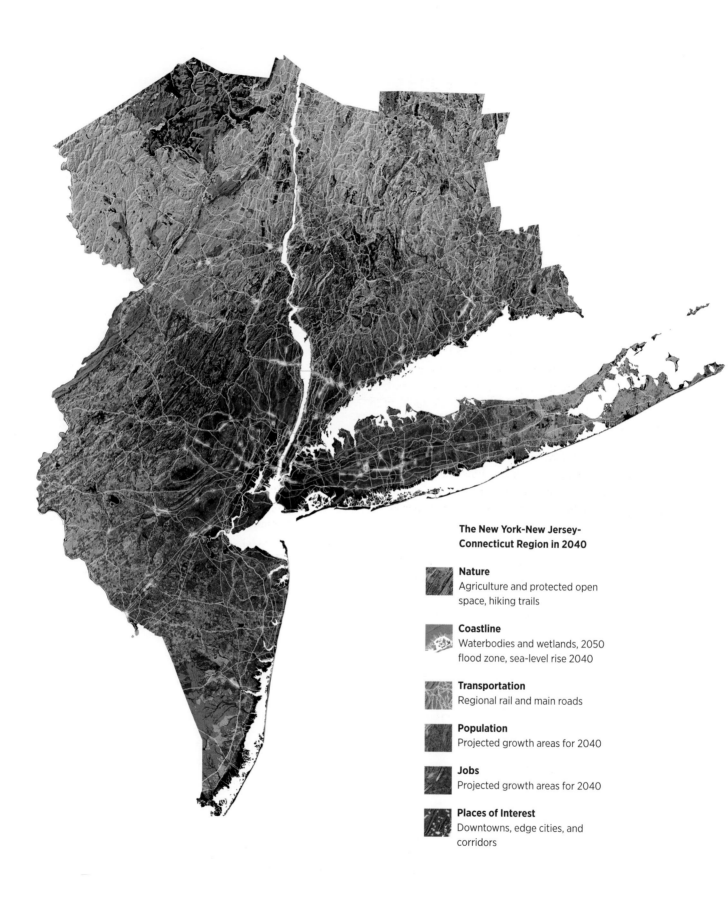

The New York-New Jersey-Connecticut Region in 2040

Nature
Agriculture and protected open space, hiking trails

Coastline
Waterbodies and wetlands, 2050 flood zone, sea-level rise 2040

Transportation
Regional rail and main roads

Population
Projected growth areas for 2040

Jobs
Projected growth areas for 2040

Places of Interest
Downtowns, edge cities, and corridors

Image: ORG Permanent Modernity
for the Fourth Regional Plan

Greetings from RPA leadership

This plan was made by listening to people.

Five years ago, we started conducting surveys, convened focus groups, and talked to a wide range of community, civic, business, and public-sector leaders to better understand the needs and concerns of everyone who calls the metropolitan area home.

What emerged was a paradox.

New Yorkers love where they live, and they believe in the region's future potential. They have seen the region face daunting challenges over the past generation and come back even stronger. This was true for everyone we spoke with: rich and poor, city dweller and suburbanite, young and old, families and single people.

But these people have also lost faith.

Regardless of where they live or how much money they make, many feel their life is too expensive, housing and jobs are too difficult to find, and the social divisions in our society run too deep.

Whether they drive a car to work, take the subway to school, or ride the bus to visit family, people are frustrated by an unreliable transportation system and congested roads. They recall the death and destruction caused by Hurricane Irene and Superstorm Sandy, and worry about the storms to come. And they despair about a future in which these problems will only get worse and threaten the success of their children.

Most distressing is the feeling that we could not solve these problems.

Over the past five years, we have spent considerable time figuring out how to address this loss of confidence. The conclusion is that the biggest challenges we face are not the result of external forces or situations beyond our control. Rather, it is the constraints we put on ourselves and our institutions.

Housing costs are too high primarily because we artificially restrict housing opportunities in the places they make most sense: near train stations and transportation links, close to jobs, and in neighborhoods with plenty of room to grow.

Our transportation system is deteriorating because we fail to invest in improvements and technology, allow costs to spiral out of control, and do not reform how these systems are governed so they function more efficiently and effectively.

Despite the impact of climate change becoming an ever-greater reality, we continue to treat each storm like a once-in-a-lifetime occurrence, instead of preparing for a radically and permanently changed environment that will reshape our region's geography.

We can secure a safe and prosperous future for the next generation if we break free from those constraints. With 23 million people and a $1.8 trillion economy—nearly 10 percent of the entire country's economy—we have the talented people, resources, entrepreneurs, creativity, and leadership to move the region forward.

But first we must shake off our old habits and assumptions and commit to not settling for anything less than the best we can accomplish. And we must have a bold plan of action that considers the needs of everyone in our region.

We offer this Fourth Regional Plan as a roadmap to making the region work for all of us.

Scott Rechler

Rohit T. Aggarwala

Tom Wright

Executive Summary

Over the last generation, the New York metropolitan region has seen sweeping change, much of it for the better. But too many people have not shared in the region's overall success. The Fourth Regional Plan provides both a vision and specific recommendations to promote growth that brings shared prosperity, equity, improved health, and sustainability for the region.

RPA provides a comprehensive perspective on the 31-county New York-New Jersey-Connecticut metropolitan region, an area that extends from Trenton to New Haven, and from Newburgh to the end of Long Island. This coastal region is defined by the housing, transportation and natural systems that sustain the most populous metropolis in the United States and a major hub of the national—and global—economy.

- 23 million residents
- 11 million jobs
- $1.8 trillion economy
- 782 municipalities
- 13,000 square miles
- 2 million acres of protected land
- 3,700 miles of coastline
- 4.3 annual trips by public transportation

The way forward

Our work on the Fourth Regional Plan began by talking with and listening to people from across the region. What we heard was that people loved living here, but also had some serious concerns. Housing was too expensive. Commutes were long and unreliable. The destruction brought by Hurricane Irene and Superstorm Sandy underscored our region's vulnerability to climate change, and raised questions about how prepared we were for the storms to come.

But the most distressing thing we heard was that many people believed these and other problems were just too big to solve.

We have spent the past five years engaged in more discussions and countless hours of research and analysis to better understand these challenges, and to find solutions.

We learned that despite the flourishing economy, future growth is far from guaranteed. The region gained 1.8 million jobs over the past 25 years, but is likely to grow by only half that number over next quarter century. And the growth we've experienced has failed to lift the standard of living for far too many households.

Yet if we change course—if we can provide the housing, commercial space, and infrastructure that is needed for all those who want to live here—the region could gain nearly two million additional jobs by 2040. More importantly, this growth could take place in a way that broadly shares prosperity and well-being, overcomes long-standing inequities, promotes a sustainable environment, and prepares the region for climate change.

Achieving this long-range vision of inclusive growth will require rethinking the institutions that govern the region and oversee its infrastructure.

The Fourth Regional Plan includes 61 specific recommendations to achieve greater equity, shared prosperity, better health, and sustainability. It also represents an important opportunity to continue—and intensify—a civic dialogue that breaks through the short-term thinking of the past.

Current trends would cut economic growth in half, while making the region more crowded and expensive. The region added 800,000 jobs over the past five years, but that's as many as we'll add over the next 25, according to current trends.

Creating more room for sustainable growth would expand economic opportunity and make the region more affordable.

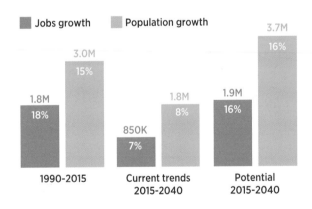

■ Jobs growth   ■ Population growth

1990-2015: Jobs growth 1.8M (18%), Population growth 3.0M (15%)

Current trends 2015-2040: Jobs growth 850K (7%), Population growth 1.8M (8%)

Potential 2015-2040: Jobs growth 1.9M (16%), Population growth 3.7M (16%)

Source: RPA, U.S. Bureau of the Census. U.S. Bureau of Labor Statistics

The current crisis

The region's economy is thriving. After the deep recession of the late 1980s and early 1990s, and the financial crisis of 2008–2009, the tri-state area bounced back. People are choosing to live, work, and visit here. New York City is now one of the safest big cities in the nation. Public health has improved, as has quality of life.

National and global trends toward urbanization have played a part in this renaissance, but intentional policy choices, such as major investment programs in both housing and transit in the 1980s and 1990s, also positioned New York to capitalize on these trends.

But this recent economic success is not guaranteed, and past development trends teach us that growth alone does not always benefit everyone.

For the bottom three-fifths of households, incomes have stagnated since 2000. More people live in poverty today than a generation ago. Those in the middle have fewer good job opportunities and chances to climb the economic ladder. There is greater income inequality in the region than elsewhere in the country.

While household incomes have plateaued, housing costs have risen sharply and are taking a larger share of household budgets. For many people, discretionary income cannot cover critical expenses such as health care, college, child care, and food.

When it becomes too expensive to live here, talented people pick up and leave for more affordable places. It's no coincidence that peak real estate prices in the mid-2000s coincided with the highest recent level of outward migration.

These dual crises of stagnant wages and rising costs are exacerbated by a legacy of discrimination in housing, transportation, education, and other policies that limit opportunities for low-income residents and people of color. Although the tri-state region is one of the most diverse in the country—nearly half of all residents are people of color, and a third are foreign-born—it is also one of the most segregated.

Growth patterns within the region have changed dramatically over the last generation. Many urban areas have been reinvigorated, but that transition has put new strains on city housing markets and suburban economies.

In the second half of the 20th century, suburbs grew quickly as middle-class and affluent city dwellers were able to take advantage of federal and local policies that promoted suburban home ownership. Cities were left behind, and struggled with growing unemployment, poverty, and crime. Over the last two decades, that trend has reversed, as people

Change in median income in the New York region, 2000–2016
Households in the lower three-fifths of the income distribution have seen little or no gains.

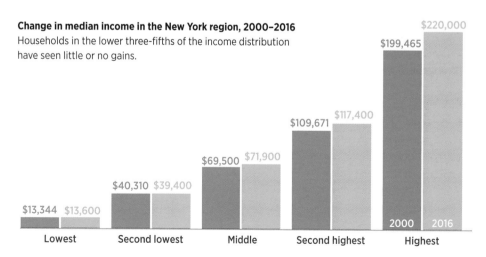

Source: 2000 U.S. Census, 2016 American Community Survey

Many people haven't shared in the region's economic growth over the last two decades.

and jobs returned to New York and well-positioned cities such as Jersey City, White Plains, and Stamford.

For many towns, villages, and rural communities, this reversal has resulted in fewer local jobs, an aging population, and a smaller tax base. And many older, industrial cities are still struggling to grow their economies.

But for New York and other growing cities, the return of jobs and people has presented new challenges: rising real estate prices and rents, families displaced by unaffordable housing, and neighborhoods that longtime residents no longer recognize as their own. This growth has also put additional pressure on the region's aging infrastructure, including subways and roads.

The failure to invest in improvements and build new infrastructure has led to disruptions and unreliable services, which are further strained by the impact of severe storms, heat waves, and catastrophic events such as Superstorm Sandy and Hurricane Irene. Lives are senselessly lost, and the economic toll registers in the billions of dollars.

Metropolitan regions around the world are taking on these problems by investing in neighborhoods and business districts; building modern infrastructure that increases capacity, improves resilience, and boosts economic competitiveness; and adopting innovative solutions to protect coastal areas.

Yet in our region, government institutions fail to make the difficult decisions necessary to address the persistent problems of affordability, opportunity, and resilience.

We haven't amended land-use and building regulations to facilitate the construction of more homes and encourage the development of communities that accommodate families of different incomes. We haven't sufficiently reformed planning, management, or labor practices to reduce the high costs and slow pace of building new infrastructure. We haven't modified tax structures to be more fair and promote a more productive and diversified economy. We haven't built new public transportation to make sure people arrive at their jobs and schools faster. We haven't done enough to update our technology infrastructure and reduce the digital divide. And we haven't invested in the physical and natural systems that make our society and economy more resilient when disaster strikes.

Throughout the region, households are spending a much larger share of their income on rents, mortgage payments, and other housing costs.

Households spending more than 30 percent of their income on housing, 2000 and 2015

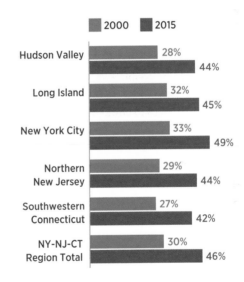

Source: 2000 US Census; 2011-2015 American Community Survey

Vision for the future

The Fourth Regional Plan is guided by four core values that serve as a foundation across issue areas.

Equity

In an equitable region, individuals of all races, incomes, ages, genders, and other social identities have equal opportunities to live full, healthy, and productive lives. The investments and policies proposed by RPA would reduce inequality and improve the lives of the region's most vulnerable and disadvantaged residents.

Goal: By 2040, the tri-state region should sharply reduce poverty, end homelessness, close gaps in health and wealth that exist along racial, ethnic, and gender lines, and become one of the least segregated regions in the nation instead of one of the most segregated.

Health

Everyone deserves the opportunity to live the healthiest life possible, regardless of who they are or where they live. The Fourth Regional Plan provides a roadmap to address health inequities rooted in the built environment to create a healthier future for all.

Goal: By 2040, conditions should exist such that everyone is able to live longer and be far less likely to suffer from mental illness or chronic diseases such as asthma, diabetes, or heart disease, with low-income, Black, and Hispanic residents seeing the greatest improvements.

Prosperity

In a prosperous region, the standard of living should rise for everyone. The actions in the Fourth Regional Plan will create the robust and broad-based economic growth needed to lift all incomes and support a healthier, more resilient region.

Goal: By 2040, the tri-state region should create two million jobs in accessible locations, substantially increase real incomes for all households, and achieve a major boost in jobs and incomes for residents in the region's poorer cities and neighborhoods.

Sustainability

The region's health and prosperity depend on a life-sustaining natural environment that will nurture both current and future generations. To flourish in the era of climate change, the fourth plan proposes a new relationship with nature that recognizes our built and natural environments as an integrated whole.

Goal: By 2040, the region should be nearing its goal of reducing greenhouse gas emissions by 80 percent, eliminating the discharge of raw sewage into its rivers and harbor, and greatly improving its resilience to flooding and extreme heat caused by climate change.

The plan is organized into four action areas that represent major challenges and areas of opportunity.

Institutions

Our infrastructure is deteriorating, and it takes too long and costs too much to fix. Housing policies, local land-use practices, and tax structures are inefficient and reinforce inequality and segregation. Public institutions are slow to incorporate state-of-the-art technology to improve the quality of services. And truly addressing the growing threat of climate change requires investments far more ambitious and strategic than we have made so far. Solving these existential challenges will require public officials and citizens to reassess fundamental assumptions about public institutions.

Transportation

Transportation is the backbone of the region's economy. It is also vital to the quality of life of everyone who lives and works here. But years of population and job growth and underinvestment in both maintenance and new construction have led to congestion, lack of reliability, and major disruptions on a regular basis. Some transportation improvements are relatively quick and inexpensive, such as redesigning our streets to accommodate walking, biking, and buses. But the region also needs to invest in new large-scale projects to modernize and extend the subways and regional rail networks, as well as upgrade airports and seaports. These investments will have far-reaching and positive effects on land use, settlement patterns, public health, goods movement, the economy, and the environment.

Climate change

Climate change is already transforming the region. Reducing the region's greenhouse gas emissions is critical, but it won't be enough. We must accelerate efforts to adapt to the impact of a changing climate.

Today, more than a million people and 650,000 jobs are at risk from flooding, along with critical infrastructure such as power plants, rail yards, and water-treatment facilities. By 2050, nearly two million people and one million jobs would be threatened. We must adapt our coastal communities and, in some cases, transition away from the most endangered areas. We will also need to invest in green infrastructure in our cities to mitigate the urban heat-island effect, reduce stormwater runoff and sewer overflows, and improve the health and well-being of residents.

Affordability

Over the last two decades the tri-state region has become more attractive to people and businesses—but it has also become more expensive. While household incomes have stagnated, housing costs have risen sharply, straining family budgets and resulting in increased displacement and homelessness. What's more, the region's history of racial and economic discrimination has kept many residents away from neighborhoods with quality schools and good jobs. Instead, many live in areas that are unsafe or environmentally hazardous. The region needs quality housing for all income levels in places that have good transit service. It must also invest in smaller cities and downtowns to boost economic opportunities throughout the region.

Key recommendations of the Fourth Regional Plan

The Fourth Regional Plan details 61 recommendations to make our region more equitable, healthy, sustainable, and prosperous. Here is an overview of the most urgent and potentially transformative ideas.

Reform regional transportation authorities and reduce the costs of building new transit projects

The Port Authority of New York and New Jersey, and the Metropolitan Transportation Authority were created in the 1920s and the 1960s to address the challenges of their respective eras. The region has evolved since then, but the agencies haven't. To fix our transportation system and expand capacity, we need to restructure the authorities that manage them.

RPA recommends reforming the governing and operating structures of both the MTA and the Port Authority to ensure they are more transparent, accountable, and efficient. Only then can the agencies regain the public's trust and support for investing in costly new projects.

Specifically, RPA recommends the governor of New York establish a new Subway Reconstruction Public Benefit Corporation to overhaul and modernize the subway system within 15 years, thereby creating a transportation system suitable to meeting the needs of the largest, most dynamic metropolitan area in the nation.

RPA also recommends the Port Authority take immediate steps to depoliticize decision-making. Longer term, the Port Authority should create independent entities to manage the daily operations of its different assets (airports, ports, bus terminal, PATH, bridges, and tunnels). The central Port Authority body could then focus on its function as an infrastructure bank that finances large-scale projects.

Price greenhouse gas (GHG) emissions using California's comprehensive approach

The region has already cut GHG emissions, but reaching the goal adopted by all three states and New York City—reducing emissions 80 percent by 2050—will require more dramatic action. RPA recommends strengthening and expanding the existing carbon pricing system, the Regional Greenhouse Gas Initiative, RGGI, to include emissions from the transportation, residential, commercial, and industrial sectors, as California has done. The three states could eventually join California and other jurisdictions to form a larger and more powerful cap-and-trade market.

The additional revenues that would be generated—potentially $3 billion per year in the three states—could be used to invest in creating an equitable, low-carbon economy and increasing our resilience to climate change.

A Subway Reconstruction Public Benefit Corporation whose sole mission is to overhaul and modernize the subways could transform the system in 15 years.

Establish a Regional Coastal Commission and state adaptation trust funds

Climate change and rising sea levels do not stop at any border, yet resilience efforts so far have been managed at the municipal and state levels, with a complex and overlapping bureaucracy and scattered funding.

RPA recommends New York, New Jersey, and Connecticut create a Regional Coastal Commission that would take a long-range, multi-jurisdictional, and strategic approach to managing coastal adaptation. The states should simultaneously establish Adaptation Trust Funds to provide a dedicated revenue stream for resilience projects. Funding should be determined by the Coastal Commission using a clear set of standards and evaluation metrics that include both local and regional impacts on flooding, ecological conditions, the economy, fiscal conditions, as well as public health and neighborhood stability, particularly for the most vulnerable and those with fewest resources.

Adopting California's approach to pricing greenhouse gas emissions could generate $3 billion a year in new revenue for our region to invest in a greener future.

Increase civic engagement at the local level and make planning and development more inclusive, predictable, and efficient

Local governments are responsible for most of the decisions that shape the daily lives of residents. Yet few residents participate in community decision-making, and those who do are not representative of their communities in terms of race, age, and income level. As a result, local institutions make decisions that often reflect the values and needs of older, wealthier, and mostly White residents rather than the overall population.

In addition, public review processes for development projects are too complex and unpredictable, which increases costs and delays, or prevents too many good projects from being completed. All too often, when government agencies evaluate projects, they fail to adequately consider effects on health, affordability, the economy, and the environment.

RPA recommends local governments engage with the public more effectively by making better use of technology and data, adopting participatory budgeting, and ensuring residents have more influence in decision-making. The planning process should be reformed to engage residents earlier in the process, establish a fixed timeline for community input and government approvals, and incorporate health-impact assessments. These initiatives will lead to decisions that better reflect community needs and aspirations.

Levy charges and tolls to manage traffic and generate revenue

There is no logic to the way we manage our limited road capacity, from the congested streets of Midtown Manhattan to our interstate highways. Now, dozens of state, local, and regional agencies are responsible for these roads, and policies vary widely and seldom use market principles to improve service.

Adding tolls to all crossings into Manhattan south of 60th Street would reduce traffic congestion in the core of the region, make trips by car more reliable and goods delivery more efficient, and free up space for buses, bikes, and pedestrians. Tolls would also generate much-needed revenue for roads and transit.

In addition to this congestion charge for the core of the region, departments of transportation and highway authorities across the region should use tolls to reduce traffic on all highways, which would make driving times more reliable while also generating revenue. Highway and bridge tolls could, in the long term, be replaced with a fee on all vehicle-miles traveled, or with tolls that vary depending on time of day and levels of congestion. Every two cents charged per mile driven on the region's highways would raise about $1 billion a year.

The Meadowlands could become the nation's first national park established to promote climate resilience.

Modernize and expand New York City subways

After decades of underinvestment, the subway system is rapidly deteriorating at a time of record ridership.

RPA recommends the creation of a special public benefit corporation to be in charge of completely modernizing the subway system within 15 years (see recommendation above). Specific proposals include accelerating the adoption of modern signaling systems, and redesigning and renovating stations to reduce crowding, make the ambient environment healthier, and improve accessibility to people with disabilities.

To accomplish these large-scale improvements in a timely way, RPA recommends the MTA adopt policies with a greater tolerance for longer-term outages (as the MTA is already doing for the L train repairs), and evaluate replacing weeknight late-night subway service with robust bus service (when streets are traffic-free). Having longer windows for maintenance work would help keep the system in a state of good repair in the long term.

The MTA should also begin to expand the subway system into neighborhoods with the densities to support fixed-rail transit, particularly low-income areas where residents depend on public transportation. These strategic extensions would provide a better, more time- and cost-effective option for more residents, foster economic opportunities, and reduce traffic congestion. The fourth plan recommends building eight new lines and extensions in four boroughs.

Create a unified, integrated regional rail system and expand regional rail

Outside New York City, our region has three of the busiest commuter rail systems in the country and bus systems that serve millions of local, regional, and long-distance trips. Funding for these systems has not kept pace with growing ridership, and in some cases has been drastically cut. NJ Transit, Metro-North, and the Long Island Rail Road need to scale up operations to serve this increased demand. RPA recommends increasing funding to these entities, and reforming their governance structures to promote innovation and coordination.

RPA also envisions a series of new projects, phased in over the next few decades, to unify the commuter rail system and expand it into a seamless regional transit system. The resulting Trans-Regional Express (T-REX) would provide frequent, reliable service, directly connecting New Jersey, Long Island, the Mid-Hudson, and Connecticut, create new freight-rail corridors, and provide additional transit service to riders within New York City. T-REX would enable the transit system to comfortably serve an additional one million people by 2040, and support a growing regional economy.

Design streets for people and create more public space

RPA recommends cities and towns across the region rebalance their street space to prioritize walking, biking, transit, and goods deliveries over private cars. Managing street space more strategically will be particularly important as shared, on-demand, and, ultimately, driverless vehicles become more commonplace. Cities and towns should take a number of measures to ensure these vehicles improve mobility and don't result in more congestion, including creating protected bus lanes, repurposing parking lanes for bus/bike lanes, rain gardens or wider sidewalks, and "geofencing" particular districts to prevent vehicle use at certain times of day.

Designing streets for people will make lower-cost transportation such as biking, walking, or riding the bus safer and more pleasant, and encourage healthy physical activity. Prioritizing public transportation is particularly important for lower-income residents who disproportionately rely on buses.

RPA also recommends larger, more crowded cities such as New York expand access to public spaces in more creative ways. This could include reopening streets and underground passageways, and integrating some privately owned spaces, such as building lobbies, into the public realm.

Expand and redesign John F. Kennedy and Newark International airports

The region's airports need more capacity to meet growing passenger and freight demand and to maintain economic competitiveness. RPA recommends phasing out Teterboro Airport, which will be permanently flooded by just one foot of sea-level rise. Improvements are already underway at LaGuardia Airport, which over the long term will need to expand capacity to handle larger aircraft.

JFK Airport should be expanded and modernized to include two additional runways, larger and more customer-friendly terminals, and significantly better transit access. Newark International Airport should be reconfigured, moving the main terminal closer to the train station on the Northeast rail corridor and freeing up more space to eventually construct a new runway. These improvements would allow the region's airports to handle a projected 60 percent increase in passengers and reduce delays by 33 percent.

Strategically protect land to adapt to climate change and connect people with nature; establish a national park in the Meadowlands and a regional trail network

Even if we aggressively reduce our carbon emissions, climate change is here to stay. Our coastline will move inland, with up to six feet of sea-level rise possible by the beginning of the next century. There will be more frequent storms and days of extreme heat. To increase the region's resilience to storms, floods, and rising temperatures, we must reconnect our communities to nature.

RPA proposes establishing a national park in the New Jersey Meadowlands, one of the Northeast's largest remaining contiguous tracts of urban open space. The Meadowlands supports a wide array of wildlife and biodiversity, and has the potential to protect surrounding communities from storm surges. A Meadowlands National Park would protect this fragile ecosystem and also help educate the public about climate change adaptation.

Redeveloping underutilized parking lots near rail stations would yield a quarter million new homes for the region.

RPA also calls for creating a 1,620-mile tri-state trail network, building on existing and planned trails and establishing new connections to create a comprehensive network linked with transit. Almost nine million residents would live within a half-mile of a trail—nearly 25 percent more than today.

Create a greener, smarter energy grid

Without significant new investment, the electrical grid will not be capable of handling increased demand due to population and job growth, the digital economy, and electric vehicles. Scaling up production of renewable energy and creating a cleaner, modern grid would also require better coordination among energy providers and regulators across the three states.

RPA recommends creating a Tri-State Energy Policy Task Force to enable a more reliable, flexible, cleaner, and greener network. This task force should develop a comprehensive plan to utilize emerging renewables such as wind, solar, and storage technology; integrate distributed generation; and make the grid smarter and more efficient. As cleaner fuels generate more power, existing electricity-supply facilities—including fast-ramping plants necessary for rapid changes—could be updated and used more effectively.

Proactive management and better design of our streets will make it easier to get around—and create better, healthier neighborhoods.

Preserve and create affordable housing in all communities

Affordability is key to giving everyone in the region the chance to succeed. RPA recommends several actions by all levels of government to protect and increase the supply of homes for households of all incomes, and create affordable housing in all communities. Many of these recommendations will facilitate the creation of new housing without additional funding. RPA also calls on cities and states to be more proactive in protecting vulnerable residents from displacement through policies that generate more permanently affordable housing and increase wealth in lower-income communities.

Municipalities should update zoning to facilitate more housing production, especially near transit. Some common-sense changes include allowing accessory dwellings, which could create 300,000 new units regionwide without any new construction. Others include ensuring all municipalities allow multifamily developments near transit stations, so residents can take advantage of technology-enabled vehicles that minimize the need for parking. Developing existing parking lots in this way would yield a quarter of a million new homes in walkable, mixed-income communities near transit.

These new homes can be accessible to all the region's residents—existing as well as newcomers—by robust enforcement of fair housing protections and a region-wide inclusionary zoning policy, thereby creating diverse, mixed-income communities.

Create well-paying job opportunities throughout the region

Increasing incomes is essential to solving the affordability challenge, and that requires a diverse economy with good jobs in accessible locations for people with a variety of skills and education levels.

Manhattan's central business district (CBD) could become a more powerful engine for the region's economy by expanding to the south, east, and west; preserving Midtown's older, less-expensive office space to accommodate different types of businesses; and creating more mixed-residential and job districts near the CBD.

Cities such as Bridgeport, Paterson, and Poughkeepsie could become regional centers for new jobs in a range of industries, by building on existing urban assets and revitalizing downtowns with financial and policy support from state government.

RPA also recommends municipalities partner with local anchor institutions such as hospitals and universities to develop career pathways for training and hiring local residents. These institutions, which have a great procurement power, can also create and support local supply chains that benefit the surrounding neighborhoods, the city, and the region as whole.

In addition, RPA urges municipalities to preserve existing industrial space for that purpose, while also creating facilities for smaller high-tech manufacturers that will drive industrial job creation in the coming decades.

From plan to implementation

The Fourth Regional Plan looks ahead to the next generation. A long-range plan allows RPA to set our sights high and not be constrained by current political dynamics. But we know a generation is too long to wait for families facing the pressures of rising rents and stagnating wages, for workers facing long and unreliable commutes, and for coastal communities on the front lines of more frequent and extreme flooding.

And so the fourth plan is the long-term strategy that also informs our short-term advocacy efforts.

If we succeed in implementing the vision and recommendations outlined in the Fourth Regional Plan, the region will be more equitable, healthy, sustainable, and prosperous. The plan provides a model for growth that creates a larger tax base to finance new infrastructure, an expanded transit network, more green infrastructure to protect us from the impacts of climate change, as well as sufficient affordable housing and other necessities that together create a virtuous cycle.

Regional Plan Association will build on the partnerships it has created through the development process for this plan to ensure its recommendations are debated, refined, and ultimately implemented. The continued success of the region and all of its residents depends on it.

New funding streams can support the recommendations of this plan.

Addressing these challenges would require significant investment.

The plan recommends ways to reform the way new rail infrastructure projects are designed and built to reduce their cost. The plan also suggests redirecting funding from low-impact programs to more effective ones. With these measures, we will be able to grow the economy, increase the tax base, and generate new revenue.

But even with significant budget savings and a growing economy, more funding would still be needed. RPA proposes new funding streams that would more fairly distribute the burden of taxes, fees, and tolls, while promoting strategic policy goals. These include sustainable patterns of development, more equitable distribution of wealth and income, energy efficiency, and climate resilience.

New or underutilized funding streams identified in this plan include:

- Pricing greenhouse gas emissions to fund climate adaptation and mitigation measures, transit, and investments in environmentally burdened neighborhoods

- Highway tolling and congestion pricing to fund investment in our highways, bridges, and transit

- Value capture from real estate to fund new transit stations or line extensions, as well as more affordable housing near transit

- Insurance surcharges on property to fund coastal climate adaptation

- Reforming housing subsidies to fund more low-income housing

What the future could look like

Jamaica

Bridgeport

Meadowlands

The Far West Side

Triboro Line

Central Nassau

Newburgh

Paterson

Inner Sound

To demonstrate how the policies and projects recommended in this plan could shape the places where we live and work, RPA described potential futures for nine "flagship" places that represent unique communities, built environments, and natural landscapes. In each flagship, we highlight the challenges and opportunities found elsewhere in the region. These narratives are intended to be illustrative and inspirational, rather than prescriptive.

- **Jamaica:** A business and cultural hub with ties to neighboring communities and JFK Airport

- **Bridgeport:** A green and healthy city along the Northeast Corridor

- **Meadowlands:** A national park for the region

- **The Far West Side:** A new anchor for the region's core

- **Triboro Line:** A new transit link for the boroughs

- **Central Nassau:** New transit links for a diverse suburb

- **Newburgh:** A model for equitable and sustainable development in the Hudson Valley

- **Paterson:** Connecting a former factory town to the region's economy

- **The Inner Long Island Sound:** Industry, nature, and neighborhoods in harmony

Values

The region's residents live in vibrant communities, share a common environment, and seek opportunities to better provide for their families. The region is also fragmented into three states and hundreds of municipalities, which often results in limited solutions and short-term thinking. To be true stewards of the region's long-term success, we must define a new path to achieve greater equity and prosperity, improve the health of residents, and secure a more sustainable environment for everyone.

EQUITY

In an equitable region, individuals of all races, incomes, ages, genders, and other social identities have equal opportunities to live full, healthy, and productive lives.

GOAL

By 2040, everyone in the tri-state region should expect to live longer and be far less likely to suffer from mental illness or chronic diseases such as asthma, diabetes, or heart disease—with low-income, Black, and Hispanic residents seeing the greatest improvements.

The investments and policies proposed by RPA would reduce inequality and improve the lives of the region's most vulnerable and disadvantaged residents.

Over the last century, urban planning and both public- and private-sector actions have undermined the basic human value that everyone should be able to live a full, healthy, and productive life, reinforcing the legacy of racism and discrimination in the U.S., and creating the region's geography of segregation, isolation, and inequality.

Policies such as unequal access to financing, restrictive covenants, blockbusting, redlining, and racial steering divided the region into largely poor communities of color and affluent, largely white neighborhoods. The infrastructure that allowed the region to grow created environmental injustices, such as urban highway construction that tore apart immigrant and communities of color, and transportation that served only some parts of the population. These cannot be forgotten, because they shaped where we live, and where we live is directly linked to our access to opportunity: the jobs we can reach, the quality of our health and schools, and ultimately, the success our children can achieve.[1]

Many of these policies exist in different forms today: discrimination in housing still uses source of income or credit scores to weed out applicants; blacklisting excludes renters who have ever been to court regardless of the reason or outcome; exclusionary zoning keeps segregation alive; inequitable school financing perpetuates unequal educational outcomes; energy and environmental policies create unhealthy living conditions; and transit services do not serve all residents equally.

Equity is also critical to the region's future health and prosperity. Metropolitan areas with greater inequality experience slower economic growth than others, perhaps because fewer are able to participate fully in the economy.[2] And racial and economic inequities impede the social cohesion needed to address the crises of declining affordability, failing infrastructure, and climate change. Done right, planning and development that achieves equity for people of diverse social identities could add tens of billions of dollars to the region's economy.[3] Done wrong, growth and technological change will widen the gulf of inequality and weaken the region's competitiveness and prosperity.

Reconnecting planning and equity

The proposals and policies in the plan could significantly expand opportunity and reduce inequality. While the plan's policies cannot alone undo the injustices of the past, its recommendations would lead to housing, jobs, transportation, schools, streets, and parks that serve everyone and explicitly reduce inequities by race and ethnicity, income, and geography. The investments proposed in the plan would also create thousands of jobs and billions of dollars in economic activity, both through immediate construction contracts and jobs and in longer-term economic growth. The distribution of those jobs and economic activity should expressly contribute to the goals of reducing inequality along racial, ethnic, gender, disability status, and other social fault lines of disadvantage. To do this, infrastructure agencies and other implementing entities must directly contribute to greater equity through contracting and procurement practices.

The Fourth Regional Plan proposes the following actions to remedy injustices of the past and present, and create a more equitable future:

Create affordable and fair housing by both strengthening disadvantaged communities and opening up exclusionary places

In 2017, the region ranked as one of the least affordable and most highly segregated regions in the country by both race/ethnicity and income. To have communities that are affordable and provide access to opportunity for everyone, government at all levels must make it possible for low-income and Black and Hispanic residents to both remain and thrive in neighborhoods where they live now, and have the choice to move to neighborhoods where they have been excluded historically:

- Protect low-income residents from being displaced from the urban areas where many reside by building wealth in communities that have suffered through disinvestment, strengthening rent regulations and protections, and ending homelessness by providing legal counsel and increased funding for affordable and supportive housing

- Strengthen and improve fair housing laws because affordable housing policies alone will not end discriminatory practices

- Promote mixed-income, multifamily housing, especially in transit-rich areas, including the region's many smaller cities, towns, and suburban areas

The New York region has the highest level of income
inequality of all major U.S. metropolitan areas, as
measured by the Gini Index of Household Inequality.

	More equal	Less equal	
New York–Northern New Jersey–Long Island, NY-NJ-PA		●	0.502
Miami–Fort Lauderdale–Pompano Beach, FL		●	0.493
Los Angeles–Long Beach–Santa Ana, CA	●		0.484
Houston–Sugar Land–Baytown, TX	●		0.478
Memphis, TN-MS-AR	●		0.478
New Orleans–Metairie–Kenner, LA	●		0.476
San Francisco–Oakland–Fremont, CA	●		0.473
Birmingham–Hoover, AL	●		0.472
United States	●		0.467
Chicago–Naperville–Joliet, IL-IN-WI	●		0.466
Boston–Cambridge–Quincy, MA-NH	●		0.465

0.45 0.46 0.47 0.48 0.49 0.50 0.51

Source: RPA

Gini Index for metropolitan areas
of over 1 million 2005–2009

- Build truly affordable housing in all communities by requiring a share of all multifamily housing be affordable, and fixing subsidy policies to expand both very low-income rental housing and non-predatory low- to middle-income home ownership opportunities

- Ensure all housing is healthy, especially because those most likely to live in older, substandard housing are lower-income residents of color who are already disproportionately likely to suffer from worse health outcomes

Make decisions more inclusively

Across the region, decision-making bodies, from local planning boards to multistate entities and commissions, should be composed of members who more closely reflect the residents they represent. More residents should be able to participate in local elections and decisions, and the decision-making process should fully account for the impact on the health and well-being of everyone. Here is how it could be done:

- Establish standards that reduce economic and health inequities.

- Reform land-use development, transportation, and facilities-siting processes so low-income residents and people of color can help shape projects from inception.

- Allow broader participation in local elections to more closely reflect the demographics of people living in the community.

Reduce inequality by expanding access to economic opportunity

Public investments recommended in the plan should reduce the racial wealth and income gaps, and be combined with actions that reduce discrimination in jobs, education, and access to services. These include reducing the disproportionately high arrest, indictment, and imprisonment rates in communities of color,[4] and improving opportunities for all formerly incarcerated individuals. The plan's recommendations would also help ensure all children have access to a high-quality education. Today, high-performing schools are largely located in high-income communities, and children living in primarily White communities are four times more likely to live near a high-performing school than children living in majority nonwhite neighborhoods. To achieve these outcomes would require the following:

- Promote equitable contracting and procurement practices through all levels of government in transportation, housing, and other capital programs that would increase the number and capacity of minority and disadvantaged business enterprises and their access to capital.

- Invest in effective workforce training programs that target disadvantaged community residents, implementing and enforcing targeted hiring policies.

- Restore regional job centers in low-income cities and promote opportunity for marginalized communities by investing in workforce development and cooperative businesses for existing residents and capitalizing on existing urban assets.

- Reduce property taxes for those least able to pay them, and consolidate and better fund school districts to help give everyone access to a quality education.

- Eliminate the digital divide with universal access to affordable, high-speed internet.

Create new relationships between communities, industry, and nature to provide dignified, productive, and ecologically sustainable livelihoods

Future economic growth should reverse the undue burden of environmental costs that previous development placed on low-income communities and communities of color. These areas house a disproportionate number of waste-transfer stations, power-generation plants, trash incinerators, landfills, regional sewage-treatment plants, and contaminated sites, and experience high levels of noise, air and water pollution, lack of green space and waterfront access, and related health problems. Black and Hispanic residents in these communities face disproportionate rates of lead poisoning and asthma.[5] Principles of environmental justice—rooted in the belief that all people, regardless of race/ethnicty, income, age, gender, or other social identity have the right to a clean and healthy environment in which to live, work, learn, play, and pray—should guide a just transition in which affected workers and communities are equal partners in a well-planned shift from fossil fuels to clean energy. To accomplish this, the region will need to undertake the following:

- Transform historically environmentally burdened neighborhoods into healthy communities by reducing pollution from ports, airports, trucks, and highways, and transitioning from polluting energy sources and incorporating cumulative impact considerations in environmental decision-making.

- Ensure our most vulnerable residents and communities are protected from extreme weather events that cause flooding and extreme heat, and have the ability to adapt and thrive in the time of climate change.

- Set aggressive goals to arrive at a low-carbon economy, while prioritizing resources toward vulnerable, disadvantaged, and frontline communities and workers

- Transition justly to a clean-energy future, ensuring grassroots and advocacy organizations are involved in the decision-making processes

- Remediate environmental hazards as the region repurposes its auto-dependent landscapes

- Connect urban neighborhoods with parks and greenery and an easily accessible regional trail network to allow everyone to benefit from the region's open spaces and natural beauty.

Invest in transportation to link everyone to more opportunities, while lowering costs for those with the least ability to pay

Communities that were once divided and blighted by urban highways should be reconnected. Access to commuter rail and public transportation should become more equitable across the region, with respect to affordability and also access to service. In 2017, MetroCards were unaffordable for one in four New Yorkers.[6] By 2040, the region's transit should enable social mobility more than ever before. This could be accomplished by the following:

- Reconnect communities divided by highway construction. The Cross Bronx Expressway, the Gowanus Expressway, the downtown New Haven portion of Interstate 91, and Route 280 in Orange and Newark are prime examples of transportation infrastructure erected at the expense of often thriving communities, many immigrant and of color, that can be decked over, buried, or removed to reverse the legacies of blight, divided communities, and pollution.

- Rebuild the subway system to reach underserved areas and improve access for the disabled and elderly without displacing long-term residents.

- Create world-class bus service that employs the best available technologies to better serve urban areas, including outside of NYC.

- Prioritize regional rail improvements with service and pricing configurations that benefit lower-income communities so they can affordably access jobs in places farther away.

- Ensure new on-demand car services are affordable to low- to moderate-income residents.

HEALTH

Everyone deserves the opportunity to live the healthiest life possible, regardless of who they are or where they live.

GOAL

By 2040, everyone in the tri-state region should live longer and be far less likely to suffer from mental illness or chronic diseases such as asthma, diabetes, or heart disease, with low-income, Black, and Hispanic residents seeing the greatest improvements.

Life expectancy has risen, but the residents of some communities still live significantly longer than others. Factors related to place, such as school quality, walkability, and air pollution, affect people's health—and these vary greatly across the region.

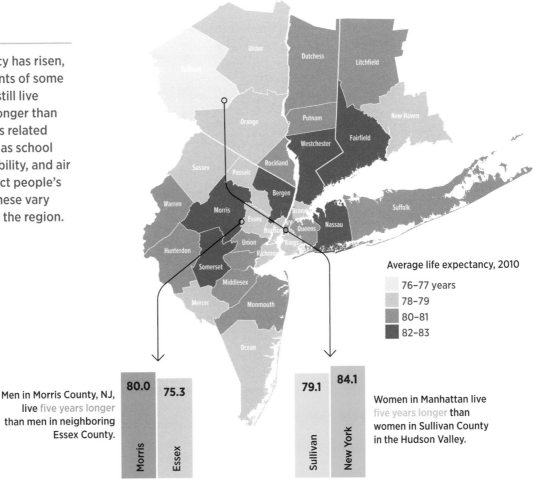

Average life expectancy, 2010

- 76–77 years
- 78–79
- 80–81
- 82–83

Men in Morris County, NJ, live five years longer than men in neighboring Essex County.

80.0 Morris
75.3 Essex

79.1 Sullivan
84.1 New York

Women in Manhattan live five years longer than women in Sullivan County in the Hudson Valley.

Source: Institute for Health Metrics & Evaluation

The Fourth Regional Plan provides a roadmap to address health inequities rooted in the built environment and create a healthier future for all.

Recent improvements in health across the New York region have not benefited everyone.[7] Too many health challenges are concentrated in poor communities of color, due in large extent to planning and other policy decisions.

Many factors contribute to the health of residents, including where affordable housing and roads are built, the transit system and other infrastructure, and preparedness for climate change. Yet planning decisions continue to prioritize efficiency over health and well-being, or reflect institutional racism and other biases. These attitudes were reproduced in many policies and practices, such as discriminatory housing policies that led to the tri-state region having one of the highest levels of segregation in the United States.[8] As a result, low-income residents and people of color are far more likely to be isolated from the resources and opportunities needed to live healthy lives.

We can reduce health inequities by making different investments and policy decisions. We can create better health outcomes in marginalized communities, while expanding our economy and protecting our environment.

After all, connecting planning and health isn't a new idea. Modern urban planning began largely in response to infectious-disease epidemics. The development of sanitation and water systems, parks, and building codes saved countless lives. The connection between planning and health was recognized in the New York metropolitan region as well. As Thomas Adams, who led the development of RPA's 1928 "Regional Plan of New York and Its Environs," told the American Public Health Association in 1926, health was "the first object," the key goal of regional planning.[9]

Reconnecting planning and health

The Fourth Regional Plan would restore the connection between planning and health with actions that would correct past injustices and improve the lives of coming generations. As described below, the plan's recommendations seek to intentionally improve health while addressing challenges in four key areas: climate change, transportation, affordability, and governance.

Reform institutions to incorporate health into decision-making

Institutional reform is a precondition to the implementation of any plan. This presents an opportunity to embrace a "culture of health." Agencies would recognize they are responsible for the public's health and make decisions through the lens of health equity. Health impact assessments would be commonplace and funding tied to outcomes. Communities would shape their own future and the health sector would be a key stakeholder in decision-making. To achieve these outcomes would require the following:

- Reorient our transit agencies toward health as part of the transformation of the way we govern and pay for transportation. Agencies should set health as a goal when evaluating planning and capital budget decisions. Health equity and the full range of social determinants of health, where relevant, should be considered. A chief health officer could promote a health agenda within the organization, guide implementation, and serve as a link to the health sector.

- Integrate health into the core missions of newly created institutions to tackle climate change. A new regional coastal commission should use health as a lens through which to communicate about climate change, and health should be incorporated into the funding criteria of an adaptation trust fund. Expanded carbon pricing together with investment in community led efforts could help ensure reductions in carbon emissions benefit the communities most exposed.

- Leverage reforms to the local planning process to make it more inclusive, predictable, and efficient to include health. Engage from the get-go all community members, especially those not traditionally included in decision-making. Incorporate health impact assessments —and technical support for them—into master planning. Leverage universities and hospitals to spur neighborhood reinvestment and promote partnerships between anchor institutions and local communities by engaging them as key partners in the process.

- Integrate health into the public realm through a new 21st century regional census agency. Start by developing consistent measures of street and public space conditions related to health. As data-driven decision-making advances, these measures could serve as inputs in street-management decisions. Prioritize street redesigns in low-income communities as a tool to improve health and increase participation in local government.

Rebuild and expand the transportation network to serve everyone

A rebuilt and expanded transportation system would connect more low-income communities, be usable by all, and limit negative environmental impacts. New rail service would open up the region's downtowns to more jobs and other opportunities, and enable more walkable communities. New York City's subways would be safer, cleaner, quieter, and fully accessible to people with disabilities. The region's bus system would be fast, reliable, and integrated with other transportation options. Fewer communities would be burdened by poor air quality. And safer streets would have more room for more people of all abilities to enjoy the health benefits of walking and biking. Achieving these outcomes would require the following:

- Create a regional public transportation network by using commuter rail to connect job centers and underserved areas throughout the region with fast, reliable service and fare structures that allow more people to afford it.

- Increase the subway's capacity and reliability. Improve the riding experience by adopting new technology for fast, reliable subway service and make riding the subway a better experience by creating spacious and healthier subway stations and making them accessible to all.

- Extend and build new subway lines to underserved areas, such as the Third Avenue corridor in the Bronx, neighborhoods along Northern Boulevard in Queens, and Utica Avenue in Brooklyn.

- Expand the transit system. Provide more and better transit options in suburban areas with affordable, on-demand service and reform and expand the paratransit system.

- Improve bus service and introduce new streetcar and light rail lines in both urban and suburban areas, connecting communities, reducing auto traffic, and promoting walkable neighborhoods.

- Remove, bury, or deck over highways that blight communities of color and repurpose them to serve the communities they are in and expand nature into urban areas.

- On city streets, prioritize people over cars by closing certain streets to cars, limiting parking in others, prioritizing pedestrians, cyclists, and sustainable transit, and making goods movement more efficient, thus reducing congestion, air pollution, and noise.

Meet the challenge of climate change by creating a healthier environment

Preparing for climate change would prevent countless injuries and deaths from extreme heat and flooding, and fewer people would be displaced or live in damaged homes. Cleaner air and water would reduce disease. And many more people, especially communities of color, would enjoy the region's abundant nature and open spaces. To achieve these outcomes would require the following:

- Create a greener and greater energy system. Modernize the electrical grid to sharply reduce carbon emissions by charging industry and consumers for the amount of carbon they produce, and investing in building energy efficiency, electric-vehicle infrastructure, and renewable energy sources.

- Protect densely populated communities along the coast from storms and flooding by deploying natural and built infrastructure and transitioning people away from places that can't be protected in a way that preserves social cohesion.

- Mitigate the urban heat island effect. Reduce rising temperatures in urban areas by creating new design guidelines and community greening initiatives to cool our communities.

- Connect open spaces. Create a tri-state trail network that connects people who have limited mobility and those without cars to nature via accessible walking and biking trails.

Create affordable and healthy communities

Measures such as fair-housing rules enforcement, land trusts, and support for homeownership will ensure that in the future, growth in the region happens in a way that benefits existing residents, particularly communities of color. More high-quality housing, jobs, public spaces, and services will result in more communities where living a healthy life is the easy choice. To achieve these outcomes would require the following:

- Provide affordable housing for all incomes, ages, races, and ethnicities through strategies such as mandatory inclusionary housing across the region, enforcement of fair-housing rules, reforms to housing subsidies programs, and incentives for transit-oriented development.

- Protect low-income residents from displacement and homelessness by preserving existing affordable housing, strengthening tenant rent protections and homeowner protections, and enabling existing residents to capture more of the wealth created from rising property values.

- Make all housing healthy housing by adopting routine inspections for health hazards in at-risk communities, new technology to detect problems, and streamlined remediation processes that address multiple hazards at once.

- Expand access to more well-paying jobs by prioritizing investments in older cities and downtowns, preserving manufacturing, and expanding affordable internet access across the region.

- Expand healthy, affordable food access in the region by prioritizing the needs of food-insecure communities, supporting a diversity of food options, and integrating food planning into regional institutions.

If implemented, these actions could help everyone lead the healthiest life possible, regardless of who they are or where they live. But for that to happen, broad consensus around challenging topics will be necessary. Health could be a way to build new alliances, promote equity, understand the true value of different investments, and promote civic engagement.

PROSPERITY

In a prosperous region, the standard of living should rise for everyone.

GOAL

By 2040, the tri-state region should create 2 million jobs in accessible locations, substantially increase real incomes for all households, and achieve a major boost in jobs and incomes for residents in the region's poorer cities and neighborhoods.

The actions in Fourth Regional Plan will create the robust and broad-based economic growth needed to lift all incomes and support a healthier, more resilient region.

The region's economy is stronger than it has been at any time since the 1960s. More than a million jobs have been created since the end of the 2008–2009 financial crisis, and the tri-state area is recognized as one of the world's leading metropolitan economies.

Yet this hard-won success is fragile. The transportation infrastructure that keeps the economy moving is deteriorating, and has little capacity to handle more people or goods. The rising cost of housing threatens to make the region too unaffordable to support all but the highest-paying jobs. And land-use and financing regulations often make it too difficult to create new jobs where they are needed most.

Recent growth has also not resulted in broadly shared prosperity. As in the rest of the country, incomes at the top have soared while stagnating for low- and middle-income households. And while New York City has seen its fastest job growth in decades, growth has slowed markedly in the smaller cities and towns in Connecticut, New Jersey, and the New York suburbs.

Reconnecting growth and prosperity

An expanding economy is essential to reducing poverty, lifting household incomes, and improving infrastructure and public services. But simply growing the economy isn't enough. Jobs need to pay enough for the average worker to get ahead. Low-income residents need the education, skills, and access to reach the middle class. Housing, taxes, and other expenses need to leave enough income left over to have a good quality of life. Public transportation, schools, health care, parks, and other public goods need to expand opportunity for those who can't afford private services.

The growing disconnect between growth and prosperity is a global crisis with a wide range of causes, from the automation of jobs that used to pay a living wage and didn't require a college degree to international markets that reduce the bargaining power of workers and suppliers.

From 1975 to 2005, nearly 9 out of every 10 new jobs in the region went to places outside of New York City. From 2005 to 2015, this was completely reversed with New York City capturing 87% of job growth.

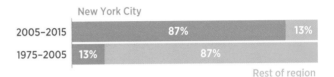

New York City

2005–2015	87% 13%
1975–2005	13% 87%

Rest of region

Source: U.S. Bureau of Labor Statistics, Moody's.com, RPA

This changing nature of work is particularly acute in the tri-state region, where middle-skill jobs are declining even faster than in the U.S. as a whole. Technology is accelerating this trend, and future disruption is all but certain. Driverless cars, for example, could displace up to a quarter million workers who drive or park cars and trucks.

Reconnecting growth and prosperity will also strengthen the bonds between prosperity, health, and the environment. Economic prosperity can only be sustained with an environment that can support a healthy population. A prosperous economy, in turn, should promote good health and a resilient natural environment. The proposals in the Fourth Regional Plan would reinforce a virtuous cycle of prosperity, health, and sustainability. Its infrastructure and energy proposals would create a low-carbon economy that creates jobs as it lowers air pollution and improves health. The plan would build the economy around walkable, transit-friendly places that bring high value, promote physical activity, and help curb urban sprawl and preserve open spaces.

Fortunately, there is much the region can do to both increase economic growth and help more people benefit from that growth. While the region's institutions can't change the trajectory of the global economy, they can expand the number and diversity of job opportunities, and provide more residents with the resources and access necessary to benefit from those opportunities.

Increase in population and jobs within a half-mile of existing subway or commuter rail station, 2015-2040

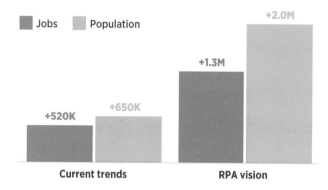

■ Jobs ■ Population

+520K +650K **Current trends**

+1.3M +2.0M **RPA vision**

Sources: Regional Plan Association; U.S. Census America Community and Longtitudinal Employer-Household Dynamics data

Transit investments and transit-oriented development can attract most of the region's new jobs and housing. Locating new development within a half-mile of a subway or commuter rail station will reduce both automobile use and the time and cost of travel. It will also increase the number of jobs within a reasonable commute distance of workers and expand the labor force available to employers.

Invest in infrastructure

States, municipalities, and regional authorities need to invest in infrastructure that both expands the growth potential of the economy and improves access to jobs and other opportunities.

- Rebuild the subway system that anchors the region's economy by adopting new technology for fast, reliable service, modernizing and refurbishing New York City's subway stations, and extending and building new subway lines to give underserved neighborhoods greater access to jobs.

- Create a fully integrated, regional transit system that includes a unified regional rail network that expands capacity for growth, greatly improves travel times and reliability, supports job growth in downtowns throughout the region, and makes commuter rail service available and affordable for riders with low-incomes.

- Reduce the cost of building transit megaprojects to build needed projects faster and cheaper.

- Create world-class airports and seaports, including the expansion and redesign of Kennedy and Newark airports, that will keep the region competitive with other world cities.

- Expand affordable internet service across the region to help close the digital divide and equip more residents with the tools to thrive in a technologically advanced economy.

- Modernize the energy grid to reliably supply an energy-efficient economy that will have a rapidly growing need for electric power.

- Reduce greenhouse gas emissions with a cap-and-trade market modeled on California's program to spur energy-efficient industries and create a revenue stream to fund the region's infrastructure needs.

Create more affordable homes

Metropolitan regions that expand their supply of inexpensive housing have faster job growth and more equitable income distributions. Cities, towns, and villages in the tri-state region need to lift constraints on creating affordable homes to allow the region to support more middle-income jobs:

- Remove barriers to transit-oriented and mixed-use development including zoning, financing, and other regulations that prevent the region from building enough homes to bring down the cost of housing.

	Car-dependent	Somewhat walkable	Walkable
Current trends	53%	19%	28%
RPA vision	30%	22%	48%

Two-thirds of all new housing can be built in pedestrian-friendly communities with access to fresh food, parks, libraries, and other amenities.

Source: Regional Plan Association; 2014 Walkscore®

- Increase housing supply without constructing new buildings by making it easier to have second and third units in single-family homes and reducing disincentives to keep available homes off the market.

- Remake underutilized auto-dependent landscapes to turn aging shopping malls, industrial parks, and commercial strips into vibrant corridors of transit-oriented jobs and housing.

Support diverse local economies

The powerful economic forces that are disrupting industries and eliminating low-skill and mid-level jobs make it even more essential to support diverse local economies that provide a broad range of career opportunities.

- Restore regional jobs centers outside of Manhattan to expand access to jobs and strengthen the economies of declining cities.

- Make room for the next generation of industry to maintain essential industrial services and maximize the number of well-paying jobs in production and distribution.

- Create partnerships between local communities and anchor institutions such as hospitals and universities to create strong neighborhood economies.

- Support and expand community-centered arts and culture to expand creative industries at both a regional and neighborhood scale.

Support racially and economically integrated schools and communities

Educational attainment remains the strongest predictor of economic success for both individuals and metropolitan areas. Regional strategies can support improvements in education by promoting racially and economically integrated schools and communities that have closed the gap in academic achievement.

- Build affordable housing throughout the region to promote mixed-income communities.

- Strengthen and enforce fair-housing laws to ensure everyone has access to places with affordable housing, good schools, and safe streets.

- Create regional school districts and services to facilitate high-performing, and racially and economically integrated schools that will improve educational outcomes.

SUSTAINABILITY

The region's health and prosperity depends on a life-sustaining natural environment that will nurture both current and future generations.

GOAL

By 2040, the region should be approaching its goal of an 80 percent reduction in greenhouse gases, and have eliminated the discharge of raw sewage into its rivers and harbor, and greatly improved its resilience to flooding and extreme heat.

T o flourish in the era of climate change, the fourth plan proposes a new relationship with nature—one that recognizes our built and natural environments as an integrated whole.

Sustainable development is defined as meeting "the needs of the present without compromising the ability of future generations to meet their own needs."[10] For the tri-state region, this means adding more affordable housing, expanding jobs and economic opportunity, and modernizing our infrastructure in ways that preserve and enhance our natural landscapes, make efficient use of land and resources, and make our air and water cleaner than they are today. It also means correcting the mistakes of the past that have left many communities to suffer heavy burdens of environmental hazards and injustices, threatening the health of their inhabitants and the region's capacity for sustainable growth.

And as the effects of climate change become increasingly severe, the need for sustainable development takes on greater urgency and complexity. The challenge is no longer to preserve the environment we have today, but to plan for the environment of the future. Making communities, infrastructure, and ecosystems resilient to change and disruption is as important as using our existing resources wisely.

In many ways, the tri-state region has one of the most sustainable economies in the United States. It generates 10 percent of the nation's economic output on less than half a percent of its land. Its population density and extensive transit network allow it to be more energy and resource efficient than most other parts of the United States. Yet its land, air, and water quality have been degraded by more than two centuries of industrialization and decades of auto-dependent sprawl, and future development will put additional strain on natural resources.

Reconnecting nature and the built environment

As the region grows over the coming decades, it is critical that we recognize that the built environment is intricately linked to the natural world. In fact, open and natural spaces are as valuable to our region as transportation infrastruc-

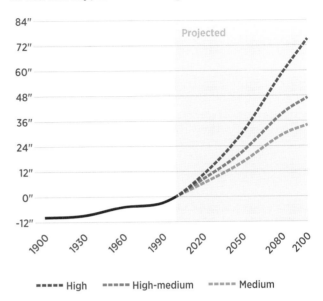

Historic sea-level rise observations and future projections for New York City / Lower-Hudson region

Source: Adapted from NPCC and New York State projections

Note: The Low scenario developed by the NPCC is not included in this chart. That scenario is dependent on a radical and immediate reduction in carbon emissions that is considered by many experts to be unrealistic, and most consider the Medium scenario to be the lower range of what may occur.

ture or any economic-development project. The return on investing in open and natural spaces is quite literally the food and water we consume and the clean air we breathe. And these resources both mitigate and help adapt to climate change by storing carbon, absorbing millions of gallons of stormwater, providing buffers that protect from storm surge and sea-level rise, and providing natural cooling to reduce extreme heat.

The proposals in the fourth plan would help restore a symbiotic relationship between the natural and built environment. They would reinforce growth where good transit service exists; reduce the number of miles traveled by cars and trucks, and accelerate the transition to clean fuels; ensure development is planned with health and access to nature in mind; create strong incentives to reduce the amount of greenhouse gas we emit; and restore and protect the natural systems that are critical to slowing and adapting to climate change.

Energy-generation capacity (MW) in the region

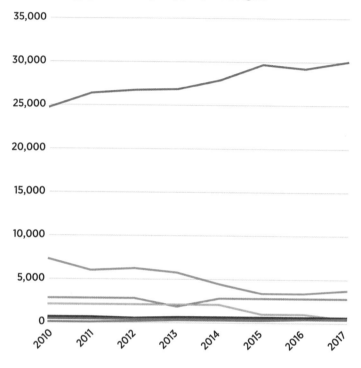

Change in generation-capacity share

—— Natural gas	11.8%	
—— Oil	-9.6%	
—— Nuclear	-0.2%	
—— Coal	-4.5%	
—— Hydro	0.0%	
	0.2%	
—— Renewables	1.0%	
—— Solar	1.4%	

Grow in ways that consume less open space and reduce greenhouse gas emissions

The most sustainable places in the region are those that are already developed. Higher concentrations of people and infrastructure make for communities that are more efficient in their use of energy, water, and other natural resources. Proposals in the fourth plan would advance solutions that encourage growth in already developed places around expanded and improved transit—from rural and suburban downtowns to urban centers.

- Remove barriers to transit-oriented and mixed-use development.

- Reduce reliance on local property taxes.

- Make a globally competitive central business district.

- Restore our regional job centers.

- Remake underutilized auto-dependent landscapes.

- Create a fully integrated regional transit system.

- Modernize the subways.

- Modernize transit systems outside of New York City.

- Improve bus service, and add new light rail and street-car lines.

- Expand suburban transit options with affordable, on-demand service.

- Reduce highway congestion without adding new lanes.

Protect open space for life-sustaining natural resources

As policies focus on growth in developed places, we must also protect the region's most important open spaces. Proposals in the fourth plan would prioritize unprotected land that provides food and recreation opportunities, stores carbon, collects storm- and floodwaters, and ensures abundant supplies of clean drinking water. It would also connect land and water systems to allow for endangered species to migrate and ensure redundancies for a more uncertain future—and to connect more communities to nature.

- Prioritize the protection of land to help adapt to a changing climate.

- Establish a national park in the Meadowlands.

- Create a regional trail network.

- Connect the region's water supply systems.

Maximize the power of nature and natural systems in and around our communities

The greatest impacts of climate change—extreme heat, flooding, and storm damage—are exacerbated where natural systems have been compromised or eliminated. The Fourth Regional Plan proposes solutions that would result in additional trees and vegetation to cool urban neighborhoods, increase wetlands, oyster reefs, and other coastal edge habitat that absorb floodwaters and mitigate the impact of waves, and more green infrastructure on our streets to capture storm water and limit the pollutants that foul waterways.

- Cool our communities.

- Stop discharging raw sewage and other pollutants into the region's waterways.

- Restore the region's harbor and estuaries.

Reduce the risks and impacts of climate change

The reality of climate change requires strategies to mitigate impact and adapt our natural environment and infrastructure. The Fourth Regional Plan recommends the region reduce greenhouse gas emissions by expanding the market for greenhouse gases by regulating automobiles and industry; change how we source, convert, and use energy in all its forms; and usher in a cleaner and more reliable energy grid. Our developed coastal areas would experience the greatest changes as sea levels rise and coastal storms become more intense and frequent. A new model of governance—a Regional Coastal Commission—funded by new state adaptation trust funds, would ensure risk in these places is limited, in a cohesive way, through protection, retreat, or innovative ways of living with water.

- Reduce greenhouse gas emissions with a cap-and-trade market modeled after California's program.

- Modernize the electrical grid.

- Scale up renewable energy sources.

- Manage demand with energy-efficient buildings and variable pricing.

- Electrify buildings and vehicles.

- Establish a regional coastal commission.

- Institute climate adaptation trust funds in all three states.

- Protect densely populated communities along the coast from storms and flooding.

- Transition away from places that can't be protected.

- Determine the costs and benefits of a regional surge barrier.

Actions

Progress cannot be maintained if we do not address a number of fundamental challenges. Income inequality is growing, and our infrastructure is deteriorating. We are more vulnerable to natural disasters. And our government often fails to make the tough decisions to fix our most pressing problems. The Fourth Regional Plan offers long-term strategies and short-term actions to ensure every resident can live in affordable, healthy communities and fulfill the promise of opportunity for all.

Fix the institutions that are failing us

Most of the public institutions that govern the region were established in a different era. Because of this legacy, the region's 782 municipalities are responsible for critical decisions about land use, property taxes, and schools—despite this structure increasing costs, inducing sprawl, and exacerbating inequality. Our transit system, for example, is technologically outdated and cannot keep pace with a growing ridership, as the institutions that oversee the subways, trains, and buses are not empowered to properly invest in and upgrade infrastructure. When faced with new challenges such as climate change, public institutions are slow to take action, and do so piecemeal and without adequate funding.

Solving such daunting problems will require public officials and citizens to reassess fundamental assumptions about public institutions. Empowered to serve the region and its residents, these bodies can and should be reformed to accelerate progress toward solving today's major challenges of affordability, infrastructure investment, and climate change resilience.

TRANSFORM THE WAY WE GOVERN AND PAY FOR TRANSPORTATION

The region's network of buses, commuter rail lines, and subways has not kept up with the tremendous growth in demand for living and working in dense, walkable communities that depend on public transportation. Despite limited new investments, on the whole, service has gotten worse. Delays and disruptions are rising, debt is increasing, maintenance and repairs are pushed off, and major capacity-expansion proposals are over budget and behind schedule—or simply not on the table at all. Meanwhile, our roads and highways, many of which are in deteriorating condition, are constantly congested.

The institutional and funding structures we have today are not capable of delivering an efficient transportation network, and should be reformed. Reducing the cost of building new projects is essential to improving the transportation network. Decision-making and regulatory and labor practices should be updated to deliver projects faster and cheaper. Agencies and authorities need to be restructured to improve accountability and prioritize service delivery and accountability. Congestion should be managed far more effectively by charging drivers in the region's Central Business District, and ultimately, on other highways and roads.

① Reduce the cost of building rail transit

Photo: MTA / Patrick J. Cashin

Rail transit projects cost more and take longer to build in the New York region than anywhere else in the world. For transit riders as well as taxpayers, that means higher costs, less reliable service, and a system that fails to reach many areas or provide affordable and frequent connections. Without a world-class transit system, access to jobs, workers, and services becomes limited and efforts to establish sustainable and energy-efficient land use are weakened. To build the next generation of transportation and other infrastructure the region needs, we must reform the entire process of building new infrastructure—from how political leaders set priorities to procurement practices and labor work rules.

The way we build large-scale transit infrastructure is too expensive and takes too long.

The huge cost of new transit infrastructure will make it nearly impossible to expand and modernize the region's overcrowded subways and commuter rails, undermining economic growth and failing to serve outlying communities. Other global cities are pressing their advantages, attracting new business, and building important economically driven infrastructure.

These extraordinarily high costs are not the fault of any single institution or individual. They reflect decades of planning and building practices, such as complicated site logistics, counterproductive regulations, complex codes, institutional inefficiencies, bonding requirements, and outdated labor practices.

As the high costs contributing to the slow pace of project delivery increase and project schedules are continually stretched, public confidence in government to deliver improvements erodes. Budgets are surpassed, deadlines are missed, and the responsible agencies struggle to complete projects.

Cost overruns and long completion times are particularly onerous when building subways and other rail transit. East Side Access (ESA), for example, cost over $519 million per mile for tunneling and track, compared with $107 million per track mile for London's new Crossrail project. With subways and commuter rails already over capacity, and the population expected to grow by four million people and two million jobs by 2040, costs and delays will only add to the frustrations of riders. And completing critical projects such as the Gateway tunnels connecting New York and New Jersey, and extending the Second Avenue Subway (SAS), will be more difficult.

Every aspect of the project-delivery process contributes to high costs and delays. Based on detailed analysis of the MTA's three megaprojects—#7 Line Extension, Second Avenue Subway, and East Side Access—high costs were driven by the political processes that govern construction, agency management and practices, and labor work rules that determine how projects are staffed and built.

- Politics and public processes lead to inaccurate budgets and timelines, lengthy environmental reviews that undervalue the economic and environmental costs of project delays, and planning decisions that engage community and business stakeholders too late in the process.

- Institutional practices include limited constructability assessments and excessive customization, fractured construction management, and an overly complex procurement process.

- Labor practices include out-of-date work rules that lead to excessive staffing and unproductive work time, requirements to use operations workforce on construction projects, and limited training capacity that is worsened by an uneven pipeline of projects that interrupts the flow of steady of work.

The entire process of budgeting, designing, bidding, and building transportation megaprojects needs to be reformed.

While the following recommendations pertain specifically to building new rail transit, many are applicable to other types of infrastructure construction.

Achieving these reforms will be difficult, requiring strong political leadership, good-faith labor-management negotiations, and a willingness to re-examine long-standing procedures and practices that have outlived their original purpose. The most critical actions include the following:

- **Make constructability a top priority of a rationalized environmental review system.** The environmental review often results in project scopes or mitigation that greatly increase construction costs, such as when access to construction sites is limited to locations and times that extend the time it takes to complete the project. While these restrictions are based on legitimate concerns, the costs of mitigation on project timelines and benefits should be weighed against community and environmental impacts; and international best practices should influence reforms that make environmental review simpler and more transparent. Federal, state, and local environmental reviews should include an independent analysis to evaluate the potential costs and disruption to surrounding communities against the costs, both financial and environmental, of the most cost-effective construction plan. Costs to the project should be given equal weight to disruption and other non-project costs.

- **Engage the public early in sustained, substantive discussion.** Environmental review is not a public-engagement strategy, and is limited to public hearings on technical documents conducted well after projects have been largely selected and designed. To get broad acceptance of system improvements, the MTA must engage the public with greater frequency, clarity, and transparency. The MTA's extensive outreach to stakeholders, as part of the planned 15-month L-train outage, is taking place years before the start of construction—an approach the agency should replicate. Another best practice adopted by the MTA is the early opening of local community outreach and education centers, such as the Second Avenue Subway Community Information Center recently opened on 125th Street and Park Avenue. These effective new efforts must be supported and expanded.

- **Adopt London's project delivery model.** Every megaproject should have a temporary organization with a focused mission of meeting project schedules. This Special Purpose Delivery Vehicle (SPDV) could be modeled on the London Underground's complex Elizabeth Line project, which was delivered on time and on budget. The SPDV would enable construction professionals more authority and accountability to control budgets, such as by giving them the ability to require supplemental funding from any agency that proposes any costly changes.

- **Maximize the land-use development potential of transportation investments.** Future megaprojects should incorporate land-use and zoning changes to capture the value created through development opportunities, while working with local communities to protect residents from displacement (link to Comm-1). New York did this as part of the #7 Line extension, in which the city prepared a former industrial area to be redeveloped into a mixed-use commercial center. ESA and SAS, whose economic impacts are more diffuse, could have leveraged redevelopment opportunities at new or existing stations to help pay for the project while at the same time addressing the region's housing and job needs.

- **Mandate design-build for all new rail lines and extensions.** The MTA should replace its traditional multistep procurement process, which is primarily useful for targeted improvements on existing infrastructure, with this increasingly accepted practice. Design-build allows greater creativity, which can lead to budget savings by mixing design and contractor teams, allowing for better and closer collaboration from the outset, and eliminating the need to reconcile designs later. Contractors are able to evaluate the constructability of designs as drawings are produced, offering suggestions on cost savings based on their experience in the field.

- **Rethink labor practices and work rules.** We should adopt the best practices other cities have demonstrated in maintaining employment and wages while delivering projects faster and at lower costs. Many project managers and contractors say work rules are a major factor driving inefficiency and higher costs. Reforming how work shifts are defined, along with overtime pay and staffing of tunnel-boring machines, could result in significant costs savings. And even wider savings could be achieved by examining the rules embedded in collective bargaining agreements.

OUTCOMES

Greater productivity and more efficient decision-making and management would result in faster and better project delivery, and allow the MTA to accelerate the construction of megaprojects. The impact of these reforms would depend on how quickly and successfully they are implemented. Delivering projects on time, on budget, and at lower costs should also boost public confidence and result in increased capital funding for infrastructure. Reforms could help implement a larger capital program with a steady pipeline of projects that could maintain or increase construction-industry employment.

PAYING FOR IT

Implementing these reforms would sharply reduce the costs of new rail projects, and could change government rules or industry practices that ultimately reduce costs for other infrastructure projects as well. Some upfront and ongoing administrative costs would be needed to introduce new management and labor processes.

② Restructure the Port Authority to function as a regional infrastructure bank

The Port Authority of New York and New Jersey has been a valuable financier and developer of critical infrastructure. In recent years, however, its operations and credibility have suffered from political interference and the inability to finance projects from which it cannot capture value, such as PATH improvements and the new Gateway Tunnel. To realize the Port Authority's potential and preserve its important mission, the entity must be reformed to increase accountability, given the ability to capture value from all of its investments, and separate operations from its historically clear mission of financing and delivering new infrastructure. This would enable the Port Authority to become the region's infrastructure bank, with assets operated by different management structures that deliver the best performance and value.

Political maneuvering, mission creep, and inefficient operations have hurt the Port Authority.

The Port Authority is a classic conglomerate. The primary advantage of such a structure is to allow profitable assets, such as the airports and Hudson River crossings, to cross-subsidize important, but money-losing, operations such as PATH and the Port Authority Bus Terminal. The structure also allows the Port Authority to plan, operate, and coordinate key elements of its transportation infrastructure.

Unfortunately, there are also significant disadvantages. Senior management, for example, with so much under its purview, is unable to undertake the kind of in-depth strategic planning that each asset requires. The Port Authority's current structure shields many underperforming assets from scrutiny. Rather than incentivizing creativity and bold actions, the multiple management layers of the Port Authority result in indecisiveness and inaction. The structure of the Port Authority as a two-state organization also makes it susceptible to abuse and political interference.

As a result, many capital projects become too expensive and are delayed, disruptions rise, debt increases, and crucial maintenance and repairs are deferred. The Port Authority is unable to meet the growing infrastructure needs of the region at a time when our aging infrastructure requires modernization and new capacity for regional growth.

The Port Authority faces many challenges, including:

- **Political interference:** Overt political interference and scandal in recent years have undermined the organization. The authority's current structure depends on the governors of New York and New Jersey to serve as the key points of political accountability and serve the public interest. They have the power to appoint commissioners and veto board actions. Gubernatorial authority and accountability, however, cannot excuse overt political interference and diversion of Port Authority resources to serve narrow political ends. A governance structure intended to safeguard the interests of both states has instead produced internal division and a lack of managerial accountability. The governors and legislatures of New York and New Jersey should agree on a series of transformational reforms that minimize the potential for political interference through greater transparency and accountability in decision-making and gubernatorial involvement.

- **Financial capacity:** The combination of the extraordinary cost of rebuilding Lower Manhattan after 9/11, and a growing list of projects that user fees will not be able to cover has turned the Port Authority into an unwieldy conglomerate of disparate entities and weakened its once-strong financial position. Major investments critical to long-term success of the region—including the Gateway project, increased capacity at JFK and Newark airports, a renovated bus terminal, and increased PATH capacity—are unlikely to be completed because the authority's cash flow and projections cannot sustain the anticipated debt service. To address the situation, the Port Authority will require new revenue sources, such as value capture, to supplement its user fees.

- **Cross-subsidization:** The practice of cross-subsidization between the authority's different business units without sufficient transparency has, over time, masked inefficiencies and inhibited much-needed investments. These inefficiencies in operations, including public security, seaports, and mass transit, have survived because the enormous profits generated by the airports and Hudson River crossings could be used to cover ongoing deficits. While transit operations will always require subsidies, the current structure has allowed costs to grow unchecked and thereby stymied innovation, such as contracting for services or merging with other public entities that could achieve economies of scale. The Port Authority should be restructured to act like an infrastructure bank, providing financing to critical initiatives, while also allowing innovative management and operations to flourish within its operating divisions.

A regional infrastructure bank would support independent entities to promote efficiency and transparency, improve service, and generate new investments.

Delivering services more efficiently and investing in the next generation of infrastructure projects will require fundamental structural change to how the Port Authority is organized and governed.

There needs to be more separation between operating the system and financing long-term capital improvements. The Port Authority's line agencies would benefit from a clearer mandate to provide the best possible service, with long-term investments planned, financed, and delivered by separate entities. Planning and investing in large capital projects, such as new tunnels or airport runways, requires a different set of competencies and authority than maintaining good day-to-day service and efficient operations. Large capital projects have economic, fiscal, and environmental impacts that extend well beyond the users of a particular facility and require a different set of political, planning, and financial expertise to execute.

Operating agencies need greater financial and performance accountability. The Port Authority's consolidated bond structure obscures how businesses are cross-subsidized and reduces incentives for efficient service delivery and capital construction. The different business units at the Port Authority, which are the by-product of a century of growth rather than any strategic plan, should be organized into distinct corporate entities with facilities that have tight operating synergies. These entities need to have clear fiscal responsibility to deliver the best service at the lowest cost, including incentive structures to drive innovation and efficiency, and be held accountable for their performance. These separate units should have expert-led governing boards that regularly hold open meetings and are required to report periodically to the public and elected officials on their operations, finances, and plans. This would allow both affected stakeholders and the media greater access to information and decision-making surrounding each of those operations.

Allowing private investors to have a stake in operations, and potentially capital investments, would help balance political decision-making with financial objectives. There may be good reasons for the Port Authority's business operations to make investments that will never yield a positive return. But these decisions must be weighed against the needs of the rest of the system, with a clear analysis of the full costs and benefits. The Port Authority has succeeded in recent years in delivering critical infrastructure projects through public-private partnerships, such as the Goethals Bridge and a future LaGuardia Airport. Leveraging the private sector through the use of well-structured partnerships could encourage innovation, discipline, and risk-transfer in the delivery of the agency's capital projects, as well as management of the agency's assets. This approach could be expanded to other business units. Having public-private partnerships manage some of the Port's assets, such as the PATH or seaport, would introduce financial incentives to decision-making to balance against other goals. There are different ways of structuring private-sector partnerships that should be carefully explored. While each operating entity may require a different approach to achieve the greatest efficiency, these reforms could be achieved without violating existing bond covenants or changing the entity's governing legislation.

Enact and implement reform recommendations

The Port Authority would be run by a chief executive, with a clearly defined role, who ultimately answers to the Board of Commissioners. New York and New Jersey governments must concur on a series of transformational reforms that minimize the potential for political interference through greater transparency concerning Port Authority decision-making, public and legal accountability, and gubernatorial oversight for their own actions relative to the Port Authority.

Much of the groundwork for essential reform has already been laid by the Special Panel on the Future of the Port Authority, which issued recommendations in 2014. Among other internal reforms, the Special Panel proposed creating a single CEO position, hired and directed by the Board of Commissioners, replacing the current chair and vice chair with two co-chairs (recommended to the board by the governors of each state), and establishing an Office of the Chair comprising the co-chairs and CEO to function as the senior operating committee of the Authority. The Special Panel's proposals would better maintain the political independence of the Authority's executives and afford them greater autonomy from undue political influence. The Authority's professional managers should be empowered—and also be held accountable—to deliver projects and provide services to the best of their abilities.

Lawmakers in each state have also proposed additional reforms to improve transparency and accountability to the public. Even as the CEO and managers are afforded more autonomy in making decisions, they should also be held accountable through clear, uniform legal obligations to provide detailed information to the public, provide protections to whistleblowers, and be subjected to uniform judicial review in the courts of either state.

The governors and legislators of New York and New Jersey should convene to reconcile these reforms and develop and pass identical comprehensive reform legislation to guide the governance of the Authority. These reforms should be enacted into law so they are long lasting, judicially enforceable, and cannot be discarded or disregarded by gubernatorial or board fiat. These steps will be necessary to re-balance the Port Authority and properly shield it from inappropriate political pressure.

Allow the Port Authority to capture more of the value it creates

As outlined in other sections of this plan, the Port Authority will be required to finance major public capital investments over the next generation, including a new commuter rail tunnel under the Hudson River, runways at JFK and Newark airports, and a new bus terminal in New York City. The Port Authority may also be asked to assume financial, design, and/or operational responsibilities for coastal resiliency measures needed to protect authority assets and the entire port region from rising sea levels and more severe storms. Even if the Port Authority succeeds in generating more efficiencies from current operations, such as the PATH system and bus terminal, it cannot finance these investments from the profits generated by the Hudson River crossings and airports.

The investments that are made will generate enormous growth and productivity that can be used to acquire additional funding. Consideration should be given to capturing some of the real estate value created by the PATH system and Gateway tunnel; charging motorists to access the airports; or redeveloping and monetizing underutilized real estate assets. The World Trade Center and certain other Port Authority real estate holdings are not core to its mission as builder and manager of transportation facilities, but they do represent valuable sources of long-term revenue. The Port Authority should determine how to redeploy its real estate holdings in a way that maximizes their long-term value, and therefore the entity's financing capacity, while minimizing the effort to manage them. This could involve engaging in joint ventures, handing off assets to real estate investment trusts, or divesting them through an IPO.

Create independent corporate entities for operating and maintaining the Port Authority's assets

The Port Authority should change the relationship between its central functions and operating assets. These should be reconstituted as independently managed units with management devolved down to the asset level, reporting on both the operational and financial performance in a clear and transparent way.

By doing so, the Port Authority would create separate corporate entities that receive a long-term franchise to operate each division of the authority's assets—airports, ports, bus terminal, and PATH—in return for a first call on revenues sufficient to pay off the related debt. These operating entities could then be organized in ways that would best serve each entity. For example, the container ports subsidiary could be operated by a for-profit entity; airports could remain quasi-independent public agencies; the PATH train franchise (which would include an ongoing subsidy rather than a payment obligation) could be operated by New Jersey Transit, the MTA, or a private transit operator.

Contracts between the Port Authority and the operating entities would specify performance standards and the flow of funds between them. The Port Authority would establish how much each subsidiary would contribute toward the Port Authority's existing consolidated bond debt service and how much Port Authority cross-subsidy (from landing fees, bridge and tunnel tolls, and real estate revenue) should underwrite critical services that need it (PATH and bus terminal operations). The operating entities would determine fares and fees to meet contract provisions, but the Port Authority could establish and enforce levels of service, asset conditions, labor standards, and other public interest conditions. Beyond these bond requirements and cross-subsidy agreements, the operating assets would have incentives to provide services at a competitive cost. They would control operating revenues and determine how to spend them, creating incentives for the operating assets to provide high-quality, cost-effective service.

Create a regional infrastructure bank

Under the structure proposed above, the management relationship between the Port Authority and its operating assets would be diminished and the financial relationship between the agency and these assets would change. In effect, the Port Authority would function as a regional infrastructure bank, collecting certain revenues from the operating units, paying consolidated debt service, and distributing surplus revenues back to the operating units or investing in new bi-state infrastructure.

Operating entities could apply for financing, and the board and management would evaluate requests based on financial and service criteria, as well as other public interests, including community, health, economic, and environmental impacts. The bank could also initiate planning for large projects, and establish single-purpose entities to design and build them, as it has done for the Gateway project.

OUTCOMES

Designating independent operating entities and converting the Port Authority into an infrastructure bank would have two primary outcomes. By creating greater transparency and independence in making capital allocation decisions, the proposal would create incentives for more efficient, customer-focused service for each of its operating subsidiaries. It would also help ensure the most important and cost-effective projects are prioritized. Both of these outcomes should increase public confidence in the authority, thus making it easier to attract public and private capital.

PAYING FOR IT

Restructuring the Port Authority would require significant legal and administrative expenses to negotiate financial structures that allocate revenues fairly while maintaining bond ratings, complying with bond covenants, providing operational incentives, and winning political approval for a governance structure that provides greater independence. But over time, the cost of delivering operations and capital projects would decrease due to the more efficient and effective structure.

③ Create a Subway Reconstruction Public Benefit Corporation

Photo: Leonard Zhukovsky

New York City's extensive subway system is the lifeblood of its economy, but faces a dire crisis. The system's infrastructure is aging and unreliable and uses outdated technology. By almost every metric, service is deteriorating. While some important improvements have recently been made by the Metropolitan Transit Authority (MTA), progress must be radically accelerated to meet demand and ensure that New York can compete for jobs with other major cities. Bringing the subway up to modern standards will need significantly more funding. But it also requires the creation of a new institution dedicated solely to fixing the problems: a Subway Reconstruction Public Benefit Corporation. This public entity would have a focused mandate, streamlined authority, and sufficient funding to rebuild the entire subway system within 15 years.

The MTA, with its current financial and operational structure, is not capable of rebuilding the subway system.

The subway system may be the spine of the city, but it is also its Achilles' heel. Surging ridership and decades of underinvestment have taken their toll. According to the Independent Budget Office, train delays have increased three-fold over the past five years—from roughly 20,000 delays a month to over 65,000—due to overcrowding, signal failures, and other daily disruptions. As the public has become increasingly aware, delays lead to overcrowding, which causes further delays and even more overcrowding. Failures and breakdowns cascade and ripple throughout the system, compounding problems and delaying riders. Stations are hot, loud, damp, and for the most part, not ADA accessible. New Yorkers now talk openly of a transit crisis that threatens the city's future.

The MTA is staffed by talented public servants, and has achieved great things over the past generation. It should be commended for repairing the subways in the 1980s and 1990s, restoring service quickly after Superstorm Sandy, extending the 7 and Q lines, and adopting a modern train control system on the L line. It recently announced plans to move to a modern fare-collection system. But the pace of these improvements has been too slow compared with the city's tremendous need for capacity expansion and modernization. Demand is growing rapidly as the city adds jobs and residents. Climate change is accelerating. And technology is raising passengers' expectations for customer service. The MTA, as currently funded and structured, cannot keep up. Unless we can find new ways to deliver improvements and modernization, the subway system will continue to slip further behind.

Fixing the subways and bringing them up to modern standards of speed, efficiency, and service must be the highest transit priority for the region. And despite strong leadership and dedicated staff, there are institutional reasons the MTA will not be able to reconstruct the subways in a reasonable amount of time. They include:

- **Competing demands:** The MTA is an enormous legacy institution responsible for funding and operating one of the largest subway networks in the world; two commuter railroads and the Staten Island Rail Road; local and express buses; and nine bridges and tunnels. In addition to operations, it is responsible for financing, designing, and overseeing all capital improvements to these properties. Although managing the subway system is tremendously complex, particularly in this time of crisis, it is just one of many competing priorities for the MTA leadership.

- **Inefficient institutional practices:** The MTA, like any decades-old large corporate institution, has acquired layers of regulations and competing organizational silos within the bureaucracy. Some of the rules that make the MTA less nimble at building megaprojects include limited constructability assessments and excessive customization, a fractured construction management process, and an overly complex procurement process that stifles innovation. Changing this structure has proven extremely difficult because it is so embedded in the legacy institutions that comprise the agency, and the different divisions have competing agendas. The agency in charge of rebuilding the subways needs to be "first among equals" in the hierarchical structure, in order to drive projects forward.

- **Anachronistic and overly burdensome regulations:** Some of the contracting, procurement and labor practices required by the MTA are inefficient and out-of-date. Contracting regulations actively stifle innovation and create costly delays. Work rules that lead to excessive staffing and unproductive work time, requirements to use the operations workforce on construction projects, limited training capacity, and project pipelines that contribute to labor shortages all increase project costs and delivery times. With his recent declaration of a state of emergency at the MTA, the governor recognized these challenges and streamlined some operations to expedite contracting and procurement, but these steps still need to be expanded and institutionalized.

- **Unclear lines of responsibility and accountability:** The MTA has an opaque structure, with different divisions going back to the legacy institutions that were merged into a single authority in 1968, a board appointed by different political leaders representing different constituencies, and complicated funding formulas that make it hard to determine who is paying what. As a result, the riding public does not know whom to credit for improvements, or blame for failures. While most riders believe the New York City mayor is in charge of subways and buses, power in fact rests with the governor, who has a plurality of appointees to the MTA board, chooses the MTA's leadership, and controls most of the funding. Until these responsibilities are clarified in the eyes of voters and transit riders, there will always be confusion about who is in charge.

- **Lack of funding:** Nobody likes to raise taxes, fees, or fares, and the current structure of the MTA and the budgeting process incentivizes politicians to defer maintenance and increase debt rather than find additional resources to pay for necessary maintenance, repairs, and expansion. But the needs of the system are clear. The MTA is $40 billion in debt, requiring 16 percent of its $15.75 billion annual operating budget to be dedicated to debt service. Its operating budget is increasingly unbalanced, with expenses growing 30 percent faster than operating revenues due to rapidly escalating employee-benefit costs and debt-service payments. Even as it must find ways to reduce operating-cost increases and reduce debt, the MTA needs additional dedicated resources of several billion dollars a year. These funds could be generated by charging motorists to enter the region's central business district and putting a price on greenhouse gas emissions from the transportation section, among other options.

Create a Subway Reconstruction Public Benefit Corporation responsible for overhauling the subway system within 15 years

To be on par with the subway systems of other major cities around the world, we need to aggressively address the backlog in critical infrastructure updates, modernize the signals system, right-size our most congested stations, and increase capacity in strategic locations. Reconstructing our subways will entail a significant increase in capital expenses, and require fundamental changes in how projects are designed, approved, and built. The scale of these governance changes is so significant, in fact, that a new quasi-governmental entity should be created specifically for that purpose: the Subway Reconstruction Public Benefit Corporation.

Give the Subway Reconstruction Public Benefit Corporation a specific mandate

A crisis demands undivided attention. A new Subway Reconstruction Public Benefit Corporation should be created with no other goal than to completely rebuild the subway system within 15 years. Without other distractions such as buses, commuter rail, roadways, and even operating the subway network, the new entity can focus entirely on subway capital construction. It can recruit leadership with specific expertise in that area, and motivate a team to meet specific goals within a specific timeframe.

The responsibilities of the Subway Reconstruction Public Benefit Corporation would be to determine the level of capital improvement required, determine how to balance construction with ongoing operating needs, identify ways to increase cost efficiencies in construction, secure the revenues needed, issue and negotiate a Request for Proposals, and oversee construction, enforcing performance measures and penalties for delays.

Allow the Subway Reconstruction Public Benefit Corporation more leeway to take a 21st century approach to capital construction

The specific structure and rules governing the Subway Reconstruction Public Benefit Corporation should be determined by the New York State governor, in collaboration with the New York City mayor and MTA leadership. Broadly speaking, its institutional structure should be designed for creative problem-solving, efficient decision-making, and accountability.

The Subway Reconstruction Public Benefit Corporation must be empowered to speed up the reconstruction process while maintaining a strong commitment to worker safety and the public interest. This may mean making it easier to engage in public-private partnerships, authorizing design-build, and revising some of the other rules and regulations that currently drive up the cost and timelines of projects built by the MTA. Today, the MTA Capital Construction Company has responsibility to deliver these projects, but it has not been given the full authority, funding, or support to do so—even as it has responsibility to deliver other capital projects.

Define clear lines of accountability

Like New York City's Economic Development Corporation (EDC), the new Subway Reconstruction Public Benefit Corporation would not be a government agency, but rather a public-benefit corporation, with a board of directors from a range of public and private-sector fields. But like EDC, the Subway Reconstruction entity would be controlled by the government—in this case, the governor of New York.

Within the Subway Reconstruction Public Benefit Corporation, accountability would be key. The decision-making process should be transparent—from what projects the new entity would undertake to what mitigation measures would be provided. Contract negotiations should identify and plan for any potential construction issues and require the builders to meet performance standards or else suffer penalties.

The Subway Reconstruction Public Benefit Corporation would be required to report on its progress on a semi-annual basis and provide justification whenever budgets or timelines are not met, thus making sure the public interest is protected.

Provide the funding necessary

Even with more efficient institutional practices and work rules, rebuilding the subway system would still significantly increase capital construction budgets. The Subway Reconstruction Public Benefit Corporation would have access to a significant portion of the existing MTA capital plan, but that would be insufficient. Identifying and securing a diverse, stable, and sizable dedicated revenue sources—such as a carbon tax, congestion pricing, value capture, charging tolls based on miles driven, and other taxes and fees—would be essential to the success of this effort.

OUTCOMES

This recommendation would end the continuous cycle of runaway construction costs and delays on capital projects. Within 15 years, the subways would be faster, more reliable, less crowded, and more efficient than they have been in decades. A streamlined decision-making and construction process would result in faster and better project delivery. With modern signalling technology, stations with platform screen doors for better safety and pedestrian circulation, and modern communications, the subway system should be able to increase its capacity significantly, and provide service to more parts of the city—all at lower costs.

In addition, this initiative would create a new model of transit governance. The Subway Reconstruction Public Benefit Corporation could, in other words, become a pilot project that informs the process for reforming the MTA itself.

PAYING FOR IT

Creating the Subway Reconstruction Public Benefit Corporation would require upfront legal and administrative costs, while reconstructing the subways would need a significant amount of funding. But in this transit-dependent region where the system is so far over capacity, the long-term return on investment on transit projects would be very high. And the lessons learned from a new institutional structure to address the MTA's most daunting challenges could be a model for other agencies that would have far-reaching impacts beyond the authority.

④ Modernize transit systems outside New York City

Photo: Nancy Borowick

Outside of New York City, the tri-state region has the three busiest commuter rail systems in the country as well as bus systems that serve millions of local, regional, and long-distance trips. Funding for these transit systems has not kept pace with growing demand, and in some cases has been drastically cut. NJ Transit, Metro-North, and the Long Island Rail Road all need to scale up their operations. These agencies must carry out the specific capital projects outlined in this report, become more innovative and better funded, and coordinate their policies. NJ Transit's bus system, along with systems such as NICE Bus in Nassau County, Bee-Line in Westchester, and Suffolk Transit also need more resources to improve service, adopt on-demand transit options, and be prepared for autonomous vehicle technologies.

Public transportation outside New York City is both hampered by lack of funding and difficult for riders to navigate.

The three railroads and dozens of public and private bus companies that make up the public transportation system outside of New York City all have certain challenges in common, while other issues are particularly acute for specific entities.

- **Inadequate funding:** All the transit systems need more resources, and NJ Transit's funding structure is the most precarious. It is one of the largest systems in the country without a designated funding stream, with state funding to the agency subject to the uncertainty of annual budget negotiations. This has resulted in a 90 percent reduction in state aid for operations since 2005, forcing fare hikes and raids of the agency's capital fund to cover operating costs. Similar funding reductions for county bus systems has also led to a downward spiral of declining service and ridership. Nassau County's NICE bus system has seen a 20 percent reduction in funding, and a 71 percent reduction in the county's support for the system since 2006.[11]

- **Political interference:** State reductions in funding and political interference (especially at NJ Transit, which is heavily dependent on annual appropriations) have consumed agency officials and thwarted their attempts at addressing the needs of the riding public.

- **Lack of investment:** Failing systems and inadequate infrastructure have led to increased delays, deadly derailments, and safety hazards. Penn Station, the western hemisphere's busiest transit hub, is unpleasant and overcrowded, despite recent efforts by the railroads to make improvements. In Connecticut, parts of the the New Haven Line—especially many of its old bridges—are in a state of disrepair. For bus riders throughout the region, funding cuts mean old buses, long waits, and deteriorating service.

- **Few resources to address inequities in the transit system:** Lack of funding has made it increasingly difficult for transit providers to accommodate the needs of low-income residents, who are particularly dependent on transit. Fares have increased and services cut because agencies have been unable to further subsidize rides or provide a system that bases fares on customers' ability to pay.

- **Poor attention to customer service and accessibility:** Rail and bus systems have been slow to adopt technology that would allow better service and coordinate trips between agencies. Navigating the many services is difficult. Many stations, particularly on the NJ Transit network, still are not ADA accessible.

Service cuts and fewer bus riders accelerate a vicious cycle. Nassau County ridership declined by 17 percent between 2006 and 2015, and Suffolk Transit reports ridership declined by 20 percent between 2006 and 2016. NJ Transit rail and bus passengers are also responding to the poor service and fleeing the struggling transit system. On the New Haven Line and Long Island Rail Road, ridership remains high, but poorly maintained tracks and old train cars limit the ability of the lines to serve a growing population. The new CT Fastrak bus rapid transit system between Hartford and New Britain in Connecticut has drawn new riders, but bus ridership in a number of urban centers, including New Haven and Stamford, has started to drop after a period of growth. New Haven saw an 8 percent drop and Stamford a 7 percent drop between 2012 and 2016.

Sound budgeting and better governance will allow operators to invest in infrastructure and focus on their customers.

More resources are needed to help NJ Transit, LIRR, Metro North, and bus transit operators improve service by doing the following:

- **Adopt sound budgeting practices and rely less on debt.** Capital funds should no longer be diverted to cover operating deficits. The operating budget should be funded by fare revenues and dedicated subsidies, taxes, and other user fees. New Jersey should replicate this structure, which is common for large public transportation systems across the country, including the MTA.

- **Ensure revenues allocated to transportation purposes are not reallocated to cover shortfalls in other areas of state budgets.** Dedicated revenues to state transportation funds must be protected from reallocation to other, non-transportation-related purposes. In Connecticut, a very small proportion of the State's general sales tax is allocated to fund transportation, but there is strong political pressure to reallocate these funds to other programs. New Jersey voters recently passed a referendum that constitutionally dedicated gas tax revenue to transportation projects. A similar constitutional lockbox in Connecticut would protect state transportation funds from being diverted for other purposes.

- **Provide more clarity and transparency about sources of funding for capital investments.** All agencies need greater clarity about how money is spent, whether it is from a legislative appropriation, a new fee/surcharge/tax, or a grant from the federal government.

- **Evaluate new revenue sources** such as revenue generated from development around stations along with other forms of value capture, or a greater allocation to public transportation from gas taxes or future vehicle miles traveled fees.

- **Improve both capital and operating efficiencies**. In addition to adopting strategies for reducing the cost of capital projects, transit agencies and service providers should look for greater operational efficiencies, such as negotiating for increased productivity in labor contracts in return for higher wages and job stability.

- **Provide transit equity to low-income, transit-dependent communities.** The many areas in the region that are transit dependent should be given priority for enhancements to the transit system, especially through improvements to the bus network, network redesigns, and other recommendations elsewhere in the plan

- **Offer discounted, needs-based fares for short trips on commuter rail lines that run through neighborhoods with many low- and medium-income households.** This would improve local mobility and encourage more riders to use public transit for short trips.

- **Emphasize customer satisfaction through integrated services.** Public transportation agencies should do more to connect with riders, involve them more in decision-making, and make their services attractive and easy to use. This will require using technology to accelerate the transition to a flexible, unified fare collection system and coordinating services that promote more intermodal trips, including with private bus carriers. Ultimately, as the system turns into an integrated regional rail and bus system, fare structures could be organized by zones, across all operators.

- **Create better intermodal connections** to provide better customer service. This could include adopting bike sharing to reduce the need for parking around commuter rail stations, and promoting innovative parking-management strategies that support on-demand services to replace surface parking.

- **Invest in infrastructure and improve service, especially in cities.** Capital budgets should be expanded to ensure the railroads and buses are able to provide safe and convenient service that is competitive. Additionally, Health Impact Assessments for transit investments can help identify the most equitable projects and their health benefits for socially vulnerable communities. This includes both maintenance and new projects to provide more capacity.

- **Plan for climate change.** As Superstorm Sandy demonstrated, much of the region's transit infrastructure is located in low-lying areas that are prone to flooding, including tunnels, rail yards, and rail lines, especially in the Meadowlands and along the Hudson River. The three transit agencies have started incorporating climate adaptation into their strategic and capital planning, but more needs to be done to address the tremendous magnitude of the challenge.

- **Explore a unified management entity and promote through-running service at Penn Station.** As Penn Station is expanded to the west (Moynihan Station) and south (Gateway), and Metro-North service is provided via Penn Access, a unified management entity, including representation from all the commuter railroads and Amtrak, should be explored to better integrate service and amenities and promote through-running. Ultimately, the system should be reconfigured to allow significantly more through-running from New Jersey to Connecticut and Long Island.

OUTCOMES

Investing in suburban transit would result in additional transportation choices, more reliable and frequent service, and better access to jobs—especially for transit-dependent households. Better transit service should succeed in getting people to choose transit over walking, which should lead to lower greenhouse gas emissions and more active lifestyles. Lastly, it would lead to less reliance on debt for future capital investments.

PAYING FOR IT

Higher gas taxes and roadway tolls, as well as a motorist tax based on the actual distance driven (vehicle miles traveled or VMT fee), would be key sources of revenue. New York would also use a portion of the sales tax, mortgage recording tax, and other levies to fund public transportation. Real estate development could also provide a new funding mechanism in certain attractive markets.

5 Charge drivers to enter Manhattan, price highways, and transition to vehicle-miles tolling

Photo: Milos Muller

As gas taxes can no longer be depended on to generate consistent revenue, there are concerns about how to finance road maintenance and upgrades at a time when transportation infrastructure needs are growing. To make up for this revenue deficit we must develop a new funding structure that is fair, incorporates new technology, and reinforces broader transportation policy goals. At a minimum, it should include consistent and fair tolling in New York City, then grow to include tolls on all major highways, and ultimately on actual miles driven.

Eroding gas tax revenues are causing a fiscal crisis.

For decades, the construction, operation, and maintenance of most of the region's roadways, as well as some public transportation, has been funded by gas taxes. But gas tax revenues have stagnated as vehicles have become more fuel-efficient, and hybrid and electric vehicles have become more popular. Raising the gas tax rate enough to compensate for the reduced demand for gasoline does not appear to be politically viable.

This funding crisis has led to widespread lack of investment and deteriorating conditions on our roadways. Every year, we spend $6 billion in capital improvements to our highways and bridges, yet they remain in such poor condition that the American Society of Civil Engineers has graded them a "D" in our region.

We need a new funding structure that is fair and reinforces other policy goals, such as managing traffic.

In the face of dwindling gas tax revenue and growing transportation infrastructure needs, we must find other ways to generate revenue, and do so in a way that reinforces other policy goals such as managing traffic, reducing driving, and redirecting people to public transportation. Relatively small reductions in vehicle volumes can generate substantial reductions in traffic congestion, as has been demonstrated in cities such as London, Stockholm and Singapore, which have successfully implemented congestion pricing.

The three revenue-generating strategies described below should build on each other as technology begins to change public acceptance of user fees based on when, where, and how much people drive.

Toll the East River bridges and avenues to the Manhattan CBD

All of the region's major crossings charge a toll, except for the four East River bridges, whose tolls were eliminated decades ago because of traffic backups at tollbooths. While keeping travel within New York City "toll-free" has been a favorite message of elected officials, the lack of tolls on East River bridges has had significant consequences, including:

- Encouraging people to drive miles out of their way to avoid the tolled crossings, causing more traffic in the most dense parts of New York City (so-called "toll shopping"). The Brooklyn-Queens Expressway, along with local streets in Lower Manhattan, Brooklyn, and Queens, are perpetually clogged with trucks and personal vehicles that would otherwise have chosen a more direct route if pricing were comparable.

- Encouraging commuters to drive instead of taking public transportation, merely to avoid the cost of a subway or bus fare. This is particularly unfair given that those who drive into Manhattan earn, on average, a higher income than those who use transit.

- Charging higher tolls at other bridges to make up for the lack of revenue. These other bridges typically serve parts of the city where there are fewer transit options, whereas those served by the free bridges typically have more transit alternatives.

A plan by Move NY calls for combining new tolls on these four bridges and north-south avenues with toll reductions on the other crossing such that all seven East River bridges and tunnels charge the same amount. This would raise more than $1 billion annually for roads and transit, depending on the toll level set, while also reducing traffic and eliminating toll shopping. To reduce backups, tolls could be collected electronically, with the price varying by time of day to encourage fewer people to drive at peak times.

Add tolls to major roads and highways

Only three major highways in the region are tolled and pay for their own maintenance: the New York State Thruway, the New Jersey Turnpike, and the Garden State Parkway. These highways are largely in good condition, although rising costs and inflation have made it difficult to keep up with needs.

But nearly all other major roads and highways are toll-free. A handful of tolled roads and water crossings fund the rest of the network, but revenue falls far short of need. It is unfair to toll only a handful of points in the network, because some users end up making up for the loss.

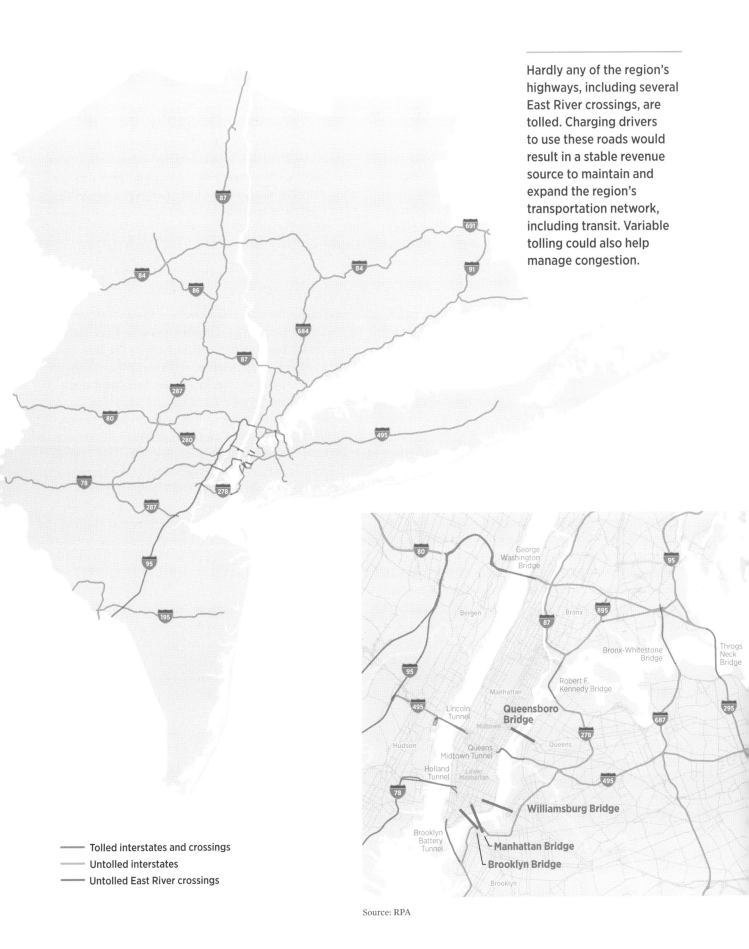

Hardly any of the region's highways, including several East River crossings, are tolled. Charging drivers to use these roads would result in a stable revenue source to maintain and expand the region's transportation network, including transit. Variable tolling could also help manage congestion.

Tolled interstates and crossings

Untolled interstates

Untolled East River crossings

Source: RPA

One solution is to charge tolls on all major roads (including interstate-designated highways, which currently ban tolling—although exceptions can be made). This can be done with electronic toll collection technology that makes tollbooths unnecessary. For only a minimal investment, physical gantries along the 1,700 miles of major roads could be eliminated and replaced with virtual gantries using GPS waypoints. Tolls could have variable prices based on time of day or level of congestion. Trucks and other large vehicles could also be charged more because of the additional wear and tear they create on the road surface.

Charge drivers for the number of miles they drive

Ultimately, the most fair way to charge people for using the road network is to base it on the actual amount of driving they do, regardless of which roads they use. Known as a Vehicle-Miles Traveled (VMT) fee or Miles-Based User Fee (MBUF), this method utilizes GPS and cellular technology, and generates enough revenue to fill the gaps in transportation budgets in all three states, as well as pay for upgrades and expansion projects outlined in the Fourth Regional Plan.

These fees are also an opportunity to use infrastructure more efficiently. Fees could be adjusted to influence travel behavior, reduce unnecessary driving, and encourage other ways of getting around (such as biking or taking the bus). Fees can be set higher or lower based on capacity, vehicle weight, or fuel efficiency.

Adopting VMT/MBUF would require all three states to coordinate implementation, which might involve establishing a regional or mega-regional organizing body similar to the E-ZPass interagency group. Ideally, federal action would also be part of the implementation to help smooth out interstate issues and create a uniform set of standards nationwide.

Although there is the potentially critical issue of the public having concerns initially about privacy due to the use of GPS and cellular technology to gather data, a transition would eventually be possible once the public was convinced appropriate measures were in place to protect privacy and delete stored records. The transition to VMT/MBUF would also be easier if the public saw the benefits of the new system, including proactive traffic management, reduced congestion, and a marked improvement in the physical condition of our transportation infrastructure. This transition would be operationally, politically, and socially sensitive, but also yield tremendous benefits to the region.

OUTCOMES

Implementing a user-fee model would result in a sustainable and stable revenue source to fix, expand, and maintain the region's roadways—and over time, would replace the gas tax. The adoption of variable tolling would reduce congestion and encourage modal shifts that lead to other changes, such as off-peak deliveries and car-free/-limited zones. Calculating tolls based on actual miles traveled would more accurately reflect the cost of driving and reduce VMT growth.

PAYING FOR IT

Implementing new tolling technologies would have significant upfront costs, but revenue generated would far exceed initial investments. If 10 cents, for instance, were charged for every mile driven on the region's highways, about $5 billion a year could be raised. Alternatively, that revenue stream could be leveraged to generate $77 billion in capital funds over 30 years. This would provide a substantial contribution to fix and upgrade our highway and transit systems, and expand transit capacity.

CREATE NEW INSTITUTIONS AND FUNDING TO TACKLE CLIMATE CHANGE

Our dense coastal region is particularly vulnerable to the impacts of climate change. With rising sea levels and worsening storms, the number of residents at risk of flooding is expected to double in the next 25 years. Our cities could have five times the number of days with extreme heat. Much of our critical infrastructure, from airports to power plants, is in vulnerable areas.

Climate and weather do not respect geographic boundaries, but the agencies responsible for adapting to climate change are limited to their state or municipal jurisdiction. As a whole, their authority and resources fall well below what's needed for a challenge of this magnitude.

The one multistate institution empowered to reduce greenhouse gas emissions, the Regional Greenhouse Gas Initiative, should expand its limited carbon-trading system to cover all sources of greenhouse gas emissions.

To lead and fund region-wide coastal adaptation, a Regional Coastal Commission should be established, with dedicated sources of funding, to develop, fund, and implement a coordinated, detailed and place-based strategy to increase resilience.

6 Reduce greenhouse gas emissions with a cap-and-trade market modeled after California's program

Photo: Wladimir Labeikovsky

The region has made significant progress in reducing greenhouse gas (GHG) emissions, but even with cleaner fuels and better technology, we will not be able to reach the goal that has been adopted by all three states and New York City of reducing emissions by 80 percent by 2050. To accomplish this, we must significantly strengthen the existing carbon pricing system of the Regional Greenhouse Gas Initiative (RGGI). Using the California model, which covers all greenhouse gases and includes transportation, buildings, and industry, as well as power generation, would result in much deeper reductions in greenhouse gases. Joining RGGI with California's market would create an even more effective program. Revenue generated from the expanded market should be invested in an equitable, low-carbon economy.

The cap-and-trade market in effect in New York and Connecticut today regulates carbon emissions only from the power sector, which represents just a small part of all emissions in the region. RGGI should be expanded to include all three states, as wellas emissions from the transportation, industrial, residential, and commercial sectors.

The way we regulate greenhouse gases leaves major sources of emissions unchecked.

New York, New Jersey, and Connecticut have each participated in the Regional Greenhouse Gas Initiative, a compact of nine northeastern states intended to combat climate change through a mandatory market-based cap-and-trade program. RGGI sets a cap on carbon pollution from the region's power plants. The cap declines every year, and has played a major role in reducing pollution from the power sector in participating states by 40 percent since 2009.[12]

But RGGI only regulates emissions from carbon dioxide, despite methane and other gases also contributing to climate change. RGGI also regulates emissions only from the electric-power-generation sector, when other sectors of the economy contribute significantly to emissions, including the transportation, residential, commercial, and industrial sectors. At a time when the federal government is retreating from reducing emissions, a more aggressive regional approach is critical.

Expand RGGI's market and join with other states to form a more powerful cap-and-trade market, and invest the revenues in mitigation and adaptation efforts

RGGI's effect on emissions would be much greater if it regulated all GHG and all economic sectors. The revenue it produces could also be invested in efforts to accelerate the transition to a greener economy. California's cap-and-trade program, which covers both all greenhouse gas emissions and major sectors of the state's economy, provides a model that RGGI can adopt and join.

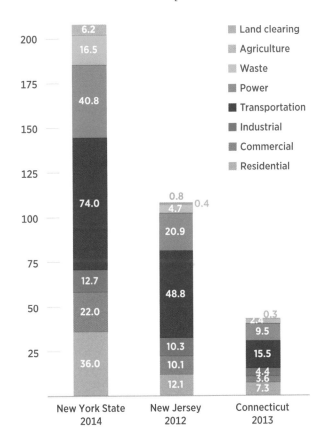

Million metric tons of CO$_2$ equivalent

Legend:
- Land clearing
- Agriculture
- Waste
- Power
- Transportation
- Industrial
- Commercial
- Residential

New York State 2014:
6.2, 16.5, 40.8, 74.0, 12.7, 22.0, 36.0

New Jersey 2012:
0.8, 4.7, 0.4, 20.9, 48.8, 10.3, 10.1, 12.1

Connecticut 2013:
0.3, 2.4, 9.5, 15.5, 4.4, 3.6, 7.3

Sources: (NY) NYSERDA, Greenhouse Gas Inventory 2014; (NJ) Michael Aucott, Marjorie Kaplan, Jeanne Herb. 2012 Update to New Jersey's Statewide Greenhouse Gas Emission Inventory. Rutgers Climate Institute 2015. (CT) Connecticut Dept. of Energy and Environmental Protection. 2013 Connecticut Greenhouse Gas Emissions Inventory.

Expand RGGI to include transportation fuels

In New York, New Jersey, and Connecticut, motorized vehicles account for a third to nearly half of all carbon emissions. Five states and the District of Columbia, including New York and Connecticut, are already collaborating to develop market-based carbon-reduction policies under the auspices of the Transportation and Climate Initiative (TCI), a collaboration of 12 northeastern and mid-Atlantic states. Research shows that a pricing policy, such as a carbon fee or mileage-based user fees, could reduce carbon emissions by 32 to 40 percent by 2030.[13] RGGI should expand its carbon market to include transportation fuels. If RGGI does not, then New York, Connecticut, and New Jersey should join with other willing states to implement transportation pricing policies.

Expand RGGI to include industrial emitters and heating fuels from the residential and commercial sectors

New York, New Jersey, and Connecticut should work with RGGI, or on their own, to expand the cap-and-trade market to include large industrial emitters and the suppliers of heating fuels, which are the primary sources of emissions in residential and commercial buildings. Like California's cap-and-trade program, fuel suppliers should be required to reduce greenhouse gas emissions by supplying low greenhouse gas fuels or by purchasing allowances to cover the greenhouse gases they produce. Including the industrial sector would also provide the opportunity to expand coverage to gases other than carbon dioxide, including methane, nitrous oxide, and numerous fluoridated greenhouse gases.

Join with California and other jurisdictions to form a larger and more powerful cap-and-trade market

Ideally, the market for addressing greenhouse gas emissions would be national or international, with all emitters participating and following the same procedures. With little chance of a national market being established in the near future, states and international partners can still create a market that would cover a large share of the North American economy. New York and Connecticut currently participate in RGGI's cap-and-trade program, while New Jersey, which was an original RGGI state, withdrew in 2011 but should rejoin immediately. The initiative should also take steps to link with the joint cap-and-trade program that currently exists between California and the Canadian provinces of Quebec and Ontario. Such an alliance would include states and provinces with a combined economy that is close to half the size of the United States economy. The two initiatives have already begun sharing information and borrowing from each other's program design, but the process should be accelerated to advance a model that can meet the objectives of steep GHG reductions.

Invest billions of dollars in revenues from an expanded greenhouse gas market into a fair and low-carbon future

Expanding greenhouse gas pricing to the transportation, residential, commercial, and industrial sectors would generate significant funds for the region and other market participants. To date, RGGI auctions have generated $2.78 billion in proceeds—nearly half of it was generated by New York, Connecticut, and New Jersey—much of which has been invested into energy efficiency, clean and renewable energy, direct bill assistance, and greenhouse gas sequestration.[14,15]

Based on California's experience and other estimates, as much as $3 billion annually could be raised by the three states. California's program, which includes electricity and industry as well as ground transportation and heating fuels, is projected to raise between $2 billion and $4 billion annually by 2020, and as much as $5 billion by 2025.[16] California's population and economy are similar in size to the nine-state RGGI region—of which New York, New Jersey, and Connecticut account for half of the revenues generated—so comparable policies here could generate up to $2.5 billion.[17] Other estimates for the transportation sector alone indicate that pricing could produce even greater revenue. The Georgetown Climate Center study—for TCI, by Cambridge Systematics—estimated that capping transportation emissions alone could generate between $1.5 billion and $6 billion annually for the 11 states and District of Columbia that participate in the TCI, depending on the price set for emissions.[18] This could translate to revenues of up to $3 billion for New York, New Jersey, and Connecticut from this sector alone.

Similar to California, revenue should be invested in places and sectors that reduce GHG emissions even further while creating a strong and equitable economy that benefits those who have been harmed most by carbon emissions and would be burdened most by increased costs passed down to consumers.

- Expand and modernize the region's transportation infrastructure to boost ridership and lower vehicle emissions. One of the most effective ways to reduce vehicle emissions is to boost ridership on mass transit.

- Provide incentives for electric vehicles and infrastructure. Demand for electric—and other alternative fuel vehicles—is on the rise, but the additional cost and lack of supportive infrastructure limit the number of vehicles on the road.

- Build resilience to climate change for critical infrastructure. Our critical infrastructure—including energy, wastewater, and transportation—still remains very much at risk from flooding and extreme temperatures caused by greenhouse gases.

- Invest in building sustainable, complete neighborhoods to reduce reliance on automobiles.

- Invest in energy rebates and improvements in neighborhoods that have been disproportionately burdened by carbon emissions and facilities. Low-income neighborhoods and communities of color have disproportionately borne the burden and environmental injustice of hosting infrastructure with local environmental impacts, such as power plants, waste-transfer stations, bus depots, etc., which directly affects the health of their residents.

- Invest in natural carbon sequestration by restoring and improving the management of natural systems, such as forests and coastal wetlands, that serve as carbon filters that remove carbon dioxide from the atmosphere and store it. The U.S. Forest Service estimates that forests offset approximately 10 to 20 percent of U.S. carbon emissions annually.[19]

OUTCOMES

An expanded greenhouse gas market will have multiple positive outcomes, most importantly the reduction of greenhouse gas emissions that contribute to climate change. By linking to other greenhouse gas markets, such as California-Ontario-Quebec, we will gain momentum toward a nationwide market. The use of a single valuation of GHGs across jurisdictions will provide incentives to implement the lowest-cost emission reductions first and offer a larger portfolio of options for emissions reductions to create a more certain market. Proceeds from the market could be used for critical investments that advance better transit, boost the electrification of our automobiles, ensure the viability of critical infrastructure and natural systems, and create more sustainable and equitable communities.

PAYING FOR IT

The costs for expanding the greenhouse gas market in our region would be covered largely by the emitters or suppliers of the greenhouse gases in the market. It is likely that some of these costs would be passed on to consumers (e.g., transportation or home heating fuel prices may rise to reflect higher costs paid by fuel suppliers). Anything passed on to consumers would likely be regressive because it would take a larger percentage from low and moderate incomes. States should ensure low and moderate income populations are protected from such increases through existing or new regulations. Investments of proceeds back into these communities, particularly low-income and working-class communities, could also help to offset any additional costs.

7 Establish a Regional Coastal Commission

Faced with the growing threat of climate change, New York, New Jersey, and Connecticut should create a Regional Coastal Commission with the mandate to protect communities from storm surges and sea-level rise, and the power to implement solutions at different geographic scales. The commission would have a dedicated focus on the region's climate adaptation needs and mobilizing resources to address them, as well as coordinating strategies, developing common standards, and prioritizing funding for region-wide resilience projects.

Coastal flooding is a regional risk that is largely managed locally.

While flooding knows no municipal boundary, the region's coastline is governed by multiple stakeholders with different rules, policies, and guidelines—and there are few incentives to collaborate or coordinate efforts. Federal minimum standards are too weak, while national flood insurance is, at best, flawed and, at worst, exacerbates the problem. The lack of guidance in terms of standards, unified science, and data across agencies and states makes it difficult to consolidate or share information or advocate for a unified long-term vision. Most of the region's municipalities have limited capacity to address coastal flooding on their own because many are governed by part-time mayors or local councils. The coastal management programs of the three states vary widely in approach, and inconsistent policies can prevent important adaptation from being implemented across state lines. At the same time, adaptation is not a singular focus of any program, nor are issues of regional significance, such as infrastructure.

The result is poor inter- and intragovernmental coordination, with conflicting interests, and communities taking actions that may have adverse impacts on surrounding communities. This fragmented governance makes it nearly impossible to address the effects of climate change in a comprehensive and effective way. As flooding affects more of the region's infrastructure, regional decision-making will become even more important to maintain services and the quality of life in individual municipalities. Without regional collaboration and stable funding, disjointed approaches and misaligned timelines will be the norm, with each community or agency competing for the same limited funding.

Create a Regional Coastal Commission to prioritize and coordinate climate adaptation.

The RCC should be modeled after successful commissions, in the region and elsewhere, that coordinate municipal and private actions to preserve and manage environmental assets. These include the Highlands and Meadowlands Commissions in New Jersey, and the Pine Barrens Commission on Long Island. Other regions, including the San Francisco Bay Area and the Chesapeake Bay region, have successful region-scale coastal management authorities. The RCC would coordinate adaptation strategies undertaken by coastal communities, develop and manage adaptation standards, and prioritize projects for funding based on the potential for region-wide resilience. Funding could come from state adaptation trust funds or from existing federal and state sources.

The commission would implement its mission through the following actions:

- Produce a regional coastal adaptation plan that aligns adaptation policies across boundaries and establishes a vision for short- and long-term adaptation.

- Develop and manage evidence-based standards to guide projects and development/redevelopment in the region's flood-prone places.

- Coordinate and encourage collaborative projects across municipal and state boundaries.

- Evaluate and award funding for projects that align with the standards established by the commission.

The commission should include each of the coastal counties plus any municipality with land at risk from flooding at six feet of sea-level rise and, as a priority, municipalities that have land within the coastal zone. This boundary could be periodically updated by the commission to account for changes in sea-level rise projections and redrawn flood maps.

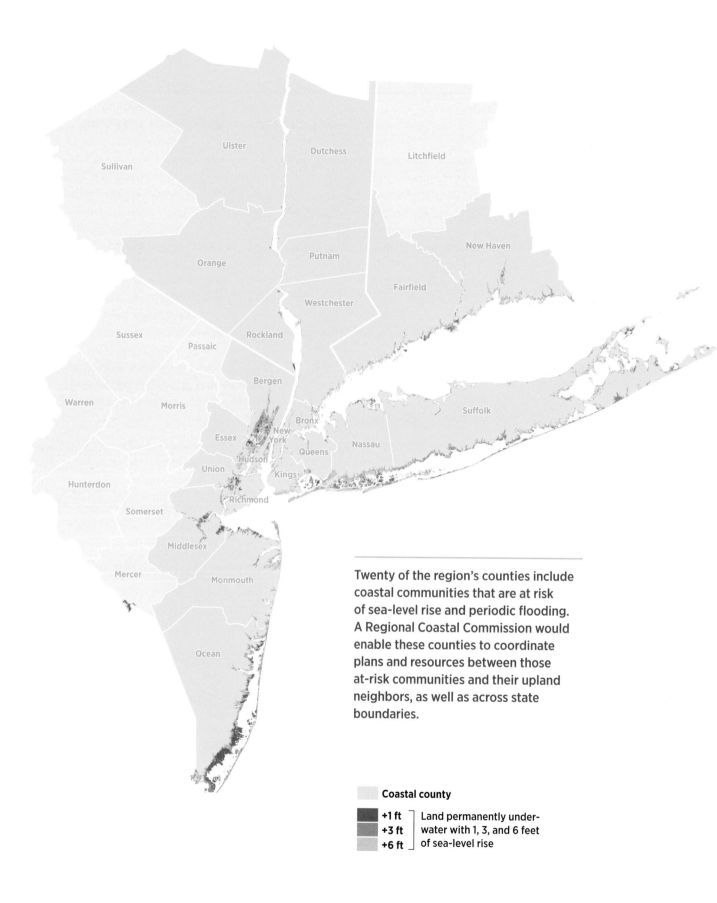

Twenty of the region's counties include coastal communities that are at risk of sea-level rise and periodic flooding. A Regional Coastal Commission would enable these counties to coordinate plans and resources between those at-risk communities and their upland neighbors, as well as across state boundaries.

Coastal county

+1 ft
+3 ft — Land permanently under-water with 1, 3, and 6 feet
+6 ft — of sea-level rise

Source: RPA

Adopt best practices of other coastal commissions

The structure and governance of the Regional Coastal Commission should be guided by the following best practices of other coastal commissions and regional collaboratives:

- **Be inclusive and cross-jurisdictional.** Members of the commission should be designated across jurisdictions and include all three states, each of the coastal counties, and a representative number from many—but not all—municipalities. The structure should allow for the free flow of information among all levels of government, even if they are not represented on the commission.

- **Represent different coastal conditions.** All types of coastal locations should be represented, including the highly developed urban shores of New York City, Jersey City, and Bridgeport, suburban communities along the back bays and barrier beaches of Long Island and New Jersey, and the undeveloped land off Long Island's east end. The region's estuary programs and reserves could serve as useful frameworks for ensuring representation from each of these different coastal locations.

- **Engage and build trust with communities.** The commission should ensure community outreach is an important part of its activities and mission,all voices are heard, and trust is established between the commission and communities. A campaign focusing on the health impacts of climate change can help sharpen priorities and translate long-term challenges into relatable issues.

- **Include elected officials.** Public officials should have a role in the commission to give it legitimacy and visibility, but the governance structure must remain independent from political cycles and direct political interference.

- **Engage across disciplines.** A key component of the commission's work would be incorporating decisions and best practices into other government agencies. RCC staff and board members should come from a variety of disciplines (environmental, health, development, transportation, etc.) to embed all aspects of adaptation planning into decisions.

- **Be informed by science, and flexible to changes.** The commission should make decisions and provide guidance based on the latest science and be flexible enough to change approaches as conditions warrant. The commission would also play an important role in communicating scientific information to government and community stakeholders.

- **Set clear criteria for adaptation funding.** The Coastal Commission would oversee and make decisions about how Adaptation Trust Fund dollars would be spent, and ensure funding allocations and project selection are guided by a clear set of standards and evaluation metrics.

OUTCOMES

With a Coastal Commission in place, the region would have a unified vision for adaptation that is informed by science, updated periodically, and tailored to the unique risks faced by different communities. Adaptation projects would proceed from planning to implementation in the places that need it most, and with sufficient funding to provide the greatest level of protection to the most people. Communities would have fewer people and less infrastructure at risk from storm flooding as well as the long-term and permanent flooding of sea-level rise. In short, our region would be prepared and taking proactive steps to adapt to the region's future coastline with reduced risk, less need for recovery following floods, and a greater knowledge of where to continue building out our region with confidence into the future.

PAYING FOR IT

The Regional Coastal Commission could be established without new revenue sources, but its effectiveness would be tremendously enhanced through the proposed state adaptation funds, which could leverage funding—or pay for altogether—sorely needed adaptation projects throughout the region. The trust funds would be organized as public benefit corporations and initially capitalized from surcharges on property and casualty premiums. The funds would be managed by each state, but oversight and authority to underwrite and allocate the funds as grants and loans would rest with the commission. Each state trust fund would finance a minimum amount of in-state projects, while residual allocations would be prioritized for projects and programs whose benefits would extend beyond jurisdictional boundaries. The grants and loans could support a range of projects, from short-term community resilience planning to long-term infrastructure finance, and could be used to leverage or match other funding sources. Through the utilization of bond leverage, the funds could operate independently and without subsidy from the insurance surcharges within a 10-year sunset period.[20]

⑧ Institute climate Adaptation Trust Funds in all three states

Image: Rafi A+U + DLAND Studio for RPA's 4C initiative

Adaptation Trust Funds (ATFs) should be established in New York, New Jersey, and Connecticut to fund high-priority projects that protect inhabitants against coastal or inland flooding. These funds would be independently managed by each state, but the ultimate oversight and authority to allocate funds would rest with an underwriting committee of the Regional Coastal Commission (RCC). The RCC would be responsible for soliciting and underwriting projects and programs that seek to advance resilience and adaptation. ATFs would be capitalized by a surcharge on a limited number of regulated lines of insurance. Over time, this revenue stream could support public bonds to finance larger infrastructure projects.

Funding for resilience measures falls well short of need, and often comes too late.

The scope and scale of actions needed to protect all of our vulnerable communities from climate change require more money than federal, state, or local budgets—or philanthropy—can currently provide. What's more, current funding mechanisms for resilience and adaptation are sporadic and unpredictable, often not becoming available until after a major disaster occurs, making it difficult for municipalities to rebuild and plan for the future. And government funding is often focused on rebuilding what existed before the natural disaster.

The need to adapt and protect our communities against climate change is an ongoing challenge, but the funding mechanisms we have today do not allow communities to plan for the long term.

More than $27 billion of the region's resiliency needs have gone unmet—a figure likely to continue increasing as natural disasters become more frequent and funding sources dwindle with every passing disaster declaration.[21]

Given changing federal priorities, it is imperative the region lead in the areas the current federal government is weakening its environmental and climate-related research: regulation, funding, and policies. Undertaking these priority initiatives will require resilience, and resources exceeding the current funding and governing paradigm.

Establish state-level trust funds to supplement and leverage existing sources

Each of the three states should establish Adaptation Trust Funds (ATFs) to finance critical adaptation projects, prioritizing regional infrastructure for transportation, energy, and water. ATFs should be capitalized by a surcharge on a limited number of regulated lines of insurance and managed by a public benefit corporation with bonding authority, created in each state, and subject to state oversight.

Building off of a long history of public trust funds, ATFs would provide the resources to incentivize collective action and policy coordination, and stimulate a range of activities from local adaptation planning and vulnerability assessments to gap financing and infrastructure development. These resources would include a range of products, such as grants, non-recourse loans, below-market loans, and prime-rate permanent loans. Resulting projects could include, but would not be limited to buyouts, contaminated-site remediation, vector borne diseases, community protection, regional infrastructure protection, adaptation planning studies, and local municipal staff training.

ATFs would provide the cash flow for the proposed RCC, and be independently managed on a state-by-state basis. The authority to underwrite, approve, and allocate funds, however, would rest with the RCC, which would also implement projects and programs that seek to advance resilience and adaptation in coordination across all three states. While each state ATF should have minimum in-state allocations, residual allocations could be prioritized for projects and programs whose impacts extends beyond jurisdictional boundaries. In particular, priority would be given to projects that work to reduce exposure of insurable assets in a manner that reduces the cost burden of premiums.

Beyond disaster-risk-reduction, the ATF could also fund both capital expenditures and ongoing programs that deliver health, equity, and environmental benefits, along with climate resilience. Examples could include restoration projects that help advance stormwater management, or local planning efforts that build and maintain social networks as a backstop to community preparedness. The underwriting of these wide-ranging interventions would be subject to a rigorous analysis by the RCC that accounts for up-to-date science, vulnerability assessments, adaptive management protocols, and community engagement.

OUTCOMES

Adaptation Trust Funds would provide the region with consistent and reliable funding for adaptation and resiliency projects. Such funding, in coordination with a Regional Coastal Commission, would enable coordinated and sufficient investments into high-priority projects to lower flood risks for the greatest number of people and the most infrastructure. With a stable and predictable source of funding, each state can plan for and implement projects before disasters strike or permanent flooding from sea-level rise affects communities, thereby reducing risk and shortening recovery periods following natural disasters, while reducing the cost burden we already pay for in energy bills, transit passes, property taxes, and other expenses that embed infrastructure upgrades and other costs that would be supported by the trust funds.

PAYING FOR IT

ATFs would be capitalized by instituting a surcharge on property-casualty insurance premiums for lines that could include homeowners, commercial, farm owners, fire, inland and ocean marine, boiler and machinery, earthquake, and private-crop products. The surcharge could be set to sunset after 10 years. Using estimates for unmet financial needs for resiliency in New York City, New Jersey, and Connecticut that were calculated by each state following Superstorm Sandy, over $27 billion was used as a starting point for needs ATFs could have met. Without utilizing leverage in the bond market, estimated insurance surcharges for the average consumer of $1 per month in Connecticut, $5 per month in New York, and $15 per month in New Jersey were used to pay for the identified unmet needs of each state over 10 years.[1]

The added costs would be borne by those who pay the insurance premiums on the lines described above, including homeowners, landlords, commercial business owners, and farmers, among others. Under this scenario, renters would not be directly affected, though landlords could be expected to recapture additional expenditures through higher rents.

Alternatively, a relatively small surcharge of between 0.5 to 1.5 percent could be leveraged by bonding in each state to develop revenue for ATFs. A 1.5-percent surcharge leveraged by bonding over the course of 20 years could cover around 25 percent of New York City's, 10 percent of New Jersey's, and all of Connecticut's unmet needs.

CHANGE FUNDAMENTAL INEQUITIES IN HOW WE GOVERN LAND USE

Local government officials have the power to allocate services, levy taxes and fees, and regulate how land and buildings are used. Municipalities make these decisions in the best interests of constituents, but they often do not result in the best outcomes. Local decision-making has led to the loss of too much open space, the building of too few homes, expensive government services, and a widening opportunity gap among residents of different income levels.

To improve outcomes for all communities, local and state policies need to move in two directions. Local governments should be given the authority and resources to make decisions that have purely local impacts, such as how to regulate their streets. They should also have more power to manage their municipal finances and diversify revenue sources.

But at the same time, states should create incentives and requirements for local governments to address issues of regional significance, including addressing the housing-affordability crisis, by reducing reliance on local property taxes, improving the planning and development approvals process, seeking cost efficiencies in the provision of local services, and creating regional school districts to promote opportunity and reduce segregation.

⑨ Reduce reliance on local property taxes

Overreliance on property taxes to fund local services creates and reinforces socio-economic inequities and skews incentives to produce less housing and more sprawl. States should assume a larger share of local school budgets, increase incentives for shared services, and encourage cities, towns, and villages to diversify their sources of revenue with income taxes or more innovative property tax structures.

Overreliance on property taxes reinforces inequities between rich and poor communities, curbs the production of multifamily housing, and encourages sprawl.

High property taxes are one of the biggest complaints of homeowners, and a frequent target of legislators. And indeed, property taxes in the tri-state region are among the highest in the United States. As a share of home values, New Jersey has the highest property taxes of all 50 states, and Connecticut has the seventh highest rates. New York is 17th and would be higher were it not for New York City, which does not need to rely on property taxes because it levies income and sales taxes.[22]

Homeowners in high-income school districts have the highest performing schools but pay the lowest property tax rates.

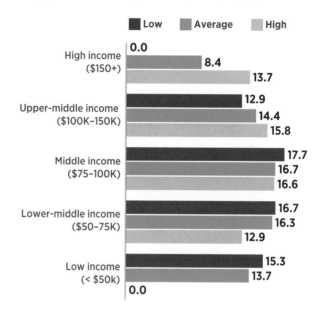

School taxes/$1,000 of property value for high-achieving, average, and low-achieving districts by median income

■ Low ■ Average ■ High

High income
($150+)
0.0
8.4
13.7

Upper-middle income
($100K–150K)
12.9
14.4
15.8

Middle income
($75–100K)
17.7
16.7
16.6

Lower-middle income
($50–75K)
16.7
16.3
12.9

Low income
(< $50k)
15.3
13.7
0.0

Source: RPA Assessment of School Performance ranked separately by state based on 4th and 8th grade test scores. American Community Survey 2015 5 Year Estimates. RPA Collection of Property Taxes from State Sources.

High property taxes are the result of a number of factors: choices of local officials and voters for types of services they want, inefficient service delivery that stems in part from a large number of small municipalities and school districts, and for many municipalities, the dearth of other revenue-source options.

Property taxes are a relatively stable source of revenue, and they are fair in the sense that property owners generally benefit from the services their taxes pay for. But when municipalities depend largely—and sometimes exclusively—on property taxes for revenue, it reinforces inequities between rich and poor communities. In less wealthy cities and school districts, municipalities make up for lower home values by cutting services and increasing property tax rates. As a result, many lower-income households end up paying a larger share of their incomes than households in wealthier communities—and often for worse service. Schools in poorer communities—where students have greater academic needs and require additional resources such as specialty teachers, equipment, and programs—have historically had the lowest budgets because they had less property tax revenue to support them. Meanwhile, schools in wealthier communities have had the highest budgets thanks to a big property tax base. Increasing state aid has narrowed this gap, but large differences between resources and needs remain.

On average, homeowners in high-income school districts pay the lowest property tax rates and have the highest-achieving schools. Homeowners in low-income districts pay higher property tax rates for schools with the lowest test scores. Interestingly, it is homeowners in middle- and lower-middle-income districts who pay the highest school property tax rates.

Overreliance on property taxes also contributes to the region's housing shortage. Communities often resist new residential development—particularly multifamily housing—out of fear that it will bring more children and add to school costs. Meanwhile, many studies have proven that multifamily housing does not add nearly as many school children as single-family homes (Joint Center for Housing Studies, *Overcoming Opposition to Multifamily Rental Housing, 2007*).

Local property taxes have also contributed to sprawl. Municipalities seeking to complement residential property tax revenue with commercial property tax and sales tax revenue have aggressively sought out the construction of new malls and retail development. Property taxes help explain why our suburbs are littered with large-footprint and underused commercial landscapes—aka, sprawl.

States have the power—and the responsibility—to address the problems with municipal property taxes.

Even though municipalities levy property taxes, the ability to reduce inequities and inefficiency in the property tax system rests with the three states.

States should relieve localities of a higher portion of their school taxes

Over the last several decades, states have already taken a greater role in funding local schools, although usually under court order.

- New Jersey's *Abbott vs Burke* case, for instance, mandated that the state provide the financial resources to ensure the students of 31 urban school districts— so-called "Abbott districts"—receive adequate public education, as required by the state constitution. Thanks to increased budgets, the performance gap between Abbott-district students and others in the state has narrowed (The Fund for New Jersey, Persistent Racial Segregation in Schools, 2017).

- New York State's highest court made a series of rulings related to the *Campaign for Fiscal Equity vs New York* finding that the state school funding system was unconstitutional, and ordered the state to provide new funding to New York City's public schools. Although some progress has been made, large gaps remain between urban and suburban schools.

- In Connecticut, building on the landmark *Scheff vs O'Neill* decision the required the state to address educational disparities in the Hartford area, a Superior Court declared in 2016 that the state's gap in test scores between students in rich and poor towns, resulting from the state's school funding system, was unconstitutional. The state's Supreme Court will hear the landmark case in 2017.

Nevertheless, the overwhelming majority of property taxes paid by homeowners and businesses goes to fund local schools. And the overwhelming majority of municipal budgets is spent on schools. Even with increases in state funding, primary and secondary schools on average still receive over half of their funding from local sources in each state, with most of that coming from local property taxes.[23]

States should increase their contributions to local school budgets, even if it means increasing state income or sales taxes, or perhaps imposing a statewide property tax. They could do so while requiring a commensurate reduction in local property taxes.

Shifting the tax base from municipalities to the state would make the overall tax system more efficient and equitable. Home owners in low- and middle-income districts would be less likely to pay higher taxes than owners in high-income districts. More education funding could be directed to the schools and students who are most in need. And there would be less incentive for towns and villages to try to stop the construction of affordable and multifamily housing or develop open space for low-density commercial space.

Provide incentives for service-sharing and consolidation

Local government is far more fragmented in the tri-state region than in other places in the United States. Outside New York City, there are 781 municipalities, 702 school districts, 491 fire districts, and dozens more authorities and special districts. Nassau and Suffolk Counties, for example, spend 45 percent more on public services and 60 percent more in property taxes than the comparably sized suburban counties of Fairfax and Loudoun in Virginia. Where northern Virginia had 17 county, town, city, village, and school district governments, Long Island had 239.[24]

Sharing services or consolidating districts could generate economies of scale, deliver services more efficiently, and reduce property taxes. States are making some progress providing grants and technical assistance to municipalities that voluntarily share services, such as fire equipment, school food, and transportation. But so far, results have been modest and diffuse. Evidently, it will take more aggressive measures from states to convince municipalities to coordinate. A new program in New York State, the County-wide Shared Services Initiative, is one approach that bears watching. It requires county officials to develop localized plans that find property tax savings from eliminating or coordinating duplicative services. Participating municipalities would be eligible for a one-time match from the state for demonstrated savings. It is too early to see results, but the requirement to develop a county-wide plan is a structure that could be enhanced and replicated.

In the longer term, states will need to provide more sustained incentives to achieve significant efficiencies. In cases of extreme inefficiency or inequity from small, fragmented districts, the state should make any state funding contingent on consolidation or an acceptable shared-services plan.

Give cities and counties the ability to diversify their revenue base

New York City and Yonkers have been authorized by the State of New York to levy income taxes. Allowing other cities, counties, and even larger towns and villages the ability to levy income taxes would lead to a more progressive tax structure and generate alternative revenue sources for communities with limited property tax bases. It would also make land-use decisions more rational by putting more emphasis on broader economic benefits rather than direct property tax ratables.

New York State also allows county and city sales taxes, whereas the other two states do not. Allowing counties and cities to levy sales taxes, while regressive, would be a means of broadening and diversifying the tax base. Municipalities would need to carefully levy the right mix of taxes to balance the revenue potential and volatility of taxes with their relative benefits.

States should also encourage municipalities to charge different property tax rates for the value of buildings than for the value of the underlying land. Taxing land at a higher rate than improvements encourages the development of vacant lots, brownfields, and underutilized properties, which could lead to more mid- to high-density, and more mixed-used development in downtowns and near transit. Where this model has been tried—in Pittsburgh, Scranton, and Harrisburg for example—more housing has been built and at greater densities than they likely would have with a traditional property tax structure.[25]

OUTCOMES

Most of these reforms would not reduce the overall level of taxation, but would shift tax burdens to make the system fairer and more efficient. Shifting more of the costs of education to the state would lower everyone's property taxes, but likely raise income, sales, and other state taxes unless the state chose to reduce spending or enact new types of taxes or fees. Municipalities and school districts with a low property tax base would benefit most. It would also increase funding to the schools and students who need it most. Sharing services and consolidation would reduce the overall level of taxation, or improve service quality, by making government more efficient. Providing municipalities with greater flexibility could provide more stability to local finances by broadening sources of revenue and helping to lessen tax burdens for households with low incomes but relatively high home values.

All of these reforms should lead to the creation of more and lower-priced housing by lowering resistance to multifamily and affordable housing and increasing incentives for owners to develop their properties. The reforms would also reduce incentives for allowing low-density commercial development—and thereby suburban sprawl—although market forces are making this less of an issue than it has been in the past.

PAYING FOR IT

Reforms should be revenue neutral in the short term and add to revenues in the long term by encouraging more multifamily and mixed-use development. Tax burdens would shift from lower- to higher-income households.

10 Create regional school districts and services

Photo: woodleywonderworks (flickr)

The region's highly segregated education system undermines equal opportunity for children in low-income and Black, and Hispanic communities, and reduces the region's economic prosperity. Segregation is supported by existing school-district boundaries that divide the region by race and income. This fragmented system also leads to inefficiencies and unfair property tax burdens. States should provide resources, incentives, and guidelines for school districts to consolidate and implement successful models of racially and economically integrated school.

The region's highly fragmented and segregated school systems contribute to wide disparities in educational achievement and tax burdens.

Educational achievement is one of the most important determinants of personal well-being, and a key to the success of the region as a whole. It is a strong predictor of personal income, upward mobility, health, and longevity—and increasingly separates prosperous from declining metropolitan areas. Unfortunately, the large gap in achievement levels that stems from a long history of inequities for poor, Black, and Hispanic families is a crisis for the region as well as the nation.

While educational outcomes are determined by many factors, including prenatal care and neighborhood conditions, the type and quality of schools can make the difference between success and failure. In the tri-state region, half of the elementary schools in predominantly low-income and nonwhite communities have low academic achievement

Low-performing schools are concentrated in low-income and nonwhite neighborhoods.

More than half of elementary schools in communities with less than $41,000 in median income are low-performing when measured by test scores. By contrast, fewer than ten percent of schools in communities with median household incomes that exceed $99,000 are low-performing. Children living in primarily white communities are nearly eight times more likely to live near a high-performing elementary school than children who live in neighborhoods where white households make up less than 10 percent of the population.

Elementary school performance by household median income of community

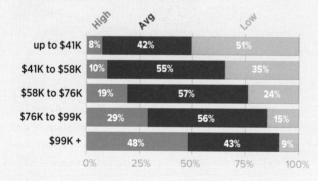

Elementary school performance by share of white population in community

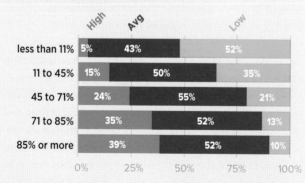

Sources: National Center for Education Statistics; NYS Department of Education; NJ Department of Education; CT Department of Education

Elementary school districts in the tri-state metropolitan area by size, race, and achievement

	School District Performance			
	HIGH	AVG	LOW	TOTAL
Less than 25% nonwhite	174	269	30	299
Very small (< 500)	28	58	12	70
Small (500–2000)	61	99	12	111
Medium (2000–4000)	53	60	3	63
Large (> 4000)	32	52	3	55
25-50% nonwhite	32	67	22	89
Very small (< 500)	1	5	2	7
Small (500–2000)	10	16	6	22
Medium (2000–4000)	11	16	2	18
Large (> 4000)	10	30	12	42
Over 50% nonwhite	2	19	23	42
Small (500–2000)	1	3		3
Medium (2000–4000)		6	8	14
Large (> 4000)	1	10	15	25
Region total	208	355	75	430
Very small (< 500)	29	63	14	77
Small (500–2000)	72	118	18	136
Medium (2000–4000)	64	82	13	95
Large (> 4000)	43	92	30	122

2011-2015 American Community Survey, 5 Year Estimates; Census School System Finance Survey for school year 2013-2014; RPA Test Schol Analysis from Fragile Success (National Center for Education Statistics; NYS Department of Education; NJ Department of Education; CT Department of Education)

when measured by fourth- and eighth-grade test scores, and only a small percentage are among the highest achieving. Test scores do not necessarily reflect the quality of instruction or leadership, but they are the best available indicator for comparing school outcomes across the region.[26] And there is ample evidence that low-income and nonwhite students who attend high-achieving and integrated schools perform better than those who attend low-achieving, segregated schools, and that higher income and white students benefit as well.[27][28]

In all three states, the large number of school districts reinforces segregation, creates inefficiencies, and unfairly distributes property tax burdens.

More than three million students attend school in 686 school districts across the tri-state region. Half of these districts have fewer than 2,000 students, and 113 have fewer than 500 students. New York and New Jersey have some of the highest numbers of small school districts in the country that are in close proximity to each other.[29]

By many measures, these small school systems are among the most racially and economically segregated in the United States. New York is the most segregated state in the nation when ranked by the exposure of Black students to White students, and New Jersey and Connecticut rank sixth and 14th, respectively.[30] By a broader measure, school segregation on Long Island is twice the national average.[31]

The segregation of our school districts is largely due to school districts being determined by municipal boundaries, with most people in the region living in segregated communities. As a result, most of the region's poor and nonwhite students are concentrated in large urban districts, while white students predominate in small suburban and rural districts.

A recent study found that, on Long Island, schools within the same school district were similar to each other, but schools in different districts were significantly different from each other, segregated by school district boundaries. A different study found that segregation in New Jersey was driven by school district boundaries, which are largely coterminous with municipal boundaries.[32]

Fragmentation also means many services cost taxpayers more than they should. Larger districts benefit from economies of scale, and therefore pay less per student for superintendents, teachers, administrative staff, transportation, and supplies than smaller districts, often without sacrificing the quality of the education.

States should provide incentives to integrate schools and combine school districts.

There is much that school districts can do, on their own or in collaboration with other districts, to reduce segregation and improve education outcomes. Where progress has been made, it has almost always been due to either federal or state action, usually in response to court orders. But the persistence of segregation after decades of court rulings requires states to be more assertive.

One way to proactively promote integration among school districts is through consolidation. States should provide incentives to collaborate and consolidate, working with school districts, counties, cities, towns, and villages to find the best regional solutions. And where incentives are not enough to achieve meaningful progress, the state should require actions among the following regionalization strategies:

- **Create county school districts:** Although many states have very successful county school districts, consolidating dozens of districts into large countywide school districts would be among the most far-reaching transformations New York or New Jersey could undertake (Connecticut would need to reconstitute county government). Such a transformation would require careful evaluation of costs and benefits, and ways of maintaining community identity and flexibility to meet local needs. Local districts could take advantage of economies of scale and have the tools and authority to promote integration on a wide scale.

- **Consolidate school districts:** School-district consolidation occurred rapidly in the early 20th century as the population shifted from rural to urban communities. Over the coming decades, the student population is again expected to shrink in many exurban and rural areas in New Jersey, the Hudson Valley, and Connecticut. Consolidating these districts would be an opportunity to expand services and lower costs. But consolidating largely white, affluent districts with neighboring nonwhite, low-income districts (Bridgeport and Fairfield, CT, for example, or Hempstead and Garden City on Long Island) would have a far bigger impact on racial integration. The Morristown and Morris Township, NJ, school districts were merged in 1973 to achieve better racial balance; to this day, the combined district remains integrated and 93 percent of its graduates go on to higher education.[33]

- **Designate regional and magnet schools:** Regional and magnet schools draw students from several districts, expand educational opportunities for all students, and can help create high-performing, integrated schools. The most prominent and successful example in the region is the Hartford interdistrict magnet program. Forty-five well-funded inter-district schools were created to attract both urban and suburban students. As a result, the share of Hartford students in racially isolated schools has been reduced from 89 percent in 2007 to 54 percent in 2014. Educational achievement is much higher for low-income students attending these schools, and suburban students who choose to attend schools with students of all socioeconomic backgrounds have positive social-emotional development.[34]

- **Allow for inter-district transfers:** Inter-district transfers allow students to choose to attend school in a neighboring district. This approach is part of the Hartford reforms and has been used in New Jersey and other states. As a tool for reducing racial isolation, the results have been mixed, and requires both parental preferences and socioeconomic background to be considered in making placements.[35]

- **Share programs and services:** Districts can share services and programs to reduce costs and expand course offerings. In New York State, the Board of Cooperative Education Services provides human resources, special education, vocational education, professional development, and other services. While less robust for promoting racial and economic integration than other strategies, it can help small districts create economies of scale and expand resources and opportunities for students in underfunded or poorly performing districts.

OUTCOMES

Each state should set a goal of increasing the number students attending high-performing, integrated schools. A reasonable goal would be to bring school segregation to the national average in 15 years, and provide direction, support, and incentives for school districts to collaborate to meet that goal. The Hartford program and other models have proven that the gap between poor and affluent students and nonwhite and white students in reading scores, graduation scores, and other achievement measures can be reduced substantially and in a relatively short period of time.

PAYING FOR IT

The most expensive element of a regionalization strategy would be the creation of regional or magnet schools. They require substantial investments and programs that both provide support for low-achieving students and attract high-achieving students. Connecticut has spent $1.4 billion to build and renovate its magnet schools and $150 million to operate them each year. But this approach also has the advantage of being voluntary for families and students. School consolidation and other approaches also require upfront administrative costs, but should save money in the long term by achieving economies of scale and reducing costs per pupil.

11 Make New York City property taxes fair

Photo: Felix Mizioznikov

New York City residential property tax bills bear little relation to property values. Tax-incentive policies for both residential and commercial properties, as well as high utility-tax rates, create further inequities. A more efficient and equitable tax system should move toward equalizing effective tax rates for all types of residential property, and relieve the hidden property tax paid by renters through utilities and rent.

For decades, New York City has had a tax system that is both illogical and inequitable.

A multitude of laws governing rates, assessments, exemptions, and valuations has left us with a backward structure in which the wealthiest people often pay the least taxes. It is not uncommon, for instance, for a longtime resident in a modest house in a working-class neighborhood to pay the same amount for property taxes as someone who has just bought a multimillion-dollar brownstone in Park Slope. A condo in Manhattan may incur the same property taxes as a condo that sold for 20 times more at the exact same time. Modest, rent-stabilized apartment buildings built 80 years ago can pay so much in property taxes that maintenance and upkeep can suffer, while apartment buildings built 10 years ago generally pay next to nothing. Properties owned by utilities are taxed at a very high rate, which gets passed on to everyone who pays an electric or water bill.

These irrational discrepancies stem from a broken taxing system that must be made fair. The New York City property tax structure features four separate tax classes, whose rates, valuation, and rules are largely determined independently of each other, resulting in imbalances. Various exemptions and policies have been instituted over the years to rectify these imbalances, such as a special tax reduction for co-op owners, and a large, long-term exemption to spur rental development. The result is a convoluted and unfair system that needs to be restructured.

Reform should aim to make property taxes more equitable without creating sharp, short-term tax increases for existing beneficiaries.

New York City should reform its property tax structure following these principles:

- Base residential housing property taxes on actual value, not type of structure

- Reduce property taxes that have a disproportionately regressive effect on low-income residents

- Put in place mechanisms to make sure renters directly benefit from any reductions in property taxes

- Reform tax exemptions so that taxpayer costs are proportionate with public benefits provided

- Make sure reforms do not unnecessarily harm residents in the short term; move smoothly and steadily toward a more logical and fair system

End the residential tax cap on title transfers

Assessed value increases for one- to three-family residential properties (Class 1) and smaller multifamily buildings (Class 2a, 2b, and 2c) are capped at a certain percentage every year in order to protect those who own properties in rapidly gentrifying neighborhoods from sharp bumps in property taxes. Because this cap is tied to the building, not the owner, it is passed on indefinitely, leading to property taxes in gentrified neighborhoods staying depressed over the long term compared with those in neighborhoods that have seen more modest price increases. These artificially low taxes also have the effect of inflating sale prices, giving an added benefit to owners in gentrifying neighborhoods and driving even higher price increases.

A more rational policy would be to tie the limitation on increases to the owner instead of the building, and end it after any part of the building transfers titles and the assessed value resets based on the current market value. This would still protect existing owners from sharp increases in property taxes, while also bringing practices in line with larger multifamily (Class 2) properties.

Equalize property tax methods between small and large properties

Buildings with either three or fewer residential units or four or more residential units play much the same role in New York City. Both are used for housing, and can be owned or rented. Yet, they are treated completely differently in the tax code. Valuation methods, assessments, tax rates, and tax caps are all calculated differently. Exemptions and abatements differ between the two types of property as well. For instance, cooperatives and condominiums have an abatement for owner-occupants, while one- to three-family homes do not. New York City should move toward a system in which small and large residential properties are treated similarly in terms of valuation, assessments, rates, caps, exemptions, and abatements.

Determine property values more accurately

The method by which multifamily properties today are assessed—according to their value as rental properties, even if they are owner-occupied cooperatives or condominiums—often leaves co-ops and condos valued significantly lower than their actual market value, especially at the high end of the market. More modest properties are therefore left to make up the difference with comparably higher taxes. A better way to value properties would be to use the same process as one- to three-family homes, which is based on the the actual sales value of comparable homes.

For rental properties, care must taken with this approach. Basing a building's taxes on the sales or refinancing price of the building itself would likely have the effect of both reducing speculation and overleveraging, as speculative sales prices would be discouraged by the resulting higher tax bills. However, basing a building's taxes on comparable sales prices would result in higher taxes for all buildings in areas of speculative price increases, which may exacerbate displacement pressures.

Owners of 1- to 3-family homes in neighborhoods with lower property values pay higher effective tax rates.

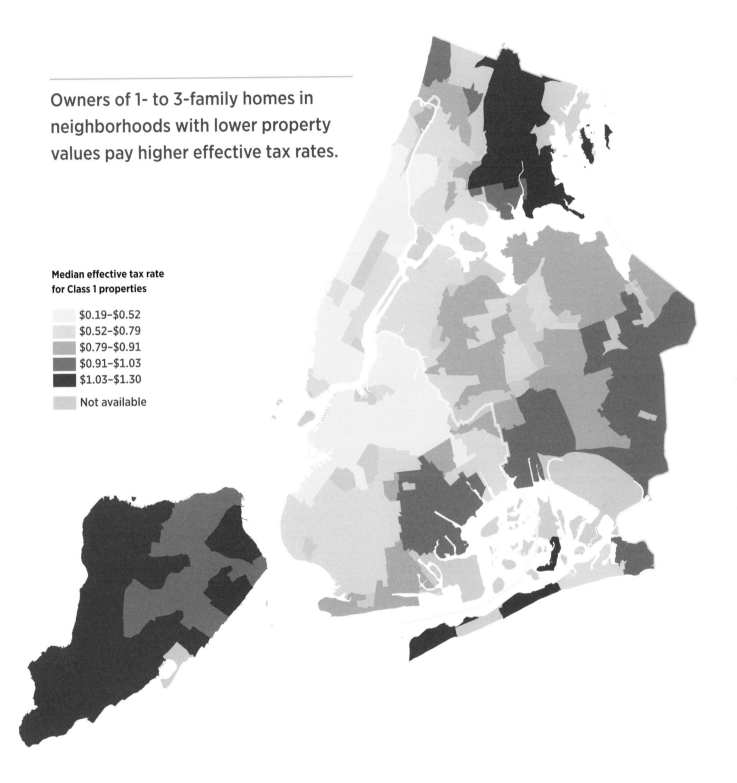

**Median effective tax rate
for Class 1 properties**

- $0.19–$0.52
- $0.52–$0.79
- $0.79–$0.91
- $0.91–$1.03
- $1.03–$1.30
- Not available

Source: NYC Independent Budget Office (IBO) 2017

Institute a direct renter's credit

The savings from any reduction in property taxes for rental buildings must be passed on at least partially to tenants, especially those who are low income. Without a direct method of delivery, these savings are not likely to be realized by tenants because of market and regulatory factors. And low-income tenants in one- to three-family homes should likewise be protected from rising rents that might come about as a result of higher taxes on the property. A direct mechanism, such as a refundable credit on state or city income taxes for renters, would ensure savings are divided appropriately between owners and renters.

Lower property taxes on utilities

Utility properties pay disproportionate real estate taxes on their holdings, accounting for 6 percent of all tax revenue while holding just 3 percent of the real estate value in the city. Since utilities are heavily regulated, this has the effect of a de facto regressive tax on all utility ratepayers, regardless of income. Capping or reducing these taxes would move the tax system overall in a more equitable direction.

Reform how multifamily and commercial exemptions are done

New York City offers tax exemptions and abatements to stimulate a certain kind of development or upgrade. Often times, however, most notably in the case of the 421a exemption for multifamily housing, instead of dedicating a set amount of money to stimulate development, the costs are left open-ended. The more a property increases in value, the greater the cost to the taxpayer.

These exemptions should be restructured to one in which a set amount of benefit is given and the value of the exemption is capped, which will ensure the public expense doesn't exceed the public benefit.

As a result of this all-or-nothing system, buildings eligible for these exemptions often pay next to nothing in taxes for decades, regardless of how valuable they are. Other buildings—often older and less valuable—then have to pick up a disproportionate share of the tax burden. Just as buildings paying too much in taxes should see their tax burdens go down, buildings benefiting from overly generous exemptions should pay their fair share.

There are also large differences in taxes on commercial properties due to tax incentive policies, most notably the Industrial and Commercial Abatement Program. While commercial taxation rates should be set separately from residential rates, incentives should be examined to provide the proper balance of commercial and residential development.

OUTCOMES

Making New York City property taxes fair and effective would result in direct savings for low-income households, and a fairer and more rational structure for residential housing overall. It would likely also have the effect of lowering housing prices in high-end, owner-occupied housing due to re-sized tax bills.

Smart property tax reform would also generate more housing production by reducing the gap in tax burden between large residences and multiple smaller units, making it more financially feasible to build rowhouses or duplexes than large McMansions, and multiple smaller condominiums instead of large penthouse apartments.

Cutting down on large incentives for multifamily residential construction would likely have a temporary negative effect on housing production. In the longer term, however, reducing the overall tax burden for multifamily housing would encourage production.

PAYING FOR IT

These reforms could be specifically designed to be revenue-neutral, meaning the savings from tax increases on one type of property would be offset, dollar-for-dollar, by decreases on others types of property. Decisions about raising more or less revenue through property taxes overall would be unaffected by this proposal, and New York City would retain the ability to make those decisions based on current fiscal conditions.

Residents who would likely see higher costs are new owners of high-cost one- to three-family homes, as well as owners of high-end cooperatives and condominiums. Existing owners of these properties would likely see lowered property values because of the higher taxes upon sale. The people likely to see lowered costs would be rental tenants of existing, older multifamily housing. City residents as a whole would also realize savings through lowered utility costs.

12 Make the planning and development process more inclusive, predictable, and efficient

The process for evaluating and approving proposed development projects is time-consuming, expensive, and inefficient. It too often excludes residents, especially low income communities of color, and it isn't creating the housing and commercial space the region sorely needs to address its affordability crisis. In order to create growth that better reflects our needs, planning and approval processes must be made more inclusive, equitable, and predictable, using the best tools available for addressing a wide range of impacts.

Complex rules exclude too many residents from the process and make it too difficult to advance worthy projects.

Each of the region's 782 cities, towns, and villages has its own process for approving development projects, zoning changes, and other land-use actions. Each state also has its own requirements for environmental review, municipal master planning, and other approvals.

And yet all of these processes have the same three problems in common: community residents feel shut out of the process until it is too late to affect decisions; developers complain that approvals take far too long and the process is so unpredictable that only the most well-resourced and patient capital can see projects to completion; and municipal officials often lack the resources to adequately evaluate proposals and efficiently move them through the approvals process.

At a regional level, this inefficiency results in too few beneficial projects reaching completion, impacting housing supply and contributing to the affordability crisis. For projects that do get finished, benefits are unevenly distributed and adverse impacts are overlooked, affecting community health and well-being.

All cities, towns, and villages should have up-to-date comprehensive plans that reflect the input and needs of residents.

Up-to-date comprehensive plans, developed with robust resident participation early in the process, both require communities to think proactively about their future and help them set out a policy framework that informs, rather than reacts to, development projects as they are proposed. These plans help communities better negotiate with developers, and give developers a clearer sense of what projects are likely to be approved.

Although New Jersey and Connecticut require municipalities to prepare and adopt a comprehensive plan every ten years in order to maintain eligibility for certain funding, they do not provide specific guidelines or requirements for incorporating community input into the planning process. Instead, municipalities typically gain input through public meetings. However, such public meetings tend to attract only a small and often unrepresentative share of the population, as many stakeholders are either unengaged or unable to attend because of work schedules, child care issues, and other conflicts. Much more needs to be done to expand the scope of engagement formats, including the use of online and social media tools. Municipalities need more guidance and training on how to effectively communicate and engage with local communities early in the process.

In New York, comprehensive planning is encouraged, but not required. Instead, the state relies on mandated environmental review to guide planning and development decisions. This means community engagement is limited

to providing input into scoping of environmental impacts, and participating in public hearings, as proactive engagement with local communities in shaping proposals and/or development scenarios early in the process is not included within the scope of the current state and city environmental review processes.[36]

All three states need a meaningful, comprehensive planning process that evaluates potential impacts and provides clear direction for future planning and development decisions. Updates should be required every ten years, with environmental review folded into the planning process. In New York City, comprehensive plans should be developed for each community board.

Give all projects a fixed timeline for community input and government approvals

Clear and predictable timelines are essential for transparent and effective community input and reliable government approvals. Without predictability and transparency, the development process can become mired in political dealings and/or the appearance of such dealings, which can result in a drawn-out, frustrating, and expensive process.

Unfortunately, outside New York City, there are often no statutory timelines, so even small projects can take years to complete—if they happen at all. Community members waste valuable time in public meetings without a clear sense of how their input is being incorporated. For developers, redundant meetings increase legal and professional consulting costs, potentially reducing the budget left over for quality design and materials. Delays can also impact developers' ability to obtain public funding and/or private financing for a project.

New York City's Uniform Land Use Review Process (ULURP) provides a good example of a clear and predictable approvals timeline, once a proposal is certified as ready for review. Once certified, ULURP guarantees that a proposed project will move through the review process with specified timelines for different agencies, community boards, and the mayor. Despite this predictability, however, meaningful community engagement does not occur early enough in the ULURP process. There is no clear process or timeline for public input before a proposal is certified as ready for review; and after certification, it is difficult to change a project in response to community feedback.

In order to be inclusive, equitable, and predictable, ULURP and other planning processes in the region need to include robust and transparent public engagement early in the planning process as alternatives are being considered and evaluated, before proposals become solidified and difficult to change. Set timelines should be specified, and a suite of engagement tools employed, to ensure meaningful contributions from a diverse group of stakeholders. The states should provide technical assistance and/or funding for municipalities to implement such engagement, with municipalities engaging with organizations within their local communities as partners to solicit community input into the process.

Evaluate projects for their impact on health, the environment, and local communities through a process that links environmental permitting and comprehensive planning

Although environmental review processes differ in each state, as well as in New York City[37], they typically require proposed projects to be evaluated on a similar set of impacts: natural habitats, air quality, water quality, traffic, noise, viewsheds, and other environmental conditions. But development projects also have important repercussions on other conditions, such as health, displacement, transit accessibility, workforce development, and fiscal balance sheets. These types of impacts are rarely included in the environmental review process. Effective analyses must capture both impacts on the natural environment and on local communities. Environmental review methodologies should take advantage of new technology, data, and research to include metrics such as formulas for calculating displacement, employing health impact assessments, and taking into consideration the social determinants of health.

Today, the environmental review process suffers from two distinct, but related flaws. First, the process is structured, by design, to identify the negative impacts of a proposed project, and not its positive benefits. For example, community services required to support a new development project can often be a flashpoint of contention, while positive impacts of a project on areas such as housing affordability may receive little attention. Second, the environmental review evaluates impacts in a very narrow geographic context that fails to include neighboring communities or the region at large—either of which may benefit or be affected negatively. Dense multifamily housing, for example, may cause more traffic or noise at one intersection, but on the whole, may generate fewer car trips than the same number of units built across a broader geography. Operating with this narrow lens, the environmental review process is very often used as a tool to delay and stop developments that may, in fact, be seen as beneficial to communities when viewed from a more holistic perspective.

Data is critical to effectively evaluating the impacts of proposed projects—and new technologies can make more data available and easier to analyze. States and/or counties must collect, maintain, and make available the information local communities need throughout the planning process. They should also provide the technical and planning assistance necessary for municipal officials, staff, and citizens to learn how to utilize the data in ways that produce better, more equitable outcomes, with greater speed and efficiency. At the municipal level, all permitting and environmental review and approvals for development projects should be coordinated by a designated municipal office or point person. At the state level, an online dashboard should be created to track local development project review and permitting. This dashboard should be accessible to the public and provide transparency and information-sharing across municipalities.

Make the project evaluation process accessible and transparent, and include the views of a wide range of stakeholders

At first glance, there seems to be an inherent tension between expanding stakeholder engagement and making the planning process faster and more predictable. Experience has shown, however, that not taking stakeholder input into account—especially early in the process—can slow down projects, or even stall them entirely. Early and inclusive participation in project planning can reduce opposition and litigation, and when combined with clear timelines and evaluation criteria, can provide greater predictability overall. Several actions by municipalities and states can help create this more virtuous cycle.

The first is to solicit the help of community-based organizations in reaching out to people who are typically underrepresented in the planning process, particularly communities of color, as well as immigrant and low-income communities. Getting their views incorporated into the project is important not only to ensure everyone has a voice in the future of where they live, but to give the municipality a better understanding of how the project will affect its residents and businesses.

Other organizations, such as health clinics, senior centers, and other community groups can also help reach out to diverse stakeholders. By serving as mediators and organizers, these organizations can coordinate community needs assessments, identify community priorities, and articulate trade-offs related to planning and development decisions.

The participatory budgeting model, which allows local community members to vote directly on how a portion of capital funds are spent in their neighborhood, could be adapted to allow local stakeholders to vote on trade-offs related to planning and development decisions (e.g., housing affordability, visual impacts, mobility, etc.).

Successful community engagement in the planning process is difficult, so states should make sure communities have the technical support and resources necessary to effectively undertake these efforts.

Promote diversity with respect to race, age, gender, and socioeconomic background on all planning and zoning boards and commissions

A substantial portion of development-application decisions are made at planning and zoning boards and commissions across the region. In many cases, these entities do not represent diverse demographic and socioeconomic backgrounds, areas of expertise, or perspectives. And with the exception of New York City's community boards, nonresident workers who often have important ties to, and care deeply about, the communities in which they work are completely excluded from community planning and decision-making, despite being important contributors to the local economy. Even in New York City, where there is more diversity on boards and commissions than in other parts of the region, community planning boards are not necessarily representative of the residents and workers in their communities.

In order for planning and development decisions to become more inclusive, predictable, and economically efficient, the boards and commissions who have the ultimate say in voting on development proposals must become more diverse and reflective of a wider range of community perspectives. Municipalities should actively work to diversify boards and commissions and create mechanisms for including the voices of nonresident workers critical to the local economy, particularly with selection of individuals for appointed and volunteer positions over which they have direct control.

OUTCOMES

Planning and development approval processes that are more predictable, inclusive, and efficient will result in projects that better reflect the needs and aspirations of local communities, and better address potential development impacts. They will also reduce project timelines, and therefore municipal and developer costs, which can translate into higher quality developments. Open-source, community-driven data tools will enable municipalities to more easily integrate planning with assessment of community and regional costs and benefits.

PAYING FOR IT

Developing comprehensive municipal and neighborhood plans with full community engagement requires significant resources for staff, outreach, and technical studies. Centralizing data sources and creating replicable tools can help reduce costs, but the commitments are still substantial, especially for small municipalities. Technical assistance for planning and data gathering and distribution are two areas where the states can play an active role in providing resources to local municipalities, either through grant funds or direct staff assistance. Some municipalities could also benefit from multi-jurisdictional planning and shared resources, a collaboration states could incentivize.

MAKE TECHNOLOGY POLICY A CORE PART OF GOVERNMENT'S BUSINESS

Technology has transformed how we communicate, shop, and consume news and information. But government institutions have struggled to integrate technology. With few exceptions, public sector agencies have been slow to leverage technology to better engage with constituents, or improve the services they provide by collecting, analyzing, and sharing relevant data. They also haven't done enough to ensure everyone has access to affordable and reliable internet service, as they have for other public utilities.

All governmental institutions in the region should promote the use of technology by setting broad objectives and encouraging pilot projects to improve services and communication with constituents. They must also increase access to affordable internet services. To support the region's hundreds of municipalities, a regional census organization that would be responsible for coordinating and disseminating essential data to improve local services should be established.

⑬ Increase participation in local government

Photo: ParticipatoryBudgeting.org

Local governments make most decisions about what gets built where—what planners call land use—as well as where public money is spent. Yet few residents participate in many types of community decision-making, and there is uneven representation by race, age, and income as well. As a result, local institutions make decisions that often reflect the values and needs of older, wealthier, and mostly white residents rather than the population at large. To promote greater participation in local government, we can use technology to broaden public engagement, adopt participatory budgeting, reform the public planning process, and give all long-term residents the chance to vote. Together, these initiatives will lead to local decisions that better reflect community needs and aspirations.

A small and unrepresentative share of the population makes critical decisions about land use, school budgets, and local services.

Whether to allow townhouses, apartments, and shops; under what conditions landlords are able to evict tenants; how to design and program public spaces; how to spend property tax revenue; and how much to invest in local schools—these are all decisions made by locally elected officials. By shaping the physical and fiscal realities of our communities, local elected officials affect how residents experience their communities every day.

But despite the outsized impact of local government, the share of people who participate in the regular workings of local democracy is extremely low. Even in high-profile mayoral elections, consistently fewer than one in three adult residents vote, and far fewer attend hearings or serve on local bodies such as the zoning boards or school boards.

The main factor driving this poor participation is the lack of a direct "reward" for participating in local government. Many people do not know what local government does or how they can affect decisions. As consumers of goods and online social networks, we are consistently given information and feedback. But as citizens, the information we receive from government can be opaque, engagement is infrequent, and there is little expectation that government will be responsive.

In some communities, there is direct exclusion from government. Across the region, 2.6 million people cannot vote in local elections because they are not U.S. citizens and tens of thousands cannot vote because they are on parole or on probation. In Port Chester, NY; Union City, NJ; Hempstead, NY; and a dozen other municipalities, more than a third of all adults are not eligible to vote. Most of these residents pay taxes, send their children to public schools, participate in the civic life of their communities, and are knowledgeable about the challenges facing their neighborhoods, yet they are barred from participating. This represents a tremendous loss to the community because these residents are typically low income and of color, and their needs can be very different than their neighbors'.

This lack of participation has very real impacts on land use, local budgeting, and school policy. Decisions about these issues reinforce the region's deepening inequality, limit economic opportunity for working families, stifle the sense of civic belonging, and lower the quality of life for many.

Local government leaders should use more of the tools at their disposal to engage with their constituents.

Improving civic participation and trust will require reconnecting residents with their government and demonstrating that participation in local democratic efforts yields results.

Expand participatory budgeting
Participatory budgeting is a process that allows community members to decide how to spend a portion of a public budget to fund improvements to schools, parks, libraries, public housing, or other public projects. By making budget decisions clear and accessible, the participatory budgeting process motivates a wide range of residents to participate in local government decisions—even those who have not been involved before.

Participatory budgeting is not new to the region, but we have a long way to go until it reaches all residents. New York City leads the country in this regard, with more than 30 city council members allocating nearly $40 million for participatory budgeting. Participatory budgeting is being considered by residents and elected officials in Hempstead, NY; Stamford, CT; Bridgeport, CT; New Haven, CT; and statewide in New Jersey. CUNY-system colleges and even an elementary school have done participatory budgeting with students. Other cities and towns in the region should follow this lead and set aside a share of their municipal budget for allocation by local residents.

Use participatory planning to design healthier communities
A lot has been learned in the last ten years about how to create better streets through design, but more of these "placemaking" projects must be built. Communities can dramatically improve quality of life and public health outcomes by connecting community destinations, and creating a sense of place around them. Including all residents in the planning process, particularly those from more vulnerable populations, will help identify the projects of most value to the community. Examples include safe routes to health in Seattle,[38] safe routes to school programs[39] and walking buses, designing playgrounds in streets,[40] using joint use agreements[41] to create more open spaces, and creating a free public water supply[42] and critical facilities in times of emergency such as cooling centers. These are all low-cost, high-impact ways to show that local public institutions are responsive to community needs.

Reform the development approvals process
Some of the most significant decisions made by local governments concern real estate development. Local governments must do more to inform the public of what projects are being considered, educate them about the broader dynamics at play, solicit their input, and keep them informed about construction updates. Among the recommendations for how to make these processes more inclusive are requiring municipal and community plans so projects reflect resident priorities, specifying timelines for community input, and working to diversify planning boards and commissions to better reflect the diversity of the communities they serve.

Make it easier and more rewarding to register and vote

Voting should be a convenient and rewarding experience. All states need to pass measures to simplify voter registration, promote early voting and voting by mail, and extend open hours at polling stations. Local elections should be scheduled to coincide with state and federal elections and communities should find more ways to reinforce the positive aspects of participating in democracy. Nobody should experience difficulty exercising their right to vote.

Give long-term residents a greater voice in local affairs

Many important decisions are made at the local level, including land use, investments in local amenities, and school budgets. In making these decisions, local government leaders better reflect the aspirations and needs of the community when they consider themselves to be accountable to all the people living in their jurisdiction. Residents, including long-term, noncitizen residents, who are invested in their community—who pay taxes, raise their families and send their children to public schools—should be able to have a say in local decisions that affect their lives. There are a range of strategies that can accomplish this goals, including publishing official documents in multiple languages, and holding hearings with translation services available. At the end of the spectrum, a few municipalities in the United States even allow noncitizen voting in limited circumstances. In San Francisco, for example, noncitizens who have children in the city's school district can now vote in local school board elections. Local governments should adopt appropriate strategies to expand participation to all residents who will be affected by their decisions.

Allow those who have served their time to vote

In New York, formerly incarcerated persons must complete parole before they can vote. In New Jersey and Connecticut, the law is even stricter, requiring completion of both parole and probation. Our three states should follow the sixteen states across the country that allow those who have served their time to be reinstated as eligible voters. We all have a vital stake in reintegrating formerly incarcerated persons back into their communities. Allowing them to exercise their right to vote is an important step in that direction.

OUTCOMES

Government must assume a more active role in efforts to widen citizen participation in decision-making, and encourage elected officials to be more responsive and in touch with the communities they represent. Changing the voting laws to permit long-term residents and those formerly incarcerated to vote will ease disenfranchisement and allow many residents who have been shut out of the process to participate. Opening the budgetary process and making the decision-making more transparent will provide residents with a better idea of what government does and how it can respond to meet their needs. Over time, all of these reforms will greatly increase civic engagement and give residents a more prominent voice in the future of their own communities.

PAYING FOR IT

Overall, efforts to increase local participation in government—such as revising voting regulations, including residents in development decisions, and adopting participatory budgeting—would involve minimal costs.

Increasing the technological capacity of local government would take more resources over the long term. State governments should make available both financial incentives and training to local governments who wish to be more innovative in their engagement with constituents.

14 Expand affordable internet access across the region

Access to high-speed internet is essential to the overall success of the region, and to growing economic and social opportunities for our residents. And yet our internet infrastructure is far behind what is available in other major U.S. cities, or internationally. High-speed digital service is available only in parts of the region, and is more expensive than in many of the region's peer metros. In order to achieve ubiquitous and affordable high-speed internet service, public-sector agencies need to coordinate and streamline access to critical infrastructure underground, on the streets, and on rooftops. They must invest in publicly accessible fiber-optic cable, and allow internet providers to innovate on last-mile solutions.

The region's internet infrastructure is expensive and unequally distributed.

The internet is already essential for many jobs, homework, research, entertainment, and, of course, connecting with other people. In the future, it will become even more essential. The number of employees who use the internet to work from home grows every year. High-quality, reliable video conferencing may become the standard in a global world. Many medical services will be delivered electronically to improve care and increase efficiency. The region's infrastructure, such as highways, the electric grid, and buildings, will be powered by the internet. If wielded appropriately, internet infrastructure can be a tool to provide economic mobility, connect people, and make our infrastructure more efficient.

Households earning twice the poverty rate or less are nearly three times more likely to be without high-speed wired internet access at their home than higher-income households.

Share of households without high-speed wired internet at home by poverty level, 2014

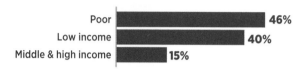

Poor	46%
Low income	40%
Middle & high income	15%

Note: Poor households with incomes below the U.S. Census poverty threshold. Low-income households with incomes above the poverty threshold but below double the poverty threshold. Middle- and high-income households with incomes that exceed twice the poverty threshold.

Source: American Community Survey 2014

A $40 monthly plan gets New Yorkers far slower internet service than residents of other cities.

Best deal under $40 by internet speed (MB), 2014

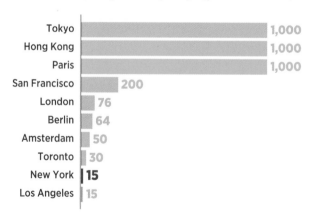

Tokyo	1,000
Hong Kong	1,000
Paris	1,000
San Francisco	200
London	76
Berlin	64
Amsterdam	50
Toronto	30
New York	15
Los Angeles	15

Source: Open Technology Institute

But the region is not necessarily on track to achieving that future. Gaining access to the internet can be a challenge for many residents. Over 23 percent of the region's households lack a wired high-speed internet connection at home, and access is unequally distributed among income levels. Only 15 percent of middle- and high-income households lack an internet connection at home, compared with nearly half of all poor households. Cost is a major factor, with few monthly subscriptions available for under $40 in New York, which can be difficult for many struggling families to afford. As a high-speed, reliable internet connection is increasingly essential for access to educational services, job opportunities, and even healthcare, this can represent a significant barrier to opportunity.

Lack of affordable internet access can represent a barrier for others as well. Internet in New York City is far more expensive than in many of its national and international peers.

These problems foreshadow what is to come if access to the internet for all types of users is not rationalized and expanded. The internet depends on a physical network of pipes, fiber-optic cables, rooftop antennas, utility poles, and data-storage centers. This physical network—and who can access it—determines the availability and cost of many other services, how equally they are distributed, and perhaps even the kind of information people have access to.

There are several reasons this physical network does not provide comprehensive and affordable service. Internet providers are private companies incentivized to serve the most profitable markets first rather than meet the region's infrastructure needs. Local government has not done enough to enable access across different public and private owners of infrastructure and buildings. Many of the various components that together make the internet—underground conduits, utility poles, rooftops, buildings—can be very difficult to access physically because they are privately owned. Conduit is underground. Buildings are not required to allow access to providers (as they are with other utilities) or be wired for fiber-optic-based service. Without rationalizing and expanding access to the internet and its underlying infrastructure, the region risks falling behind in a world in which everything will depend on the internet.

Make it easy for competitors to enter the market

As the region looks to restore its infrastructure and ensure equity, health, and prosperity, it is time to reimagine how internet infrastructure is built and managed. After all, the internet was developed by the U.S. Department of Defense, and its early development was driven largely by government and academic needs. But its broad-based deployment to consumers was achieved by private companies. With lagging and uneven service, it is time for government in the region to take a leadership role in the provision of this increasingly essential infrastructure. This has already been happening in many places across the United States. In a region with so many municipalities and different needs and capacities, no single strategy will work everywhere. But the following proposals can apply in a range of contexts to improve planning, investment, and outcomes.

Expand public ownership and partnerships with service providers

States should proactively incentivize and support publicly owned internet infrastructure and provide technical assistance to local government around data collection, business models, and policy options. In turn, counties and councils of governments, and sometimes municipalities, should take a leadership role in exploring what broadband solutions work for them. And under any scenario, municipalities should ensure fair wholesale access to their internet infrastructure for all users, even when it is privately owned.

In locations facing major redevelopment, needing other public investment, or with poor internet service, municipally-provided broadband may be the best course of action. Counties and municipalities could partner to create service districts that have the authority to finance and build infrastructure that could be owned entirely by local government or other partners. These service districts could be financed through private-sector partnerships, with the goal of building public-access networks to a specific building or node. Priority would be given to major redevelopments and low-income areas, and to making infrastructure more resilient in the flood zone. Third-party providers could then compete to supply innovative last-mile solutions, and state and local economic-development agencies could work to incentivize this collaboration. In places where there are sufficient internet offerings, renewed franchise agreements could be an opportunity to expand wholesale access to the internet and increase competition.

Reform how we manage our underground assets

One of the biggest barriers is the difficulty of accessing the infrastructure. This is particularly true for assets below ground, especially in Manhattan, much of whose web of assets under its streets is more than 100 years old. The challenge has three components: lack of shared knowledge of what infrastructure is located where, lack of coordination on street digging and other related actions, and lack of a publicly accessible conduit that would make it easier for different companies to utilize the underground infrastructure. Together, this represents a big challenge not only to internet access, but also to other utilities, transportation investments, green infrastructure, and better public use of underground spaces.

Municipalities should create dedicated authorities to not only issue permits for street work but proactively plan and coordinate between different actors, ensuring "dig once" policies are implemented with maximum efficiency. Any entity that digs up a street should also be responsible for building public conduit and laying public fiber-optic networks. As part of that process, municipalities and other public entities should inventory and open up any public assets—for example, by connecting to the fiber-optic network owned by the MTA.

Open access to other critical public assets

While underground utilities are the biggest challenge to access, other public assets can also be difficult to get to. "One touch make ready" and "dig once" policies can ensure that if one utility is installing infrastructure using utility poles or digging underground, other critical infrastructure work, including the installation of internet infrastructure, is completed as well, saving time and money.[43] Street-design codes can incorporate various points in which to access the conduit and where infrastructure such as Wi-Fi kiosks or small cell towers could be connected. Building rooftops and facades can also be important assets in the installation of mesh networks. Creating a clear process for public use of public buildings and other assets would enable exploration of different technology options.

Make sure every building is wired with fiber-optic cable

Private assets will also be critical in getting access to the internet. Currently, energy, water, and sewage utilities have the right to access any given property they serve, but that is not the case for internet infrastructure, which hinders its deployment. In addition, just like underground, the building's own infrastructure is in a state of free for all—with different utilities building separate infrastructure. Building codes and other regulations should be updated to require enabling access to utilities and connecting every place in the building via fiber-optic cable. There is also an opportunity to incorporate new technology needs into building standards such as LEED certifications.

Ensure everyone has low-cost options for connecting online

Low-income populations face a particular challenge in connecting to the internet. To correct that, an affordable internet option should be built into municipal broadband and franchise agreements. Free internet service should be provided in all libraries and schools. Models for offering free Wi-Fi via advertising could also be combined into a municipal broadband model. Finally, encouraging the creation of mesh networks would provide an alternative, particularly during emergencies. Mesh networks are networks of multiple nodes connected wirelessly to each other to form a web. This design provides resiliency during emergencies because if one node fails, information can be moved through other nodes. The low cost of the infrastructure and ease of installation also make them low-cost to the consumer.[44] Making financing, training, and critical assets available to mesh networks such as on rooftops and buses, municipalities can create a low-cost community-driven alternative.

Government needs to create capacity for internet infrastructure planning and investment

These actions depend on the three states and New York City to create or expand their capacity to plan for internet infrastructure, make investments and finance them, develop innovative business models and partnerships, and manage assets.

Each state has different contexts to build on:

- **New York City:** Emphasis should be to prioritize investments in public conduit in challenging terrains such as Manhattan, and opening up a digital right of way.

- **New York State:** Create incentives and technical assistance for small municipalities to work together. Streamlining the franchise agreement process and helping municipalities band together would reduce red tape.

- **Connecticut:** Major capital investments are needed for the state to catch up, in particular, building public-peering points (places where different internet networks can connect).

- **New Jersey:** Ensure equal access to utility poles and remove legal barriers to community internet networks.

OUTCOMES

The region should see the following direct outcomes:

- Streamlined and fairer access to various types of public infrastructure

- Access to privately owned infrastructure, with fair terms, to serve public needs

- Enough capacity and access to support innovative last-mile business models

Secondary outcomes should be more competition—and therefore more options and lower prices—around providing internet and related infrastructure. Low-income areas in particular would benefit from more public and private investments in internet infrastructure and the creation of mesh networks as low-cost, resilient options.

PAYING FOR IT

While investing in the region's internet infrastructure and related assets requires an upfront investment in both capacity-building and capital investment, it is the type of infrastructure that can pay for itself and even generate new revenues for cash-strapped municipalities. Additionally, because it is inherently easy to share internet infrastructure, there is great potential for public-private partnerships. Exactly how much the region ultimately would pay for this infrastructure would depend on how streamlined a process localities can create to expand internet access. A benchmark cost for connecting a home to the internet via a fiber-optic cable is $1,500. This means that for $6 billion, the same cost as for phase II of the Second Avenue subway, we could connect half of the region's households to very fast internet.

⑮ Create a Regional Census to support better use of data for public purposes

Photo: RPA

Data can be a powerful tool for government and communities. A wide range of applications can help improve traffic safety, empower civic engagement, identify sources of pollution, and prevent flooding. Yet government has lagged behind the private sector in its ability to collect, analyze, and disseminate data. A new regional census organization should be created to expand the capacity of governments and residents to use data for the benefit of communities and to address issues of cybersecurity.

Government does not have the capacity to provide and manage data that is critical for the region.

Planning for the region's future depends on the availability of good data. We need to know which neighborhoods are the most attractive, how technology is changing travel patterns, and what new industries are emerging and which are at risk. To take action, policymakers need information on the loss of open spaces, which communities struggle more with health issues, and how climate change impacts infrastructure.

Federal data resources such as the U.S. Census, the Bureau of Labor Statistics, and the United States Geological Survey, in collaboration with state governments, have for decades been the established sources of data. But recent advances in technology have made it possible to collect, analyze, and disseminate a vast amount of data that could help us better understand the world. Most government entities, however, have been slow to adopt these new technologies and adjust policy needs. In fact, basic data collection at these agencies is even at risk of cutbacks for both budgetary and political reasons. Public-sector agencies don't collect data consistently or share it with the public, and government has been reluctant to require aggregated (anonymized) data collected by the private sector to be shared or disseminated more broadly.

In 2012, New York City enacted an open data law to accelerate data use by the city and residents, making it a national leader in data policy. New York City's Open Data portal, established as a result, contains data as varied as a detailed inventory of all the trees in the city, temporary street closures, and filming locations. The Mayor's Office of Data Analytics, founded at the same time, aggregates and analyzes data from across City agencies to help make public services more efficient.

Many municipalities and public sector agencies, however, don't have the funding or technical expertise to provide these services. New data tools also raise concerns about hacking and cybersecurity as well as privacy, including data captured on street cameras. Data concerning race and ethnicity could theoretically be used in discriminatory ways. And any data-driven application that is connected to the internet might be hacked.

Establish the Regional Census to help the public sector better serve constituents

Since its inception in 1840, the U.S. Census Bureau has facilitated tremendous public and private innovation. Counting people in a given tract of land on a regular basis helps federal and state government allocate scarce resources. The census gives valuable information to companies seeking to expand their market base, and researchers studying socioeconomic trends. The process of counting and calculating census data has also triggered innovation in and of itself: IBM's first contract, for example, was to build a tabulator for the Census Bureau.[45]

Fifty years into the digital age, we need a new regional institution to further advance that development of data that is of particular relevance to the metropolitan economy and civic functions, just as the U.S. Census did on a national level. A regional census would not compete with the nationwide census, but rather would augment it; and the standards, methods, and governance it develops could be deployed in other states and nationwide.

For the most part, the regional census would serve as the strategic planner, capacity builder, and synthesizer of data to complement public-sector agencies across the region. While data might still be collected by multiple private and public-sector entities, the Regional Census would coordinate and standardize data collection and dissemination.

In some cases, the Regional Census would collect data that is not the responsibility of any single agency, and also provide the technical expertise agencies need to implement policies, evaluate technologies, and set security and privacy policies. As a result, municipalities would be better equipped to improve resiliency, utilize real-time data on vehicle movement from sources such as bus and truck fleets, and evaluate on-demand transportation services and dynamic tolling technologies.

Designate a nonprofit organization as a home for the Regional Census

A Regional Census would be a nonprofit organization funded by both the public sector and philanthropy, such as the New York Public Library. It could be based at an academic institution to provide independence and allow more direct connections to researchers. The board of the Regional Census would be composed of public-sector representatives and members of the community, academia, and the private sector.

One model for the Regional Census is the Array of Things in Chicago, an innovative partnership between the University of Chicago, the Argonne National Laboratory and the city government. The Array of Things measures data on such things as air quality, climate, and traffic to better understand and improve cities.

The Regional Census should provide data resources and technical support to public entities who seek it out. The census should also develop best practices on protecting privacy and civil rights, and ensuring cybersecurity, with a standing opt-in policy on anonymizing personal data. Expanding the use of open-source software should be a priority, as it allows for greater community collaboration on security and does not bind the agency to one vendor for servicing, thereby potentially reducing costs.

Expand the scope of data-driven decision making for the public good

The Regional Census would prioritize the collection of local data, and a multi-stakeholder process would define more specifically what data is needed. This could include data about land use, zoning, and finance data, standardized across municipalities. It could also include building-level data about energy and water use, or indoor air pollution; real estate sales, evictions, and foreclosures; as well as traffic, transit, and street conditions.

Some of this data is currently collected by private entities such as ridesharing companies, but as it has public significance, should be released—at least in an aggregate fashion—to benefit the public good.

A critical element of the regional census mission would be to enable collaboration among different levels of government, by creating and releasing data targeted to specific policy goals rather than simply identifying problems.

The data developed by the Regional Census could also be utilized to formulate regulations in areas such as transportation and health using real-time data at the appropriate geographic scale.

Enhance regional capacity to develop data and new business models

To facilitate the collection and dissemination of data, the Regional Census would create and release a set of developer tools via Application Programming Interfaces (APIs). APIs are standard protocols for building software to facilitate communication between various software components. Data related to the Regional Census would include guidelines about privacy and security issues as defined by the organization's board of trustees.

For some datasets, there could be an opportunity to release the data as a product, creating a data marketplace in which private companies could pay to access API with guaranteed service levels, thereby helping fund the Regional Census and spurring further innovations in data collection.

OUTCOMES

The Regional Census would provide more technical capacity for municipalities and agencies to collect and utilize data for policy-making and improving services. Data could be used to increase transparency and government engagement with constituents; facilitate planning and decision-making; and also be able to respond to privacy and cyber security concerns. Community groups would be able to engage in citizen science projects and advocate for data needs and concerns. This would enable better collaboration between municipalities, while businesses would more easily be able to find new opportunities.

PAYING FOR IT

The cost of the census would depend on the breadth of its mandate. It could start relatively small with state funding and focus on a few key data sources and issues. The agencies, county governments, and municipalities that use the organization's services could provide further financing as it takes on additional responsibilities. The census could also generate revenue from contracting its services.

Create a dynamic, customer-oriented transportation network

Transportation is the backbone of the region's economy, and is essential to the quality of life for all residents. Yet the region has outgrown an aging transportation system that is increasingly unreliable and unable to respond to changing needs, technology, and travel patterns. Years of underinvestment in both maintenance and new transit systems during a time of rapid economic and population growth have led to congestion, delays, and deteriorating infrastructure. Many improvements could be made quickly and inexpensively at the local level, such as prioritizing people over private automobiles to make city streets and suburban roads safer and more pedestrian friendly.

But the region also needs large-scale transportation projects to better serve the residents of this dynamic, growing metropolitan region. Transforming the fragmented commuter rail network into a comprehensive regional rail system would greatly expand capacity and reduce travel times throughout the region. Strategic investments in the subway system would make it reliable, comfortable, and fast—and accessible from more neighborhoods. Traffic congestion would be sharply reduced. An integrated network of buses, light rail, and affordable on-demand car services would transform aboveground transit. High-speed rail connections and modernized airports and seaports would improve global connections and intercity travel.

CREATE A FULLY INTEGRATED REGIONAL TRANSIT SYSTEM

Every day, hundreds of thousands of people travel into and out of Manhattan from the suburbs on the region's commuter rail system—the nation's largest. Yet, even this extensive system cannot meet the capacity and service needs of a growing region, especially for reverse direction, off-peak, and suburb-to-suburb travel. There is, for example, no easy way to commute from Brooklyn to a job on Long Island. Nor can travelers easily get to Connecticut from New Jersey without a complicated transfer in Manhattan. Many parts of the network, including the critical Penn Station gateway and the trans-Hudson River crossings, are over capacity and risk catastrophic failure. Equally important, many suburbs and places in the outer boroughs of New York City are not well served by commuter rail, despite having the density to support it.

The most urgent need is to invest in significantly improving rail and bus service across the Hudson River. Subsequently, the region should undertake a phased strategy to unify the fragmented commuter rail network into a fully integrated rail system, the Trans-Regional Express (T-REX). This complex project would take decades to complete and cost billions of dollars, but would dramatically transform transportation services and options.

16 Build a second bus terminal under the Javits Convention Center

Photo: RPA

Building a second bus terminal in the basement of the Javits Convention Center to consolidate intercity buses would free up 30 percent of the gates at the existing Port Authority Bus Terminal at 42ⁿᵈ Street. It would also expand options and reduce travel times for many New Jersey commuters. Along with new rail capacity from RPA's proposal for through service at Penn Station, these two facilities would provide improved service, redundancy, and enough Trans-Hudson capacity until the existing terminal reaches the end of its useful life in the next 20 to 25 years.

New Jersey commuters need a new bus terminal.

The Port Authority Bus Terminal is in dire need of renovation and expansion. Bus ridership is at record levels, yet service is unreliable, passenger conditions are dismal, and the building itself hasn't been updated since the 1980s and is in a state of deterioration. What's more, demand for bus travel is expected to increase by 38 percent in the next 30 years. Commuters in much of northeastern New Jersey have no choice but to rely on buses to get into Manhattan—at least until the Gateway and additional trans-Hudson rail service is introduced as part of a regional rail system.

Because it is at capacity, renovating and expanding the terminal in place will be difficult and disruptive to the densely developed area that surrounds it. The Port Authority is currently studying a plan that would build additional floors to the existing facility to maintain operations while rebuilding the four floors below, but its feasibility and costs are still unknown. Building a new, larger terminal on a different site, which the Port Authority previously proposed, is constrained by a lack of land and is incompatible with the surrounding redevelopment of the West Side. Building a terminal in New Jersey to intercept bus riders before they reach the Central Business District has also been studied, but this would require the construction of a new rail service (and trans-Hudson crossing) to take commuters to their final destinations in the city.

Two bus terminals are better than one.

In the long term, rail service should be expanded to serve residents of northeastern New Jersey and dramatically improve their commutes, which would reduce the need for commuter buses. This expansion, however, would require the creation of a unified and expanded regional rail system that could be implemented in the next 20 to 40 years. Until then, a comprehensive solution must be implemented to improve commuting options for those 229,000 people who rely on buses every day.

Construct an underground bus annex in the Javits Center
The Javits Convention Center is a multiblock site that is adjacent to the Lincoln Tunnel. Its lower level, currently used for overflow exhibit floor space and conferences, could be converted into a bus terminal. Buses could either connect directly into the Lincoln Tunnel via underground tunnels, thus avoiding all vehicular traffic, or reach the tunnel via entrances along the West Side Highway.

A new bus terminal on the lower level of the Javits Convention Center would relieve pressure at the existing bus terminal on Eighth Avenue. It could accommodate all intercity bus services and serve as a storage facility for commuter buses during the day. Some commuter service could also be provided at the new Javits bus terminal; as the office district on the far West Side of Manhattan grows, commuters may find it more convenient to arrive at Eleventh Avenue than Eighth.

The lower level of the Javits Center, and a possible southern extension to 33rd Street, is large enough to accommodate more buses than the current PABT, but ridership levels of a facility this large would overwhelm the #7 train upon which many travelers would rely. But even a facility of a more limited scale, roughly half the capacity of the current terminal, would be large enough to house all intercity buses, which would free up 30 percent of the gates at the existing bus terminal.

Consider using part of the lower level at Javits for freight deliveries
The lower level of the Javits Conference Center could also be used as a consolidation and transloading center for freight deliveries, wherein large trucks from the Lincoln Tunnel would have their goods transferred to smaller electric vehicles for Manhattan deliveries. This would help reduce truck traffic in the city—despite the demand for online shopping and instant deliveries increasing in the coming years.

Renovate the PABT on Eighth Avenue
Consolidating intercity buses at a new Javits terminal would free up 63 intercity/mixed gates at the bus terminal on Eighth Avenue to be used exclusively as commuter buses, making it easier and far less costly to spruce up the existing station and provide basic upgrades for commuters. The additional capacity could be used to accommodate the growing demand for commuter buses.

Build new trans-Hudson crossings and redevelop the existing PABT once it has exceeded its useful life
Travel demand across the Hudson River will continue to grow in the coming decades. In fact, within the next 25 years, it is expected to be at capacity even after two new bus terminals and the Gateway tunnels have been built. At that point, a new rail tunnel connecting 57th Street and the New Jersey Palisades should be built, tying in with and allowing passenger service on the Northern Branch, West Shore, and Susquehanna lines. This new rail service, along with bus intercept facilities in New Jersey, would sharply reduce the number of bus riders, potentially allowing the Eighth Avenue bus terminal to be demolished and redeveloped, and generating revenue to help pay for the rail improvements. The new line would turn down Third Avenue in Manhattan to 31st Street, connecting with Crosstown Service/Gateway. Additional phases of the regional rail system would bring more service west of the Hudson and connect to new service throughout the region.

A new bus terminal under the Javits Convention Center would relieve pressure at the existing bus terminal on Eighth Avenue. It could accommodate intercity buses and some commuter service, as the Far West Side of Manhattan grows into a major office district. This rendering is just one way the new facility could be designed.

Image: Perkins Eastman

OUTCOMES

The two bus facilities would improve commuting in significant ways:

- Travel conditions would be greatly improved at the current bus terminal on Eighth Avenue, thanks to reduced crowding and wait times as well as better passenger amenities.

- Riders destined for Hudson Yards and other locations west of Tenth Avenue would enjoy an additional terminal option and reduced travel times.

- Capacity would be sufficient for bus riders through 2040, but a decision to build more rail capacity or rebuild the existing terminal must be made in the next five to ten years.

- Redundancy would be provided, in case service to one bus terminal or Penn Station is disrupted.

- Intercity bus services would be consolidated, removing buses from unloading or parking on streets.

- Redeveloping part of the Eighth Avenue site would remain a possibility.

PAYING FOR IT

The cost of the second terminal would depend on its size, its design, and whether it could be connected directly to the Lincoln Tunnel. Total costs would likely be less than the $3.5 billion the Port Authority had previously allocated to replace the 42nd Street terminal. In the long term, the 42nd Street terminal will need to be replaced, either with additional rail capacity or with a smaller terminal. In either event, development on some or all of the existing PABT site would pay for a substantial portion of a new rail tunnel or bus facility. A full analysis of all costs and benefits should be performed and evaluated against other alternatives, including the Port Authority's most recent proposal to rebuild the existing facility in place.

17 Build new rail tunnels under the Hudson and East Rivers

Photo: MTA / Patrick-Cashin

The region is in dire need of a new train tunnel under the Hudson River. Planning and engineering for Amtrak's Gateway project are underway, but must be accelerated. It must also be modified to include an extension to Queens. As currently planned, Gateway service dead-ends at Penn Station. Extending the tracks to Sunnyside Yards in Queens would provide tremendous benefit to the region by providing travelers with direct crosstown service between New Jersey and Long Island, and greatly increase the efficiency of train movements—increasing capacity across the Hudson River by an estimated 38 percent, and across the East River by 68 percent. Getting shovels in the ground is of critical urgency to the region's economic vitality and quality of life.

Gateway must proceed as quickly as possible, but the project won't be enough to address the region's trans-Hudson needs.

Despite existing train tunnels being at capacity for a long time, and flooding from Superstorm Sandy accelerating the need to conduct extensive repairs to them, the Gateway project is not expected to be completed until 2026 at the earliest. Considering the daily delays NJ Transit commuters and Amtrak travelers suffer every day, this is simply unacceptable.

What's more, the Gateway project as planned—with service terminating at Penn Station—will not by itself provide enough long-term capacity or connectivity for a growing metropolitan region. Instead of stopping at Penn Station, Gateway should continue across Manhattan and under the East River, and connect to the Amtrak rail yards in Sunnyside, Queens. A through-running operation would allow trains to run much closer together, increasing the capacity of the station by 30 percent or more.

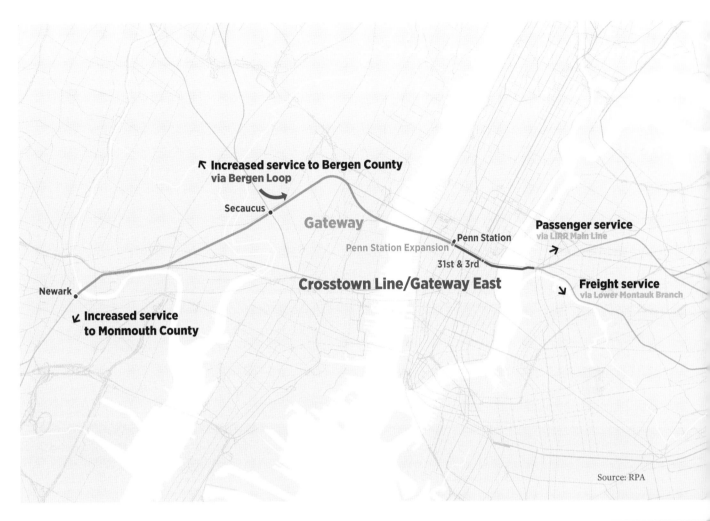

↖ Increased service to Bergen County
via Bergen Loop

Secaucus

Gateway

Penn Station Expansion

Penn Station

Passenger service
via LIRR Main Line
↗

31st & 3rd

Newark

Crosstown Line/Gateway East

**↙ Increased service
to Monmouth County**

Freight service
via Lower Montauk Branch
↘

Source: RPA

Extending the Gateway
tunnels east to Sunnyside
Yards in Queens will
allow through running
service from New Jersey
to Long Island.

Instead of terminating at Penn Station, extend Gateway to Sunnyside Yards in western Queens to provide crosstown service

As critical as it is to get the Gateway tunnels under construction as soon as possible, the project should be modified to extend through Manhattan and into Sunnyside Yards in Queens.

By providing crosstown service, passengers could travel directly between New Jersey and Long Island, thus increasing regional connectivity while also drastically increasing the capacity of the investment. A through-running configuration, with fewer and wider platforms at Penn Station, would allow for an additional six to nine trains per hour under the Hudson River on top of the additional 24 trains the new Gateway tunnels would allow. These 30–33 trains represent up to a 68 percent increase of what can run under the East River today.

This additional capacity could be used to provide new rail service in parts of New Jersey that are currently reliant on commuter buses (Bergen Loop). Old rail lines in Middlesex, Ocean, and Monmouth counties could be reactivated and connected into the NJ Transit system and Manhattan—greatly improving commuting times and reducing vehicular traffic in New Jersey and across the river.

Building crosstown tracks would also provide additional redundancy across the East River in the event service in the existing tunnels were disrupted.

Build a station at Third Avenue

A new rail station should be built at 31st Street and Third Avenue to provide New Jersey commuters with better access to the region's greatest concentration of jobs, in East Midtown. This station could also ultimately serve as a major hub station linking crosstown into the larger regional rail system proposed in this plan.

Use the new through-running tracks for freight during off-hours

Gateway East could become an important intra-regional freight rail line by connecting New Jersey's rail freight network and Port Newark–Elizabeth with the Lower Montauk freight line in Queens. This would allow goods currently carried by trucks from New Jersey to Queens and Brooklyn to be shipped overnight via rail, thus reducing the number of noisy and polluting trucks crossing the two rivers and traveling through New York City.

At least one tunnel should be constructed to accommodate rail cars with a height clearance of up to 21 feet to enable the operation of freight during off-hours.

OUTCOMES

By increasing the passenger capacity of the proposed rail tunnels across the Hudson River, Gateway East would support additional employment growth in Manhattan and distribute benefits to New Jersey and other parts of the region. By providing more rail service, it also supports a region with more sustainable land use and energy use, and jobs in locations that can be accessed by a larger number of neighborhoods and residents. Specifically, the project would bring about the following benefits to the region's residents:

- Direct access to the East Side of Manhattan for New Jersey residents

- New direct rail service from Bergen, Passaic, Rockland, and Orange counties

- Expansion of rail service in Middlesex, Monmouth, and Ocean counties

- Substantial reduction in both the number of cars and commuter buses traversing the Hudson River, and congestion and pollution in New Jersey and Manhattan

- Redundancy in the event of a catastrophic event (flooding, terrorism, etc.)

- The opportunity to create an intra-regional freight rail service that would reduce the number of trucks traversing major vehicular water crossings and New York City

PAYING FOR IT

The Gateway Project as currently conceived is expected to cost $24–29 billion, including $17 billion for the tunnels alone. Turning it into a real crosstown service by extending tracks to Sunnyside Yards would add $4 billion in construction costs, plus indirect costs that can be as high as the construction costs. Like other major capital investments, a key to financing crosstown is to reduce the cost of building big rail projects.

Some of the revenue needed could come from new real estate development near the new Third Avenue station on the East Side of Manhattan or a ticket surcharge, but most would require a new revenue source, such as carbon pricing or new tolling.

18 Expand, overhaul, and unify the Penn Station Complex

New York's Penn Station, the busiest station in the Americas, is a congested, uninviting, and dangerous underground complex. It needs to be transformed into an expansive and gracious hub for an expanding rail network. Current plans to expand the station complex with a new Moynihan Station across Eighth Avenue and Penn South—a terminus for the proposed Gateway tunnels—should be enlarged to create a unified complex with room for more people and trains, through-running service for both commuter and intercity rail service, and an inspiring design that brings in light and air and pedestrian spaces. Madison Square Garden will need to be relocated to improve security and bring light and air into the terminal.

Penn Station is overcrowded, confusing, and substandard.

Long reviled for its cramped conditions and uninspiring design, Penn Station has become increasingly dysfunctional, as ridership into the station has nearly tripled in the last 25 years—a level of use never contemplated by the station's architects. Concourses and platforms are narrow, and vertical circulation to the platforms is inadequate. The station lacks basic amenities such as clear signage and comfortable waiting areas. With no natural daylight or other obvious visual markers, it's easy to get lost. The station also has little to no presence from the street, and pedestrian conditions surrounding Penn are poor.

These problems will be further compounded in the future, as travel across the river increases in the coming decades. Work trips alone are projected to increase by 24 percent or more by 2040, depending on growth in all trans-Hudson travel and the amount of new rail service that connects to the station.

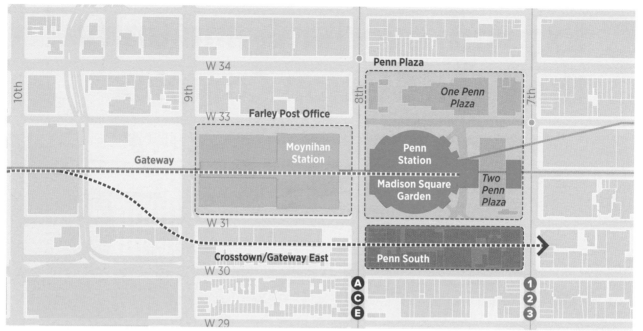

Source: RPA

New York's Penn Station is not a single structure, but rather a vast complex.
In addition to the superblock that extends from 34th Street to 31st Street and Seventh to Eighth Avenues, Penn Station will soon include the Farley Post Office building, which is being renovated into a new train hall dubbed Moynihan Station. Amtrak has also been studying extending Penn Station south as part of the Gateway project to build new train tunnels under the Hudson River.

Unify the Penn Station complex into an inspiring gateway to New York

New York's Penn Station is already a vast complex that extends over two square blocks and three underground levels. In 2020, a new train hall in the Farley Post Office building will be added to this complex, a project known as Moynihan Station. And the Gateway project, currently in the planning stages, will further extend Penn Station southward. These investments will expand the station's footprint, relieving congestion and finally providing the opportunity to gut-renovate Penn Station.

Create inviting new entrances at Seventh Avenue
Penn Station deserves to have a great presence in Midtown Manhattan. Today's main entrance at 32nd Street is cramped and unwelcoming; it should be widened and expanded. A new great entrance to the station should also be built on the corner of Seventh Avenue and 33rd Street by turning part of 33rd Street into a civic plaza. With new architectural elements running from 31st Street to 34th Street, Penn Station could also have an improved, uniform presence at the street level along three city blocks.

Underground, there are also great opportunities to improve pedestrian conditions, even without removing Two Penn Plaza and its myriad vertical columns through the station. The Long Island Rail Road concourse, which runs under 33rd Street, should be widened and shifted north. Ceilings should be elevated for better light and air. The Hilton Corridor under 32nd Street should also be widened and extended eastward to connect Penn Station with the subways at Broadway and Sixth Avenue. Finally, the central concourse should also be widened and extended southward to connect to Track One (and later to Penn South), removing the B-level (Amtrak waiting room level) under Two Penn Plaza and lining up the NJT concourse with elevation at the A-level (the same level as the LIRR concourse).

A proposal by Vishaan Chakrabarti and PAU envisions gutting Madison Square Garden, removing the floors and exterior curtain wall, and keeping just the structural skeleton of the building clad in glass.

This intervention, combined with the complete removal of the B-level concourse beneath MSG, would eliminate over 200 columns from the platforms—freeing up more space for stairs and passenger queuing, and removing all of the barriers between the tracks and platforms. The glass curtain wall would be open at street level to provide 360° access to the station—similar to many traditional stations.

Complete Moynihan Station

A new train hall in the Farley Post Office is under construction and should be completed by 2020. Moynihan Station, as the train hall will be called, will accommodate Amtrak's main waiting room, its Acela lounge, and many of its back-office functions, freeing up valuable space at the existing Penn Station. The project's completion should proceed without delay, including a new mid-block passageway to Ninth Avenue.

Move Madison Square Garden

Madison Square Garden's 10-year special permit is up for renewal in 2023. It should not be renewed. By removing the sports arena and theater, Penn Station's underground complex will gain much-needed natural light and air, and significantly improve pedestrian circulation and safety.

Previous schemes have suggested replacing Madison Square Garden with a new head house with retail and office space. A recent proposal instead envisioned removing the floors of the arena and its exterior curtain wall, but keeping its structural skeleton and cladding it in glass. Combined with removing one of Penn Station's underground concourses (on the B-level), this would eliminate over 200 columns from the platforms—freeing up significant space for pedestrian circulation, including stairs and escalators.

Amtrak should move forward with this scheme. The building's glass curtain wall should be open at street level to provide 360° access to the station, and the 33rd Street plaza should be extended to Eighth Avenue. Only the station's three north-south concourses and two or three east-west corridors should remain to better distribute passengers, facilitate orientation, and better integrate the station with the future Penn South.

Build Penn South for running service between New Jersey and Queens

As part of its Gateway proposal to build two new rail tunnels under the Hudson River, Amtrak has been studying extending Penn Station southward, down to 30th Street. The most recent proposal is for a new station, named Penn South, with five platforms and eight tracks, four of which could be extended to Queens in the future.

A far better scheme would be to build the station for through-running trains from the get-go. Because running trains straight through the station is so much more efficient than having trains terminate at Penn and turn around, fewer tracks and wider platforms could be built, while still accommodating up to 33 trains per hour.

In fact, Penn South as is currently proposed—with four stub-end tracks and five platforms of varying widths—would make it much more difficult to retrofit the station into through-running in the future. Instead, the Gateway tunnels to New Jersey should be extended to Sunnyside Yards, with two new tunnels and an intermediary station at Third Avenue.

To facilitate pedestrian circulation in Penn South, a new underground east-west concourse should be built, roughly between 30th Street and 31st Street, bookending the improved LIRR east-west concourse at the northern edge of the station.

Improve pedestrian conditions at the platform and track level

While a wholesale reconfiguration of platforms and tracks isn't feasible in such a high-traffic station, some improvements should be made to increase station capacity, reduce congestion on the platforms, and enable through-running regional rail. These include:

- Widen select platforms in the center and southern end of Penn Station. This would result in the removal of a number of tracks.

- Replace escalators with stairs and elevators on the more narrow platforms to allow for greater vertical capacity.

- Simplify the station and improve vertical circulation by removing one of Penn Station's underground levels and creating a more straightforward circulation scheme for the other level across the entire station complex.

- Remove as many old columns (from the original Penn Station) and other nonessential platform elements as possible to increase existing platform capacity.

- Install high-density signaling system in East River tunnels to increase their capacity and improve the reliability of the service.

OUTCOMES

The result of these investments and reconstruction would be a unified Penn Station complex with modern amenities and the capacity to serve a growing region. New York City and the region would finally have a station that reflects its status as a global economic hub and gateway to the metropolitan region. Commuters, intercity passengers, and visitors would enjoy the conveniences of a modern transportation hub, arriving in a station that is no longer dreary and unpleasant, but a place to linger and enjoy.

PAYING FOR IT

Much, if not all, of the costs for a new Penn Station should be paid for from the value of real estate development that will be created either directly, from air rights that are released, or indirectly, from increases in the value of existing buildings near the site that would benefit from proximity to a redesigned hub that attracts more travelers and becomes a destination itself. For example, moving Madison Square Garden could create more than two million square feet of additional development rights that could be used near the station.

19 Combine three commuter rail systems into one network

Image: ORG Permanent Modernity for the Fourth Regional Plan

The region's aging commuter rail network leaves many parts of the region poorly served or without rail service at all. It wasn't designed for today's travel patterns and has little capacity for future growth. A series of new projects, phased over the next few decades, should combine the three commuter railroads into a unified system that vastly improves mobility throughout the region. The resulting Trans-Regional Express (T-REX) would provide frequent, consistent service directly connect New Jersey, Long Island, the Mid-Hudson, and Connecticut; and allow the region's economy to continue growing.

The region has outgrown its commuter rail network.

The region's three commuter railroads—Long Island Rail Road, Metro-North Railroad, and New Jersey Transit— are an amalgamation of rail lines built largely by private railroads more than 100 years ago. This aging system was designed to get people in and out of Manhattan when the metropolitan area was less than half the size it is today. It poorly serves job centers outside of Manhattan, leaves many places without any rail service at all, isn't configured to serve today's 24-hour, multidirectional travel patterns, and is straining to serve the number of riders it has today, much less tomorrow.

More specifically:

- Many assets—from stations and signals to tracks and interlockings—are well past their useful life or don't meet modern standards.

- All service ends in Manhattan, preventing trains from traveling through from one part of the region to the other, and reducing the capacity of the system overall.

- While ridership is growing the fastest outside of morning and afternoon rush hours, service continues to be much worse on most lines at those times than during their peak.

- Reverse service into many job centers with strong growth potential, such as Bridgeport or Hicksville, is poor—and limits the ability of those downtowns to grow into major economic hubs. Some large downtowns such as Paterson have no direct service at all.

- Many residential areas with densities to support commuter rail service don't have it, including much of Bergen, Passaic, and Monmouth counties.

- Service is too infrequent or too expensive for many residents in Bronx, Brooklyn, Queens, Hudson, and Essex counties.

- Many parts of the system are already operating well past their capacity, including the rail tunnels under the Hudson River used by all New Jersey Transit trains, Penn Station, and Metro-North's New Haven line. Over the next 25 years, the number of people commuting from the suburbs into Manhattan could grow by as much as 34 percent, much more than the current system can handle.

- Fragmented control of the system among the different railroads makes it difficult to plan for upgrades and repairs, or provide holistic, integrated service.

Many of New York City's peers, such as Paris and London, have transformed their traditional commuter rail systems to run more like urban metro systems. With more frequent and convenient service to, in, and through the city centers, those systems have increased businesses' access to a large and varied labor pool. They have also given residents access to more jobs and more housing choices. New York's disjointed system is holding us back from becoming a truly integrated and economically powerful region.

Convert the region's three commuter lines into a unified system to increase capacity, expand options, and reduce travel times

The region must modernize, integrate, and expand its commuter rail network to keep up with a growing region, as well as changing technology and service demands. Unifying the network into a Trans-Regional Express service that vastly improves mobility throughout the region will require major infrastructure upgrades to integrate its different components and then expand it. Some actions, like building additional tunnels under the Hudson and creating a more functional Penn Station, address urgent needs and should begin immediately. Others will take a decade or more to be planned and approved. But all improvements should be designed to allow future projects to rationalize and synchronize service as they expand capacity.

Based on an analysis of existing deficiencies, future demand, and project feasibility, a fully integrated regional rail system could be built in three phases.

Phase 1: The Crosstown Line creates through-running service from New Jersey to Long Island

The Crosstown line builds on Amtrak's Gateway plans to build new rail tunnels under the Hudson River and expand Penn Station. These tunnels and tracks should be extended to build new tunnels under the East River to provide a new through-running Crosstown service between New Jersey and Long Island. Instead of a terminal, RPA's proposed Penn South would become a through-running station with two tubes extending east to Queens. A new station on 31st Street and Third Avenue would provide suburban commuters access to southeast Midtown. The Crosstown line will address the immediate crisis of declining service across the Hudson while creating a range of new benefits:

- It would provide capacity for six to nine more trains per hour from New Jersey than the Gateway project as it is currently planned, and result in a total of 30 to 33 more trains from both New Jersey and Long Island into Penn Station.

- NJ Transit riders would have direct service to Manhattan's East Side, and Long Island Rail Road riders would have a second East Side destination, in addition to the Grand Central LIRR station currently under construction.

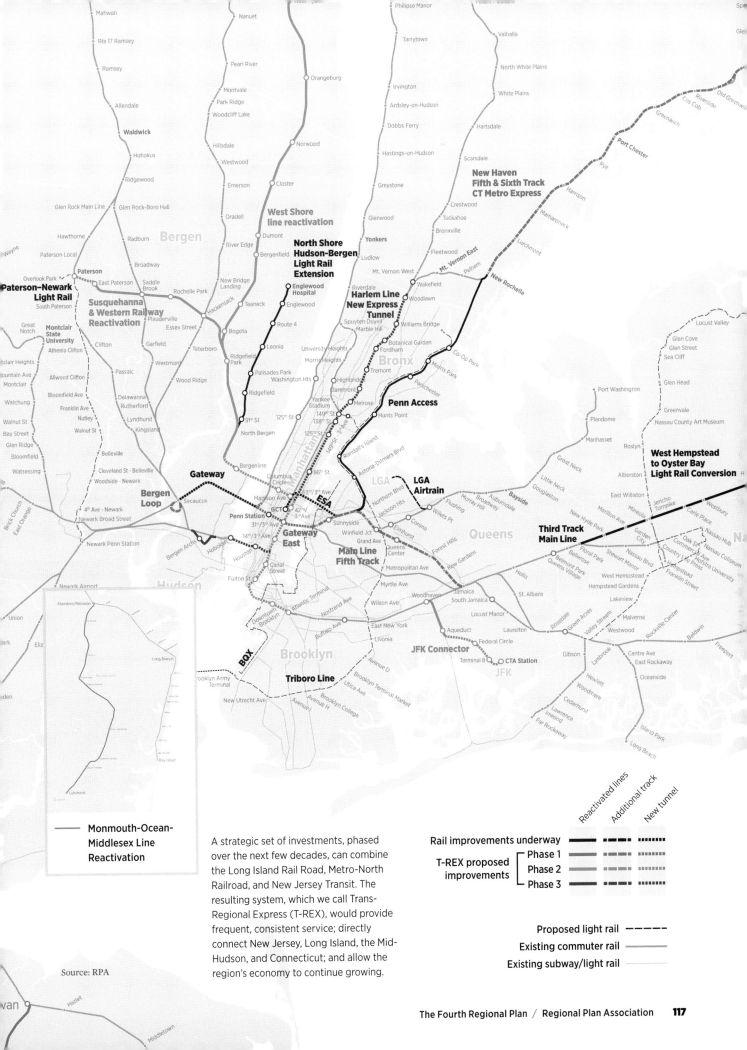

A strategic set of investments, phased over the next few decades, can combine the Long Island Rail Road, Metro-North Railroad, and New Jersey Transit. The resulting system, which we call Trans-Regional Express (T-REX), would provide frequent, consistent service; directly connect New Jersey, Long Island, the Mid-Hudson, and Connecticut; and allow the region's economy to continue growing.

Source: RPA

Monmouth-Ocean-Middlesex Line Reactivation

Rail improvements underway

T-REX proposed improvements
Phase 1
Phase 2
Phase 3

Reactivated lines   Additional track   New tunnel

Proposed light rail
Existing commuter rail
Existing subway/light rail

Proposed Regional Express (RX) service map

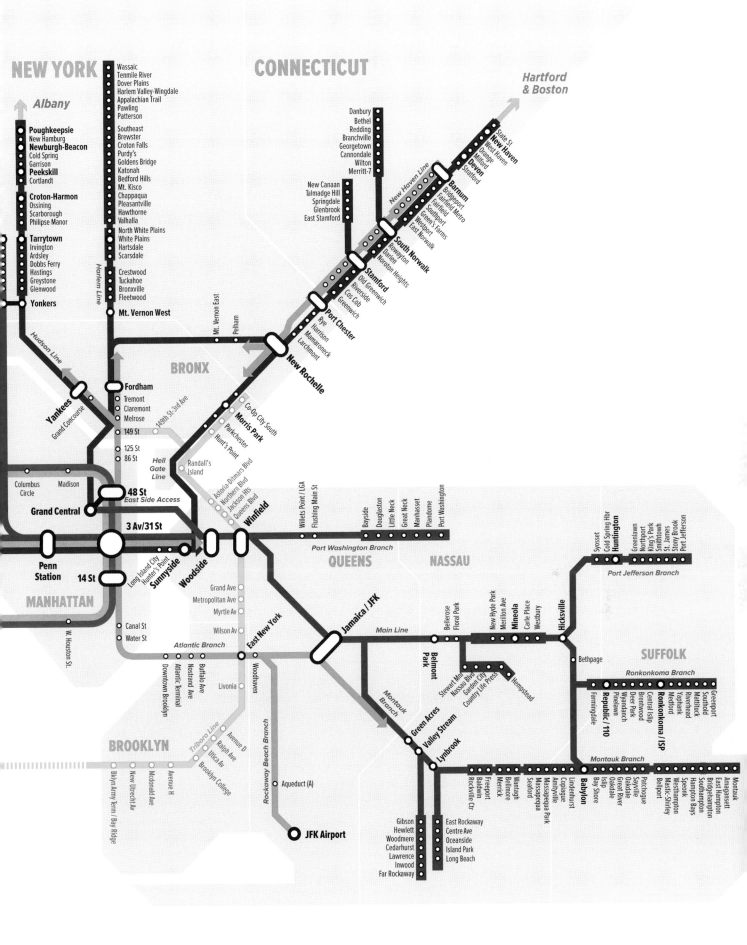

NEW YORK

Albany

Wassaic
Tenmile River
Dover Plains
Harlem Valley-Wingdale
Appalachian Trail
Pawling
Patterson

Poughkeepsie
New Hamburg
Newburgh-Beacon
Cold Spring
Garrison
Peekskill
Cortlandt

Croton-Harmon
Ossining
Scarborough
Philipse Manor

Tarrytown
Irvington
Ardsley
Dobbs Ferry
Hastings
Greystone
Glenwood
Yonkers

Southeast
Brewster
Croton Falls
Purdy's
Goldens Bridge
Katonah
Bedford Hills
Mt. Kisco
Chappaqua
Pleasantville
Hawthorne
Valhalla
North White Plains
White Plains
Hartsdale
Scarsdale

Crestwood
Tuckahoe
Bronxville
Fleetwood

Mt. Vernon West

Harlem Line

Hudson Line

CONNECTICUT

Hartford & Boston

Danbury
Bethel
Redding
Branchville
Georgetown
Cannondale
Wilton
Merritt-7

New Canaan
Talmadge Hill
Springdale
Glenbrook
East Stamford

State St
West Haven
New Haven
Orange
Milford
Devon
Stratford
Barnum
Bridgeport
Fairfield Metro
Fairfield
Southport
Green's Farms
Westport
East Norwalk
South Norwalk
Rowayton
Darien
Noroton Heights
Stamford
Old Greenwich
Riverside
Cos Cob
Greenwich

New Haven Line

Mt. Vernon East
Pelham
Port Chester
Rye
Harrison
Mamaroneck
Larchmont
New Rochelle

BRONX

Fordham
Tremont
Claremont
Melrose
149 St
125 St
86 St

149th St-3rd Ave
Co-Op City South
Morris Park
Parkchester
Hunt's Point

Hell Gate Line

Randall's Island

Yankees
Grand Concourse

Columbus Circle
Madison

48 St
East Side Access

Grand Central

3 Av/31 St

Penn Station

14 St

MANHATTAN

W. Houston St.

Canal St
Water St

Astoria-Ditmars Blvd
Northern Blvd
Jackson Hts
Queens Blvd

Long Island City
Hunter's Point
Sunnyside
Woodside
Winfield

Willets Point / LGA
Flushing Main St

Port Washington Branch

Bayside
Douglaston
Little Neck
Great Neck
Manhasset
Plandome
Port Washington

QUEENS

NASSAU

Syosset
Cold Spring Hbr
Huntington
Greenlawn
Northport
King's Park
Smithtown
St. James
Stony Brook
Port Jefferson

Port Jefferson Branch

Grand Ave
Metropolitan Ave
Myrtle Av
Wilson Av

East New York

Jamaica / JFK

Main Line

Bellerose
Floral Park

New Hyde Park
Merillon Ave
Mineola
Carle Place
Westbury

Hicksville

Bethpage

SUFFOLK

Ronkonkoma Branch

Greenport
Southold
Mattituck
Riverhead
Yaphank
Medford
Ronkonkoma / ISP
Central Islip
Brentwood
Deer Park
Wyandanch
Pinelawn
Republic / 110
Farmingdale

Atlantic Branch

Downtown Brooklyn
Atlantic Terminal
Nostrand Ave
Buffalo Ave
Livonia
Woodhaven

BROOKLYN

Triboro Line

Avenue H
New Utrecht Av
Mcdonald Av
Avenue D
Ralph Av
Utica Av
Brooklyn College

Bkyn Army Term / Bay Ridge

Rockaway Beach Branch

Aqueduct (A)

JFK Airport

Belmont Park

Stewart Mnr
Nassau Blvd
Garden City
County Life Press
Hempstead

Montauk Branch

Green Acres
Valley Stream
Lynbrook

Gibson
Hewlett
Woodmere
Cedarhurst
Lawrence
Inwood
Far Rockaway

East Rockaway
Centre Ave
Oceanside
Island Park
Long Beach

Freeport
Baldwin
Rockville Ctr

Wantagh
Bellmore
Merrick

Lindenhurst
Copiague
Amityville
Massapequa Park
Massapequa
Seaford

Babylon
Bay Shore
Islip
Great River
Oakdale
Sayville
Patchogue
Mastic-Shirley
Bellport
Westhampton
Speonk
Hampton Bays
Southampton
Bridgehampton
East Hampton
Amagansett
Montauk

Montauk Branch

Source: RPA

- The additional capacity would allow old rail lines to be reactivated, and large parts of Monmouth, Ocean, and Middlesex counties could gain direct rail access into Manhattan.

- New Jersey commuters would be able to go directly to Jamaica to board the JFK AirTrain, and LIRR riders could travel directly to the rail stop for Newark Airport.

- The additional East River tunnels would provide greater resiliency in case of flooding, terrorism, or other disruptions.

Phase 2: Additional trans-Hudson and East Side service, and restored passenger service in northeastern New Jersey

Before 2040, it is expected that the Gateway/Crosstown tunnels will also be at capacity. And even though 2040 sounds like a long way off, planning and building infrastructure of this scale can take decades, so it really shouldn't be too long before we begin to plan for the next set of trans-Hudson tunnels. Additional rail tunnels from Union City, NJ, to 57th Street in Midtown would provide the next trans-Hudson capacity expansion after Crosstown reaches full capacity. New tunnels at 57th Street would also allow for the restoration of passenger service on the West Shore line, a portion of the Northern Branch line, and the Susquehanna lines in Bergen, Passaic, and Rockland counties. These areas are almost exclusively served by express buses today. The completion of this portion of the system would likely reduce the demand for express buses significantly enough to enable the Port Authority to replace its current bus terminal with either a smaller Manhattan facility or bus intercept facilities in New Jersey.

Beyond providing new rail service to many New Jersey communities, this second phase of the proposed regional rail network would provide a new north-south transit service on the East Side of Manhattan from 57th Street, running south under Third Avenue, and making four to five stops to Lower Manhattan, a corridor that currently is only served by the Lexington Avenue subway. This service could obviate the need to construct the lower portions of the Second Avenue Subway. This "Manhattan Spine" would be connected to the Crosstown line via a new hub station located at 31st Street and Third Avenue, allowing a seamless transfer between the Crosstown and the new service that would run along 57th Street and down Third Avenue.

The Manhattan Spine would continue to run downtown, stopping at Fulton Street and Water Street, and then into Downtown Brooklyn, where it would connect with the Long Island Rail Road at Atlantic Terminal. This portion of the line would provide robust and speedy rail transit service to parts of outer Brooklyn and southeastern Queens, which currently have limited transit options. A short extension to JFK Airport would also be made using part of the existing Rockaway Beach Branch line, south of the Atlantic Branch, along with the construction of a short new segment with two new stations at the airport.

These investments would provide the following benefits:

- Transit capacity to support the continued expansion of the region's economy

- Vastly improved service and much shorter travel times for residents of Bergen, Passaic, and Rockland counties

- Reduced crowding at Penn Station

- Elimination of the need to build a large bus terminal

- Possible elimination of the need for building the lower portions of the Second Avenue Subway

- Direct service connecting New Jersey, Manhattan, Brooklyn, Queens, and JFK Airport

Phase 3: Completing a fully interconnected regional rail network

The final phase of constructing the regional rail system entails completing the uptown portion of the Manhattan Spine to connect to the Bronx, Westchester, the Hudson Valley, and Connecticut, and the lower trans-Hudson tunnels that would complete a "Jersey Loop" that connects to service in the north to Hudson County.

The Uptown portion of the Spine would provide relief for Metro-North's Park Ave Tunnel, which currently runs at capacity. The completion of Penn Access, a project to add tracks and a station on the Hell Gate line so that Metro-North Railroad's New Haven line trains can directly access Penn Station, should reduce stress on the Park Avenue Tunnel, buying some time for Metro-North. But the project will not ultimately divert any riders bound for the East Side. The Uptown portion of the Manhattan Spine, however, would provide relief, paralleling the Park Ave Tunnel along Third Avenue, providing a new express track through the Bronx from Mott Haven to Woodlawn, and seamlessly connecting the Mid-Hudson and Connecticut into the new regional rail system.

The lower leg of the Jersey Loop will provide a third new set of trans-Hudson tunnels, reducing future congestion, improving access to Hudson County, creating opportunities for more direct travel within the region, and providing additional redundancy. The construction of this new tunnel could also serve as a replacement for the Uptown PATH, which has tunnels over a century old, small stations, an inefficient junction, and a terminal at Hoboken that limits capacity and performance and is costly to maintain. On the New Jersey side of the Hudson River, the tunnels will lead to a station at Hoboken/Newport and a new station in Jersey City Heights via the Bergen Arches, eventually connecting into the existing NJ Transit system.

This expansion would allow for the complete unification of the regional rail network, with the following improvements:

- Less crowding, improved reliability, and more service for Metro-North riders

- Direct access through Manhattan from Westchester, the Mid-Hudson, and Connecticut, to New Jersey and Long Island

- Transit service for Bronx residents in the Third Avenue corridor, which today has very poor transit access

- Direct access to JFK Airport from the Bronx, Westchester, Mid-Hudson, and Connecticut

- Expanded service for residents of Hudson County and reduced crowding for New Jersey Transit riders at Penn Station

- Elimination of the need to replace the PATH Uptown line

Provide frequent service in all directions

The physical connections described above would allow for transformative improvements to rail service. Instead of long wait times, passengers in Bronx, Queens, Hudson, Westchester, and Nassau counties would have access to more subway-like frequencies—in both directions. Passengers in Bergen, Passaic, Monmouth, Hudson, and Essex counties would have access to the rail network with consistent service. Finally, an intercity express service would offer faster speeds, lower fares, and more direct service between major hubs—from New Haven to Trenton, and from Poughkeepsie to Ronkonkoma.

All of these services would be overlaid in a Trans-Regional Express (T-REX) system that combines the territories of all three commuter railroads, and complements and connects to the New York City subways and PATH.

In much of the region, the service would provide a consistent level of service: every 15 minutes throughout the day and every 10 minutes during the traditional peak periods. Such a schedule would reduce the physical stress placed on the system and allow it to be used throughout the day as a viable transit option.

The system could be managed either by combining the existing railroads into one operating agency, or by creating a regional coordinating entity that would be responsible for coordinating schedules, fares, and operations among the three railroads. The service could be operated by the existing public authorities or by private concessions, such as the London Overground.

OUTCOMES

The regional rail proposal would dramatically increase rail capacity across the Hudson River, provide additional layers of redundancy for the region's transit system, and bring rail service to currently unserved areas of New Jersey. It would improve the region's rail service by standardizing fares, headways, service routings, rolling stock, and transfer arrangements to create a coherent and integrated system. Travel times would be reduced from well over an hour to less than half an hour for many commuters, and traveling would be far more predictable. The system as a whole would be significantly more resilient with multiple options for rerouting service or taking alternative routes. As a result, the region would be able to attract and sustainably accommodate far more economic growth. Many residents who can't reach or afford rail service today would be able to use it on a regular basis.

PAYING FOR IT

The system would be built out over several decades. The cost of the tunnel is likely to be in line with costs for other rail projects in the New York City region, although these costs are likely to change over the different phases of the project. Without reforms to bring down project costs, it will be nearly impossible to afford these improvements. However, implementing this regional rail program does provide opportunities for savings from economies of scale and standardized construction practices, and by obviating the need for other projects. For example, the regional rail system would result in a smaller bus terminal than currently planned, and could obviate the need for the southern portion of the Second Avenue Subway, saving tens of billions of dollars. The sources of revenue would need to include substantial federal revenue, as well as dedicated revenue from new sources, such as mileage-based fees for automobile and truck travel or carbon pricing that could provide revenue for a range of transportation projects.

REBUILD THE SUBWAY SYSTEM

The New York City subway system was in crisis in the 1970s, when trains were covered in graffiti and crime was commonplace. Despite the many improvements since those dark days, the subways are facing another crisis, with overcrowded trains, unpleasant stations, and all-too-frequent delays and system failures. Investments in new trains, technology, and maintenance have not kept pace with growing ridership, thus contributing to a deteriorating system that is a deep source of frustration for New Yorkers and threatens the economic vitality of the region.

Creating a modern subway system will require accelerating the adoption of new technology, dramatically improving station appearance and amenities, and extending lines to underserved areas. To complete this massive undertaking, we must make a firm commitment to embrace innovation and restructure how the subway operates and finances improvements. This investment will justify the large upfront expense, as New York will have a reliable and efficient subway system that is accessible to all residents and worthy of its status as serving a major global city.

20 Adopt new technology for fast, reliable subway service

Photo: Siemens

As every New Yorker knows, the city's aging subway system is terribly congested and unreliable. New technology can dramatically increase both the capacity and reliability of the subways, but the pace at which the MTA adopts technological innovations is glacial. Wi-Fi in stations wasn't made available until 2017, years after other cities. Our refusal to embrace fare-collection technology or to acquire a more state-of-the-art train signalling system also has us behind the times. And driverless or even single-driver trains still seem light years away. Even if it is more difficult to upgrade old systems than build new ones, the MTA must accelerate the adoption of new technology to meet the needs of a growing ridership.

Outdated technology hobbles New York City subways.

Growing subway ridership is straining the system and exposing the negative effects of decades of underinvestment and lack of innovation at the MTA. Subway performance has declined steadily over the past three years, causing stress and aggravation for riders. Technology has the potential to improve capacity and reliability, but the MTA is dreadfully slow at adopting innovation.

Signal-related problems account for well over half of all subway delays. Upgrading to the more efficient Communications-Based Train Control (CBTC) signaling system would be the single best way to increase capacity and improve reliability on the subway system in a relatively short amount of time. And yet, the MTA continues to adopt CBTC at a slow pace. Since 1999, when the agency began upgrading signals, only the L line has fully implemented CBTC, with the #7 line coming on in 2018. It could be 50 years before CBTC is installed throughout the system.

Other technological innovations are also progressing very slowly. Subway stations only just acquired Wi-Fi and cell service in 2017—years after other metro systems. The magnetic Metrocard has kept fare collection stuck in the 1990s, despite cities all over the world having adopted "tap" technology long ago. Driverless subways—or at least subways with only one operator instead of two—are within reach, but the MTA has not been capable of taking that leap.

The New York City subways are old, and upgrading such systems is harder than building new ones. But other cities, including Paris and London, whose systems are at least as old as ours, are adopting technology to improve capacity, reliability, and customer satisfaction.

Use technology to dramatically increase both the capacity and the reliability of the subway system

Just as technology is transforming all different aspects of modern life, it can—and should—transform the way public transportation is operated. Dynamic information about crowding conditions, events, incidents, and current train locations can and should make more efficient use of the infrastructure that is already in place and inform passengers in real time.

Modernizing our subway technology could shave precious minutes off the average commute, while also improving reliability and resiliency—two of the most crucial drivers of the region's success and prosperity.

Accelerate the adoption of modern signaling systems

Using radio signals, fiber optic lines, and advanced computer software, Communications-Based Train Control allows each train to know precisely where it is relative to the train in front of it so they can run more closely together. This real-time information about each train's location can be shared with customers so they can make more informed decisions about their travel choices. Overall, CBTC lowers maintenance costs, improves efficiency, and when hurricanes and rising sea levels threaten more frequent flooding, provides more resiliency—because CBTC equipment is either waterproof or relatively easily removed and reinstalled.

CBTC could be deployed across the system in 10 to 15 years by taking the following steps:

- **Simplify the installation of the new signal system.** The MTA currently requires the existing fixed-block signaling system to be upgraded and retained as a backup as the new CBTC signals are installed. The MTA should instead simply install CBTC alongside the current fixed-block

signaling system and test in the background while the existing system continues to authorize train movements. Once CBTC testing is complete, the old fixed-block system could simply be deactivated and left in place—potentially serving as a backup in case issues arise after the installation—and eventually removed over time. This approach would have the added benefit of limiting the amount of track access required for the installation.

- **Eliminate the legacy analog interlocking equipment.** After track circuits, signals, and train stops—the last vestiges of the legacy signaling system— are removed, the agency could use axle counters as a backup to continue tracking and protecting trains.

- **Guarantee track access and extended work windows.** Track work is complicated and expensive on a 24/7 system. Closing the subways on weeknights and/or for more extended time periods would create more opportunities for track installation and testing of the equipment—and reduce costs. Only 1.5 percent of weekday riders use the system between 12:30 am and 5 am. The overwhelming majority of people who ride the subway during the daytime would benefit from the better, more reliable, cleaner, and better-maintained system that weeknight closures allow. Of course, whenever lines are shut down, the MTA will need to make sure riders are not left stranded. New bus service should be provided to mimic subway service on traffic-free streets, and with shorter waiting times than today's overnight subway service.

- **Accelerate the procurement of new subway cars.** The MTA could further accelerate the adoption of CBTC by retiring its oldest train sets early, and assigning specific fleets to specific lines.

Reform the operations rule book to reflect the opportunities provided by new technology

Wages and benefits account for 40 percent of the cost of operating the subways. As we invest in technology, we must take advantage of the opportunities technology provides to change the responsibilities of MTA's workers, or potentially reduce the number of those positions through natural attrition at the agency—to lower operating costs and/or redirect savings to infrastructure upgrades.

For example, one of the benefits of CBTC is that it is capable of determining the cause of an emergency brake application, allowing the conductor to address the situation more quickly. Yet MTA work rules for the L line have not been revised to reflect this opportunity, requiring conductors to continue the practice of walking the length of the train anyway, which further delays operations.

New signals needed within five years

Line	Service	Track Miles	Age	Capacity	Growth	Score
Lexington Ave Line (MN)	④⑤⑥	37	9	6	3	18
63rd St Line (MN)	ⓕ	21	6	6	3	15
6th Ave Line (MN/BK)	ⒷⒹⓕⓜ	23	9	4	2	15
Astoria Line (MN/QN)	Ⓝ Ⓠ	13	6	6	3	15
Broadway Line (MN/BK)	Ⓝ Ⓠ Ⓡ	30	9	4	2	15
Crosstown Line (QN/BK)	Ⓖ	13	9	4	2	15
Queens Blvd Line (QN)	Ⓔⓕⓜ Ⓡ	53	6	6	3	15
42nd St Shuttle (MN)	Ⓢ	1	9	4	1	14
8th Ave Line (MN/BK)	ⒶⒸⒷⒹ	53	6	6	2	14
Broadway - 7th Ave Line (MN)	①②③	50	6	6	2	14
Fulton St Line (BK)	ⒶⒸ	30	9	4	1	14
Liberty Ave Line (QN)	ⒶⒸ	7	9	4	1	14

Line Evaluation

New signals needed within ten years

Line	Service	Track Miles	Age	Capacity	Growth	Score
Archer Ave Line (QN)	ⒺⒿⓏ	5	6	6	1	13
Nassau St Loop Line (MN)	ⒿⓏ	5	6	6	1	13
4th Ave Line (BK)	Ⓓ Ⓡ Ⓝ	20	6	4	2	12
Lenox Ave Line (MN)	②③	6	6	4	2	12
Myrtle Ave Line (QN)	ⓜ	6	3	6	3	12
Rockaway Line (QN)	ⒶⓈ	23	9	2	1	12
Eastern Parkway Line (BK)	②③④⑤	17	6	4	1	11
Jerome Avenue Line (BK)	④	19	6	2	2	10
Pelham Line (BK)	⑥	23	3	4	3	10
Brighton Line (BK)	Ⓑ Ⓠ	28	3	4	2	9
Clark St Line (MN/BK)	②③	4	6	2	1	9

Line Evaluation

New signals needed within 15 years

Line	Service	Track Miles	Age	Capacity	Growth	Score
Nostrand Ave Line (BK)	②⑤	5	6	2	1	9
Sea Beach Line (BK)	Ⓝ	16	6	2	1	9
Culver Line (BK)	ⓕⒼ	42	3	4	1	8
Jamaica Line (QN/BK)	ⒿⓏⓜ	22	3	4	1	8
Concourse Line (BK)	ⒷⒹ	17	3	2	2	7
Second Ave Line (MN)	Ⓠ	5	3	2	2	7
West End Line (BK)	Ⓓ	18	3	2	2	7
White Plains Road Line (BX)	②⑤	26	3	2	2	7
Dyre Ave Line (BX)	⑤	11	3	2	1	6
Franklin Ave Line (BK)	Ⓢ	1	3	2	1	6

Line Evaluation

Source: RPA

Modern signals could be installed across the entire subway system in 10 to 15 years, dramatically increasing capacity.

The table to the left ranks the subway system's 36 lines, based on age of signals, lack of peak-hour capacity, and potential for population growth along the corridor. Higher scores indicate more urgent need for modern signals.

CBTC Prioritization
— Completed/Underway
— 5-year
— 10-year
— 15-year

Another example of the MTA being reluctant to change institutional practices is the lack of progress in transitioning to One Person Train Operation (OPTO). With the help of new cameras and CCTV monitors that let train operators at the front of the train view the entire length of the platform, operators (at the front of the train) could close the doors (in the middle of the train), while conductors could be redeployed to stations and other important positions. The MTA should use its next contract negotiation with labor to draft a schedule to start the full conversion of the subway to OPTO over the next five to 10 years.

Fully automate the subway

Ultimately, MTA subways should transition to fully automated trains, as evidence shows driverless subways are safer, more energy efficient, and more flexible than human-operated trains—with reduced maintenance costs. Once CBTC is fully installed, the MTA should move to eliminate train operators altogether and operate a driverless subway.

Replacing the train operators with technology could save the agency billions of dollars annually in labor costs. Alternatively, the MTA could redeploy operators as roving train agents who are responsible for customer assistance and respond to medical emergencies or crises.

Make the subway smart and on-demand

As fiber-optic cable is laid, CBTC is adopted, next-generation fare payment systems come online, and stations and trains are equipped to measure performance, occupancy, and the environment, vast amounts of information are being generated that could help the MTA operate the subway very differently than it does now.

Equipped with this data, the MTA could start piecing together over the next few years a much more complete picture of the operational environment and start sharing it with customers. It isn't difficult to imagine riders receiving information on their smartphone about delays so they can explore alternatives. Signage in stations should be dynamic, diverting passenger flows to keep people moving during incidents. The MTA should leverage the new contactless fare collection technology to support both fare pricing based on means and dynamic pricing to further encourage passengers to divert to a less-crowded subway line or the bus during events or incidents.

Looking farther into the future, one can imagine passengers' smartphones anticipating travel patterns based on travel history and preferences. When passengers enter a subway station, the MTA could know they are destined for a specific place and customize its trains' operations based on that demand—thus skipping through stops and adding service when needed.

Tying all of these technologies with those coming online in the future will allow the MTA to operate the subways in ways we cannot even completely imagine—but this will happen only if the agency embraces innovation.

OUTCOMES

Modernizing the subway with newer equipment will improve reliability and provide greater redundancy. Modern train control would make the subway safer and increase system capacity, thereby reducing congestion (if paired with other "brick and mortar" investments) and creating space for growth. It would also lower operating and maintenance costs by hundreds of millions of dollars annually. Finally, it would allow the MTA to improve the distribution of employees to better serve customers.

PAYING FOR IT

RPA estimates that it would cost about $27 billion, or $1.8 billion annually over the 15-year life of the plan, to fully implement CBTC on the subways. This estimate includes the cost of installing the system and upgrading interlockings and other associated investments. These costs could likely be reduced if the implementation of CBTC is streamlined. It's a very significant investment, and cost is the main reason the technology isn't being implemented more rapidly. At the current pace, the MTA would take more than 50 years to complete the changeover. RPA proposes accelerating the process, as well as prioritizing major lines so New Yorkers and others can receive the benefits of CBTC sooner.

21 Modernize and refurbish New York City's subway stations

Photo: Nancy Borowick

New York City's subway stations are crowded, noisy, and uncomfortable. For people with disabilities, four in five stations are inaccessible. The MTA must make significant investments to improve air quality and the overall station environment, and ensure all stations are ADA-compliant. This will require more elevators; widening entrances, corridors, and platforms; adopting a variety of strategies to improve ventilation and reduce heat; and building platform screen doors.

New York City subway stations are unpleasant and unhealthy.

Compared with many global cities with exceptional subway stations, New York City falls woefully short. Its stations are stifling hot in the summer, become damp when it rains, and have poor air quality and deafening noise levels when trains enter and leave. Crowded platforms keep trains from moving through the stations quickly and pose hazards for passengers, who also struggle with confusing signage and a lack of information. In many stations, there is peeling paint and cracked tiles; rats scurry on the tracks looking for trash left behind by travelers. Fewer than one in five stations are accessible to people with disabilities.

A region that depends so heavily on public transportation deserves subway stations that are safe and comfortable.

While moving passengers from one place to another is the main function of the subway system, making sure customers are comfortable and safe as they enter the station from the street and wait for their train is an essential part of the service. There are a number of ways to improve the experience.

Make all stations ADA-accessible

Only 82 out of 472 stations are accessible (or partially accessible) to those with physical disabilities. Being able to access the platforms from the street without needing to take stairs is important not only to those in wheelchairs, but also to the elderly and people with children in strollers who have no choice but to take the subway. The MTA currently has a waiver from the Americans with Disabilities Act that allows it to get by with making only 100 key stations accessible. This is unacceptable, particularly as the population ages. The MTA should accelerate adding stair-free access to 10 to 15 stations annually, with a goal of reaching 100 percent access by the 2040s.

Reduce crowding in stations

Thirty stations across the network are too small for the amount of pedestrian traffic they experience every day. Substantial investments are necessary to improve pedestrian flows and reduce congestion. These projects will be significant undertakings, costing on average hundreds of millions of dollars per station. But the return on "right-sizing" would include an increased capacity of the system beyond the station itself as a result of the improved speed and reliability of the trains traveling through.

Specific actions to "right-size" subway stations include:

- **Build larger and more accessible entrances.** These egress points should ideally be located within buildings or pedestrian plazas, and include escalators and elevators. Stations should be accessible to all users, including the elderly, the disabled, travelers with luggage, and parents with strollers.

- **Redesign and enlarge corridors and mezzanines.** Stations with clear sightlines are less confusing and easier to navigate. Major hubs such as Union Square and Herald Square should be completely rebuilt to create large column-free areas and wider walkways. In smaller stations, columns should be removed wherever possible to ease traffic flow.

- **Remove obstacles and widen platforms.** To move riders on and off of them quickly, station platforms should be decluttered of anything nonessential—such as newsstands that could be placed on the mezzanine—and in some cases widened. Vertical circulation could be improved by adding new stairways, escalators, and elevators. Riders would reach their destinations faster, and trains would spend less time in the stations.

In the longer term, like many metros around the world, stations could be rebuilt to separate the flows of pedestrian traffic going in opposite directions, thereby reducing congestion and improving throughput.

Reduce heat in stations

The extreme heat inside subway stations in the summertime—often well over 90 degrees—is not only unpleasant, it's also a health hazard. There are a number of ways to mitigate this:

- **Adopt regenerative braking on trains.** While traditional brakes release heat when activated, regenerative braking systems capture the heat energy and store it in a battery. This has the dual benefit of reducing both the amount of heat generated by braking trains as well as the amount of energy required to operate the subway.

- **Install modern signals.** Communications-Based Train Control (CBTC) enables trains to maintain a constant distance from each other using their current forward inertia and only applying the brakes when absolutely necessary. By reducing the stop and go of most manually operated trains, CBTC can reduce the amount of heat generated from unnecessary braking that radiates inside the tunnels and stations.

- **Lower the weight of subway cars.** According to the MTA itself, new subway cars could weigh as much as 2,000 lbs less than those in use today. This would decrease train power draws by 2.5 percent, and thereby the amount of heat.

- **Change how subway cars are air conditioned.** Air conditioning on subway cars increases the temperature on the platform, and moving from a sweltering station to a relatively cold car is unhealthy. Lowering the amount of air conditioning and exploring other ways to cool trains would help in this regard. Better ventilation over the tracks could also help divert some of the heat, although this solution would not be feasible in many of the older stations.

Image: ORG Permanent Modernity for the Fourth Regional Plan

- **Design and engineer future subway lines to generate less heat.** "Humped tracks," for example, harness the power of both gravity to assist with acceleration as trains leave the station, and braking before trains enter the next station. Curves in tracks can also be designed in a way that reduces the need for unnecessary braking between stations and maximizes the benefits of coasting.

- **Improve ventilation plants.** Better ventilation—in stations or even in tunnels—helps alleviate heat in the stations. Unfortunately, only 60 percent of ventilation facilities are in a state of good repair. Strategies to improve station ventilation and cooling may be considered part of public transit bonuses for real estate development.

- **Investigate using pumped groundwater to cool stations**, as was recommended by the MTA's Blue Ribbon Commission on Sustainability.

This is the subway system New Yorkers deserve—with platform screen doors, better elevators, less congested platforms, and more light and air.

Thirty of the MTA's 472 subway stations are too small for the pedestrian traffic they experience every day, and should be improved with bigger entrances, wider walkways, and redesigned platforms.

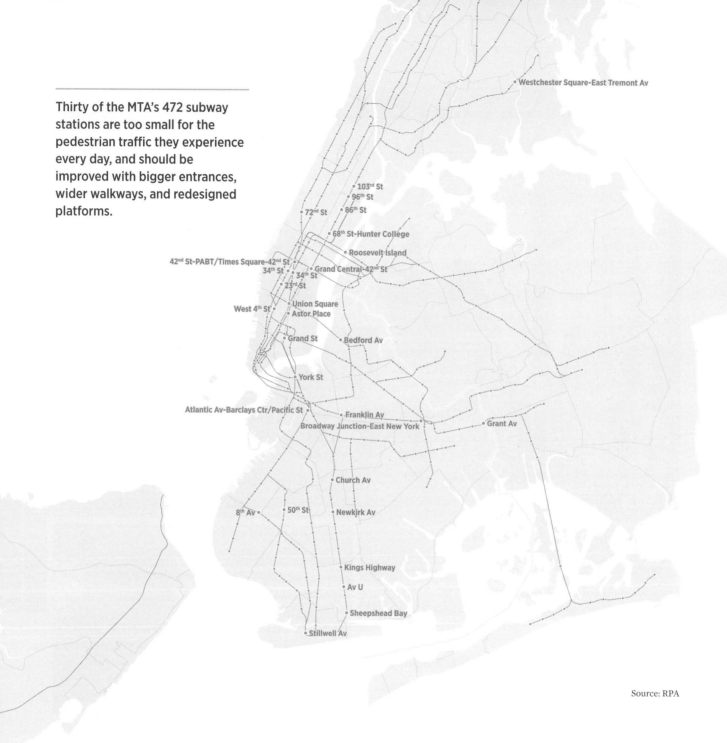

Source: RPA

Improve air quality in stations

- **Eliminate diesel vehicles and equipment.** The MTA should retire its diesel-powered service vehicles that emit "black carbon," a health hazard, and replace them with all-electric-power equipment.

Reduce noise in stations

- **Smooth the rails.** Continuously welded rail eliminates joints in the tracks, reducing noise and improving the smoothness of the ride. The MTA has installed continuously welded rail in a handful of places, and ultimately, should install it system-wide. In the shorter term, elimi-

nating these joints around stations and on the express tracks running through local stations would help reduce noise in stations.

- **Install quiet rail or low-vibration track in all stations.** Railroad ties encased in concrete-covered rubber and neoprene pads (instead of the traditional wood ties in concrete), combined with continuously welded rail, would further reduce vibration and noise. The new stations on the Second Avenue line have installed these systems, and the difference is noticeable.

- **Add sound-absorbing panels.** Most subway stations are finished with tiles or stone, which exacerbate and amplify noise. Low-maintenance sound-absorbing panels made of fiberglass or mineral wool have been installed in the new stations on the Second Avenue Subway, and should be made standard across all stations in the MTA network.

Platform screen doors would provide a dramatically more comfortable traveling experience

Although platform screen doors—glass and steel walls with doors placed between the tracks and the platform—can be very expensive and complicated to install, they would have a tremendously positive impact on the passenger experience.

Full-height platform screen doors would allow stations to be air conditioned (or heated in the wintertime), and would substantially reduce noise and passenger exposure to particulates. Altogether, they would radically improve the health of the station environment.

Even half-height platform screen doors would:

- Save lives, by preventing people from falling (or being pushed onto the tracks)

- Prevent trash from entering the tracks, thereby reducing delays caused by track fires

- Secure subway tunnels from unauthorized access

- Increase platform capacity, ease pedestrian flow, and enable trains to enter and depart stations faster

- Allow for better temperature control

Installing platform screen doors has significant cost implications. Most of the system's platforms would need to be reinforced to bear the load, and columns would potentially need to be removed to make space for unimpeded movement. Maintaining the doors would also increase operating costs. That said, there is also a cost savings to implementing platform screen doors from reduced litigation and track cleaning. Finally, platform screen doors would require the MTA to standardize its fleet of trains to ensure both sets of doors align.

Opening up stations to light and air would give the subway a more prominent presence in the urban fabric—and help with orientation below ground

Breaching the plane between the street and subway stations underground would bring natural light and air into the subway system. It would also give transit a more visible presence at the street level. Unfortunately, over the last 10 years, subway stations were built very deep underground to avoid utilities and reduce surface disruptions during construction. Nevertheless, many existing stations could be daylighted, thanks in large part to pedestrianization efforts to widen sidewalks and create more public plazas throughout the city.

Bringing light and air into stations also opens up the possibility of installing green walls and other natural finishes to help cool and filter the air. Cities around the world are experimenting with bringing nature into man-made environments; New York City subways should explore similar interventions.

OUTCOMES

These investments will make stations healthier and less crowded. The additional space and improved vertical circulation will increase the throughput of the subway and its reliability by reducing delays (dwell time at stations). It will make the subway accessible to the segment of our population that avoids it today, and allow it to continue to serve an aging population. Improving the environment of our stations will decrease medical costs over time by protecting riders' hearing and respiratory systems, along with substantially reducing stress. Finally, improvements such as platform screen doors will save lives, eliminating the 50 or so deaths per year caused by riders falling onto the tracks.

PAYING FOR IT

Improvements to the stations should be partially paid for by the local property owners who would benefit from the investments. This could be done through a value-capture mechanism—a property-tax surcharge for commercial land owners and new residents. Where Business Improvement Districts exist, resources could be leveraged to help improve and maintain underground spaces, as has been done with surrounding streets and public open spaces. Advertising as part of screen doors and other installations could also be a source of revenue.

22 Build new subway lines to underserved areas of the city

Photo: MTA Capital Construction / Rehema Trimiew

New York City has one of the world's biggest subway systems, but some areas of the city are poorly served. While better bus service has helped, there are still large parts of the city, including low-income neighborhoods dependent on public transportation, that are out of reach of any transit. Building new subway lines or line extensions in the South Bronx, southeast Brooklyn. and eastern Queens would reduce travel times and fully connect these communities to the city's transit system—and thereby job opportunities.

Many New Yorkers are not served by the subway.

Even though New York City has the most extensive subway system in the Americas, less than two-thirds of the city's population actually lives within walking distance of a station. This lack of access is particularly acute in Queens, where fewer than four in 10 residents can walk to the subway. Over the last few years, the city has initiated a Select Bus Service (SBS) program to mitigate this lack of access, but the results have been mixed—SBS has been slow to be implemented, and is simply not on par with subway service.

New Select Bus Service began in 2013 in order to improve the limited transit options along Nostrand Avenue in outer Brooklyn. In the future, densities along that corridor could justify extending the subway line down Nostrand to serve many more customers.

And so the city is full of neighborhoods that aren't served by the subway or SBS, even though their densities justify it (roughly 20,000 people per square mile, or the average density of Middle Village or Canarsie). Of those, many are low-income neighborhoods, where households are particularly dependent on public transportation.

High-density, low-income neighborhoods with poor access to transit include:

- The Third Avenue corridor and the southeastern sections of the Bronx

- East Harlem and the Lower East Side in Manhattan

- Areas in central/northeast Queens, including North Corona, College Point, Pomonok, and Fresh Meadows

- Vast areas of southeastern Brooklyn, including Flatlands, Canarsie, and Marine Park

Provide subway service to all mid- to high-density neighborhoods—particularly those with low-income residents

Providing good transit options to all high-density neighborhoods, with a special focus on those where low-income households live, is a top priority. The regional rail proposal described in this plan, dubbed T-REX (Trans-Regional Express) would provide subway-like service and fares at commuter rail stations within the city. In the longer term, it would also provide new service in neighborhoods without rail access. The proposed Triboro line would also provide new rail service to residents along that corridor.

Beyond these neighborhoods, there are others where new subway lines or extensions of existing lines are needed. They are typically high-density and low-income neighborhoods, with no subway service—although occasionally new lines are recommended to open up new housing and employment opportunities, or to increase line capacity. For example, extending the #1 line to Red Hook or the D line to the East Bronx could be justified in the future if these areas continue to develop.

A handful of strategic subway extensions could dramatically improve access in dense, low-income neighborhoods. More than a third of all New Yorkers don't live within walking distance of a subway or train station. Many—for whom transit access is disproportionately important—are low-income and/or live in neighborhoods that are dense enough to justify rail service.

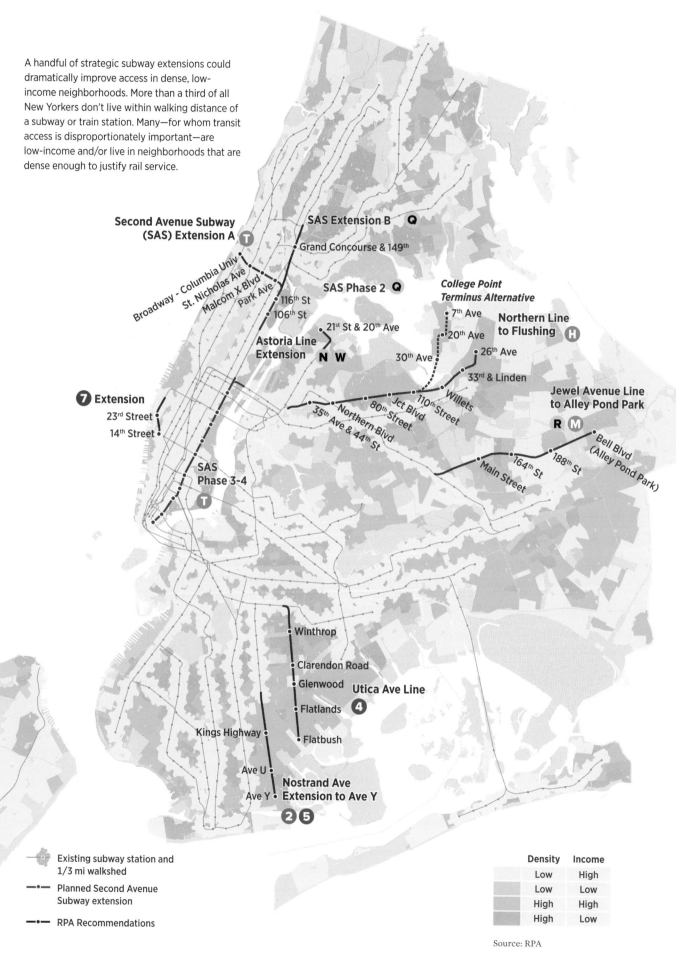

Second Avenue Subway (SAS) Extension A **T**

SAS Extension B **Q**

Grand Concourse & 149th

Broadway – Columbia Univ
St. Nicholas Ave
Malcom X Blvd
Park Ave

116th St
106th St

SAS Phase 2 **Q**

College Point Terminus Alternative

7th Ave
20th Ave

Northern Line to Flushing **H**

21st St & 20th Ave

Astoria Line Extension **N** **W**

30th Ave

26th Ave

33rd & Linden

7 Extension

23rd Street

14th Street

35th Ave & 44th St
Northern Blvd
80th Street
Jct Blvd
110th Street
Willets

Jewel Avenue Line to Alley Pond Park

R **M**

164th St
188th St
Bell Blvd (Alley Pond Park)

Main Street

SAS Phase 3-4 **T**

Winthrop

Clarendon Road

Glenwood

Utica Ave Line **4**

Flatlands

Kings Highway

Flatbush

Ave U

Ave Y

Nostrand Ave Extension to Ave Y

2 **5**

Existing subway station and 1/3 mi walkshed

Planned Second Avenue Subway extension

RPA Recommendations

Density	Income
Low	High
Low	Low
High	High
High	Low

Source: RPA

Each of the new lines and/or extensions are proposals that should be further evaluated by the Metropolitan Transportation Authority and the City of New York to determine whether their benefits justify their costs.

The Bronx

Third Avenue in the Bronx developed into a very dense neighborhood more than 100 years ago, but ever since the elevated line was torn down in the 1970s, the neighborhood has had very poor access to transit. The T-REX proposal would provide robust transit service to this neighborhood by converting Metro-North's commuter rail into a rapid-transit service. A terminal for the proposed Triboro line would also be located on Third Avenue at 149th Street, connecting that neighborhood to Queens and Brooklyn.

Second Avenue Subway extension

The Second Avenue Subway should be extended from its current terminus at 96th Street to the Grand Concourse line, connecting with the 2 and 5—and with T-REX at 149th Street. Extending the Second Avenue Subway to the Grand Concourse would increase service on the underutilized line, and provide Bronx residents with better access to jobs on the East Side of Manhattan.

Queens

Large parts of Queens are not on the subway system—although many of these neighborhoods have Long Island Rail Road stations. Ridership is very low at these stops because service is infrequent and expensive. The T-REX proposal includes a more frequent subway-like service at these stations—and adds eight new stations in Elmhurst, Corona, Rego Park, Rochdale, Laurelton, and South Jamaica. The Triboro line will provide service to places such as Middle Village and Glendale, connecting to the Crosstown T-REX lines at Winfield Junction and the Manhattan Spine/Atlantic line at east New York. While the T-REX and Triboro would address transit deserts in Queens, the remaining gaps should be filled with new subway lines and extensions, including:

Northern Boulevard Line

A new 3.7-mile Northern Boulevard line should be built to serve the neighborhoods of Jackson Heights, North Corona, North Flushing, Mitchell-Linden, and College Point. The line would run from 36th Street and Northern Boulevard to Willets Point, continuing east to serve north Flushing and Mitchell-Linden, or turn north to pass under Flushing Bay to College Point.

Jewel Avenue Line

The proposed 5.7-mile Jewel Avenue line would bring service from the Queens Boulevard line to the transit deserts of Pomonok and Fresh Meadows in Central Queens. It would bookend the new T-REX Metro service along the LIRR main line in Hollis and Queens Village.

Astoria Line Extension

Ridership on the Astoria line is expected to increase dramatically as the population grows in western Queens. A new terminus and yard capacity/train storage would allow for more frequent service to accommodate that new demand. Instead of today's two-track stub-end terminus with no storage, a new yard should be constructed on an industrial site on the northern side of Ditmars Blvd along 20th Street. With this new yard, the line could be extended west toward the East River to cover a part of Astoria that is dense and currently far from the subway. The extension would also place the line within walking distance of Astoria Park. Although this short new extension would be only 0.8 miles long, it would upgrade line capacity and reliability.

Manhattan

Only a few pockets of Manhattan are not covered by the subway. The T-REX would provide new transit options in the borough's busiest corridors, and improve coverage for the edge of the Upper West Side. It would also make it easier to get across town at 57th Street and Houston Street, and to travel up- and downtown on the East Side along Third Avenue. After these improvements, the places that still lack coverage would include theFar West Side in Midtown north of 42nd Street, the Lower East Side (east of Ave A), and East Harlem.

Second Avenue Subway and Crosstown 125th Street

The Second Avenue Subway should be extended from its current terminal at 96th Street to 125th Street and Park Avenue, and then continue westward along 125th Street to Broadway. In just three miles, it would cover the unserved lower-income neighborhoods of East Harlem and Harlem, and connect to seven subway lines (four stations), the T-REX at Third Avenue, and the 125th Street Metro-North station. The extension should also plan for a separate Second Avenue extension up to the Bronx, as described earlier.

Photo: MTA

The 7 line was extended from Times Square to Hudson Yards in 2015, giving subway commuters easy access to a growing part of the city. Other line extensions in Brooklyn, Queens and Manhattan would, similarly, improve commutes.

#7 Line Extension to Chelsea and Meatpacking District

Extending the #7 train from its current terminal at 34th Street down to 14th Street would improve access to the underserved areas of Chelsea and Meatpacking, and allow for more office and job growth. The extension would also improve access to the Hudson River waterfront from all parts of the city, and would connect the #7 with the L and A/C/E lines. RPA proposes extending the line on a gradual diagonal from 25th Street and 11th Avenue to Ninth Avenue and 14th Street, with a Station at 25th/23rd between Eleventh Avenue and Tenth Avenue. A subterranean pedestrian corridor would connect the L and #7 along 14th Street between Eighth Avenue and Ninth Avenue. After the new terminus at 14th Street, the line would extend down Hudson Street to 11th Street to restore the tail-end tracks. This extension should be designed so as not to preclude future extensions, including to New Jersey.

Brooklyn

Brooklyn has experienced tremendous growth over the past two decades, mostly in areas already served by the subway. The next wave of growth is likely to occur in Crown Heights, Brownsville, East New York, Flatbush, Midwood, and the Flatlands, which will put tremendous stress on the existing subway system. The T-REX Atlantic line would provide supplemental capacity for some of these neighborhoods, while others would benefit from the Triboro line. But even with these two services, several neighborhoods in southeastern Brooklyn would still be unserved. They are East Flatbush, Flatlands, Marine Park, Mill Basin, and Sheepshead Bay.

Utica Avenue Line Extension

A new subway line should be built under Utica Avenue, from Eastern Parkway to Flatbush Avenue, extending the #4 by four miles. The Utica Avenue subway would bring new rapid transit service to parts of Crown Heights, East Flatbush, Flatlands, Marine Park, and Mill Basin. It would also connect the rest of the city with Jamaica Bay—specifically, Floyd Bennett Field and Marine Park. Several of these neighborhoods are already served by express buses, but bus service is slow and only peak-period/peak-direction. The City of New York recently funded the MTA to study this line, and an assessment should be forthcoming.

Nostrand Avenue Line Extension

The Nostrand Avenue line should be extended 2.7 miles south to Avenue Z. This short extension would enable the #2 and #5 subways to provide service to the remaining portions of the Flatlands, Midwood, Marine Park, and Sheepshead Bay. A direct connection to Marine Park/Floyd Bennett Field would be possible if a pedestrian/bike bridge were constructed over Shell Bank Creek.

Staten Island

Staten Island poses difficult questions about investments in public transportation. The borough's current population and job densities make it difficult to justify the large capital expenditures rail requires. But extending the proposed Triboro system via a new tunnel under the Narrows and integrating the SIRT operation into the Triboro line could have multiple benefits. This improvement would directly connect passenger and freight rail service from geographic Long Island to Staten Island for the first time. SIRT customers would also gain the ability to reach parts of Brooklyn, Queens, and the Bronx, and connect to over a dozen subways and regional rail.

OUTCOMES

These new services would substantially reduce commute times for New Yorkers and improve access to neighborhoods, which means more choices for jobs and housing. Expansion of the mostly underground subway system would reduce the number of surface transit trips and ease traffic congestion, providing more space for repurposing of roadways for pedestrians, cyclists, and goods transporters. There are also opportunities for more redevelopment around stations, in some cases short-term, and others in the future. Finally, these improvements would substantially improve access to major open spaces, such as Alley Pond Park and Floyd Bennett Field.

PAYING FOR IT

These improvements would be funded through state and federal grants, along with revenue-backed financing. The MTA should also take advantage of opportunities to capture some of the value of real estate development that could occur along the corridors as a result of the new subway service. In most cases, these projects would only be feasible with reforms to planning, approving, managing, and constructing rail projects RPA is also is proposing as part of the Fourth Regional Plan.

ADAPT STREETS AND HIGHWAYS FOR A TECHNOLOGY-DRIVEN FUTURE

Streets and roads comprise the largest part of the region's public spaces. Over the last century, they have been dominated by the automobile. Instead of cars, however, people, bikes, and public transit should be given priority on the streets of cities and major downtowns. Even in suburban areas, roads should be designed to accommodate a range of users. On-street transit systems should be recalibrated and expanded to better serve more communities. Highways should be better managed to reduce congestion and increase reliability; and, in some urban neighborhoods, highways should even be removed, buried, or decked over to reconnect divided communities burdened by traffic and pollution.

Advances in technology provide new ways to manage streets and roads, while improving mobility. On-demand vehicle services can extend the reach of the public transportation network in lower-density communities. In the city, technology-enabled services such as ridesharing and, soon, driverless vehicles, could result in streets with less parking and more space for transit, walking, and biking. And throughout the region, variable road tolls could help reduce congestion and generate much-needed revenues for infrastructure upkeep and improvements.

23 On city streets, prioritize people over cars

Photo: New York City Department of Transportation

Street space is at a premium in this region. New York and other cities are particularly crowded, with pedestrians and cyclists competing for space with buses, cars, taxis, trucks, and emergency vehicles. Fortunately, there are a number of actions we can take to more actively manage and design our streets and roads to prioritize moving people and goods more efficiently and safely, while reducing air pollution, and absorbing rainwater.

Although some progress has been made, automobiles continue to dominate our streets and roads.

In a dense region like ours, the demand for street and road space will always outpace the supply. The allocation of space leaves too little room for walking, biking, and transit, largely the result of decisions made throughout the 20th century. Progress has been made: New York City's efforts to make streets safer has succeeded in cutting the number of annual traffic fatalities nearly in half, from 400 in 2000 to 229 in 2016. New York City has also built 1,200 miles of bicycle lanes, dozens on public plazas, and 15 Select Bus Service routes with more planned by 2030. One of the city's jewels, Prospect Park, has recently been closed to cars. Jersey City introduced bike-share services in the last year, and White Plains has plans to improve bike and pedestrian infrastructure.

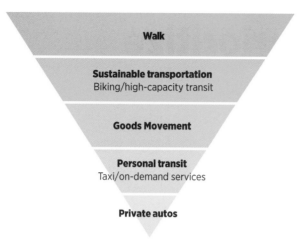

Street design and management practice should be turned upside down to prioritize pedestrians, cyclists, and transit users, followed by goods movement, shared services, and, finally, the private automobile.

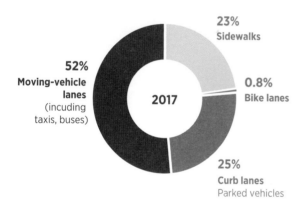

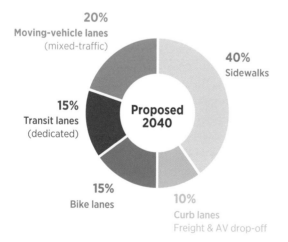

Less than a quarter of all New York City street space is dedicated to sustainable modes of transportation today; by 2040, it should be 80 percent.

Source: RPA

But too many of our streets are still unsafe and given over to automobiles. Less than a quarter of all New York City's street space is dedicated to sustainable modes of transportation—walking, cycling, and exclusive bike lanes—and most of this is concentrated in Manhattan and denser parts of the city. The vast majority of our streets and roads are handed over to automobiles, taxis, and transportation-network companies' delivery vehicles, freight trucks, construction equipment, garbage trucks, buses, and emergency vehicles. Many of these vehicles serve vital purposes, but they also cause air and noise pollution, clog up streets and roads, cause crashes, and generally increase the stress levels of drivers and pedestrians alike.

By not managing roads effectively, valuable space isn't used efficiently. Buses with dozens of passengers are stuck in the same traffic as vehicles with one passenger. Delivery and garbage trucks are free to make their runs at any time of day—even the busiest times. Clean, electric vehicles aren't given any preference over vehicles that burn gasoline and cause air pollution. It costs more to take the bus or the subway into Manhattan than to drive over four of the East River bridges. Car owners are provided free or heavily subsidized parking even though that land could be used for other purposes. And too little has been done—particularly outside New York City—to make streets safe.

We must rationalize how we use our streets and roads. Not only is it vital for public health and quality of life, but also critical to the region's economic vitality.

Proactive management and better design will make it easier to get around and create better, healthier neighborhoods.

The revolution in transportation that is occurring now, as on-demand, shared, and autonomous vehicles become more popular, is opening up a world of opportunities to manage and design our streets more strategically. Technology-enabled vehicles have the potential to make traveling much more efficient, reduce traffic, and dramatically cut back on the amount of parking a city needs. Municipal planning and transportation departments must harness the power of these new technologies to turn our city streets into healthy, active, and green spaces where people can reach their destinations efficiently and in a variety of ways. And planners and developers must prepare now for a future with new transportation technology and autonomous vehicles that reduce demand for parking.

Address the needs of neighborhoods with the worst pedestrian conditions

While streets and roads need to be improved across the region, certain places require more urgent attention. They are places that have the essential elements of what makes streets great for people—high concentrations of people and jobs, and high intersection densities—but that fail by other measures, such as number of crashes, air quality, tree-canopy coverage, and access to transit and bike infrastructure. In New York City, many of these neighborhoods are located in the Bronx and Manhattan, while outside the city, they are concentrated in western Nassau, southern Westchester, Hudson, and Essex Counties.

Charge drivers for the luxury of driving in the busiest parts of the region's core

Severe traffic congestion could be reduced by charging drivers a toll to enter Manhattan's central business district (CBD), along 60th Street and from the East River bridges. RPA has long supported congestion charging as a way to reduce traffic both in the CBD and in upper Manhat-

In an era of shared vehicles and, ultimately, driverless vehicles, traffic on city streets must be managed to prioritize people, bicycles, and buses over cars, with some room left over for green infrastructure.

tan, Brooklyn, and Queens. One of these proposals, Move NY, would combine new tolls with toll reductions on less-traveled routes farther from the core. Improvements in bus service and rationalizing fees for all for-hire vehicles would further reduce traffic in the CBD.

On city streets, use policy and design to prioritize walking, biking, and transit over cars

In cities and downtowns, decades of auto-oriented design and management practices must be upended to prioritize walking, biking, and transit, followed by goods movement, on-demand services, and finally, travel by private automobiles. This new street hierarchy would be transformative. In New York City alone, 80 percent of street space could someday be allocated to walking, cycling, and public transit, up from approximately 25 percent today.

To help make this transition, New York City should:

- Be given the authority by the state to have local control of traffic enforcement cameras

- Widen sidewalks over time to make them accessible for people of different abilities

- Build on the Select Bus Service Program by improving all major bus routes with designated lanes, and work with the MTA on transit-signal priority and modern fare collection

- Adopt bikeshare citywide, providing the subsidies needed so it reaches all five boroughs and is affordable to all residents

- Implement and expand the city's bicycle network; turn all painted bike lanes into separated bike lanes and build high-capacity bike parking stations

- Build more bicycle-only lanes on East River crossings, especially the Brooklyn Bridge, even if it requires repurposing vehicular traffic lanes

- Reform parking policies, ending free parking both on- and off-street; reducing overall number of parking spaces; and converting parking to wider sidewalks and parklets, for freight drop-offs and future autonomous vehicles

- Substantially reduce the number of parking placards issued for city employees

- Ban driving in Central Park and other city parks, opening up space for pedestrians and bikers

- Integrate new pedestrian boulevards, such as a re-imagined Broadway, into the proposed Tri-State Trails network

While some of this change would require large-scale street reconstruction projects, low-cost treatments such as paint, bollards, signage, and greenery could make a substantial difference in the near term.

In dense commercial areas, create car-free or low-car and low-emission districts

The densest parts of the city, where sidewalks are crowded and transit options are strong, should become either car-free pedestrian districts with no access for private automobiles, or low-car zones with very limited auto access, permitting only local residents, emergency vehicles, and local deliveries.

One way to transition toward these car-free and low-car districts is to organize more regular street closures. Neighborhoods could be car-free during times of high traffic—on Halloween, for example—or throughout the summer, or on weekends.

Use technology to manage traffic throughout the day

Just as technology is multiplying the number of ways people can get around—with on-demand, shared, and ultimately autonomous vehicles—technology can also multiply the number of ways cities can manage traffic.

Digital signage could notify people when streets are temporarily closed to traffic. Technology already allows drivers to navigate the city through apps that report traffic crashes, speed traps, and street closures in real time. "Geo-fencing" technology could even more proactively redirect drivers to avoid particular streets during peak travel periods or districts prioritized for pedestrians and cyclists during weekends.

To integrate technology into street management, cities should:

- Improve driver awareness of policies with temporal information on streets and curbs reducing confusion and improving compliance. This would require revising future street geodata (e.g., NYC's LION dataset) to include information on timesharing and time-based curbside restrictions, if/when applicable

- Use image analytics and license-plate recognition to support real-time parking information and enforcement

- Introduce digital wayfinding signage, particularly for shared spaces, expanding on such existing technologies as LinkNYC and MTA's On the Go kiosks

- Anticipate the need for future wayside digital technology with expanded sidewalks and curb bulbs at intersections

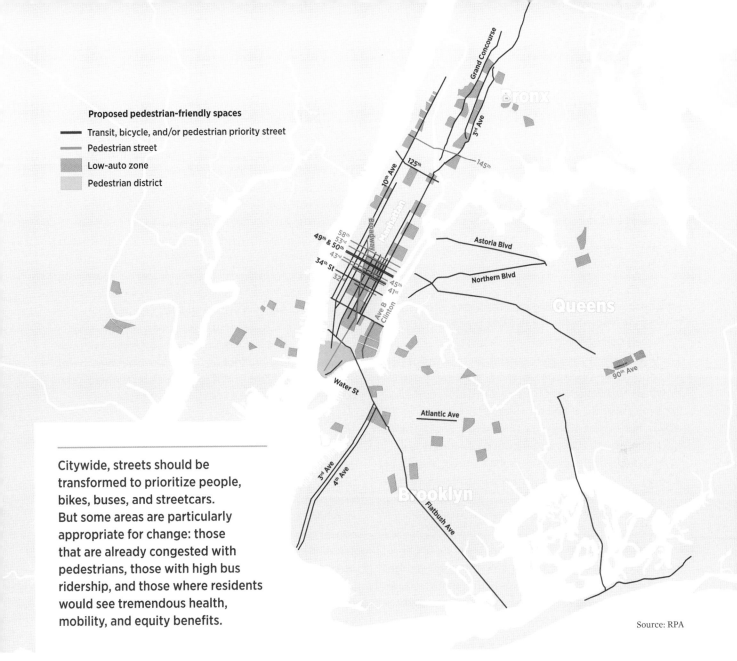

Proposed pedestrian-friendly spaces

— Transit, bicycle, and/or pedestrian priority street
— Pedestrian street
▮ Low-auto zone
▮ Pedestrian district

Citywide, streets should be transformed to prioritize people, bikes, buses, and streetcars. But some areas are particularly appropriate for change: those that are already congested with pedestrians, those with high bus ridership, and those where residents would see tremendous health, mobility, and equity benefits.

Source: RPA

Green the streets, improve health, and strengthen the urban ecosystem

There are many reasons to green the streets. More trees and landscaping make for a more pleasant streetscape, giving people places to sit and relax. They help clean the air, reduce heat, and absorb noise. They also absorb rainwater, and reduce storm-water runoff and flooding from heavy rains, especially in low-lying areas. New York and other communities should build on successful initiatives to improve the urban ecosystem—and boost public health—with bioswales, street trees, landscaping, and permeable pavement.

Promote efficient, environmentally friendly solutions to lower truck traffic for goods distribution

A functioning economy requires not just the movement of people, but also goods. Millions of shipments get delivered by truck every day—a number that could grow exponentially with e-commerce. Although New York City does not have a consistent or strategic delivery-management system, it is starting to address this through a new urban freight plan. Deliveries would cause less traffic if cities implemented the following measures:

- Designate more truck parking and loading areas, even if it requires eliminating on-street parking

- Repurpose curb space for wider sidewalks and loading zones

- Use textured pavement to delineate and designate areas for deliveries on shared streets

- Provide incentives for off-hour deliveries, pedestrian deliveries, and deliveries with nonmotorized vehicles

- Adopt low-emission zones in dense urban areas that ban or restrict high-pollution vehicles

- Enforce anti-idling programs, and transition truck fleets to electric and alternative-fuel vehicles

Adopt single-stream recycling and other waste-management measures to reduce traffic and sidewalk crowding

Waste and waste pickup have a big impact on our streets. Trash bags are strewn along already narrow sidewalks, attracting rats and giving off foul smells in the summer heat. Hundreds of sanitation trucks are deployed every day—some for commercial waste and recycling, others for residential waste and recycling. They crowd city streets, slowing traffic and fouling the air. And recycling rates are still very low.

A unified, single-stream recycling system should be adopted for both commercial and residential waste in New York City. In a single-stream system, all recyclable waste is collected by the same trucks, to be sorted into different streams—paper, metals, plastic, etc.—by special facilities. Single-stream systems have been adopted in thousands of municipalities across the U.S., and despite more upfront capital costs, they dramatically reduce the number of sanitation trucks on the road, boost recycling rates, and cut back on the amount of trash trucked to landfills.

Other waste-management measures should be taken to reduce traffic and sidewalk crowding, including:

- Rationalize and consolidate private commercial-waste collection

- Require trash bags to be placed in reusable bins, such as recessed bins at the curbside, instead of loose on the sidewalk

- Explore shared municipal binning, instead of curbside pickups at individual homes

- Explore requiring pneumatic waste-collection systems in all large new-housing, and commercial developments

Democratize planning for small-scale changes to local streets so government can focus on broader citywide challenges

The New York City Department of Transportation oversees one of the most complicated urban transportation networks in the world. Managing 6,000 miles of streets and highways, nearly 13,000 signalized intersections, 800 bridges and tunnels, and many other infrastructure elements is a massive undertaking, and means the DOT cannot be involved at the hyper-local level. But communities could be empowered to make targeted decisions about their local streets.

San Francisco, for example, recently launched Ground-Play, a multiagency effort to empower local leaders to make community-driven changes in their neighborhoods. GroundPlay identifies specific criteria for projects up-front, and then devolves some planning and design responsibility so citizens can work with their neighbors on public street art, plazas, and certain pedestrian safety projects.

New York City should consolidate the myriad of application-based processes different city agencies already run into one well-branded and unified entity. Empowering communities to take ownership of their streets would foster a culture of planning and vibrant street management.

OUTCOMES

The shared public street space is likely to change more dramatically than any other part of the urban environment over the next few decades. With the proactive planning and management recommended here, these changes would result in streets that can move more people and goods in fewer vehicles, provide more options for getting around, improve health by making it easier and more enticing to walk or take a bike, and create public spaces that encourage positive social interactions. Scarce urban space currently used for parking and storing cars would be freed up for more productive activities. The region as a whole would be more competitive in attracting businesses, residents, and tourists.

PAYING FOR IT

Many of the actions—redesigning the physical streetscape, implementing new technologies, putting in new bike and transit lanes and plazas—come at a substantial cost. An appropriate revenue source would be a share of congestion charges for entering the central business district or higher municipal parking curb-use fees that would also limit car use. Other actions would have a low monetary cost, such as regulations to limit car or truck use, but require a workable political consensus that is often difficult to achieve. Both short- and long-term success would depend on maintaining momentum from recent successes and replicating those successes in more locations and cities, effectively demonstrating benefits of more transformative change, and enlisting local organizations and business improvement districts to design district or neighborhood solutions.

24 Improve bus service, and introduce new light rail and streetcar lines

Riding in a bus or streetcar on a city street is as important as riding beneath that same street on a train, but receives far less public attention. Infrequent availability and slow speeds have led to falling bus and streetcar ridership. But with the right combination of smart technology, greater availability, faster travel times, and new lines, riding a bus or streetcar would no longer be the last and least desirable option in the region's transit system—it may even be the first.

Buses and light rail lines are underappreciated transit options.

In the urban center, low-density suburbs, and everywhere in between, buses and light rail lines must be actively managed to remain competitive with other ways of getting around.

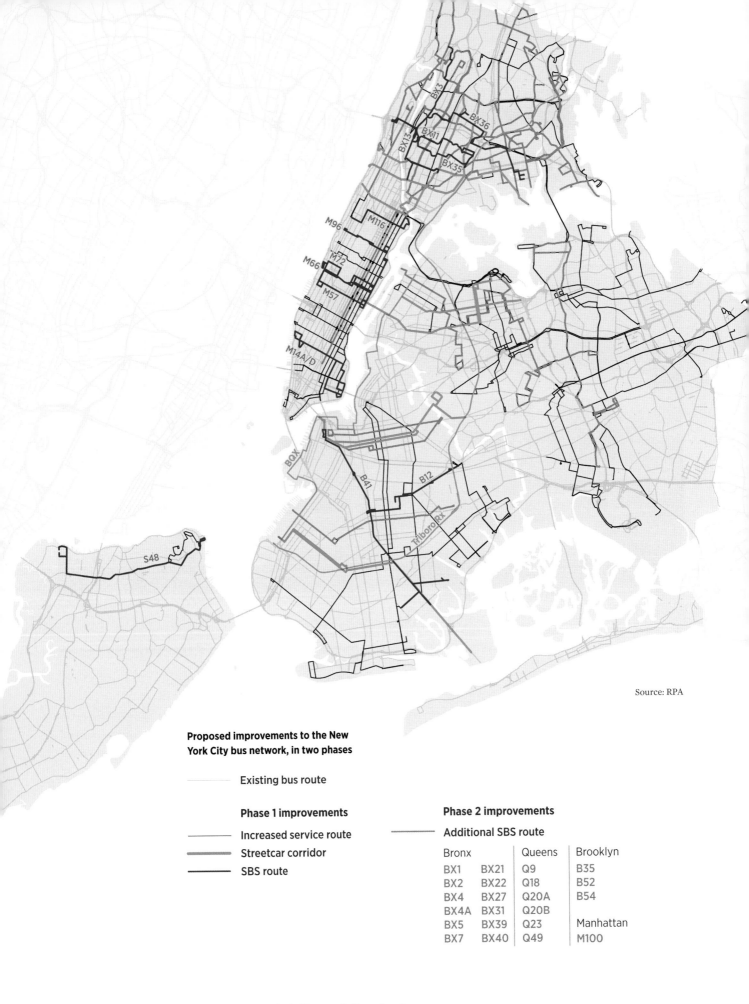

Proposed improvements to the New York City bus network, in two phases

——— Existing bus route

Phase 1 improvements

——— Increased service route

——— Streetcar corridor

——— SBS route

Phase 2 improvements

——— Additional SBS route

Bronx		Queens	Brooklyn
BX1	BX21	Q9	B35
BX2	BX22	Q18	B52
BX4	BX27	Q20A	B54
BX4A	BX31	Q20B	
BX5	BX39	Q23	Manhattan
BX7	BX40	Q49	M100

Source: RPA

Buses should no longer be the stepchild of the transit system. Bus riders deserve comfortable rides and convenient amenities. A handful of bus hubs, such as this one in Jamaica, Queens, can serve as regional transportation centers and serve the surrounding community.

In New York City, dramatically improve commutes with the Triboro line, additional Select Bus Service, and new streetcars

There are a number of opportunities for improving how New Yorkers get around, without having to build any new tunnels.

Activate the Triboro line

The Triboro line would run for 24 miles from Co-op City and/or 149th Street and Third Avenue in the Bronx to Bay Ridge in Brooklyn, providing new passenger rail service on an existing, underused freight right-of-way. As a circumferential line, the Triboro would intersect with 17 subway lines and four commuter rail lines along its route. It would provide better north-south transit service between Brooklyn, Queens, and the Bronx—a need that is growing as job growth accelerates in the boroughs (more than 50 percent of New York's job growth in the last 15 years has occurred outside Manhattan).

The Triboro line would increase connectivity between the boroughs and to Manhattan-bound subway lines. It would increase reverse-commute access to the suburbs for residents of the boroughs through outbound Metro-North and Long Island Rail Road services.

Triboro could be built faster and more cheaply than other recent, large-scale transit projects in the New York region because most of its right-of-way already exists.

Launch new SBS routes

NYC DOT's Select Bus Service (SBS) doesn't have all the features of Bus Rapid Transit (BRT), but it does offer off-vehicle fare collection and a combination of preferential lanes for buses, queue-jumping traffic signals, and longer station spacing. NYCDOT should add 15 more routes to the program. The bus lines with the highest use and the slowest speeds should be converted to SBS to improve transit service in Lefferts Garden, Ridgewood, Mott Haven, Riverdale, Soundview, and Jackson Heights, among others. Savings from SBS lines' greater efficiency and lower operating costs should be dedicated to increasing their availability and improving access to the subway system. Many other bus lines could also be simplified and redesigned for faster service.

Build light rail and streetcars

A proposal to build a light-rail line along the Brooklyn and Queens waterfront, a project known as BQX, has kicked off a lively public debate about reviving rail lines in New York, as many cities around the world have done in the last decade.

Surface rail can operate faster and be more flexible than buses on narrow streets, and can—and in most cases, should—trigger new development near stations. Eight streetcar routes should be considered in Brooklyn, Queens, and the Bronx. Depending on how well these projects progress, 22 more routes should be considered for either streetcars or SBS.

Invest in better fare collection for all buses

The MTA and other surface transit providers should accelerate the adoption of contactless fare collection to allow riders to tap in their fare as they step onto the bus, eliminating delays caused by passengers paying in cash or dipping their magnetic fare card as they do today. Although transitioning to contactless fares will be complicated and expensive, it will cost less than installing off-vehicle fare collection at kiosks along all routes and all stops, including more than 16,000 bus stops in New York City alone. As an added bonus, the same contactless card could be used universally on all transit systems across the region.

Outside New York City, increase bus service where possible

Outside New York City, many bus routes struggle with low ridership and high per-passenger costs, while others serve their communities well and have the potential to provide better service with more investment.

A comprehensive analysis of six suburban bus systems identified:[46]

- 31 routes with high ridership and low speed should receive operational improvements such as queue jumping, signal priority, and designated bus lanes where appropriate.

- 64 routes with high demand relative to cost should be considered for more frequent service.

- 22 routes that are run at the extremely high cost of more than $10 per rider should be assessed for alternative services, such as on-demand shuttles.

Launch new surface transit on dedicated rights-of-way where possible

To support population and employment growth in New York City and the region's other cities, public transportation providers should introduce new service or improve existing service along certain corridors. Of particular interest are corridors that:

- Connect to an existing transit corridor

- Connect two major subcenters

- Have a major employment center at one end to serve as anchor

- Run through places that can, over time, accommodate new, dense, walkable communities

- Exist in congested parts of the roadway network, so exclusive lanes can attract people away from their cars

Connecticut's new Fastrak service—a bus rapid-transit system between Hartford and New Britain—is proof that providing dedicated lanes for bus service can dramatically cut travel times, improve reliability, and increase ridership. There are three other corridors in the region that should make similar investments in either light rail or Bus Rapid Transit.

For each of these corridors to succeed, they must be developed along with the creation of more compact and walkable transit-friendly communities. Stations along these corridors should be optimized for drop-offs as on-demand and autonomous vehicles gain in popularity, providing critical "last-mile" access to the corridor from less-dense suburban communities.

Passaic/Essex Corridor: Paterson to Newark

The Passaic/Essex corridor spans a distance of 14 miles from the city of Paterson to downtown Newark. Restoring service on this line—the former Newark Branch of the Erie Railroad—would be transformative for Paterson, as well as for Clifton, Nutley, and Belleville. To maintain compatibility with existing freight service on part of the line, the new passenger service should be light rail (instead of BRT). Many of the nine train stations have been torn down, but their original sites should be evaluated for future stops.

The Interstate 287 Corridor

The Interstate 287 corridor extends for 30 miles, from Suffern in Rockland County, over the Mario Cuomo (Tappan Zee) Bridge, to Port Chester in Westchester. There is excel-

lent Metro-North rail service to New York from the three Westchester communities of Tarrytown, White Plains, and Port Chester. But east-west transit service—both to feed the Metro-North line and for local travel within and between Westchester and Rockland—is slow, unreliable, and hampered by congested roads.

Exclusive lanes for buses and three-or-more-occupant carpools should be implemented on I-287 from West Nyack to the Tappan Zee Bridge, and then from Tarrytown to White Plains. This would involve a combination of new right-of-way using surplus land along I-287 and rededicating lanes, either permanently or for certain times each day. The lanes would have direct busway tie-ins to the rail stations in each of the three Westchester cities, and would offer more local bus services.

Nassau Corridor: Oyster Bay to West Hempstead

The Nassau Corridor spans from Valley Stream on its southern end to the Oyster Bay at the north, a total of 22 miles in length. Two lightly used LIRR lines with low usage could be converted to light rail or BRT—either of which would provide more frequent service and lower operating costs. More frequent service could also help to establish a new north-south transit alternative, and both better serve existing land uses and jumpstart new development along the line.

OUTCOMES

Implementing all of these bus, streetcar, and light rail improvements could lower transit speeds for as many as a billion rides per year. Faster and more reliable service, shorter wait times, and more convenient and comprehensive service would reverse the decline in bus ridership such that the number of riders would grow faster than the population. Reliable service could reduce the growth of transportation network companies for surface-transit trips and mitigate rising congestion on New York City streets.

PAYING FOR IT

Better bus service can also be cost effective, as the expense of additional service could be partially offset by higher bus speeds that shorten route times. And routes that are to be reinforced should be selected in part because of their high ridership potential, which would result in a relatively low cost per rider. New BRT, streetcar, and light rail lines can employ tax-increment financing and other forms of capturing a reasonable portion of increased real estate values to pay for improvements.

Proposed network changes to the suburban bus network
These routes were selected for their potential ridership,
based on the density between centers.

Bus Rapid Transit (BRT)/Light Rail Transit (LRT)

Operational improvements,
such as signal priority or designated lanes

Increased service

Assess for alternative service,
such as on-demand shuttles

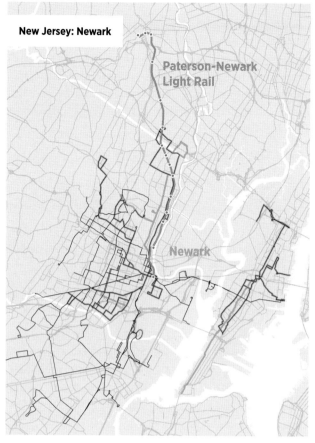

New Jersey: Newark

Paterson-Newark
Light Rail

Newark

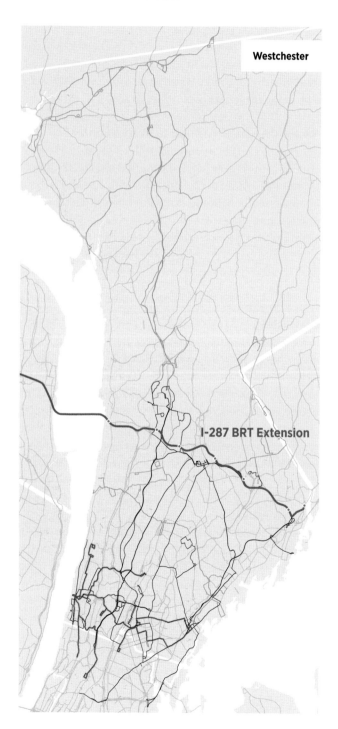

Westchester

I-287 BRT Extension

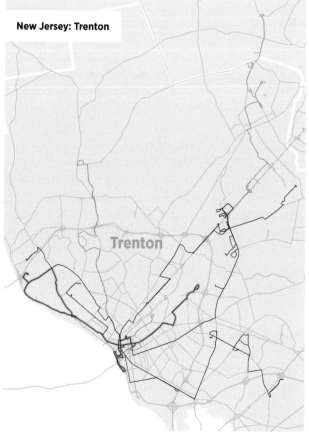

New Jersey: Trenton

Trenton

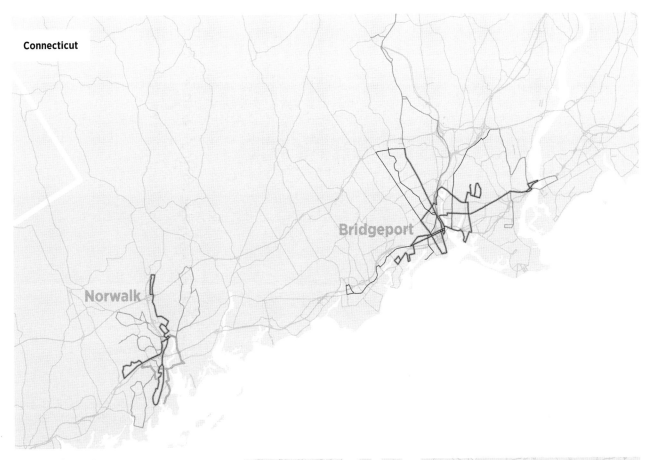

Connecticut

Norwalk

Bridgeport

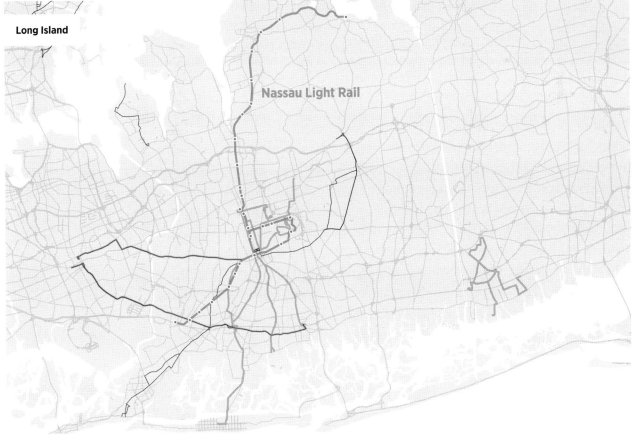

Long Island

Nassau Light Rail

Source: RPA

25 Expand suburban transit options with affordable, on-demand service

Photo: Jason Doiy

Car-dependent suburbs are becoming less competitive as both young adults and a growing senior population are looking to drive less. Yet the effectiveness of fixed-route transit such as rail and bus will always be limited in areas that are sparsely developed. Technology now provides an answer to this dilemma, making it possible to link bus and rail service with options ranging from biking and walking to car-sharing and van services. With proper government oversight, private on-demand car services, electric vehicles, and shared autonomous vehicles can provide better service at a lower cost. Where destinations are closer together, fixed-route bus lines may continue to be the best option. The public sector will need to manage this change with a focus on equity to make sure new technology-enabled services are affordable and accessible for all.

Image: ORG Permanent Modernity for the Fourth Regional Plan

Transit options in the suburbs are lacking.

Suburbs were designed and built for automobile travel. When residential densities are too low and destinations too scattered, operating a comprehensive public transportation network isn't viable. Although some corridors can support adequate bus service, residents mostly rely on cars for most, or even all, their daily trips. Traffic is choking many parts of the region; for low-income residents, needing a car to get to work can be cost-prohibitive; and for many others—including the disabled—getting around can be a real challenge.

An established commuter rail network helps anchor the region, providing many suburban residents access to New York City's enormous and rapidly growing job base. But not all suburbs currently have good rail options, as commuter rail fares are out of reach for many moderate- and lower-income families, while access to many commuter rail stations is limited due to insufficient parking or poor local transit connections. As a result, many families—especially those with low to moderate incomes—rely on bus service for their commuting needs.

Shared, on-demand, and driverless vehicles can extend the reach of the commuter rail system into the suburbs, making it easier for people to commute without having to drive and park at the train station. And the acres of parking that surround stations can be transformed into walkable neighborhoods with new apartments, shops, and offices.

Technology changes the mobility equation.

Technology has already changed the way we get around—but much more change is coming. On-demand services can enable custom routing and scheduling, with the possibility of limited ride-pooling. Where a large bus on a fixed route following a fixed schedule may be an inefficient and infrequent option, Transportation Network Companies (TNCs) can group people heading in the same direction at the same time by providing a small van to take them to their destinations quickly, efficiently, and at lower cost than traditional suburban cab service. As more customers use shared, on-demand services, the more competitive these services become compared with cars. Information technology also offers the promise of unified payment systems that facilitate trips involving multiple modes of travel.

Today, these services rely on human drivers. But innovation is moving quickly, and autonomous—or driverless—vehicles could be the norm within the next decade or two. That transition is likely to trigger even more changes to the way people get around, further lowering the cost of transportation in low-density suburbs.

Technology can improve the mobility equation if we implement the following policies:

Reinforce fixed-transit routes where there is sufficient ridership, or where new development will justify it in the future

There are places in the region where public buses operating on a fixed route and schedule are essential, including Route 8 from Trumbull Mall to Bridgeport in Connecticut; Route 110 from Amityville Railroad to Halesite in Suffolk County on Long Island; and Springfield Avenue from Irvington to Newark Penn Station in New Jersey. These fixed routes can help reinforce denser land-use patterns and better designed road corridors with pedestrian and other amenities.

Use on-demand services to supplement existing transit service

On-demand services are currently provided by the private sector, while most fixed-route transit is provided by the public sector. Government should take the lead in collaborating and coordinating services better in the future. NJ Transit, Bee Line, NICE, and other suburban bus providers, for example, could partner with technology companies to provide better service at lower costs. Different models for these partnerships could include:

- Government agencies providing subsidies to individuals who wish to use TNCs to reach designated destinations (e.g., a train station, or major employment hub) instead of providing direct bus service. The fare subsidies could also be given to specific customers—like people with disabilities—in lieu of providing paratransit service.

- Public transportation providers setting ambitious service-performance metrics for private companies to follow when providing transit services. Contracting does not automatically lead to better service quality or lower costs, but done strategically, it can promote the public interest. Transparency in the contracting process, strict enforcement of performance metrics, and labor protections are critical to success. As stated in a recent Transit-Center report: "Poorly written or otherwise ill-conceived contracts can lock public agencies into bad contracts that erode the status quo and miss opportunities for improvements."[47]

- Public transportation providers contracting out for back-end technology from TNCs to help make daily operations more efficient.

- Private institutions such as hospitals, universities, or other large employers collaborating with TNCs to provide faster, more efficient services for their target populations—while also supporting transit for other groups.

Offer incentives to shift riders to on-demand service to get to the train station instead of building more parking facilities

On-demand TNC cars have started to compete with local taxis and car services to provide "last mile" service from train stations. So far, change has been limited because for many commuters it is still faster and cheaper to drive their own car, especially when they already have a parking space.

But when a municipality needs to build a new parking structure or acquire land for more surface parking, it should consider redirecting those funds to subsidies for commuters who choose to be dropped off at the train station, whether by a TNC, taxi, or car service, instead of parking at the station all day.

Summit, NJ, has undertaken such a pilot project. Instead of building a new $10 million parking lot, the municipality launched a pilot project to subsidize TNC trips for its residents. The pilot's participants contribute $2 toward the cost of a trip to or from the station to anywhere in Summit, and the township picks up the rest of the tab—for a total of $167,000 a year, which is a fraction of the debt service cost of a new parking garage, to say nothing of the opportunity cost of the land. The program has had mixed success for a variety of reasons, and Summit continues to experiment with the model to promote participation at a cost the city can handle. Regardless, this business model offers strong potential if it can be scaled up.

Redevelop parking lots near train stations

Municipalities and transit agencies that own land near commuter rail stations should consider redeveloping and monetizing these assets. As on-demand, shared vehicles, and then autonomous vehicles become more widely used, the need for parking will be reduced, particularly directly adjacent to the station. The public entities in charge of providing parking at train stations could redevelop their land into housing or commercial space and create a more walkable neighborhood around the station. The revenue generated from the sale could be used to subsidize TNC trips for residents who choose to be dropped off instead of driving themselves.

The potential for these parking lots to provide housing, jobs, and tax revenue is enormous. Even after reserving space for parking and pickups and drop-offs at the 353 commuter rail stations in the region, more than 7,500 acres of parking lots could be reconfigured and redeveloped to create more than 250,000 new homes and the shops, parks, and community services needed to support them.[48]

Leverage on-demand technologies to improve and expand paratransit

Approximately 1.3 million people in the region have an ambulatory disability, namely a difficulty walking or going up stairs. And with an aging population, the number of people with ambulatory disabilities will likely increase. Their transportation needs are not being met. The number of paratransit trips in NYC has tripled since 2000, but the current system is slow and unreliable. Booking a trip requires 24-hours notice, and service is often delayed. To meet these challenges, the MTA is looking to improve services using up-to-date technologies. But beyond the paratransit needs of NYC, there is also an opportunity to use on-demand platforms or similar technologies to expand services both across the region and for other vulnerable users. Examples include food shopping and helping expectant mothers or parents with children get to a doctor. Provided there are incentives and design standards for accessible vehicles, TNCs could be a more affordable and efficient alternative to conventional publicly operated paratransit services—this approach should be explored by the city and other public operators in the region.

Stay ahead of the technology: Remain wary of the pitfalls, but be ready to adopt new opportunities

The advent of on-demand, shared, and autonomous vehicles could yield great benefits both for those who can't or don't wish to own a car, and for transit providers who could cut their costs. But there are concerns to stay aware of.

Technology evolves quickly, and technology companies will always be ahead of the curve. But it is important for the public sector to invest in technology-savvy employees and be flexible in the procurement process to stay nimble. TNC companies are for-profit businesses and although public-private partnerships can be very productive, the public sector must be diligent about requiring and enforcing service-performance measures, collecting data, and keeping their private providers' fares affordable.

As driverless vehicles increase the convenience and reduce the cost of traveling, measures must be taken to ensure they do not simply encourage longer travel distances, generate more traffic, and cause more sprawl at the suburban edge. This may require other strategies to mitigate long-distance travel, such as pricing and land-use controls.

OUTCOMES

With proactive planning and innovative policies, on-demand services and autonomous technologies should drive the costs of mobility down in suburban areas while significantly improving access for lower-income riders or riders with disabilities. These services would improve safety for the elderly, women, and young people during late nights and weekends. Over time, they would also free up parking spaces for repurposing as new public spaces, affordable housing, bike lanes, or freight pickup and drop-off zones. The goal is to create an integrated mobility system that gives users multiple options for fixed-route transit or on-demand mobility.

PAYING FOR IT

The cost of improved service would be partially covered by the efficiency gains of on-demand transportation and eventually the labor savings through autonomous operation. However, local subsidies would likely be required to provide greater frequencies in less dense places. These subsidies could eventually be paid for through value-recapture as parking lots are redeveloped for other higher-value uses over time.

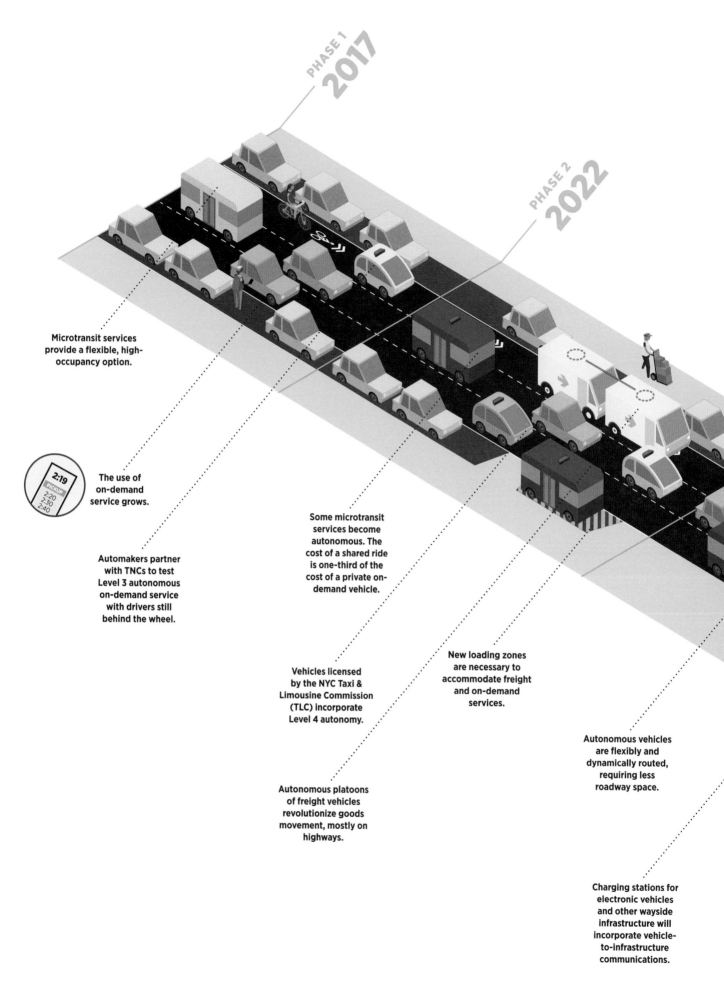

PHASE 1
2017

PHASE 2
2022

Microtransit services provide a flexible, high-occupancy option.

2:19
PICKUP
2:20
2:30
2:40

The use of on-demand service grows.

Automakers partner with TNCs to test Level 3 autonomous on-demand service with drivers still behind the wheel.

Some microtransit services become autonomous. The cost of a shared ride is one-third of the cost of a private on-demand vehicle.

New loading zones are necessary to accommodate freight and on-demand services.

Autonomous vehicles are flexibly and dynamically routed, requiring less roadway space.

Vehicles licensed by the NYC Taxi & Limousine Commission (TLC) incorporate Level 4 autonomy.

Autonomous platoons of freight vehicles revolutionize goods movement, mostly on highways.

Charging stations for electronic vehicles and other wayside infrastructure will incorporate vehicle-to-infrastructure communications.

The road to autonomous vehicles in the region

PHASE 1
Automated features continue to improve and become less expensive, while car ownership declines.

PHASE 2
Fully autonomous vehicles are on the market, but AV and legacy vehicle mix results in uneven traffic improvements.

PHASE 3
Autonomous conversion of light-duty vehicle fleets increases from 15 percent in 2030 to 75 percent in 2040.[49]

PHASE 4
Street design and land-use planning are permanently altered to make way for pedestrians, cyclists, and public spaces—in both urban and suburban streets.

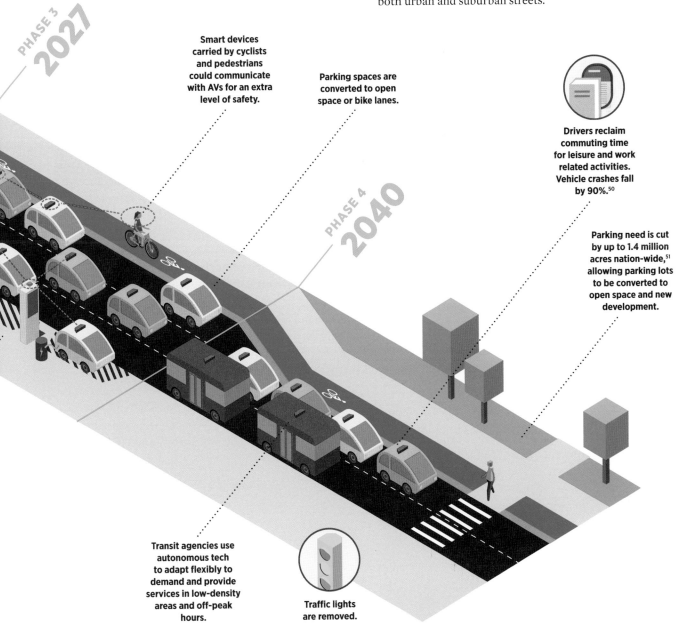

PHASE 3
2027

PHASE 4
2040

Smart devices carried by cyclists and pedestrians could communicate with AVs for an extra level of safety.

Parking spaces are converted to open space or bike lanes.

Drivers reclaim commuting time for leisure and work related activities. Vehicle crashes fall by 90%.[50]

Parking need is cut by up to 1.4 million acres nation-wide,[51] allowing parking lots to be converted to open space and new development.

Transit agencies use autonomous tech to adapt flexibly to demand and provide services in low-density areas and off-peak hours.

Traffic lights are removed.

26 **Reduce highway congestion without adding new lanes**

Photo: Shutterstock / barbsimages

Sitting in traffic is still a frustrating daily experience for many of the region's residents who must drive a car to get to work or run errands. The last 50 years have demonstrated that wholesale highway expansions don't solve traffic issues long-term. The only way to address congestion effectively is to manage traffic. This can be done using a range of tools, including removing physical bottlenecks, prioritizing multi-occupancy vehicles, and charging users to drive at the most congested times.

The New York region has the worst congestion and the most unreliable commutes in the nation.

The region's highway network is chronically congested. At all hours of the day, backups delay commuters, truck drivers, residents, and visitors alike. Some congestion occurs after an incident, such as a crash, breakdown, or construction work. Commutes that used to take 20 minutes now routinely take 30—and can sometimes take 45. Valuable hours are lost, which ultimately drains the economy—on top of causing stress, which can translate into deeper health hazards.

Expanding the highway network to ease congestion is no longer an option. In addition to an overall lack of available land, the region has learned that new highway lanes will fill up again in a matter of months or years. Diverting drivers to public transportation is worthwhile, but difficult, as taking the bus is rarely faster than driving, and rail infrastructure is tremendously expensive to build. Developing more compact neighborhoods will also help reduce traffic, but only in the long term.

And we don't have that time. The region is choking on its traffic.

Today's highway system can be more reliable—and even gain some capacity.

We will never be able to meet the ever-growing demand for highway space by increasing the supply of highways. But we can get more out of existing infrastructure by eliminating the handful of bottlenecks that cause recurring problems, making travel movements more smooth and efficient, and using tolls to discourage or redirect travel, thereby reducing highway congestion without having to add new lanes.

Eliminate recurring highway bottlenecks

Key pinch points in the highway network cause a disproportionate number of delays. Many are due to the age and inadequate maintenance of our highway infrastructure. Major roadways and bridges are over half a century old, and need constant repair to meet modern standards, while more than 1,000 bridges are considered structurally deficient. Where feasible, departments of transportation should analyze choke points and prioritize them according to congestion.

In general, three types of improvements are the most effective in addressing recurring bottlenecks:

- **Install breakdown lanes.** Disabled vehicles having no place to park while waiting for emergency assistance or repair causes major backups. The Cross Bronx Expressway and 25 miles of I-278 between New Jersey and Queens are particularly problematic. The installation of breakdown lanes should be prioritized based on the frequency of accidents, low travel speeds, and proximity to existing breakdown lanes.

- **Add lanes where roadways narrow for short stretches and merges occur.** Lanes should be added based on the severity of the congestion and the availability of space to add lanes.

- **Widen ramps or add exit lanes.** Certain ramps and exit lanes are no longer adequately sized to accommodate current demand—a result of a highway system that has not been recalibrated to more recent land use changes and travel patterns. One particularly striking example is the exit for I-80 off of I-287, a major interchange in New Jersey, where westbound traffic has dramatically increased since the interchange was built. Long queues extend back into the travel lanes and create a safety hazard.

Smooth the flow of vehicles

Traffic flow is most affected by sudden stops, many of which could be avoided with more widespread use of effective traffic-management policies.

Speed harmonization involves warning motorists and modulating speed limits in real time to reduce sudden stops that reverberate through the network. Speed harmonization, which is not in place in the region, can reduce serious crashes and their related traffic congestion consequences by at least 25 percent.

Ramp metering, which has been deployed successfully for decades on the Long Island Expressway, uses traffic signals at highway entrance ramps to more evenly insert vehicles into the flow of traffic. NYSDOT is already installing ramp meters at 13 locations along I-87/I-287 in Rockland and Westchester counties. This system should be installed wherever there is recurring congestion and there is sufficient space to hold waiting vehicles on the ramps.

Encourage group travel

Vehicles that carry a larger number of passengers—be they carpools, minivans, or large buses—should be given preferential treatment on highways. The most effective way to do this is to designate certain moving lanes for higher occupancy vehicles (HOV). Even though HOV lanes have been widely adopted across the U.S., there are only about 50 miles of HOV lanes in the region.

The most efficient HOV lane, by far, is the two-mile approach to the Lincoln Tunnel in New Jersey that is reserved for buses heading to the Port Authority Bus Terminal. While a typical traffic lane carries approximately 3,000 people in 2,000 cars each hour, the XBL lane can carry over 30,000 people in 700 buses during that same time period. The Port Authority should therefore convert a second lane of the Lincoln Tunnel for buses only.

Other good candidates for HOV lanes are on the New York State Thruway in Rockland County from West Nyack to the Mario Cuomo Bridge, and segments of Interstate 287 in Westchester County.

HOV lanes should be created by converting existing travel lanes rather than by adding new lanes to existing roads, which encourages further sprawl. And no new HOV lanes leading directly into Manhattan should be created, as this would encourage added car traffic in Manhattan and be a disincentive to use public transit.

Charge tolls that vary according to congestion levels

Only a very small share of the region's highways is tolled today. Charging drivers to use highways—or any part of the region's entire road network—would not only raise revenue, but could also be used to manage traffic. Tolls could have variable prices based on time of day or level of congestion, encouraging drivers to travel at off-peak times, use a less-crowded part of the road network, or redirect drivers to public transportation. Strategic toll-setting can be a tremendously effective tool to control congestion and ensure reliability on the road network.

Open up more highways to truck traffic

The movement of goods in the region is hampered by many segments of our highway network not allowing truck traffic, forcing trucks to use other, more-circuitous routes and ultimately clocking in additional miles on our already-congested highways.

Some of these truck-free roads were built as parkways, whose many features (such as tight turning radii, narrow lane widths, and low overhead clearances) would need to be reconstructed—a prohibitive price tag. But other highways could, with more minimal interventions, be retrofitted to allow trucks or, at least, lighter commercial vehicles. This would reduce the total number of miles driven by trucks in the region, and alleviate pressure on the most congested parts of the network.

Highways that could be opened up for lighter trucks include the Belt Parkway, FDR Drive, Henry Hudson Parkway, Cross Island Parkway, Ocean Parkway, and Jackie Robinson Parkway.

Continually reevaluate the opportunities offered by technology

Few cars are driverless today, but the autonomous features already standard on modern cars are changing the way cars "interact" with each other and with highways, and are an opportunity to make driving safer and more efficient. They reduce stop-and-go driving and create traffic flow that is safer and higher-capacity. They give drivers up-to-the-minute information about upcoming incidents and travel speeds, and suggest alternative routes.

In the next decade, as fully autonomous vehicles become more commonplace, transportation departments will have the opportunity to make our highways "smart"—using virtual cordons, geo-fencing, driving fees, and other measures to direct drivers toward or away from particular routes. Autonomous vehicles may be able to operate in platoons (groups of vehicles following each other at constant and identical speeds), which could increase highway capacity by 25 percent or more.

OUTCOMES

These actions would help decongest our highways by eliminating bottlenecks and allowing traffic to flow more smoothly. Moving from an unmanaged to managed highway network will increase both safety and road capacity. These steps would prepare the region to adopt to new autonomous vehicle technologies that will drive additional efficiencies and allow us to rethink how we use highways.

PAYING FOR IT

Most of the recommended traffic-management policies could be implemented with minimal capital investment. While actions to eliminate physical bottlenecks can cost in the tens or hundreds of millions, these improvements could be paid for using revenue from new tolls on interstates and major highways, along with the eventual transition to fees based on the number of miles motorists drive.

㉗ Remove, bury, or deck over highways that blight communities

Photo: ORG Permanent Modernity

In the middle decades of the 20ᵗʰ century, carving limited-access highways through the middle of neighborhoods and city districts was considered the unavoidable price of progress toward the all-important goal of increasing traffic flow. These highways continue to blight and divide neighborhoods, many of which were and still are low-income communities of color, limiting access to open spaces and negatively affecting public health. State departments of transportation should prioritize improving highway segments that cause the most harm to neighborhood health, prosperity, and cohesion, and work with communities and municipalities to remove or transform them into community assets.

Urban highways have caused severe damage.

Whether the roadways were sunk in trenches, elevated above, or built at grade, they broke up neighborhoods, resulted in dangerous and noisy streets, and led to high rates of asthma and traffic accidents. The most problematic examples include the Cross Bronx Expressway, Brooklyn-Queens Expressway, and Sheridan Expressway in New York; Interstates 280 and 78 in New Jersey; and Route 34 and I-95 in Connecticut.

In other cases, highways were built at the water's edge or in parks, mainly because that land was already publicly owned and planners at the time wanted to create parkways. Roads that cut off access to rivers and park space include the Belt, Henry Hudson Parkway, Hutchinson River Parkway, FDR Drive, and Sheridan Expressway in New York; Route 21 and Route 29 in New Jersey; and Route 8 and Route 34 in Connecticut.

State DOTs should work with communities to transform urban highways and repair the harms of the past.

In all but a few cases, removing these highways entirely is not possible due to high costs and disruption. Moreover, residents and businesses have made long-term decisions based on the access these roads provide, and eliminating them without a comparable alternative would create additional problems for neighborhoods.

There are, however, many segments of highways that can and should be removed because they are underused or there is an alternative nearby. In other cases, highways can be replaced by a different type of road, such as a boulevard with trees, less traffic, and pedestrian and bicycle amenities. Depressed roadways can be decked over and rebuilt with new housing or open space that reconnect the community to the street grid. Finally, certain highways can be rerouted underground—or "buried"—to eliminate their street-level impact and make land available for housing or open space.

The following highway improvements have been recommended based on costs, benefits, and the impacts of both action and inaction. State departments of transportation should launch a new program in collaboration with cities and local communities to implement solutions for these highways.

Restore Van Cortlandt Park

Sixty years ago, Van Cortlandt Park, one of the crown jewels of the New York City park system, was chopped into six pieces with the construction of three highways. A 0.4-mile segment of the underused Mosholu Parkway between the Major Deegan Expressway and Gun Hill Road should be considered for removal or burial, which would create safe east-west pathways in the park and restore its value as a place for recreation.

Reclaim the Brooklyn-Queens Expressway

The stretch of the Brooklyn-Queens Expressway (BQE) running through downtown Brooklyn is being considered for redesign or reconstruction by state officials, although burying this obtrusive highway instead would dramatically improve the community's access to the waterfront. Decking over stretches of the BQE in Carroll Gardens would provide opportunities for new housing. In Williamsburg and Greenpoint, the public realm below and around the BQE could be dramatically improved, as community members and elected officials have requested.

Deck over trenched highways such as the Cross Bronx in New York City, Interstate 280 in Newark and East Orange, and Route 8 in Bridgeport

Several segments of the region's highways can easily be decked over for new development or open space without affecting traffic patterns. In addition to mending scars left by the highway, decking over also mitigates the visual, noise, and air-quality impacts of the highways on nearby residents. Decking over would create more valuable land on the deck itself and in adjacent areas that be could be used to defray the cost through residential or commercial developments.

Thirteen segments of six highways in New York City have been recommended for decking over: the Cross Bronx, Bruckner, Gowanus, Brooklyn-Queens, Trans-Manhattan, and Van Wyck expressways. Decking over those stretches could amount to 100 acres of new land. Parcels on the FDR Drive should also be further evaluated for cantilevered development over the highway.

In New Jersey, Interstate 280 could be decked over in Newark and East Orange, which would restore the street grid and knit back together neighborhoods. In Bridgeport, Connecticut, a short depressed stretch of Route 8 between Pequonnock and Highland avenues could also be decked over.

Boulevard the Sheridan and Prospect Expressways in New York City, Route 29 in Trenton, and Route 34 in New Haven

In 1989, the West Side Elevated Highway in Manhattan was dismantled and turned into a boulevard, West Street, which has since helped nearby communities reconnect with the Hudson River waterfront and led to the building of the Hudson River park, one of the city's most treasured parks. The last segment of the elevated highway, from 60th Street to 72nd Street, should also be taken down.

In the Bronx, after years of advocacy from organizations such as the South Bronx Watershed Alliance, a 1.25-mile stretch of the Sheridan Expressway is being turned into a boulevard. Current plans, which include new crosswalks, other pedestrian improvements, and lining the street with trees, could be improved by further narrowing the road from three lanes down to two in each direction. The freed-up land could be used for open space and community amenities, which are of far greater benefit to the nearby communities.

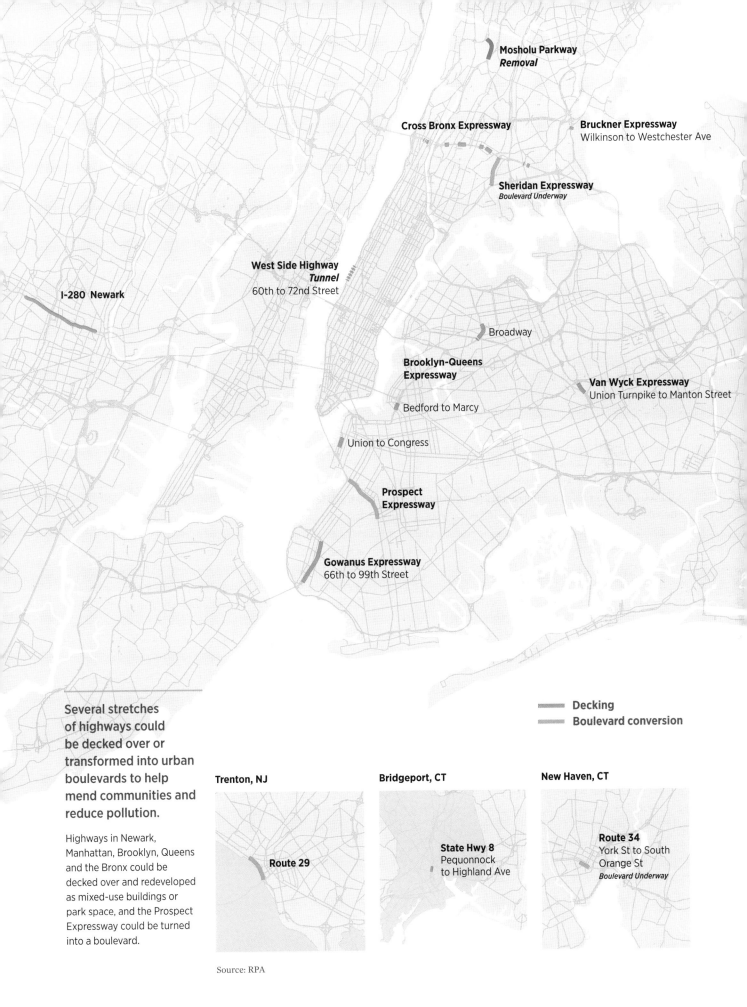

Mosholu Parkway
Removal

Cross Bronx Expressway

Bruckner Expressway
Wilkinson to Westchester Ave

Sheridan Expressway
Boulevard Underway

West Side Highway
Tunnel
60th to 72nd Street

I-280 Newark

Broadway

Brooklyn-Queens
Expressway

Van Wyck Expressway
Union Turnpike to Manton Street

Bedford to Marcy

Union to Congress

Prospect
Expressway

Gowanus Expressway
66th to 99th Street

Decking
Boulevard conversion

**Several stretches
of highways could
be decked over or
transformed into urban
boulevards to help
mend communities and
reduce pollution.**

Highways in Newark,
Manhattan, Brooklyn, Queens
and the Bronx could be
decked over and redeveloped
as mixed-use buildings or
park space, and the Prospect
Expressway could be turned
into a boulevard.

Trenton, NJ

Route 29

Bridgeport, CT

State Hwy 8
Pequonnock
to Highland Ave

New Haven, CT

Route 34
York St to South
Orange St
Boulevard Underway

Source: RPA

Decking over below-grade highways can stitch neighborhoods back together at the same time opportunities are created for open space, green infrastructure, and adjacent neighborhood development.

Image: DLANDstudio

Route 34 in New Haven is being turned into a boulevard, reducing the roadway's width and adding pedestrian amenities and new development.

Other opportunities to boulevard existing highways include:

- The Prospect Expressway in Brooklyn: From Third to Church avenues, a distance of almost two miles, it should be narrowed to one lane in each direction, opening up land for a new bicycle "highway," residential development, and public spaces.

- Route 29 in Trenton: A project that has been discussed for decades, it would convert a mile-long stretch of limited-access highway between Trenton's downtown and riverfront. Tying the road back into the city grid and adding pedestrian features would have tremendous social and environmental benefits.

OUTCOMES

These actions would stitch together neighborhoods, restore communities, and improve local mobility. They would create over 100 acres of reclaimed land for development of housing, mixed uses, or open spaces. Removing, burying, and decking over the region's highways will improve the health of communities by mitigating some of the noxious air and noise impacts. It would also reconnect parks and other open spaces for recreational purposes such as walking and biking.

PAYING FOR IT

The cost of these interventions would be significant, and funding would need to be prioritized within state and city transportation budgets. For example, the New Haven Route 34/Downtown Crossing will cost an estimated $74 million, while some of the more extensive projects will cost far more. Many of the benefits, however, can be monetized in a short time period, including selling off parcels of land for redevelopment, which would add valuable real estate to the tax rolls. Other benefits have longer payback periods, such as better public health outcomes and cities with more development and a higher tax base.

CREATE WORLD-CLASS AIRPORTS AND SEAPORTS

**N**ew York's dynamic economy depends on international trade and connections, yet the region's critical transportation links—its airports, seaports, and railway lines—lag behind global peers.

To maintain New York's position as a hub for trade, business, and tourism, we must modernize and expand critical transportation infrastructure. Kennedy and Newark airports should be expanded to increase capacity and alleviate persistent delays. Investments in railways in the Northeast Corridor could dramatically reduce travel times to Washington, D.C., and Boston. Modernizing seaports and freight-distribution systems would improve efficiency and make them more environmentally friendly.

These large-scale projects would be expensive and complex, and could require significant changes to the agencies and authorities that oversee these facilities. But keeping the region connected to the world is critical to its continuing economic growth and prosperity.

28 Expand and redesign Kennedy and Newark airports

Image: Gensler for the Fourth Regional Plan

Our three airports must be significantly improved in order to meet growing demand and keep the region globally competitive. John F. Kennedy International Airport should be expanded and modernized to include two additional runways, larger and more customer-friendly terminals, and significantly better transit access. Newark International Airport should be reconfigured, moving the main terminal closer to the train station on the Northeast rail corridor and freeing up more space to eventually construct a new runway. These improvements could accommodate a 60 percent increase in airline passengers, and reduce delays by 33 percent.

The region's airports have the worst delays in the nation and do not have the capacity for the expected growth in passengers.

Today, our three major airports rank first, third, and fourth for worst delays in the nation. And while air passenger travel demand could increase by 60 percent in 2040 (and double by 2060), it is obvious our airports will not be able to meet that demand and keep us competitive on the global scale. Unfortunately, expanding any of these airports presents major environmental challenges for adjacent communities and natural ecosystems.

The customer experience—from access to the airport to amenities inside the terminals—is also uneven and subpar when compared with international peers. Even with the success of AirTrain at JFK and Newark, transit access to the airports is not optimal, and traffic congestion on nearby roads and highways makes flying even more uncertain and time-consuming.

Climate change poses an additional challenge to our airports. Teterboro Airport, currently the airport of choice for general aviation flights (primarily corporate business flights), will likely need to close later this century due to the risk of rising sea levels.

Expand airports to bring delays down to the national average of ten minutes, and accommodate future growth

Many improvements could help reduce delays and handle additional passengers at JFK, Newark, and LaGuardia, including implementing new air traffic control technology, improving intercity rail service, and expanding service at other airports in the region. But the only thing that would significantly increase capacity at these major airports is building new runways.

Of the three airports, LaGuardia is the most land-constrained and lacks the facilities for international service, while JFK and Newark are better suited for expansion—which will be necessary to accommodate the anticipated overall growth in air travel, and to absorb both the many commercial flights from LaGuardia and those displaced by the closing of Teterboro.

Expand JFK on both the air-side and land-side

JFK will eventually need two new runways, larger, better-designed terminals, and new transit service that supports a one-seat ride through to Manhattan. The plan must include protection from storm surges, and the restoration of Jamaica Bay.

- **Construct a new 9,000-foot departure and arrival runway west of the terminal area.** A second 7,000- to 8,000-foot arrival runway will eventually be needed either adjacent to this western runway or between the two eastern runways. All new runways should be built to minimize the impact on Jamaica Bay.

- **Consolidate the six existing terminals into four larger common-use facilities**, with all gates available to all airlines.

- **Reconfigure the central terminal area** to improve service with open and spacious terminals, business centers, and customer amenities that would be competitive with cities such as Singapore, Amsterdam, Madrid, and London.

- **Rebuild and expand on-airport AirTrain stations at JFK.** Parts of the existing AirTrain alignment could be rebuilt in the central terminal area to better integrate it with the existing or new terminals, giving passengers better or equal access to the check-in hall as well as curbside. The rebuilt station would be designed to accommodate longer trainsets and to facilitate one-seat ride service to the central business district (CBD).

- **Create an express one-seat ride to Manhattan instead of extending the existing AirTrain.** The new airport service would be an outgrowth of RPA's regional rail plan. The Rockaway Beach Branch would be reactivated for passenger service from Atlantic Avenue, where it would connect to the new regional rail line at Howard Beach with two dedicated tracks for the airport service. The new airport express service would provide a quick one-seat ride from Midtown Manhattan, Lower Manhattan, and Downtown Brooklyn to JFK utilizing a new East River crossing. There would be at least four trains per hour with an average wait time of seven minutes.

- **Protect JFK from storm surges.** Unlike LaGuardia and Newark airports, JFK Airport is not significantly affected by sea-level rise, although the entire airport is vulnerable to flooding and therefore requires protection from storm surges.

- **Strengthen connections between JFK and downtown Jamaica.** Downtown Jamaica should be redeveloped in tandem with the airport. In particular, hotels and other hospitality services should be located downtown, preserving on-airport capacity for terminals, runways, and freight facilities.

- **Protect and restore Jamaica Bay.** Given the environmental impact of constructing one or two new runways into Jamaica Bay, various mitigation measures should be implemented by the Port Authority. First, every acre of habitat affected by the construction of runways should be restored elsewhere throughout the bay. Emphasis should be placed on restoring the salt marshes and maritime forests, as well as filling the holes made by excavations and restoring other bird sanctuaries away from flight paths. Further, the Port Authority should establish a Jamaica Bay Restoration & Resilience Mitigation Fund that will serve to fund research, restoration, and adaptation efforts to make Jamaica Bay and its communities more resilient. The fund could be managed in cooperation with a group such as the Science and Resilience Institute at Jamaica Bay or the NY-NJ Harbor Estuary Program. Funds could be raised out of the Port Authority's general budget or a dedicated per-flight user fee. Further, the Port Authority should ensure the airport is among the most sustainable in the world, from including green infrastructure to carbon offsetting programs.

Source: RPA

To reduce delays, handle expected growth, and improve the customer experience, Kennedy airport will need to expand. A new departure-and-arrival runway west of the terminal area will eventually need to be joined by a second runway. A reconfigured central terminal area with open, spacious terminals would be linked to a rebuilt AirTrain that would connect to a one-seat train ride from Midtown, Lower Manhattan, and Downtown Brooklyn.

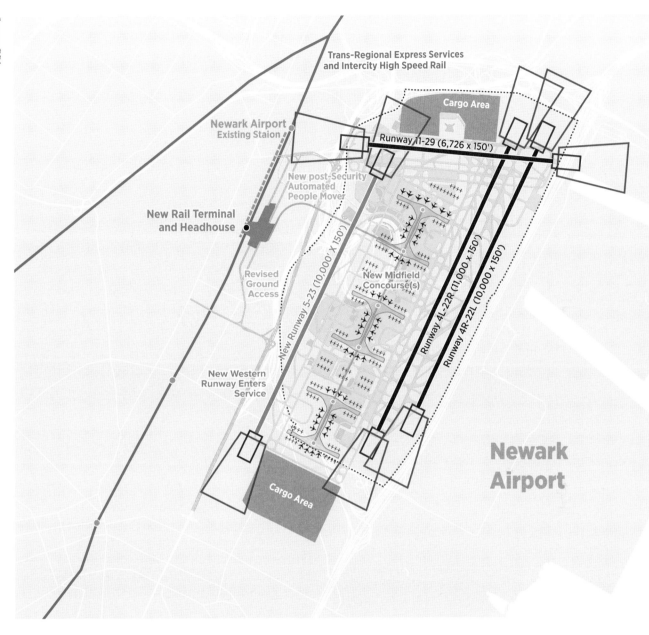

Trans-Regional Express Services and Intercity High Speed Rail

Cargo Area

Runway 11-29 (6,726 x 150')

Newark Airport
Existing Staion

New post-Security
Automated
People Mover

**New Rail Terminal
and Headhouse**

New Runway 5-23 (10,000' x 150')

Runway 4L-22R (11,000 x 150')

Runway 4R-22L (10,000 x 150')

Revised
Ground
Access

New Midfield
Concourse(s)

New Western
Runway Enters
Service

Cargo Area

**Newark
Airport**

After a rebuilt Terminal A reaches the end of its useful life, Newark Airport should be reconfigured to bring the terminals directly to the rail station served by Amtrak, New Jersey Transit, and PATH. The airport will need to be extended south for new cargo operations, and a new runway on the western side of the terminal will soon be needed.

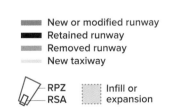

New or modified runway
Retained runway
Removed runway
New taxiway

RPZ
RSA

Infill or
expansion

Source: RPA

Reimagine Newark Airport

Newark Airport should be reconfigured with a new main-terminal entry connected to public transit, a new western runway, and a midfield concourse. The airport should also be extended south for aircraft parking, add a modernized and more accessible air cargo area, and reduce noise impacts from the new western runway. Comprehensive adaptation solutions would address the risk of flooding of Newark Airport, the I-95 corridor, and the New York and New Jersey port facilities.

- **Build Terminal A and AirTrain with a maximum 30-year design life.** Construct the new Terminal A to operate for the next 30 years or more, until it would eventually need to be razed to make way for the construction of a new runway. The AirTrain system could be a short-term solution, or be replaced by a more-frequent bus service until a new system is in place in 10 to 20 years.

- **Extend Newark Airport south to create a new cargo area, and improve airfield operations.** At only half the size of JFK's, Newark Airport's airfield is constrained. To accommodate future expansion, a portion of the new midfield concourse, and cargo operations, the airport will need to expand its footprint. The logical place for this expansion is to the south of the existing airfield, using a 600-acre industrial/commercial area between the airport and the old Central New Jersey rail line.

- **Consolidate the existing Terminals C and B at the Northeast Corridor (NEC) rail station**, with either one or two midfield concourses for boarding planes, and a new people mover serving the midfield concourses. Terminal A would be served by buses in the interim and eventually phased out after its useful lifespan, with terminal services moved to the NEC rail station. This new multimodal hub will streamline the customer experience and result in more passengers getting to and from the airport by public transit.

- **Extend the PATH to Newark Airport**. The new NEC headhouse would place the PATH at the entrance of the airport, making it effortless to transport baggage from transit to check-in. An extension further south to Elizabeth should be explored, which would open access to the airport to surrounding communities for travel and employment.

- **Construct a new 9,000-ft runway on the western side of the airfield** after terminal consolidation to the new headhouse on the Northeast Corridor is complete and the central terminal area is reconfigured.

- **Adapt Newark Airport for storm surges and sea-level rise.** Along with the Port of New York and New Jersey and the I-95 corridor, Newark is at risk of frequent flooding, with certain areas becoming permanently flooded once sea-level rise reaches six feet.

OUTCOMES

The JFK and Newark airport expansions will greatly improve the overall flying experience and accommodate more passengers. Expected outcomes include:

- Direct one-seat ride access to the Manhattan CBD in 30 minutes or less

- 104 million passengers served annually at JFK

- 69 million passengers served annually at Newark Airport

- Delays reduced from an average of 15 minutes today to the national average of 10 minutes

- Expanded job opportunities in downtown Jamaica and Newark, and at both airports

- Improved protection from storms and sea-level rise

- Replacement of every acre of habitat in Jamaica Bay lost during construction

PAYING FOR IT

Airport expansion will be one of the most expensive infrastructure projects the region will need to undertake over the coming decades. Total costs for both airports are estimated at $48 billion—$27 billion for Newark Airport and $21 billion for JFK—which would be paid for by Port Authority airport revenues derived primarily from airline fees and passenger facility charges. This level of investment would only be possible if airport subsidies to other Port Authority operations are phased out over time. Few major airports around the world subsidize other activities as New York does.

Airport expansion will likely require a buyout of a few dozen residential properties to the north of the JFK runways, and industrial and residential properties to the south of Newark Airport.

Mitigation measures should include a one-for-one replacement of any acres of natural habitat lost as the result of construction, with emphasis placed on restoring salt marshes and maritime forests, as well as filling holes made by excavations to fill the bay. A Jamaica Bay mitigation fund should also be established to fund research, restoration, and adaptation efforts.

Build fast and affordable rail service in the Northeast Corridor

29

Image: Amtrak

With a new, dedicated two-track right-of-way, Amtrak service from New York City to Washington, D.C., could reach speeds of over 200 mph, reducing travel time in half to 90 minutes. From New York to Boston, two additional tracks between New Rochelle and Bridgeport, and rerouted service through Hartford, would allow trains to reach 125 to 160 mph, cutting trip times by almost one hour. These investments would dramatically increase intercity and commuter-rail capacity in the Northeast Corridor (NEC), and reduce traffic congestion.

Slow and unreliable rail service in the Northeast weakens the U.S. economy.

The Amtrak line between Washington, D.C., and Boston via New York City, known as the Northeast Corridor, is by far the busiest in the country. But, because of high ticket costs, slow speeds, and unpredictability in service, it is still barely competitive compared with driving and air travel. In fact, the NEC is far slower and less reliable than intercity train service in any other major region around the world.

Decades of underinvestment are largely to blame—as is Amtrak's having to share the tracks with commuter railroads and freight trains. There are several major bottlenecks with insufficient capacity to accommodate all users. Fares are relatively high—unaffordable for many—as a result of Congress requiring Amtrak to be financially self-sufficient at the national level, and service on the NEC being used to subsidize routes with lower riderships in other parts of the country.

Both policy changes and physical investments will be required to create fast, reliable, and affordable service in the NEC.

The Northeast Corridor, which extends from Virginia to Massachusetts, represents one-fifth of the U.S. economy. A functional intercity rail system would bolster the national economy and help keep the tri-state area economically competitive. But creating fast, reliable, and affordable service on the NEC will require both changes to the way Amtrak is governed and major investments in infrastructure over the next two decades.

- **Reform the NEC governance and operating model** to include a public authority that would control the corridor's infrastructure and grant concessions to private operators. The model is similar to the UK rail system where Network Rail is the national infrastructure operator and the Department for Transportation grants operating concessions to private service providers. This would keep the public in control of the asset and long-term planning, but create incentives for more efficient operations.

- **Stop using NEC revenues to cross-subsidize the national rail system**, which starves the NEC of funds to improve capital assets along the corridor and provide a balanced fare policy.

- **Upgrade infrastructure and address major bottlenecks**, including $21.1 billion in state-of-good-repair backlog needs (moveable bridges, power, etc.) and billions more to address existing bottlenecks where limited tunnel capacity, at-grade junctions, and other physical conditions constrain throughput and reduce reliability.

- **Increase frequency of service and lengthen trains**. Intercity trains are six to eight cars, versus 10 to 14 cars for commuter trains. Making these trains longer and adding more trains per hour would substantially increase the supply of service along the corridor. Creating uniform rolling stock for intercity service would simplify operations and combine first, business, and coach classes on one train. To support the recommended increase in service, new crossings will be needed at the region's core across both the Hudson and East rivers.

- **Introduce a high-speed rail service between New York City and Washington, D.C.,** To substantially improve service over the next 20 to 30 years, two new tracks dedicated to high-speed trains traveling in excess of 200 mph should be added. In the long term, new stations in Philadelphia and Baltimore will be needed to speed up service through those two metropolitan areas and to help reduce NYC to DC travel times to 90 minutes from the current 175 minutes for Acela, and 200 minutes for regional service.

- **Substantially upgrade service from New York City to Boston**. Aside from addressing a handful of critical bottlenecks, two major investments will be required to improve service between New York City and Boston. The first is two new tracks between New Rochelle and Barnum Station in Bridgeport, to support increasing intercity service frequency between NYC and BOS while also adding intra-state service and more traditional commuter services to NYC. The second investment needed is new intercity express alignment between New Haven and Providence via Hartford, to increase speed and improve resilience.

  This leg of the NEC is unable to support true high-speed service (186 mph and above) due to the physical rail alignment and insufficient separation between track centers. Alternatives include the two "off-corridor" alignments proposed by the Federal Railroad Administration in its NEC Future analysis. The preferred alternative is to use the existing corridor, which would support economic growth in cities in a high-density corridor along the New Haven line.

- **Explore options to improve service to Albany and points north**, including Albany service out of Grand Central run by Metro North. Improvements could include electrification to Albany with better transit access to destinations between Albany and Poughkeepsie. Another option to consider is overnight trains to Montreal and Buffalo: Little new infrastructure aside from rolling stock (sleepers) would be required, and scheduling could open up access to popular destinations such as Montreal and Niagara Falls.

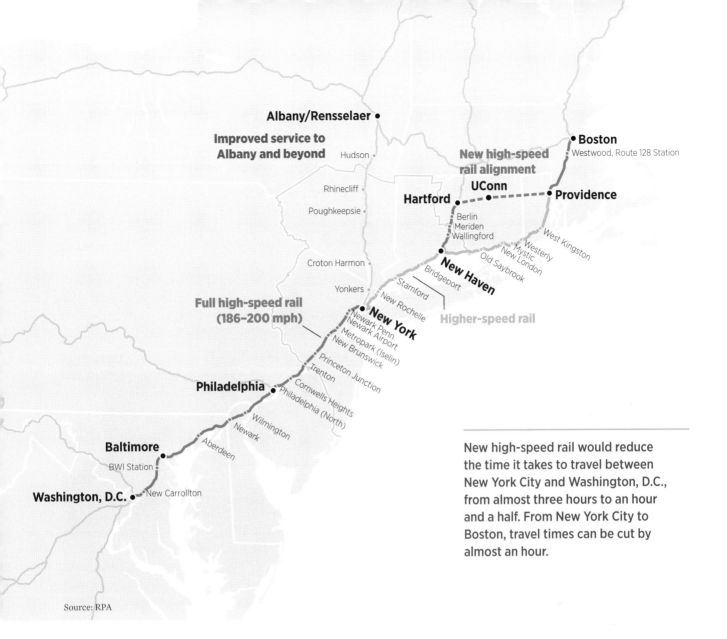

Albany/Rensselaer •

**Improved service to
Albany and beyond** Hudson •

**New high-speed
rail alignment**

Rhinecliff •

UConn

Poughkeepsie •

Hartford

• Boston
Westwood, Route 128 Station

• Providence

Berlin
Meriden
Wallingford

West Kingston

Croton Harmon •

New Haven

Westerly
Mystic
New London
Old Saybrook

Yonkers •

Stamford

Bridgeport

New Rochelle

**Full high-speed rail
(186–200 mph)**

• New York
Newark Penn
Newark Airport
Metropark (Iselin)
New Brunswick

Higher-speed rail

Princeton Junction

Trenton

Cornwells Heights

Philadelphia •

Philadelphia (North)

Wilmington

Newark

Aberdeen

Baltimore •

BWI Station •

Washington, D.C. • New Carrollton

New high-speed rail would reduce
the time it takes to travel between
New York City and Washington, D.C.,
from almost three hours to an hour
and a half. From New York City to
Boston, travel times can be cut by
almost an hour.

Source: RPA

OUTCOMES

The proposed recommendations would dramatically transform
intercity rail service, and result in the following outcomes:

- Higher frequency and faster service that would improve access
  to job opportunities for residents of the region. Regional service between NYC and Philadelphia would be faster than existing commuter service between Stamford and NYC.

- A more affordable and reliable service would divert more
  intercity auto, air, and bus travelers to rail. This would free
  up highways for freight and local traffic, and airports for
  longer-haul flights.

- Higher capacity on the NEC would allow for simultaneous
  growth in commuter, regional, and intercity services.

- Greater accessibility and more convenient scheduling could
  draw more riders to other (non-NEC) intercity routes.

PAYING FOR IT

Funding for NEC improvements would come from conventional
sources such as federal grants and loans, and expanded local
contributions—a mixture of track fees and passenger ticket
surcharges. Additional funding/financing might be possible
from public-private partnerships, with firms acquiring equity
in the infrastructure as part of investing in modernization and
capacity improvement, or as part of an operating concession. A
return on investment is possible today due to the higher fares
charged on the NEC.

30 Modernize the region's seaports and expand rail freight access

Photo: RPA

Seaports serve a critical function within the region's economy, moving goods from abroad to a large consumer market and supporting thousands of industrial and service jobs. Although the region's seaport is the second largest in the United States, it is far less efficient than others, and fails to take advantage of the region's extensive rail network. A new governance structure, and more investment in port facilities, rail connections, and access roads could lead to more port-related jobs and revenue, a bigger regional economy, and less truck traffic.

Our seaports are inefficiently managed and fail to take advantage of our rail network.

The Port of New York and New Jersey is the second largest seaport in the nation, handling over six million containers and millions of tons of bulk cargo annually. But the port's facilities are inefficiently managed. Terminals are not state of the art, and little investment has been made in the new technologies that would allow for reductions in air and water pollution. Lack of automation and outmoded management practices have kept labor costs high and reduced the port's output. Connections to roadway networks are inadequate, and nearby roadways are often congested. While other ports around the country turn a profit, the Port of New York and New Jersey barely breaks even—at times even requiring a subsidy. The port's deficiencies are enabled by a governance structure that provides insufficient transparency and incentives for efficient operations.

The Port of New York and New Jersey also sits in the middle of one of the densest rail networks in North America, yet hardly any of the region's freight is moved by rail.

Nearly all the goods imported through the seaports are carried to their final destinations by truck, despite record congestion on roads and highways. Freight rail could provide a more reliable and efficient alternative—a single freight railcar can eliminate four truck trips—especially given the dense concentration of rail infrastructure in the tri-state area. But there are few rail lines dedicated to freight, and passenger rail operators typically refuse to allow freight operations on the busier parts of their network. The result is a segregated and underused rail network.

Modernize, rationalize, and expand our seaports

Transforming our seaports into 21ˢᵗ century facilities and turning a profit will require physical investments and governance changes, including:

- **Reform the governance of the seaports to incentivize greater efficiency and modernization of the infrastructure.** This could be achieved by giving the seaports greater operational and financial autonomy from the Port Authority of New York and New Jersey, increasing transparency and accountability within the ports.

- **Close and redevelop both the Red Hook container terminal and the southern Brooklyn (Sunset Park) seaport facilities.** Both of these facilities are outmoded and have poor links to transportation. Their operations should be consoli-

dated to ports in Staten Island and New Jersey, freeing up land for new parks, housing, and light industrial uses.

- **Expand Staten Island's New York Container Terminal to include the long-planned Port Ivory redevelopment.** The port is well connected to the highway and rail networks, especially with the recent completion of the new Goethals Bridge. The direct ramps from the bridge to the port that have been proposed should be built.

- **Modernize and improve access to Port Newark–Elizabeth Marine Terminal.** The port should be densified, from five container stacks to seven, and its efficiency increased. More automation will enable it to increase throughput and revenue. Local road access should be improved to all facilities, including preferential treatment for trucks.

- **Prepare Bayonne Peninsula for growth.** In 2010, the Port Authority bought 130 acres in Bayonne for a mix of residential development and future port use. As part of this initiative, truck access to the peninsula must be improved by rebuilding and expanding the NJ Turnpike extension and interchange—a long-delayed project. The residential developments being built adjacent to the future port should be designed for a soft, transitional edge between residential and industrial uses. The Port of Los Angeles has done this successfully.

- **Protect seaports and surrounding critical infrastructure from sea-level rise and storm surges.** By virtue of their operating requirements, seaports are already fairly resilient. But with additional investments, ports could be designed to serve as buffers to help protect other vulnerable infrastructure nearby. Port Newark–Elizabeth Marine Terminal, for example, could help protect Newark International Airport and the I-95 corridor.

- **Reduce noxious impacts to adjacent communities.** Ships, on-dock equipment, and trucks are all sources of air, noise, and light pollution. The ports should provide shoreside electrical power to docked ships, allowing them to turn off their polluting engines. All the gantry cranes that have not yet been electrified should be. Only electric vehicles should be used for container movements within the ports. The Port Authority should take aggressive steps toward cleaner trucks—expanding the truck-replacement program, requiring low-emission vehicles as a default, and ultimately mandating a transition to electric trucks once they've become commercially viable. Light and noise abatement programs should be expanded, and measures should be taken to create transitional areas around the ports to buffer communities from those impacts.

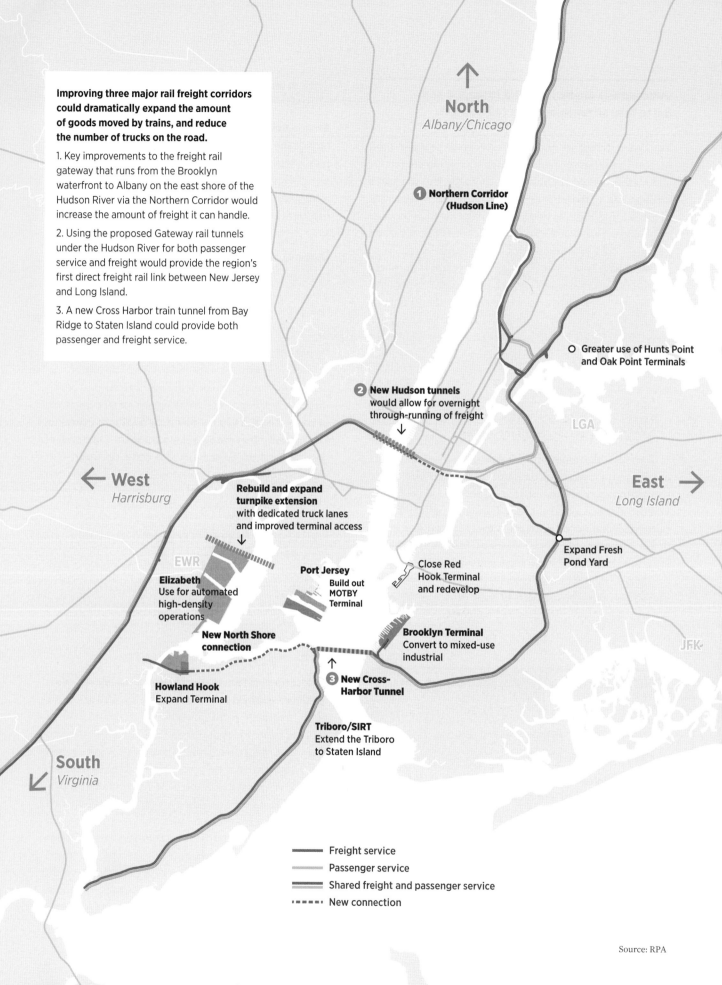

Improving three major rail freight corridors could dramatically expand the amount of goods moved by trains, and reduce the number of trucks on the road.

1. Key improvements to the freight rail gateway that runs from the Brooklyn waterfront to Albany on the east shore of the Hudson River via the Northern Corridor would increase the amount of freight it can handle.

2. Using the proposed Gateway rail tunnels under the Hudson River for both passenger service and freight would provide the region's first direct freight rail link between New Jersey and Long Island.

3. A new Cross Harbor train tunnel from Bay Ridge to Staten Island could provide both passenger and freight service.

↑
North
Albany/Chicago

**1 Northern Corridor
(Hudson Line)**

○ **Greater use of Hunts Point
and Oak Point Terminals**

2 New Hudson tunnels
would allow for overnight
through-running of freight
↓

LGA

← **West**
Harrisburg

East →
Long Island

**Rebuild and expand
turnpike extension**
with dedicated truck lanes
and improved terminal access
↓

**Expand Fresh
Pond Yard**

EWR

Port Jersey
Build out
MOTBY
Terminal

**Close Red
Hook Terminal
and redevelop**

Elizabeth
Use for automated
high-density
operations

**New North Shore
connection**

Brooklyn Terminal
Convert to mixed-use
industrial

JFK

Howland Hook
Expand Terminal

**3 New Cross-
Harbor Tunnel**

South
Virginia

Triboro/SIRT
Extend the Triboro
to Staten Island

——— Freight service
——— Passenger service
━━━ Shared freight and passenger service
∙∙∙∙∙ New connection

Source: RPA

Reduce truck traffic by promoting the use of rail for freight

Giving freight access to existing and future passenger rail facilities, and developing new routes for both passengers and freight, would radically transform the way freight is shipped within the region, reducing truck traffic and cutting operating costs.

- **Allow freight and passenger rail to share track infrastructure.** Desegregating the rail network by encouraging freight service on passenger lines, and passenger service on freight lines, would increase the efficiency of the entire rail network, and would get thousands of trucks off the road. In order to overcome the operational and infrastructure hurdles, the three states should provide financial incentives to railroad operators (passenger and freight) to open up their physical infrastructure to one another's operations. Developing infrastructure and operating standards to provide certainty to operators will be critical to the success of the system.

- **Strengthen the existing northern freight rail gateway.** The northern freight rail gateway extends from the Brooklyn waterfront through Brooklyn, Queens, and the Bronx, then up the East Side of the Hudson River. Thanks to the Oak Point Link connection and other improvements made over the years, this line now runs both passengers and freight service—and could accommodate more, as the Hunts Point market expands in the future. Oak Point Yard in the Bronx and Fresh Pond Yards in Queens are two facilities that should be improved and expanded in the near future to strengthen rail-freight access to points north.

- **Build Gateway for freight rail too.** The proposed rail tunnels under the Hudson River, a project known as Gateway, should be extended to Queens and designed to accommodate both passenger and freight services. Freight traffic could travel through Manhattan during off-peak periods, and connect the ports in New Jersey with the Lower Montauk line, a dedicated freight line that serves an industrial area and connects to Fresh Pond Yards and eventually the LIRR Main Line. This would be the region's first direct freight rail link between Long Island and New Jersey, and likely provide a service that would be more competitive than trucks—resulting in reduced traffic through Manhattan, Brooklyn, Queens, and Nassau County.

- **Extend the Bay Ridge line to Staten Island.** A new tunnel from Bay Ridge to Staten Island could provide freight access from New Jersey to Brooklyn via Staten Island. It could also provide valuable passenger service from Staten Island to Brooklyn by extending the Staten Island Rapid Transit System into the proposed Triboro line—providing direct access to Brooklyn, Queens, and the Bronx. This proposed tunnel would be significantly shorter than the Cross-Harbor Tunnel currently under study, and would open up countless transit options for Staten Island residents. This route would also connect the New York Container Terminal at Howland Hook directly to Long Island.

OUTCOMES

These proposals would result in a modern and efficient seaport that would be a good neighbor to surrounding communities and return a profit to the public to invest in other regional infrastructure investments. They would also encourage the diversion of more goods to rail by sharing freight and passenger assets.

PAYING FOR IT

The new investments would be partially paid for by reforms requiring renegotiated leases or assessments on lease-holders for capital investments. Another source of funds would come from the redevelopment of surplus facilities, such as Red Hook. The Port Authority should assess whether an outright sale or long-term land lease is the most viable option. Track/tunnel access fees paid by the private railroads could also help fund the capital improvements and would be a source of revenue to maintain the infrastructure over the long haul. Traditional funding sources from the federal government, such as Railroad Rehabilitation and Financing (RRIF) loans, should also be pursued.

Rise to the challenge of climate change

Climate change is already transforming the region. The coastline is shifting inward, and homes, businesses, and critical infrastructure are more prone to flooding. By 2050, more than two million people and 60 percent of the region's power-generating capacity, as well as dozens of miles of critical roads and rail lines, will face a high risk of flooding—some of it permanently underwater. The number of days of extreme heat, which are far more threatening to human life than any other impact of climate change, will multiply by five.

We must accelerate efforts to both adapt to climate change and reduce the region's contribution to this global problem. This includes adapting coastline communities to permanent and periodic flooding; strategically protecting open space with the most potential to absorb carbon dioxide and stormwater; planting more trees and vegetation in urban neighborhoods at risk of extreme heat; upgrading water and sewer infrastructure; and modernizing and greening the energy grid. Doing so will not only mitigate the impact of storms and heat, but also create a new relationship with nature that will improve the health and well-being of residents, now and in the future.

ADAPT TO OUR CHANGING COASTLINE

Our coastal region is particularly vulnerable to the impacts of climate change. Many communities, especially those in the floodplain where more than two million people will be living by 2050, could become permanently flooded due to rising sea levels. Critical infrastructure, such as public housing, hospitals, airports, rail yards, power plants, refineries, and other industrial sites would also be at risk.

Walling off the entire shoreline is neither financially feasible nor environmentally sound. In areas with high concentrations of people, we will need both natural and engineered solutions to keep communities safe and resilient to flooding. For other places at particularly high risk or with low densities, such as barrier beaches, back bays, and wetlands, a phased approach will be needed to transition away over time.

Fortunately, there are innovative ways to adapt coastal areas and dense urban centers while also restoring natural systems that provide multiple benefits. Rising seas could provide an opportunity to better integrate nature into our communities, with small waterfront parks and a new national park in the Meadowlands in New Jersey.

31 Protect densely populated communities along the coast from storms and flooding

Over the centuries, the region has made major investments along its coastline. Homes, businesses, rail lines, airports, factories, power plants, and other infrastructure has been built in places that are now threatened by the effects of climate change, primarily storm-related flooding and permanent sea-level rise. Adapting these densely populated communities and critical infrastructure is complicated and expensive, and special consideration will be required in socially vulnerable neighborhoods. But where the densities justify it, investments must be made in resilience projects that will ensure the region continues to thrive in the era of climate change.

Some of the region's densest communities, and much of its infrastructure, are highly vulnerable to catastrophic flooding due to sea-level rise and storms.

Today, more than one million people in the region live in flood-prone areas, with more than half a million living in dense urban areas, and 385,000 people working there. One-third of the residents in these at-risk communities are elderly, low-income, disabled, or otherwise socially vulnerable.

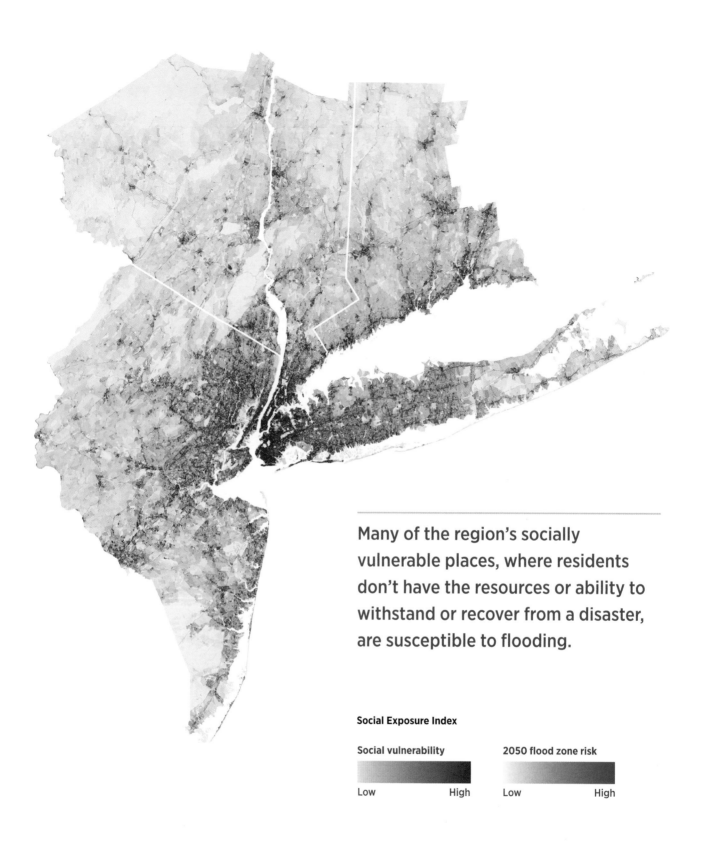

Many of the region's socially vulnerable places, where residents don't have the resources or ability to withstand or recover from a disaster, are susceptible to flooding.

Social Exposure Index

Social vulnerability

Low   High

2050 flood zone risk

Low   High

Source: RPA analysis of Federal Emergency Management Agency, The Nature Conservancy, National Oceanic and Atmospheric Administration, US Census Bureau, and United States Geological Survey data

Surges from Superstorm Sandy breached many of the barriers and sea walls in our coastal urban centers, damaging over 600,000 homes in 2012, claiming the lives of 60 people, and bringing parts of the region to a grinding halt. When the urban core shuts down, the economy slows and the transportation network and waste treatment plants no longer function, threatening the safety and livelihoods of communities.

Efforts to improve resilience have been inconsistent and wholly insufficient. Although few programs have the funding to be fully implemented, some local resiliency projects are underway, thanks in part to the innovative Rebuild by Design initiative, New York City's Special Initiative for Rebuilding and Resiliency, and other state and local efforts. While many communities are beginning to address the increased frequency of coastal flooding, most have not started planning for the long-term consequences sea-level rise will have on neighborhoods and infrastructure.

Promote long-term local and regional adaptation measures

The future of the entire region depends on whether we can adequately protect the urban core from catastrophic emergency flooding and adapt to the permanent flooding caused by sea-level rise. Building a large surge barrier to protect the core is one solution to evaluate, but there are many unknowns about the effectiveness, impacts, and costs of a barrier. Even in a best-case scenario, it would take many years to plan and construct a barrier, and require local adaptation strategies to address sea-level rise, wind, and inland flooding.

In any given community, a combination of resilience strategies will most likely be necessary, including traditional "gray" infrastructure (berms and levees, sea walls, and pumps), natural strategies such as restored wetlands and floodable land, as well as policy changes such as zoning codes and land acquisition. Such comprehensive adaptation planning can create synergistic benefits (e.g., berms that create public open space, or buyouts that open up land for new mitigation infrastructure), while adaptation strategies should be evaluated for their cumulative effects.

Complete resilience projects that are currently underway
In New York City, progress on the city's $20 billion Special Initiative for Rebuilding and Resiliency is being made. A new resilient boardwalk and dune system along the Rockaways has been completed, and rock barriers in Sea Gate have

been established. The state bought out 300 homeowners in Staten Island's Oakwood Beach to demolish the houses and return the land to nature. But the list of planned projects far exceeds the list of completed ones, including the most ambitious out of the Rebuild by Design initiative slated for the Lower East Side (due to break ground in 2019) and Lower Manhattan as well as the new oyster reef being designed off the coast of Staten Island, due to begin as soon as 2018. Full funding of all of these very expensive projects has been a factor, as has the slow-but-necessary pace of community planning, and state and other permitting.

Bridgeport, Connecticut, Hoboken, New Jersey, and a handful of communities in the New Jersey Meadowlands have also been slowly progressing through design, planning, and permitting of Rebuild by Design projects to stem storm surges and minimize flooding from stormwater. Other less-ambitious efforts, including home and street elevations, construction of seawalls and bulkheads, and installation of pumps are taking place in communities throughout the urban core. For many communities, waterfront parks—which in many places effectively serve as the first line of defense against coastal flooding—can be designed to provide even better protection.

For many projects, the focus has been much more on addressing storm-related flooding than on the effects of sea-level rise. As coastal cities implement short- and mid-term resilience projects, they must also start planning now for the permanent flooding from sea-level rise and higher storm surges. And the range of options for addressing these risks—from hard or hybrid infrastructure to nature-based solutions—should be considered based on community needs and risk factors.

Provide the financial and technical support for municipalities and communities to advance their own resilience planning
All coastal cities and towns should have comprehensive, long-term adaptation and resilience plans with site-specific recommendations for their most at-risk areas. These should not only consider storm surges, but also the long-term impacts of sea levels rising. States should lead the way by requiring agencies that have land and assets in flood-prone areas to formally include climate change planning in their long-term plans. New York State's Community Risk and Resilience Act, which adopted official sea-level-rise projections and requires the consideration of flood risk, is a step in this direction. Agencies and utilities responsible for the region's critical infrastructure must also assess their risks and adapt to future conditions.

Municipalities and communities should be provided with technical and financial support to understand the risks, evaluate trade-offs, and pursue the resilience strategies that meet their needs, with priority given to historically marginalized and underserved communities. This support could come from states and counties, or from a peer-to-peer network such as the New York Region Climate Action Network, that would allow communities to exchange knowledge and resources and have a unified voice for adaptation funding and policy reforms.

Communities with a large number of low-income residents and public housing in high-risk flood zones—such as neighborhoods along New York City's Rockaway barrier beach—would require a different approach, as typical tools such as buyout programs and protective infrastructure would not ensure the safety of residents. Edgemere residents working in partnership with the New York City Department of Housing Preservation and Development have started investing in waterfront parks that, in addition to being community amenities, provide short-term protection against storm surges until a real transition away from the neighborhood can take place.

Create a comprehensive, long-term regional adaptation plan
Ultimately, the Regional Coastal Commission should coordinate and work closely with all levels of government to plan for and implement priority adaptation projects by investing revenues from the Adaptation Trust Funds. The Commission would oversee the creation of a comprehensive, long-term, regional adaptation plan that would identify areas at greatest risk and help implement projects that are complementary and effective.

OUTCOMES

If short- and long-term adaptation is properly planned for and adequately funded, the region's urban core could continue to thrive and grow, with significantly reduced risk from catastrophic and long-term sea-level rise flooding. Some areas would see decreases in population and increases in natural systems. Others would receive more protective infrastructure—ideally combined with community uses—along with more resilient development.

Reaching that goal would require the following milestones:

- By 2020, every coastal urban center should have an adaptation and resiliency plan with specific projects outlined. A network would be in place to share information among municipalities and across boundaries. Planning for sea-level rise would be integrated into adaptation and resilience strategies. Ground would be broken and work underway on many of the ambitious adaptation projects being planned today.

- By 2030, most, if not all, of the adaptation projects that today are planned or underway would be completed. Hundreds of thousands of residents would live with minimized risk of catastrophic flooding, and the majority of projects outlined in new adaptation and resiliency plans would have completed planning stages and be starting construction. Municipalities would have collaborated through a Regional Coastal Commission to complete an integrated and comprehensive urban adaptation plan. Low-lying communities would begin to implement projects and policies to respond to the permanent flooding from sea-level rise that would be starting to affect a number of communities.

- By 2040, coastal urban centers would be working together to complete projects in the comprehensive plan and make adjustments as sea-level rise increases.

PAYING FOR IT

Completing adaptation projects would require tens of billions of dollars over the next few decades. Funding for most of the projects underway has come from the federal government in the form of disaster relief, or occasionally from preventative programs such as the Hazard Mitigation Grant Program from the Federal Emergency Management Agency (FEMA). To supplement federal revenue and ensure a more stable and reliable source of funding, the fourth plan recommends the development of state Adaptation Trust Funds. We must also address further challenges to implementation, including outdated regulations and bureaucracy, as well as the political will, to succeed. Projects should be evaluated using benefit-cost analyses that take into account environmental and social impacts. Communities should be offered incentives for regional coordination and hazard mitigation, similar to the NFIP Community Rating System program, which reduces flood insurance premiums up to 50 percent if concrete efforts are made to strengthen resilience.

32 Transition away from places that can't be protected

Photo: RPA

In a region with 3,700 miles of shoreline, the impact of climate change on coastal areas from rising sea levels and more intense flooding presents major challenges to infrastructure and the health and safety of residents. Increased funding will be needed to rebuild to higher standards of resilience and invest in protective measures to keep water out. While we cannot wall off the entire shoreline, we can help communities determine how and where to spend limited dollars to protect the most people and critical infrastructure. A phased approach over the long term will be required to reduce and ultimately remove development from the highest-risk flood zones. Other measures such as elevating buildings, changing zoning codes to account for sea-level rise and flood risk, and buying out the owners of properties most at risk will all be important tools in making this transition.

The developed coastal areas of the region are at significant risk from rising seas and increasingly destructive storms.

Superstorm Sandy galvanized the region to plan for coastal storm surges. A variety of adaptation plans and projects are underway, but few grapple with the difficult reality of sea-level rise and the permanent inundation it will bring to the lowest-lying areas. Communities that have settled on barrier beaches, back bays, and river floodplains are at particular risk, and within a few decades will need to be relocated.[52] A small number of communities in New Jersey and on Staten Island and the south shore of Long Island have already begun to encourage residents to sell their property and move away. Many more communities need to plan for this transition—in the New Jersey Meadowlands, Long Island's south shore, and the iconic Jersey Shore—and will need technical assistance to do it right. A further challenge is programs to buy out homeowners: while effective in the early stages of transition, buy-out programs will not be financially sustainable as currently conceived when entire communities need to be relocated.

Gradually move housing, commerce, and infrastructure away from low-density, flood-prone areas to higher ground

Implementing this transition is imperative for our survival, but will involve difficult decisions and actions, as these shoreline areas contain active communities with homes, businesses, and essential services, many of which must be relocated. As sea levels rise and land becomes permanently inundated, retreat is inevitable, whether it is well-managed or left to market forces. We can, however, ease climate adaptation by phasing in measures over time, curbing new development, and providing strong incentives and support for people to relocate.

The process for getting to resilience in less-dense communities involves the following steps:

Know what's at risk

Using federal flood maps, repetitive loss data, and storm surge and sea-level rise models, municipalities should comprehensively analyze which areas are at greatest risk. There are numerous free, user-friendly, web-based tools (such as the Coastal Resilience tools from The Nature Conservancy and Rutgers University, and Climate Central's Surging Seas tools) along with government, universities, and non-profit organizations that can provide support. Additionally, a peer-to-peer network of municipalities such as the New York Region Climate Action Network allows for the exchange of ideas and best practices concerning long-term adaptation. High-quality and accessible data is critical for informing which combination of adaptation strategies is best-suited for the community.

Place a moratorium on new development in areas at greatest risk of flooding and destruction

Once the areas at greatest risk are identified, a moratorium on new development in these places should be put into effect. It is the responsibility of the government (federal, state, and local) to ensure additional residents will not be put in harm's way.

Plan for long-term adaptation

Municipalities with high-risk coastal areas should comprehensively overhaul local zoning and building codes to reflect the realities of climate change and its consequences. Zoning regulations should be updated to discourage growth in high flood-risk areas and encourage growth and redevelopment in low flood-risk areas. Building codes in all waterfront communities should be adapted to make any future development or redevelopment in lower-risk flood zones more resilient.

Implement phased-in, long-term adaptation plans

Although a moratorium combined with zoning and building code updates will help guide new development in the right direction, plans will be needed to adapt existing development in flood zones. Long-term adaptation plans that set goals for waterfront areas and consider the many adaptation tools will allow municipalities to phase in different adaptation steps. In the short term, structural measures such as seawalls, bulkheads, and pumps may be the best option; in the long term, managed retreat from the waterfront could be the ultimate step. Municipalities should consider integrating these plans in upland areas by, for example, rezoning higher ground for higher density, where appropriate. The plan should lay out the transition across phases that align with increasing climate risks.

Improve buyout programs

Ultimately, many municipalities may determine that retreat from the most at-risk areas is the best option to keep residents out of harm's way. Underutilized as a tool today, buyout programs should be strengthened to optimize their potential as a feasible and effective adaptation strategy. Programs will need to[53]:

- Rethink the purpose and timeline of buyouts so they are not just made available after a disaster

- Include more standardization across states

- Create permanent and sufficient funding streams

- Be integrated into the local adaptation plan, and designed to better accommodate renters and multifamily buildings

- Provide flexibility and support to participants throughout the process, continuing beyond the official transfers of property

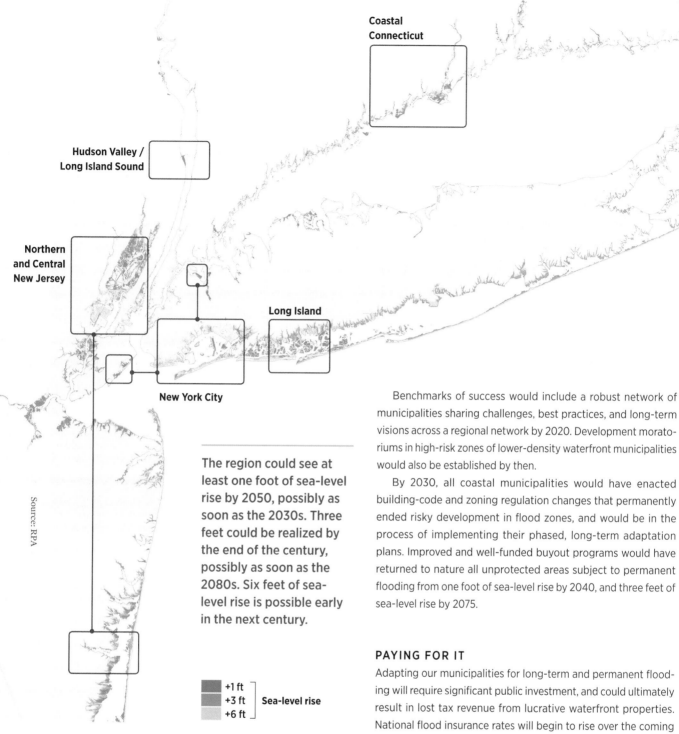

Coastal Connecticut

Hudson Valley / Long Island Sound

Northern and Central New Jersey

Long Island

New York City

Source: RPA

The region could see at least one foot of sea-level rise by 2050, possibly as soon as the 2030s. Three feet could be realized by the end of the century, possibly as soon as the 2080s. Six feet of sea-level rise is possible early in the next century.

+1 ft
+3 ft   Sea-level rise
+6 ft

OUTCOMES

In the short term, an increasing number of municipalities would acknowledge the areas at greatest risk of flooding and destruction, and future development there would cease. Over time, building codes and zoning regulations would be updated, discouraging growth in the flood zone and encouraging resilient growth on lower-risk land as municipalities develop phased adaptation plans. Enhanced buyout programs and reliable adaptation funding would allow communities to make the transition, and much of the waterfront edge would be returned to nature to serve as a natural buffer from floods.

Benchmarks of success would include a robust network of municipalities sharing challenges, best practices, and long-term visions across a regional network by 2020. Development moratoriums in high-risk zones of lower-density waterfront municipalities would also be established by then.

By 2030, all coastal municipalities would have enacted building-code and zoning regulation changes that permanently ended risky development in flood zones, and would be in the process of implementing their phased, long-term adaptation plans. Improved and well-funded buyout programs would have returned to nature all unprotected areas subject to permanent flooding from one foot of sea-level rise by 2040, and three feet of sea-level rise by 2075.

PAYING FOR IT

Adapting our municipalities for long-term and permanent flooding will require significant public investment, and could ultimately result in lost tax revenue from lucrative waterfront properties. National flood insurance rates will begin to rise over the coming years, perhaps making affordability along the coast even more difficult and buyouts a more attractive option. All adaptation tools—from walls and pumps to buyouts—will require a large and stable source of funding.

In the long run, some costs could be offset by a reduced need for municipal services (evacuation, closed roadways, repairs to infrastructure) and personal expenditures (flooding repairs, mold, loss of workdays, health issues). Lost tax revenues can be restored by developing lower-risk areas, if the community has such land available. The high cost of adapting and retreating from the waterfront underscores the importance of developing Adaptation Trust Funds.

33 Establish a national park in the Meadowlands

Image: MIT CAU + ZUS + Urbanisten

Despite decades of industrial activity, the New Jersey Meadowlands remains the largest remaining wetland system in the region. It is also likely to be one of the first places to be permanently inundated from sea-level rise. Building on the work of local conservation groups, the state should work with the federal government to make the Meadowlands a national park to demonstrate how properly managed natural landscapes can help mitigate the impacts of climate change. A national-park designation would also help preserve and restore the Meadowlands' natural habitats, protect nearby communities, and make it a recreational resource for the entire region.

Of all of the places in the region challenged by increased flooding from climate change, the New Jersey Meadowlands is at greatest risk.[54]

The immense concentration of infrastructure that exists in the Meadowlands—warehousing and distribution facilities, commuter and intercity rail, roads and bridges, energy transmission facilities—is vital to the economy and transportation needs of the tri-state region, and indeed the entire Northeast.

But by the end of this century, permanent flooding from sea-level rise will likely displace between 4,000 and 8,000 Meadowlands residents, and cost 51,000 jobs (as defined by today's district). The lives of another 40,000 people will be disrupted by periodic flooding from increased precipitation and storm surges, while infrastructure will be threatened by more frequent flooding and saltwater intrusion—a particularly vexing problem given the area's concentration of hazardous-waste sites.

Park boundaries will expand as the sea level rises and communities recede from the water's edge. Starting with existing natural, vacant, or publicly owned lands, the park boundaries would be drawn and redrawn as the coastline changes, to protect residents outside of the park.

Source: RPA

Starting park boundary

Boundary with sea-level rise of 1 foot

Boundary with sea-level rise of 3 feet

Boundary with sea-level rise of 6 feet

The Meadowlands is one of the Northeast's largest remaining contiguous tracts of urban open space, one that supports a wide array of wildlife and biodiversity thanks to the work of advocates and state officials. Although it is a scarred vestige of what it once was, the Meadowlands still provides critical ecosystem functions, including nutrient cycling and flood storage, while supporting critical fish and wildlife biodiversity. The Meadowlands has been designated as a regionally significant natural resource by the U.S. Environmental Protection Agency and the U.S. Fish and Wildlife Service.

As the impacts of climate change accelerate, the natural and human communities of the Meadowlands will face even greater risks, putting in jeopardy the natural and human-made systems connected to it.

A new Meadowlands National Park would help the region adapt to climate change, and serve as a model for the rest of the country.

National parks are typically selected for their natural beauty, unique archeological features, or historical significance. The Meadowlands represents a new opportunity for the National Park Service to identify and promote the value natural landscapes can provide in protecting people from the effects of climate change.

Designating the Meadowlands a National Park would make a strong statement about the role public institutions can play in climate change resilience. Leadership from the public sector on climate change has been inconsistent. The National Park Service, among the more well-established and trusted institutions in the country, could turn the tide and persuade other agencies to prioritize climate resilience.

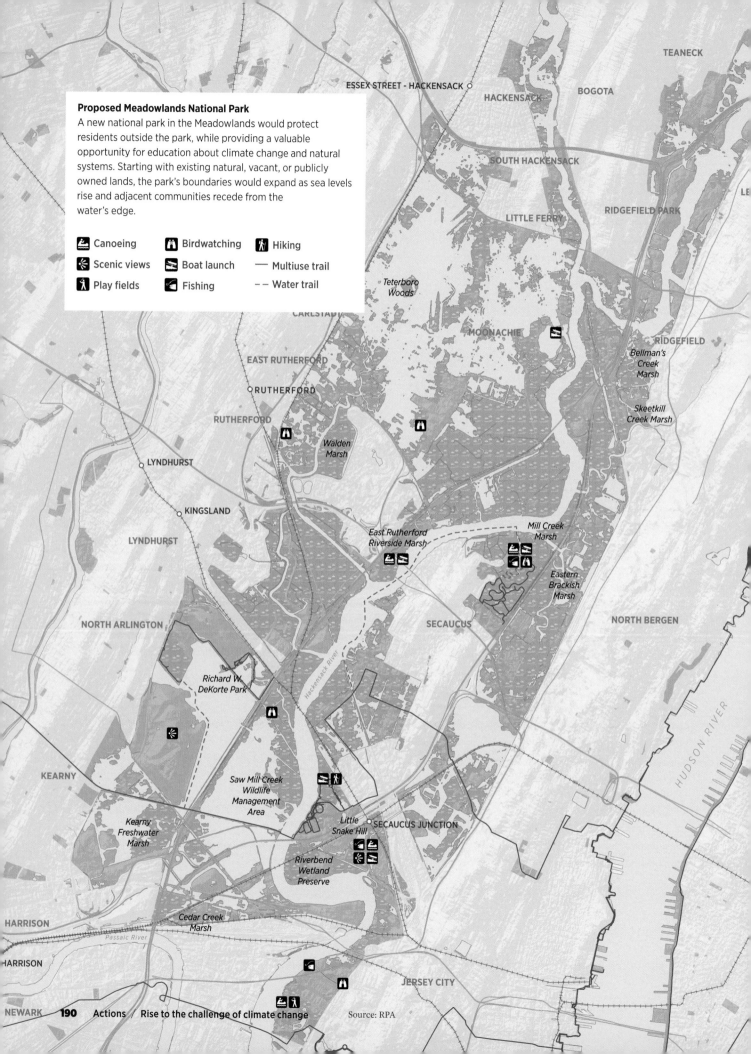

Proposed Meadowlands National Park

A new national park in the Meadowlands would protect residents outside the park, while providing a valuable opportunity for education about climate change and natural systems. Starting with existing natural, vacant, or publicly owned lands, the park's boundaries would expand as sea levels rise and adjacent communities recede from the water's edge.

🛶	Canoeing	🔭	Birdwatching	🚶	Hiking
🎿	Scenic views	⛴	Boat launch	—	Multiuse trail
🤸	Play fields	🎣	Fishing	--	Water trail

TEANECK

ESSEX STREET - HACKENSACK

HACKENSACK

BOGOTA

SOUTH HACKENSACK

RIDGEFIELD PARK

LITTLE FERRY

LE

Teterboro
Woods

CARLSTADT

MOONACHIE

RIDGEFIELD

Bellman's
Creek
Marsh

EAST RUTHERFORD

Skeetkill
Creek Marsh

RUTHERFORD

RUTHERFORD

Walden
Marsh

LYNDHURST

Mill Creek
Marsh

KINGSLAND

East Rutherford
Riverside Marsh

LYNDHURST

Eastern
Brackish
Marsh

NORTH ARLINGTON

SECAUCUS

NORTH BERGEN

Hackensack River

Richard W.
DeKorte Park

HUDSON RIVER

KEARNY

Saw Mill Creek
Wildlife
Management
Area

Little
Snake Hill

SECAUCUS JUNCTION

Kearny
Freshwater
Marsh

Riverbend
Wetland
Preserve

HARRISON

Cedar Creek
Marsh

Passaic River

HARRISON

JERSEY CITY

    Source: RPA

With other urban coastal areas around the United States facing similar challenges, the park would provide a model that is consistent with the mission of the National Park Service. It would preserve a unique ecosystem and one of the most battered natural systems in the country. It would educate the public on what urban wetlands mean to us today, and how climate change could redraw coastlines in the future. And it will inspire this and future generations to protect these vital assets and develop innovate ways to adapt to a changing environment.

A national-park designation could help provide the resources and legal framework to help the Meadowlands's unique ecosystem continue to recover from its industrial legacy, and restore additional wetlands and other natural features that would help absorb floodwater from storm surges as well as rising seas. Park boundaries would grow as seas rise.

A national park at the Meadowlands would also provide a unique opportunity to both educate local and national visitors about the effects of climate change, and strategize how to mitigate its effects—all in an urban context, where some infrastructure is too critical to be removed, but can be rebuilt to higher standards of resilience.

Creating a new national park is complex, but could follow these general steps:

Adopt a new master plan

In order to become a national park, the State of New Jersey, the federal government, and local Meadowlands stakeholders—residents, workers, business owners, infrastructure managers, and other local institutions such as the Sports and Exposition Authority and the Meadowlands Conservation Trust—must first reach consensus on a vision for the Meadowlands, and a plan to get there. A new master planning process for the Meadowlands District should be stakeholder-driven and aim to develop a vision and timeline for the new National Park.

Seek national-park designation

The State of New Jersey and park advocates should work closely with the National Park Service and members of Congress to begin the process of getting the Meadowlands designated as a national park. The National Park Service will perform a special resource study to determine the area's potential, after which the sponsoring lawmakers can introduce legislation in Congress.

Transfer land

As the study and potential legislation are considered, the State of New Jersey, the Sports and Exposition Authority and the Meadowlands Conservation Trust, and municipalities within the designated boundary should prepare to transfer all parks, protected wetlands, vacant land, and landfills, as well as relevant state-owned property (approximately 10,000 acres) to the federal government to serve as the foundation of the new national park.

Focus federal funding

Federal funding should be secured to buy out owners of property to be added to the park in phases, starting with the land at greatest risk of flooding. Additionally, federal programs should be used to help facilitate improvements in and around the park, including contaminated site cleanups, public access infrastructure, and educational signage—complementing and leveraging financial commitments made by New Jersey.

OUTCOMES

A Meadowlands National Park would offer a unique opportunity to restore a significant natural system, and turn the risks and challenges of climate change into a national asset. The park would help protect residents and businesses. It would also introduce a groundbreaking model of a national park that could be replicated across the country.

PAYING FOR IT

Galvanizing support for the Meadowlands as a new model of a national park will require focused regional, state, and municipal planning and advocacy. An initial vision could be developed with foundation funding and used to inform the master planning process, which will be funded by the state. Once a consensus vision has been reached, efforts to secure federal and private funding for improvements and infrastructure adaptation can be made. A Meadowlands Buyout Program, created in partnership with the state of New Jersey and the federal government could aggressively buy out high-risk properties in communities such as Teterboro, Little Ferry, and Moonachie, transferring purchased land to the National Park Service. Once active, funds from the state Adaptation Trust Funds could leverage funding opportunities in the Meadowlands.

34 Determine the costs and benefits of a regional surge barrier

Photo: RPA

Multiple projects are underway to protect specific neighborhoods from coastal storm-surge flooding, but a larger-scale approach—such as a regional barrier system—must be evaluated against other alternatives, as extreme storms are likely to become more frequent and intense. The Army Corps of Engineers should lead a comprehensive study to determine the need, cost, and feasibility of a regional surge barrier, emphasizing the impacts on communities and the region's ecosystem. This should be done in partnership with relevant public agencies, the region's academic institutions, and experts from private organizations and nonprofits.

Much of the region's population and economy surrounds a complex water system that's vulnerable to extreme weather events.

The region's core has the highest concentration of people, jobs, and infrastructure, much of which are at significant risk from storm-surge flooding. Superstorm Sandy brought the core to a halt and left behind tens of billions of dollars in damage to infrastructure, homes, businesses, and other property. Investments in resiliency projects after Sandy were made at the local level to protect those communities, but many others will still be vulnerable.

With this in mind, it is necessary to determine whether an investment in a regional surge barrier system will be needed over time and what impacts it could have. The most frequently considered barrier design would entail constructing a five-mile long "Outer Harbor Gateway" across the New York Bight from Sandy Hook to the Rockaway Peninsula, in addition to a barrier at the East River.

Such a project would introduce an engineered system to a complex network of more than 30 rivers and streams. These include the Hudson, Passaic, Hackensack, and Raritan rivers; over a dozen tidal straits, such as the East River and Long Island Sound; and nearly forty bays, inlets, and coves, including Jamaica, Newark, and Raritan bays.

Constructing a surge barrier has the potential to protect critical infrastructure and hundreds of thousands of residents and businesses from the effects of storm-surge flooding. There are nevertheless many unknowns about the impacts of building a storm-surge barrier on the interconnected network of natural systems as well as key questions around social impacts, governance, funding, and decision-making that need to be answered.

The full costs and benefits of a surge barrier should be evaluated before a decision is made to proceed.

Given the potential impact on the region's residents, jobs, infrastructure, and property, the costs and benefits of a regional surge barrier need to be studied. In 2016, the U.S. Army Corps of Engineers (the Corps) began scoping for the New York/New Jersey Harbor & Tributaries Focus Area Feasibility Study, which will identify measures and alternatives to address coastal risk and determine potential future actions, which are likely to include a regional surge barrier. The study will result in a Chief Engineer's Report to Congress, which could eventually lead to funding for the implementation of the measures recommended.

As part of this study, the Corps should break out the proposed surge barrier into a more comprehensive study that invites research across scientific disciplines. In particular, the Corps should provide the funding for hiring the region's academic institutions and private and nonprofit experts to help determine the need, cost, and feasibility of a regional surge barrier, emphasizing the impacts on communities and our complex ecosystem. Experts in policy, governance, and land use should each determine the potential implications to their respective fields.

Particular emphasis should be placed on the following topic areas and considerations:

Effectiveness

- **Failure rate and lifespan:** Determine how often and under what conditions the barrier could fail, as well as the lifespan of an effective barrier.

- **Sea-level rise:** Because surge barriers do not protect against permanent flooding from sea-level rise or the inland flooding caused by stormwater, investments will still need to be made to protect or move populations and infrastructure. The rate of sea-level rise must also be factored in when determining the design, scope, and estimated completion date of any potential new surge barrier.

- **Frequency of closure:** The effectiveness, costs, and impacts of a surge barrier will depend on how frequently it is used. Frequent closings would raise maintenance costs and cause greater ecological impacts, but public or political pressure could lead to closing it even when there is only minimal risk of flooding. Infrequent closings could raise damage risks, and bring into question the ecological, political, and financial costs of building a surge barrier that is seldom used.

- **False sense of security:** Even areas protected by a surge barrier could end up needing additional protectio against inland flooding, sea-level rise, and high winds—as well as storms that could occur before a barrier is built. The decision to proceed with a barrier may create a false sense of security that could lead to delays in improving site-level resilience or transitioning away from high-risk locations—or cause them to be canceled altogether.

Ecology

- **Salinity/tidal area:** Barriers have been shown to alter the circulation of water in and out of the system, regardless of whether they are open or closed. Estuaries—where freshwater and saltwater meet and the fish and wildlife therein depend on a given range of salinities—can be particularly affected.

- **Water quality:** When closed during a storm, a barrier will contain all of the water that normally flows out of the system naturally, as well as any accumulated stormwater, potentially concentrating pollutants and nutrients in the system.

- **Sediment:** Sediment distribution, which is necessary for wetland survival, could be altered or impeded by a barrier. Additionally, the bottom substrate in sites such as the Hackensack, Passaic, and Hudson rivers has been found to contain industrial pollutants that could be affected by changes in the system from a barrier.

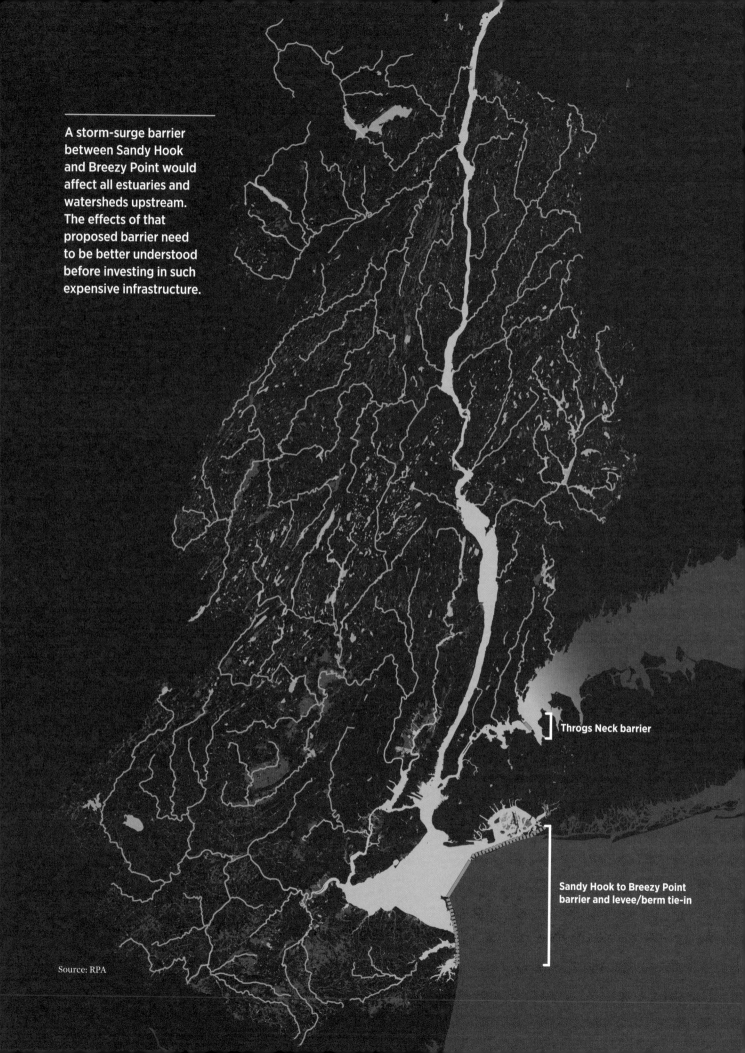

A storm-surge barrier between Sandy Hook and Breezy Point would affect all estuaries and watersheds upstream. The effects of that proposed barrier need to be better understood before investing in such expensive infrastructure.

Throgs Neck barrier

Sandy Hook to Breezy Point barrier and levee/berm tie-in

Source: RPA

- **Anadromous fish and wildlife migration:** The estuary is home to a number of fish and wildlife that migrate in and out of the system over their life cycle (including shad, striped bass, blue fish, blue crabs, and young eels). It should be determined what level of interruptions to access would be harmful to migrating species.

- **Resident fish and wildlife habitat:** Resident fish and wildlife in the estuary find their niche on the bottom of the system based on a variety of factors ranging from substrate type, surrounding vegetation, water depth, etc. Any changes to the dynamics of the system could make portions of the estuary uninhabitable to resident species, such as the Shortnose Sturgeon, which lives in the Hudson River and is considered endangered. This designation ensures that any potential impacts on their habitat must be taken into account before any changes to the system are made.

- **Potential greenhouse gas emissions:** Changes to the salinity of an estuary system that is rich in nitrogen could lead to a chemical reaction wherein the potent greenhouse gas nitrous oxide is created.

Social/Political

The proposed development of a surge barrier has led to heated, politically charged debates for a number of reasons detailed below.

- **Constituents inside/constituents outside:** As it is impossible to build a system that can protect the entire region from storm surges, many of the region's residents would still be left without protection should a barrier be built. Debates over this dynamic could make the project complicated to design and approve.

- **Resilience funding:** There is a risk that a surge barrier could divert funding from other needed projects. For example, many adaptation projects, including large resilience investments being made in places such as New York City's Lower East Side and Hoboken in New Jersey, do not yet have full funding. Additionally, other infrastructure, including transit, wastewater, and energy systems face significant shortfalls in funding designated for maintenance.

- **Two states + New York City:** Responsibility for the barrier, including who would determine when it should be closed and opened, will need to be assigned. Although many other municipalities would be protected by a barrier, the outer harbor gateway would require bi-state cooperation between New York and New Jersey for a multibillion dollar project that has different benefits and consequences for each state. New York City—which would see perhaps the greatest benefits from the project—has already come out firmly against such a project, choosing instead to invest in local resilience measures.

OUTCOMES

A comprehensive study that evaluates all of the potential benefits and costs of a regional surge barrier system, weighed against other adaptation measures, would provide critical information to decision-makers and the region's residents about whether and when a regional surge-barrier system should be constructed. Without answering the questions described above, arguments in favor or against such a system would be based largely on incomplete information, conjecture, and emotion.

PAYING FOR IT

Estimates for constructing a barrier range from $10 billion to $36 billion, with annual maintenance costs estimated between $100 million and $2.5 billion. Currently, the region's planned adaptation projects are not yet fully funded, nor are upgrades to our transportation, water and wastewater, energy, and other critical pieces of infrastructure. Paying for a surge barrier will require new streams of funding that wouldn't compromise local adaptation funding sources, and will sufficiently cover the necessary annual maintenance costs that ensure the system functions properly for decades to come.

BRING NATURE INTO OUR COMMUNITIES

After decades of development that prioritized the construction of roads and buildings without much concern for the environment, many of our streams, forests, and floodplains have disappeared. As a result, heat is trapped and magnified, especially in cities; polluted stormwater and untreated sewage flows into waterways; and residents everywhere have too few opportunities to enjoy open spaces and cultivate a healthy connection to nature.

We can address these issues by first recognizing nature as a vital component of cities that is woven into the the built environment and integral to the health and well-being of residents. With more trees, rain gardens, and green roofs in our neighborhoods and downtowns, we can help prevent sewer systems from overloading and discharging pollutants into waterways. These improvements would mitigate rising temperatures and help restore the region's harbors and estuaries, while also creating a healthier and more pleasant place to live.

35 End the discharge of raw sewage and pollutants into waterways

Photo: Borough of State College

A majority of the region's waters, despite significant improvements in recent decades, are still so polluted they contribute to health risks and are unfit for swimming, fishing, or supporting a biodiverse environment. The main recurrent sources of pollution, stormwater runoff and the discharge of combined stormwater and untreated sewage, will only get worse as climate change brings more frequent and intense storms. The federal government, states, and municipalities should work together to eliminate all combined sewer overflow by 2040. This will require incorporating green infrastructure strategies into building and zoning codes, and strengthening clean-water standards. We can accelerate this process by establishing neighborhood green districts that implement pilot projects, and by imposing a stormwater utility fee to fund and advance new infrastructure initiatives.

Raw sewage and other contaminants flow into our harbors, rivers, and streams, increasing health risks and reducing biodiversity.

Many of the region's sewer systems were built to collect stormwater together with domestic sewage and industrial wastewater. Unfortunately, in times of heavy rain, these systems overflow. In 39 municipalities across the tri-state region, there are 702 combined sewer overflow outfalls—places where untreated human and industrial waste, plus contaminants and debris, gets discharged directly into our rivers and ocean when there are periods of heavy rain.

Each year, more than 27 billion gallons of untreated wastewater and polluted stormwater discharge from 460 combined sewer overflow (CSO) outfalls into New York Harbor alone,[55] with another nearly 300 CSOs in waterways throughout the region. These outflows present significant ecological and public health issues, as they generate algal blooms, reduce water quality and biodiversity, increase shellfish-bed and beach closures, and create the potential for waterborne-disease outbreaks. More sewage and pollutants will spill into these waterways as climate change brings intensified storms, threatening wetlands, oyster beds, and other natural systems that protect against flooding.

Communities that discharge raw sewage into waterways are required to have a plan to separate older-style combined sewer systems, store excess sanitary waste and stormwater until it can be treated, or otherwise control the discharges. Municipalities that are prepared for the future by scaling efforts to eliminate the discharge of polluted stormwater and untreated sewage into our waterways by 2040 will be better positioned to attract residents, businesses, and tourists with access to clean water.

New York City has adopted an approach that combines "green" and "grey" infrastructure improvements to reduce CSOs, investing $1.5 billion in public funds in green storm-water runoff mitigation strategies by 2030, and an additional $1.6 billion in grey infrastructure, including treatment-plant upgrades and the construction of large retention tanks to hold overflows until the polluted water can be treated. These investments will help the city reduce CSO discharges by approximately eight billion gallons per year.

Communities outside New York City in the Hudson Valley, northern New Jersey, and coastal Connecticut have fewer concentrations of CSOs, but the pollution and harm they cause are still significant, at 6.3 billion gallons per year. Like New York City, these areas are implementing plans to reduce flow through green and grey infrastructure investments.

Eliminate CSOs by 2040 with state leadership, inter-municipal coordination, and new financing tools

Traditionally, municipalities have eliminated CSOs through costly sewer projects that separate the combined, single-pipe system into different sewers for sanitary and stormwater flows. While this may be an effective strategy, it would be cost-prohibitive and logistically challenging to complete throughout the region, particularly in the most densely developed cities.

To achieve zero CSO outfalls by 2040, municipalities will need to put a greater emphasis on a green-infrastructure-centered approach that uses nature-based features such as parks, greenways, bioswales and rain gardens to soak up stormwater before it reaches the sewer. States should set strong water-quality standards that exceed federal minimums and encourage municipalities to deploy these green infrastructure strategies. Municipalities will need to invest in these systems using new financing tools, and plan at the watershed level.

Grey infrastructure is considerably more costly and has fewer co-benefits, but can remove greater quantities in a single project, and works best in places such as Manhattan where bedrock lies below the surface and doesn't allow for water infiltration.

Set state baseline requirements for incorporating green infrastructure strategies into municipal building and zoning codes

Incorporating green roofs, rain gardens, permeable pavement, and water-retentive cisterns into new and renovated large-scale developments can reduce the load on a community's stormwater management system. State planning and environmental protection agencies should require a higher standard of green infrastructure in all local building and zoning codes. In addition to reducing stormwater overflows, the cooling effect of green infrastructure has the benefit of mitigating the effects of urban heat island. Standards and practices should be updated as measurement and monitoring programs of green infrastructure installations determine the best applications for different conditions.

Daylight streams as part of a comprehensive green infrastructure strategy

Uncovering streams that were buried or otherwise covered in pavement—known as daylighting—can also reduce the load on the stormwater system and alleviate the risk of flash flooding. Although daylighting streams can be complex and expensive, it could mitigate flooding risk, improve habitat,

The region's 702 Combined Sewer Overflow outfalls release untreated water directly into waterways, causing algal blooms, threatening habitat and biodiversity, closing beaches, and creating the potential for waterborne illnesses.

Kingston

Poughkeepsie

Waterbury

Newburgh

New Windsor

New Haven

Highlands

Bridgeport

Norwalk

Irvington

Yonkers

Paterson

Hackensack

Ridgefield Park

North Bergen

Kearny   Weehawken

Harrison   Hoboken

Newark   Jersey City

New York City

Elizabeth

Bayonne

Woodbridge

Perth Amboy

Annual Discharge

— 1B gal
— 500M gal
— 100M gal

○ No data

Data: New York State Department of Environmental Conservation, New Jersey Department of Environmental Protection, Connecticut Department of Energy & Environmental Protection, New York City Department of Environmental Protection and provide aesthetically pleasing natural landscapes in urban communities that could boost surrounding property values. Recent projects in Yonkers, NY, and Stamford, CT, demonstrate the high return on investment of restoring buried or culverted streams.

States should develop evaluation metrics to identify the best daylighting opportunities, informed by historic ecologies, maintenance operations, and stewardship opportunities, as well as additional co-benefits such as recreational opportunities, potential community spaces, and the ability to measure success post-implementation. Such a cost-benefit analysis would provide a roadmap for future daylighting projects.

Develop stormwater utility-fee systems to fund and advance green infrastructure projects

Stormwater utility fees provide both a dedicated revenue stream for stormwater management programs and a way to incentivize property owners to adopt best practices in green infrastructure and low-impact development. Water authorities should institute stormwater fee systems that charge property owners based on the area of impervious cover and how much stormwater flows off of the property. The revenue could be used to upgrade and maintain stormwater management systems and fund stream-restoration projects. Cities across our region could structure their utility-fee systems in ways that best suit their built environment, and establish different rates based on property types.

Evaluate proposals for green districts at the watershed level

Green districts are a way to focus on green infrastructure projects in a distinct geographic area in order to see quick returns on investment. Although green districts are not appropriate in every context, they can help catalyze change. These projects are typically easier to implement when states and municipalities agree on the process for designating green districts, and what kind and how much funding they'll each ultimately receive.

Some green districts are quite large, such as a network of interconnected parks, while others are no bigger than a neighborhood. For example, Philadelphia has had success implementing green infrastructure projects in small, concentrated clusters that gradually radiate out as they increase in size and area over time.

Communities seeking to transition some of their auto-dependent landscapes into complete neighborhoods should designate them as green districts in order to focus attention and investment where it could have the most impact.

OUTCOMES

Eliminating the occurrence of CSOs and capturing more stormwater would help end the continuing pollution of the region's waterways, particularly from heavy stormwater runoff. It would also increase biodiversity and healthy habitats, and allow for more water-based activities such as swimming and fishing. More of the region's waterways would become healthier and more attractive for communities, attract visitors, and improve the well-being of residents.

PAYING FOR IT

Eliminating all 702 CSOs across the region would require significant investments in a variety of projects, including green and grey infrastructure. Regional cost estimates are difficult to quantify given the differences in approaches, but New York City has estimated the cost of green infrastructure to be about $1 to $2/gallon of CSO avoided. Grey infrastructure is considerably more costly and has fewer co-benefits, but can remove greater quantities in a single project. It is likely the final price tag will be at least $10 billion. Achieving this goal by 2040 would require a combination of state and local funding. State funding for watershed wide projects and incentives could leverage municipal green infrastructure and daylighting projects. Stormwater utility fees based on the amount of impervious surfaces could substantially fund local shares.

36 Restore the region's harbor and estuaries

Photo: Wayne Marshall

Centuries of development and industrialization have reshaped and impaired our region's harbor and estuaries. In recent years, progress has been made protecting these intricate and fragile ecosystems, but sea-level rise and more frequent storms threaten to erase these gains—and in fact, further disrupt them. Restoring wetlands, nurturing oyster beds, and providing pathways for migration of habitat as sea levels rise will ensure the harbor and the region's estuaries remain essential economic, ecological, and recreational resources.

Climate change threatens to overwhelm recent progress made restoring the New York-New Jersey harbor and the region's other estuaries.

The harbor between New York and New Jersey is part of a vast estuary that has nurtured life and commerce since the earliest human settlement, as have other estuaries along the coasts of Connecticut, New Jersey, and New York. The harbor estuary is particularly complex, comprising more than 30 rivers and streams, including the lower Hudson, Passaic, Hackensack, and Raritan rivers; over a dozen tidal straits, including the East River and a portion of Long Island Sound; and nearly 40 bays, inlets, and coves, including Pelham, Jamaica, Newark, and Raritan bays. These comprise tens of thousands of acres of wetlands, parks, beaches, and piers, support maritime and recreation industries that include the East Coast's busiest port, and are a critical habitat for numerous species that are essential to the region's ecosystem.

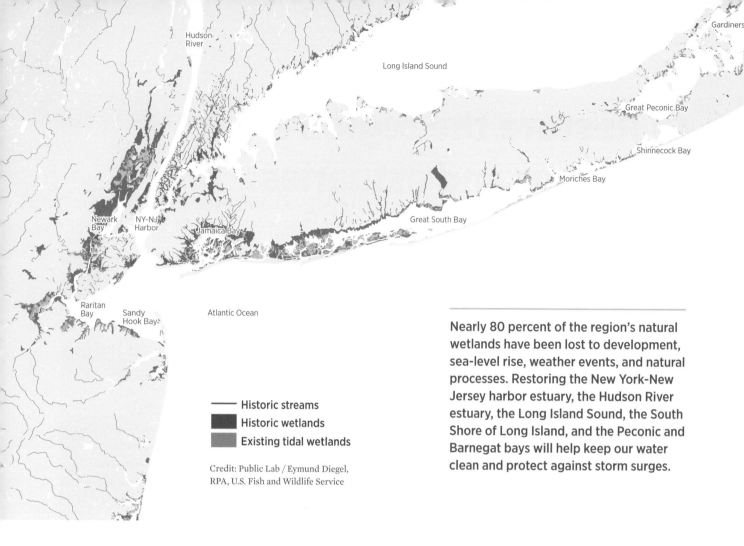

Historic streams
Historic wetlands
Existing tidal wetlands

Credit: Public Lab / Eymund Diegel,
RPA, U.S. Fish and Wildlife Service

Nearly 80 percent of the region's natural wetlands have been lost to development, sea-level rise, weather events, and natural processes. Restoring the New York-New Jersey harbor estuary, the Hudson River estuary, the Long Island Sound, the South Shore of Long Island, and the Peconic and Barnegat bays will help keep our water clean and protect against storm surges.

Centuries of development have resulted in the loss of around 78 percent of our historic wetlands in these estuaries[56]; trade and commerce have dredged away habitat from the bottom of our waterways; dams have reduced the flow of water into the system; and industrialization has left behind a legacy of contaminants in landfills, Superfund, and brownfield sites.

Thanks to four decades of better environmental policies, parts of the harbor estuary are beginning to thrive again. But the consequences of climate change threaten to roll back the progress that has been made. Increased precipitation will result in greater volumes of stormwater runoff and combined sewer overflows, washing more contaminants into local waterways and threatening water quality. Greater frequency of high-intensity storms will result in storm surges and wave action that threaten fragile estuarine ecosystems. And the rapid rise in sea levels will advance faster than our marshes and wetlands can respond, thus threatening their survival.

Increased flooding from storms and rising seas also threatens to unlock contaminants currently held in place in Superfund, brownfield, and other contaminated sites, as well as at landfills in low-lying areas. The changing climate will modify our natural systems and put at risk the economic, ecological, and recreational assets that are essential to the region's quality of life.

Scale up efforts to clean, restore, and maintain the harbor estuary

A comprehensive strategy for the harbor and other estuaries must maintain existing estuarine habitats; restore lost habitats, including wetlands and oyster reefs, through innovative new projects; provide pathways for wetlands to migrate up-land as sea levels rise; and shore up and clean low-lying contaminated sites at risk of flooding. For each approach, performance standards should be developed, and projects monitored to ensure necessary adaptations are made as sea-level rise and other climate consequences play out.

Maintain existing estuarine habitats
Estuarine habitats, including wetlands and other aquatic vegetation, serve as the breeding grounds and nurseries for many species of birds, fish, and other wildlife, ensuring the

continued biodiversity of the estuary. While existing federal and state policies serve to protect most of the region's remaining wetlands, some remain vulnerable to development. Protecting remaining habitats will require updates to current regulatory mapping (New York State's wetland maps are over 30 years old); policy shifts (freshwater wetlands of less than 12.4 acres in New York are not currently protected); and additional federal and state investments in acquisition of priority sites and programs to maintain habitat, particularly as the threats from climate change and invasive species will only accelerate. Finally, recent research has uncovered the rich biodiversity of the Hudson Canyon, the 400-mile extension of the Hudson River Valley into the Atlantic Ocean. As we learn more about this critical feature, additional steps should be taken to protect the canyon and designate it as a National Marine Sanctuary.

Restore lost habitat

Increasing the amount of wetlands and other estuarine habitats through restoration will not only benefit the natural environment, but also help protect our coastal communities. These benefits include storm-surge absorption, wave mitigation, carbon sequestration, and pollutant trapping.

The Army Corps of Engineers should invest additional resources into efforts to restore ecosystems in the estuary, as they are in places like Jamaica Bay and the Hudson River. Buyout programs in the region should also consider restoration opportunities as criteria, and funding should be allocated to support restoration of natural systems, in addition to purchasing and clearing sites. Finally, regulations around permitting should be updated to ensure innovative projects such as daylighting streams, and oyster-restoration initiatives like the Billion Oyster Project in New York Harbor, can proceed quickly and easily.

Provide pathways for wetland migration

It is estimated that one foot of sea-level rise would affect as much as 52 square miles of remaining wetlands in the region, while three feet would affect approximately 80 square miles, and six feet would affect around 106 square miles.[57] Pathways for wetland migration will need to be determined and regulated to ensure the survival of wetlands as seas rise. New mapping efforts, updated policies, land acquisition and protection, and community land-use changes should all ensure pathways for migration exist. State permitting regulations should be updated to enable the adaptation of coastal and estuarine habitat while also protecting communities through the use of living shorelines—the human-made shoreline treatments that mimic natural features that can mitigate the effects of flooding, such as dunes and wetlands.

One model for encouraging the use of such techniques is Maryland's Living Shoreline Protection Act of 2008, which requires soft shoreline stabilization techniques be used for erosion control unless the permit applicant can demonstrate that a harder stabilization technique is necessary.

Shore up and clean contaminated sites

An analysis of remediated and contaminated sites at risk of periodic and permanent flooding should be carried out to determine which sites are at greatest risk of being inundated in ways that release contaminants into the estuary. Contaminated sites at greatest risk should be fast-tracked for cleanup or shoring-up to prevent the release of contaminants. Policies that regulate private sites with chemicals and contaminants should be updated to ensure the consequences of climate change are factored into hazard planning.

OUTCOMES

These policies and practices would lead to increased acreage of protected wetlands; land-use changes that permit wetland migration; more innovative restoration projects throughout the estuary that plan for wetland migration in the face of sea-level rise; and a change in practice around how contaminated sites are regulated and managed. By 2040, we should have a healthy and clean harbor that is ecologically vibrant and supports a growing population, with access to more recreation and maritime jobs, and that helps keep us safe from the storms and flooding from a changing climate.

PAYING FOR IT

Restoration will require both reprioritization of existing funds and increased resources. A greater share of Army Corps funding should be directed toward natural restoration. The state buyout program and conservation funds should be directed toward protection and restoration of critical estuarine habitat as well as pathways for migrating habitat. Adaptation projects seeking funding through the proposed state adaptation trust funds should receive higher scores for protection, restoration, and migration considerations. Federal and state cleanup funds should be prioritized for sites at greatest risk of inundation and releasing contaminants.

③⑦ Cool our communities

Cities, with their heat-trapping buildings and pavement, are particularly susceptible to the extreme heat caused by climate change. The urban heat island effect magnifies the impact of high temperatures, worsens air quality, threatens public health, and strains the energy grid. Federal, state, and local authorities should aggressively pursue measures to mitigate the impacts of high temperatures—including greening initiatives, revised building guidelines, and stronger social programs—to keep residents and buildings cool, and infrastructure functioning.

Extreme heat is a grave threat to our urban residents.

Extreme heat poses a far bigger threat to human life than other climate change effects such as extreme flooding, particularly in cities. Between 2000 and 2012, extreme heat was responsible for 162 deaths in New York City alone—almost half of which were attributed to just two events in 2006 and 2011.[58]

Unfortunately, the number of "extreme heat event" days is expected to multiply fivefold in the next 30 years from 11 to 55 days in New York City; from eight to 55 in Newark; and from six to 31 in Hartford. Deaths could double by mid-century.[59]

Heat events also pose significant economic risks. Between 2002 and 2009, heat waves were responsible for $5.2 billion in health costs due to premature deaths, with an additional $179 million due to heat-related illnesses.[60] Communities with large populations of children and the elderly, and households with low incomes are especially at risk for both health and economic impacts.[61]

Although extreme heat kills more people, on average, than any other type of extreme weather event, the majority of adaptation funding provided in recent years has gone toward protecting against storm surges rather than reducing the effects of heat.[62]

Prepare for the inevitable rise in temperatures and manage extreme heat by making our cities greener

Cities and states should employ a variety of strategies to alleviate the heat-island effect in urban communities. These include greening infrastructure, neighborhood-based heat-event relief programs, and the more widespread use of heat-reflective building materials.

Institutionalize greening initiatives and relief programs at the community level

Restoring natural systems, green infrastructure installations, and replacing impervious surfaces with porous pavements are primarily regarded as stormwater management strategies. But they have the additional benefit of reducing urban heat-island effects. These actions also beautify neighborhoods and reduce their carbon footprint. Utilities and municipalities can promote greener neighborhoods by adopting rebate programs such as the Portland, Oregon, "Treebate" initiative, which provides ratepayers with a credit toward their stormwater and sewer bill for planting a tree on their property. Agencies with jurisdiction over streetscapes can also consider replacing concrete road medians with gardens or lining the street with trees, which helps reduce ambient temperature and stormwater runoff, and improves the quality of life.

Neighborhoods with little greenery and higher concentrations of asthma patients, senior citizens, or low-income residents are particularly vulnerable to extreme heat events.[63] Approximately 93 percent of the most socially vulnerable neighborhoods in our region have high concentrations of impervious surfaces coupled with low amounts of tree coverage, making them very or extremely vulnerable to heat.

Developing community outreach initiatives around extreme heat issues can empower community members and relieve these public health concerns. Community-managed rooftop gardens and street-tree initiatives can provide work for local residents, as well as cool the buildings they cover. Heat-stress initiatives can be incorporated into grade-school curriculums to encourage smart decisions about outdoor activity during extreme heat events. Officials should target these initiatives toward neighborhoods identified by RPA's Heat Vulnerability Analysis.

Require major urban projects to be green

Extreme heat can be mitigated by adjusting how we design and construct our built environment. Buildings in urban areas need to adopt robust building-code standards that put more focus on efficient insulation to minimize air conditioning usage during summer months, when stress on the electrical grid is highest. In addition, developers, state agencies, and regional transportation agencies should replace highly absorbent infrastructure materials with more reflective ones wherever feasible. For example, "white-topping" an asphalt roadway with concrete overlays to increase the streetscape albedo has been done on highways surrounding Denver, Colorado. Planning for urban streetscapes should also include using permeable and water-retentive pavements in select areas, such as truck-restricted corridors and pedestrian-only walkways.

Use pilot programs to measure the impact of natural approaches, and design community-based solutions

State agencies and planning officials should develop pilot programs that expand urban forestry, green infrastructure, and stream daylighting approaches, measuring the cooling effect on ambient temperature of immediate surrounding areas. This would help municipalities identify nature-based cooling solutions that would work best for their communities, while also developing a better case for utilizing green infrastructure solutions for stormwater and extreme-heat mitigation. Measuring effects on multiple scales could inform how future projects' success is defined, and to inform the parameters of innovative financing mechanisms such as social-impact bonds. Understanding a project's effect on the cooling and water management of a community facilitates implementation of and investment in later projects.

Trees, green roofs, and other vegetation can help cool urban communities by deflecting radiation from the sun and releasing moisture into the atmosphere.

Image: Only If + One Architecture for RPA's 4C Initiative

OUTCOMES

A proactive approach toward cooling our region's communities would yield opportunities for critical and multiple benefits to arise, including:

- Reduced heat stress in vulnerable communities and heat-related fatalities during extreme heat events

- Improved knowledge about heat-mitigation strategies

- Reduced stormwater runoff

- More attractive public spaces, which in turn could encourage economic investment into the area and uplift communities

- More jobs in low-income communities to green buildings and public spaces

- Stronger ties among community members who work together at community gardens and other outdoor spaces

PAYING FOR IT

State and local expenditures in the form of tax breaks, utility rebates, and other financial incentives, such as cool roofs and better building materials, would leverage localized UHI-mitigation strategies. Meanwhile, large-scale mitigation strategies such as increasing the urban tree canopy, replacing streets with "cool pavements," and installing green infrastructure will require large investments from municipal, state, and federal governments, as well as nonprofits. For example, New York City's Million Trees Initiative was able to meet its goal two years ahead of schedule and with expansive reach, with help from the nonprofit New York Restoration Project, which raised $30 million to implement the plan. Municipalities will also need to account for the ongoing maintenance costs of these projects. Some projects that have multiple benefits, such as climate adaptation or stormwater management, could leverage funding from federal or other sources that might be more readily available to implement cooling measures. These high up-front investments could help control healthcare expenditures in vulnerable communities and spur more economic investment in "newly green" communities.

IMPROVE THE NATURAL AND BUILT SYSTEMS THAT SUSTAIN US

To most of the world, the tri-state region is largely known for its vibrant downtowns, diverse communities, and iconic buildings. But it also features spectacular natural landscapes such as the Hudson Highlands and the Jersey Shore, and hundreds of thousands of acres of underappreciated forests, farmland, and waterways that protect and sustain the region's communities.

A changing climate is adding greater urgency and different strategic direction to the cause of sustainability and management of natural resources. Unprotected open space should be preserved as it absorbs carbon dioxide and heat, supports diverse habitats, helps species to migrate, and is a source of clean water and food. Connecting these open spaces with a system of trails would maximize their value for both climate adaptation and recreation. Infrastructure should be made more resilient to help communities respond to storms, flooding, drought, and heat, while water sources and supply systems should be protected from multiple risks.

By using and maintaining these natural resources in a more strategic way, we would be able to enhance the symbiotic relationship between the environment and growing communities.

38 Prioritize the protection of land to help adapt to a changing climate

Photo: William Avery Hudson

State and local governments and land trusts should prioritize the protection of natural and agricultural lands to promote healthier communities and adapt to a changing climate. This requires greater collaboration between community organizations and government, increased funding, and updating of prioritization criteria. This criteria should include consideration of the land's potential to store carbon, capture and filter stormwater, and protect the drinking-water supply. The land to be protected must support biodiversity, allow for habitat migration, increase regional food production, and offer recreational benefits.

Too few of our open spaces are protected, and the limited funding available to preserve them does not reflect today's biggest environmental challenges.

Open spaces and agricultural lands provide tremendous benefits to the region and its residents. They provide us with abundant and clean water, reduce air pollution, and protect a range of habitats for numerous species, as well as providing an opportunity to connect with and experience nature. But in a growing region like ours, these open spaces are at risk. While nearly 70 percent of our region's land is undeveloped, only 21 percent is permanently protected, leaving too much vulnerable to future development. Many state programs—such as New York's Environmental Protection Fund, New Jersey's Green Acres, and Connecticut's acquisition program, as well as private nonprofit land trusts—have been established to identify and acquire priority parcels for permanent protection, but are woefully underfunded.

In this situation, when demand for funding is high, the current criteria for determining which parcels should be prioritized for acquisition are outdated. They do not reflect the most critical challenges we face in the era of climate change, which brings greater risk of flooding, droughts, and threats to our natural habitat.

State and local governments and land trusts should prioritize the protection of natural and agricultural lands using new criteria that emphasize climate and community benefits.

In order to maximize their limited funds, state preservation programs and land trusts should adopt new criteria to identify and prioritize the acquisition of land best suited to protect and mitigate the effects of climate change, particularly in the communities that are most vulnerable. Building on the work done by The Nature Conservancy and Scenic Hudson, these criteria should include:

- **Climate mitigation:** Because forests have the capacity to store large amounts of carbon, protecting swaths of unprotected forest will help mitigate carbon emissions and slow the pace of climate change while we transition away from greenhouse gas-emitting fuels.

- **Flood resilience:** Open spaces and agricultural land absorb water. Protecting these spaces in areas that are susceptible to flooding can help reduce damage to our communities. "Flood farms," an innovative concept advanced by PORT + Range in the fourth plan's 4C Initiative, are marginal agricultural lands protected and used to absorb riverine or storm floodwaters conveyed to the site. Flood farms could offer a new source of income for farmers on marginal lands, or a reason to prioritize agricultural-land protection.

- **Natural species protection:** Some land parcels are particularly important for protecting animal species and giving them routes to migrate northward, as the climate warms and ground conditions change.

- **Local food production:** As farms across the country become increasingly susceptible to drought, it is important to protect the most fertile agricultural land and expand the opportunity to grow more food regionally.

- **Community health & well-being:** It is critical to protect open spaces that ensure a high-quality drinking-water supply for a growing population. Land that gives the region's residents access to nature also has important health benefits.

Using the criteria above, RPA identified nearly 237,000 acres of high-priority unprotected open spaces with multiple overlapping benefits.

Increase state funding for open-space-acquisition programs
Each state in the region should increase the funding dedicated to preserving open spaces and agricultural land, and make long-term investments to ensure they are protected. Across the country, such measures enjoy wide support from the public, with many statewide and municipal ballot measures to create new public funds for parks and land conservation having been approved. Once each state has agreed on the prioritization of open spaces and agricultural lands, a bond initiative should be pursued to raise the needed funds.

Pursue broader collaboration between government and community-based groups to protect open spaces and farmland
Preserving farmland requires creativity, perseverance, and greater collaboration between all interested parties. A good model for collaboration to preserve farmland is Scenic Hudson's Foodshed Conservation Plan, which brings together rural communities dependent on agriculture and city neighborhoods seeking fresh food. The plan rightly calls on federal, state, county, town, village, and New York City participation in the effort.

Large clusters of
open space, which are
critical to biodiversity,
community resilience,
health, and quality of life,
are concentrated in the
Catskills, the northern
Croton watershed, and
in the New Jersey and
Hudson Highlands.

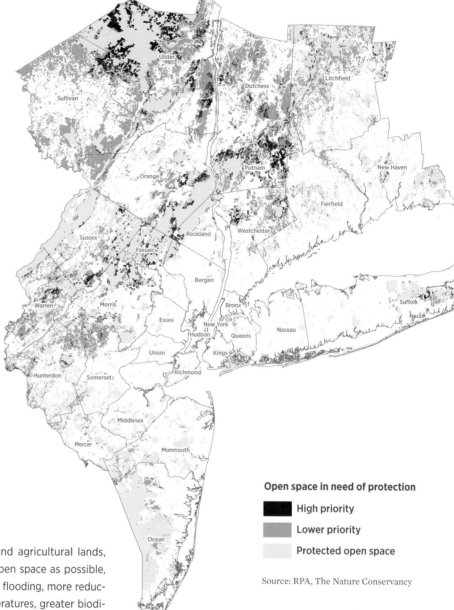

Open space in need of protection

■ High priority

■ Lower priority

□ Protected open space

Source: RPA, The Nature Conservancy

OUTCOMES

Strategically protecting open spaces and agricultural lands, instead of simply preserving as much open space as possible, would result in greater resilience against flooding, more reductions in greenhouse gases, cooler temperatures, greater biodiversity, stronger local economies, and healthier communities. In particular, this would lead to preservation of the most fertile and economically viable farmland; forests that absorb carbon and clean the air; and trails that connect communities to nature and allow species to migrate as the environment changes. This strategy would be the most cost-effective from an economic and environmental perspective. It would result in cleaner and more abundant drinking water, fewer people with chronic diseases caused by air pollution, fewer deaths from extreme heat, and more secure access to local and regional food. Incomes would be higher and unemployment lower in some of the most economically depressed areas of the region. More people would be able to walk, bike, or use a wheelchair to get to the region's natural landscapes. Finally, prioritized protection would allow for strategic partnerships across governmental jurisdictions and among different land conservation groups that would help ensure the protection and stewardship of these critical places for generations to come.

PAYING FOR IT

Over the past 20 years, New York, New Jersey, and Connecticut have spent a combined $1.3 billion of environmental protection and acquisition program funding to protect about 200,000 acres of open space (not including coastal wetlands). Additional funding will be needed to protect high-priority portions of the region's 3.9 million acres of unprotected open space. In combination with legally and politically appropriate land use regulations, changing the criteria to reflect current priorities around climate change will allow funding to have a greater impact. The Nature Conservancy, Scenic Hudson, RPA, and others have developed different models that can be expanded and improved.

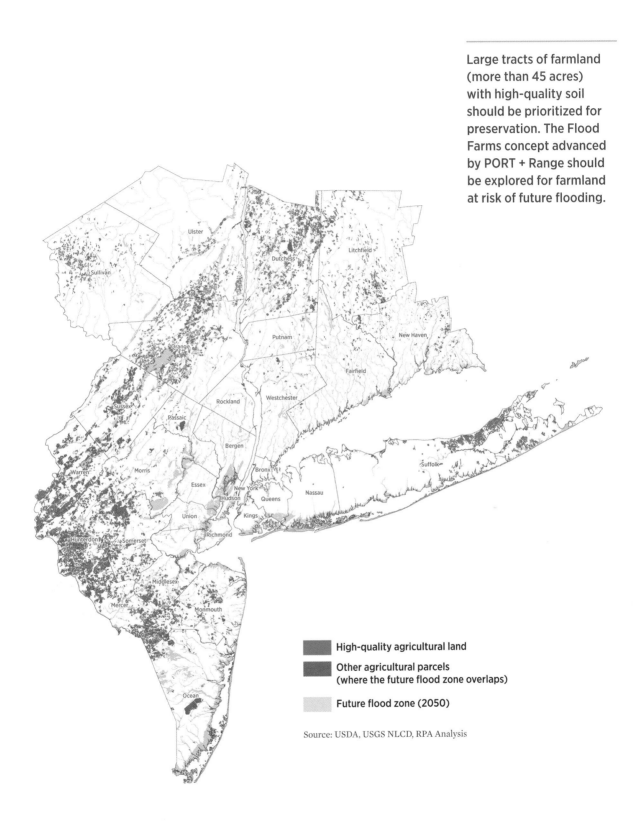

Large tracts of farmland (more than 45 acres) with high-quality soil should be prioritized for preservation. The Flood Farms concept advanced by PORT + Range should be explored for farmland at risk of future flooding.

High-quality agricultural land

Other agricultural parcels
(where the future flood zone overlaps)

Future flood zone (2050)

Source: USDA, USGS NLCD, RPA Analysis

"Flood farms," an innovative concept advanced by PORT + Range in the fourth plan's 4C Design Initiative, are marginal agricultural lands protected and used to absorb riverine or storm floodwaters conveyed to the site. Flood farms could offer a new source of income for farmers on marginal lands, and a reason to prioritize the protection of agricultural land.

Farmer stewardship
Large-scale restoration efforts require a cooperative and dedicated local knowledge base and workforce to grow, build, and care for the new landscape.

Flood farm
Private landowners receive credits and conservation subsidies by providing ecosystems services that expand the floodable public infrastructure along the water.

Flood park
Variable topography on lands adjacent to rivers improves floodwater storage, increases groundwater recharge, and restores floodplain habitat important for migratory birds

Public access to river
Waterfront access to the Wallkill River provides residents and visitors with public space amenity and recreation.

Preserved croplands
High-value cropland is protected with opportunities for erosion control, drainage buffers, and other ecosystem services at scale.

Image: PORT + Range for RPA's 4C Initiative

39 Create a tri-state trail network

Image: PORT + Range for RPA's 4C Initiative

The tri-state region includes hundreds of iconic parks and landscapes, from the forested open spaces of the Catskills, Highlands, and Pinelands to the sandy shores of New Jersey and Long Island. But these spaces are largely disconnected from each other and from the population centers that use them. Linking these areas of precious natural beauty would boost recreational opportunities, catalyze economic development, and enhance the biodiversity of our natural systems, leading to better health and quality of life for our residents. Federal, state, and local governments should collaborate with land trusts, trails groups, and other partnerships to develop an integrated network of biking, hiking, and walking trails from underutilized rights-of-way such as roadways, rail lines, transmission lines, and pipelines.

The region's abundant natural resources are out of reach for too many people.

Our region is rich in natural and recreational resources, including large tracts of protected and unprotected open spaces, parks, agricultural lands, waterways, and estuaries. But we often overlook these natural wonders, thinking of them as individual places disconnected from each other, instead of as a part of a regional ecosystem. This lack of connection diminishes our ability to access the wide variety of natural beauty, openness, and geographies that exist in the region today. It reduces awareness and experience of the natural environment and opportunities for environmental stewardship and open-space protection.

Connect the region's open spaces with an accessible trail network

Connecting disparate open spaces can help us think of the region as an ecosystem—one that happens to have communities in it—and value our natural environment. A trail network weaving throughout every part of the region and beyond should be developed with existing and planned trails in combination with rights-of-way for pipelines, transmission lines, railways, roadways, and natural features such as beaches and waterways. When complete, the network would include user-friendly biking, hiking, and walking trails that connect the region's treasured open spaces to each other and to our communities.

Fortunately, our region is already home to a number of clusters and arteries of trails of local, regional, and national importance, from the Appalachian Trail to the East Coast Greenway and smaller systems of hiking trails within parks. Even though many of these trails are not physically connected to each other, it would take just a few key investments to create a tri-state trail network of some 1,620 miles. This trail network would put almost nine million of the region's residents within a half-mile of a trail—nearly 25 percent more than today.

There will be many challenges to implementing such a comprehensive trail network. On any stretch, there are likely to be conflicts and barriers, from competing uses and issues of liability to privacy concerns and local opposition to lack of funding for planning, construction, and maintenance of the system, among other issues. To overcome these challenges, we propose the following:

Organize a coalition to promote a regional trail network

The coalition would prioritize trail segments most relevant to regional connectivity, allocate funding, and provide support, data, and other resources to local governments and trail groups. Federal, state, and local government should collaborate with land trusts, trails groups, and other partnerships to develop this integrated network.

Secure funding for planning, implementation, and maintenance

In other regional trail networks across the country, fundraising and allocation of trail funds operate on both a local and regional scale. While a regional coalition might oversee fundraising and allocation of federal and foundation trail funds, particularly for the design and engagement phases of trail building, in some cases construction and maintenance of regional trails would rely heavily on state and local sources, or fundraising on a local scale.

Define design guidelines to support universal access

While some trails are natural and rugged, others should be designed to be accessible to a range of users, including those with limited mobility.

Create safe and user-friendly connections between trails and nearby transit

The complete network would run within a half-mile of 111 regional rail stations, plus 237 New York City subway stations and 13 PATH stations. Safe pathways and wayfinding signage between transit stations and trails would facilitate use, but would require policies and investments to enhance safety and operation.

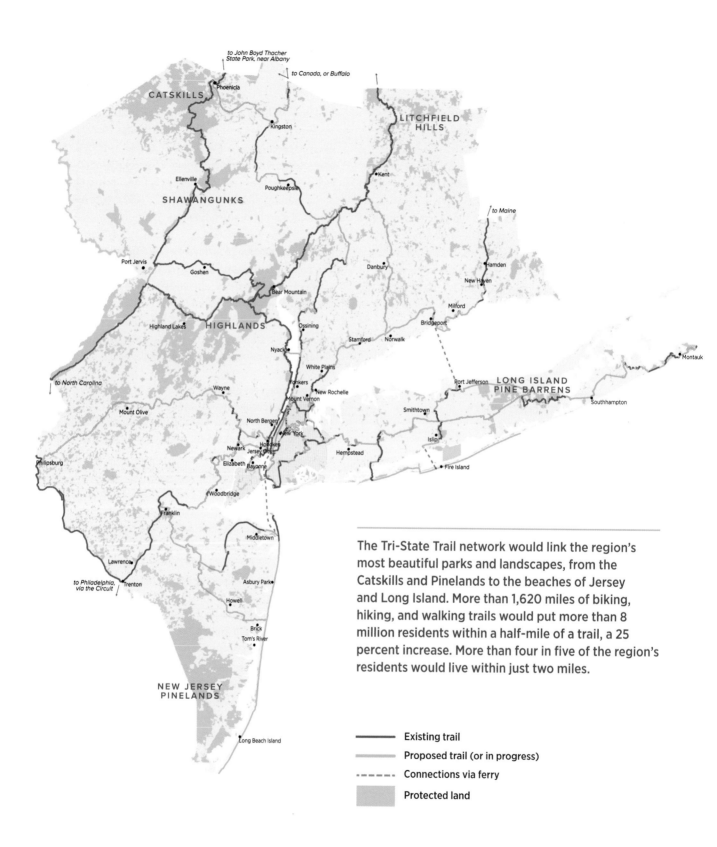

The Tri-State Trail network would link the region's most beautiful parks and landscapes, from the Catskills and Pinelands to the beaches of Jersey and Long Island. More than 1,620 miles of biking, hiking, and walking trails would put more than 8 million residents within a half-mile of a trail, a 25 percent increase. More than four in five of the region's residents would live within just two miles.

———— Existing trail

———— Proposed trail (or in progress)

------ Connections via ferry

▆ Protected land

Source: RPA

Image: PORT + Range for RPA's 4C Initiative

OUTCOMES

When complete, the network would facilitate connections to nature, promote health, well-being, and economic activity, and foster stewardship of our natural resources. A regional network would put almost nine million people within a half-mile of a trail—trails that would connect to over 70,000 acres of protected and/or publicly owned open spaces. Access to green and open spaces is increasingly being linked to health benefits, including lower rates of obesity, greater activity levels, lower levels of depression, reduced allergies, and higher self-esteem, among others.[64]

The network would also pass through 287 of the region's municipalities, opening up economic-development opportunities around tourism, recreation, and hospitality. In New York, the Hudson River Valley Greenway alone generates an estimated $21 million annually in economic activity from visitors to the communities along the trail during its annual month-long Ramble event.[65]

The network would also help to expand rail access to open spaces. Today, rail service provides connections to around 330 square miles of open space, and the regional trail network would boost that number by an additional 1,200 square miles, allowing greater access to city residents without cars.

Finally, as climate change alters the habitat of our region's wildlife, trails could provide an opportunity for habitat migration. To maximize the benefit of this opportunity, final planning and design for the trail system should factor in species migration and include habitat-friendly crossings, particularly along highways.

The Regional Trail Network would help establish the tri-state region's reputation as a place where communities have direct and easy access to an interconnected network of natural and open spaces for everyone to enjoy.

PAYING FOR IT

Building a regional trail network will require funding for planning, design, construction, and maintenance. One model is to combine philanthropic support with federal and state funding and partnerships at the local level, which was used in networks such as The Circuit around Philadelphia, PA, and could be replicated throughout the tri-state region. Increasingly, metropolitan planning organizations and state agencies recognize the importance of investing in multimodal transportation, including biking and walking. Ensuring line items in transportation budgets for trails will help advance those solutions.

Additionally, land trusts such as the Trust for Public Land and Scenic Hudson can play an important role in prioritizing open-space acquisition or securing easements for lands that contribute to the network. Finally, ensuring there are plans and adequate funding for maintenance and programming will be critical to the network's success. An umbrella group that helps coordinate activities and supplement funding carried out by regional and local groups such as the New York-New Jersey Trail Conference and the D&R Greenway will help ensure the network thrives.

40 Upgrade infrastructure to high standards of resilience

The region's critical infrastructure, already struggling with the effects of age and underinvestment, is also facing additional threats from climate change. Superstorm Sandy demonstrated how flooding from storms can wreak havoc on the power, transportation, wastewater, telecommunications, and social-service systems, but the gradual rise of sea levels also threatens to inundate dozens of critical facilities in the coming decades. Higher temperatures and more-intense precipitation can also exacerbate existing weaknesses in our infrastructure. The region must not only upgrade and repair assets such as power plants and wastewater treatment facilities to withstand the threats of climate change, but also redesign critical systems like energy and telecommunications so that disruptions are as limited as possible, and do not lead to cascading failures across multiple systems.

Most of the region's infrastructure is not capable of withstanding the effects of climate change.

In the coming decades, our critical infrastructure will not just face threats from powerful storms, but from rising sea levels and temperatures as well. By 2050, nearly 60 percent of the region's power-generating capacity will be at risk of flooding, along with 21 percent of public housing units, 40 percent of wastewater treatment plants, 115 rail stations, and dozens of miles of subway and commuter rail routes. Superstorm Sandy caused power outages for more than eight million people, severely damaged public transit, and dumped billions of gallons of untreated sewage into our waterways. Regional infrastructure in the lowest lying areas will begin to experience frequent or permanent inundation from sea-level rise, including two airports (Teterboro and, without continued investment, LaGuardia), critical roads and railways, more than 35 major wastewater treatment plants, and over 1,600 sites with hazardous chemicals, in addition to vital economic and cultural assets, from public beaches to Giants Stadium.

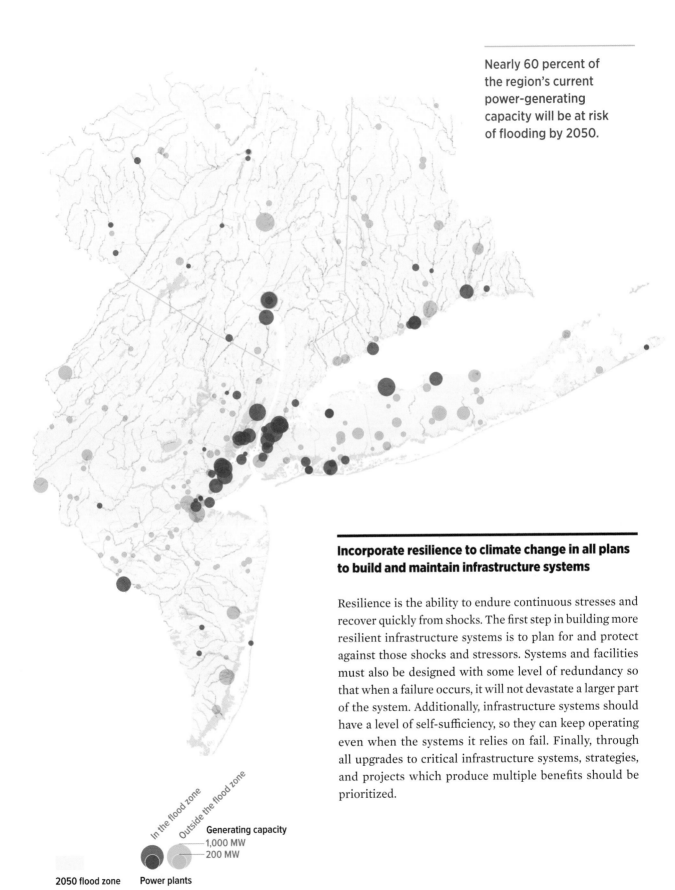

Source: U.S. Energy Information Administration, RPA

Nearly 60 percent of the region's current power-generating capacity will be at risk of flooding by 2050.

In the flood zone

Outside the flood zone

Generating capacity
1,000 MW
200 MW

2050 flood zone   **Power plants**

Incorporate resilience to climate change in all plans to build and maintain infrastructure systems

Resilience is the ability to endure continuous stresses and recover quickly from shocks. The first step in building more resilient infrastructure systems is to plan for and protect against those shocks and stressors. Systems and facilities must also be designed with some level of redundancy so that when a failure occurs, it will not devastate a larger part of the system. Additionally, infrastructure systems should have a level of self-sufficiency, so they can keep operating even when the systems it relies on fail. Finally, through all upgrades to critical infrastructure systems, strategies, and projects which produce multiple benefits should be prioritized.

Image: ORG Permanent Modernity for the Fourth Regional Plan

As older, dirty power plants are retired and replaced with smaller, more efficient facilities, valuable space can be freed up for parks and other community amenities.

Resilience against climate change must be at the center of plans to repair and replace aging infrastructure

As facilities and systems are upgraded, replaced, or preserved, anticipating the effects of climate change continues to be critical to the longevity of facilities. This could take different forms depending on the type of infrastructure and its vulnerabilities. But planning should nevertheless include elevating, flood-proofing, and/or relocating facilities; reducing the carbon footprint; expanding facility capacity to better deal with extreme conditions such as greater heat and more precipitation; and extending the life of the investment. In recent years, the New York State Governor's Office of Storm Recovery and the New York City Mayor's Office of Recovery and Resiliency have been established, and many state, local, and regional agencies have begun to incorporate climate change resiliency into their work. New Jersey, Connecticut and all municipalities should follow the lead of New York State in passing legislation to adopt sea-level rise projections, and mandate the consideration of climate change in projects.

Design and build in redundancy so systems continue to function even when a failure occurs

Precaution and planning go a long way toward preventing failures, but cannot eliminate them entirely. By working redundancy into our critical infrastructure systems disruption is kept to a minimum. This can look different depending on the type of infrastructure. Innovations in the energy sector such as microgrids allow for better distributed energy resources and can be isolated from the macrogrid when necessary—benefitting those inside and outside the microgrid. Green infrastructure-like bioswales and rain gardens help absorb stormwater, reducing the chance of an overwhelmed sewer system releasing untreated water. For transportation infrastructure, the proposed Gateway project to construct two new rail tunnels under the Hudson River would both increase capacity and create redundancy if one or more of the existing tunnels need to be shut down.

Make systems more self-sufficient to avoid cascading failures across different systems

A failure of one critical system can lead to a domino effect, causing many more to fail. For example, a power outage can disrupt the function of wastewater treatment plants. Fortunately there are innovations that can mitigate cascading failures by keeping facilities and networks at least partially functioning, even when related systems are disrupted. Many of these adaptation strategies involve backup power or cogeneration, such as with wastewater treatment plants and pumping stations, or for cell towers and data centers. Excellent examples include the NJ Transit Grid, a $400 million initiative to both protect a portion of the NJ Transit system from interruptions to the centralized power grid and incorporate green energy production; and NYC's Red Hook Mesh Network, a community-built WiFi network that keeps communications functioning 24/7—even during disasters.

Prioritize infrastructure projects and upgrades that provide multiple benefits and/or regenerative functions

There are many ways to make critical infrastructure more resilient while at the same time providing additional benefits to the surrounding communities and region. Natural and nature-based solutions, in particular, can help accomplish this. For example, cleaning up contaminated sites using phytotechnology, where specific plants are used to extract contaminants from the soil, also increases green space and absorbs stormwater. Microgrids and other upgrades to the energy grid increase the share of renewable energy sources, while green infrastructure that alleviates storm drainage not only reduces the sewage wastewater treatment plants must

process, but also helps cool urban areas, thereby improving the community's overall health and well-being. One of the biggest impediments to most of these strategies is the need for skilled workers to implement them. However, this can also be an opportunity for local-workforce development, if implemented properly.

Innovate the way resilience is funded by linking adaptation with infrastructure and economic programs

While funding to build and maintain critical infrastructure is not at all sufficient to address all the needs, it still represents more money than is currently allocated for climate change adaptation projects in general. By linking adaptation to infrastructure spending, there is more funding for adaptation and infrastructure programs that are able to withstand current and future hazards. The proposed state adaptation trust funds could provide gap financing to enhance adaptation improvements as part of infrastructure projects.

OUTCOMES

Over the next decade, larger-scale systems should be overhauled, with rapid growth in the number of microgrids and other strategies that create self-reliance and redundancy. There should be an acceleration in preparing land for permanent inundation through remediation, and protecting or relocating critical facilities such as train lines and power plants. By 2040, all systems—from power to transportation, wastewater, hospitals, and schools—should be able to withstand greater natural and man-made stresses with minimal disruption, and provide a greater and more diverse set of benefits.

PAYING FOR IT

The cost of adapting our critical infrastructure to new standards of resiliency varies widely depending on the project and type of infrastructure. To complete all necessary upgrades to the region's critical infrastructure would cost tens of billions of dollars, although these expenditures would defray even larger costs resulting from damage to these facilities from flooding and other climate impacts. Funding for projects would be incorporated into agency capital programs and distributed among federal, state, and local sources. The state adaptation trust funds proposed by RPA could supplement this funding for high-priority investments.

41 Connect the region's water supply systems

Photo: Eileen_10

The region has been able to develop, grow, and thrive in large part because of a steady supply of clean drinking water. The water originates in the New Jersey Highlands, the Catskills, the Delaware River Valley, and Long Island aquifers. Despite their close proximity, these water systems are isolated from each other, with a few exceptions. As the risk of disruption increases because of climate-change-induced drought, heavy precipitation, and saltwater intrusion, as well as terrorism, redundancy in our water systems is essential. We should invest in bi-directional connections between the region's major water systems so that all residents will have access to clean drinking water at all times.

The region's disconnected water-supply systems face increasing risks from extreme weather conditions and climate change, as well as terrorism.

In addition to sprawling development, pollution, and aging infrastructure, our water sources now face a new threat: climate change, which causes saltwater intrusion into aquifers, more extreme patterns of drought and heavy precipitation, and changing snowpack dynamics. They are also vulnerable to terrorist attacks. Yet coordinating policies and taking action is difficult. The systems that deliver our drinking water are based on political boundaries, unlike the aquifers from which they are sourced. A complex web of public water agencies, water districts, investor-owned utilities, and private wells is distributed across multiple layers of political jurisdictions.

On Long Island, for example, 2.6 million people rely on an overused sole-source aquifer that is vulnerable to contamination from septic systems, industry and stormwater runoff, and saltwater intrusion exacerbated by sea-level rise and the destruction of wetlands.

Photo: Halfpoint

which has one of the most sophisticated water-supply systems in the country, is currently taking steps to preserve its level of redundancy through its Delaware Aqueduct Bypass project. There are still critical groundwater-recharging lands that remain unprotected, however, particularly places like Long Island, where aquifers are being pumped faster than they can recharge.

Contamination from both non-point-source and point-source pollution continues to threaten the region's drinking-water supply. The most effective protections to the water supply include ending the discharge of raw sewage into our waterways and the cleanup of brownfields and Superfund sites. Changes made today would affect the drinking water a decade from now, as contaminants travel slowly through the ground.

Implement sound water-management practices

Compared with many other parts of the country, the New York Region faces fewer challenges from drought or overuse. Yet the magnitude of the effects climate change has on our water is unknown, and therefore sound water management is critical. To limit our vulnerability to less-predictable water supplies, we need more sophisticated drought monitoring and management, audits to determine the amount of water lost due to faulty infrastructure, aquifer storage and recharge (for both reserves, and to prevent saline intrusion), and encouraging the reuse of reclaimed water for certain purposes.

Connect the region's water-supply systems

Even if the water supply is preserved and conserved in the ways described above, part of the region's water supply could still fail for a number of reasons, potentially leaving millions of people temporarily without clean water. Connecting the region's water-supply systems would create redundancy that would be lifesaving if drought, contamination, or saltwater intrusion were to interrupt the water supply to a part of the region. It would also allow repairs to existing infrastructure by temporarily sourcing water from another system. The U.S. Environmental Protection Agency classifies the connection of systems to diversify the water supply as a "no regrets" adaptation strategy, which means there are significant benefits regardless of the rate of climate change.

There are national and local precedents for connecting water supplies. Many interconnections already exist, though most are between smaller systems, and some have been inactive for decades, such as the several smaller systems in the Hudson Valley that maintain interconnections with New

Overcome the physical and institutional barriers to protect and connect the region's water-supply systems

The region's freshwater supply is one of its most valuable resources. We must maintain its abundance and ensure its safety against the threats of contamination, overuse, climate change, and terrorism. We must protect its sources, manage its consumption wisely, and create a more connected network to ensure that even during an emergency, the tap does not run dry.

Protect the sources of the region's drinking water from contamination and over-withdrawal

The region has made great strides in protecting the integrity of its water supply in recent decades. The 1993 Long Island Pine Barrens Protection Act in New York and the 2004 Highlands Water Protection and Planning Act in New Jersey preserved large areas where critical sources of drinking water were threatened by development. New York City,

York City's aqueducts. Since 2016, Newburgh's interconnection to the Catskill aqueduct proved critical in mitigating a public health crisis when their main reservoir was contaminated from a toxic chemical spill at Stewart Air National Guard Base. A 1980-81 drought in New Jersey became so severe a temporary connection to New York City's water supply was constructed across the George Washington Bridge—but never utilized and soon thereafter dismantled. The 2007 New Jersey Department of Environmental Protection Interconnection Study found utility interconnection opportunities not only improved water delivery during droughts and other emergencies, but also improved operations under normal conditions. New York City also explored the potential of an interconnection with neighboring water supplies in New Jersey across the Arthur Kill, and of reviving existing but antiquated connections with Nassau County to augment supply during construction of the Bypass Tunnel project under the Hudson, and subsequently to provide backup supplies for either party during an emergency.

These and past proposals to connect water-supply systems across jurisdictions have generally failed due to regulatory, political, and cultural challenges. Interconnection projects face a complicated maze of state and local regulation and utility contracts, ecological concerns, and different water treatment systems and standards. For example, the New York City-New Jersey interconnection would require approval or permits from at least 21 local, state, and federal agencies, and at least 17 for the proposed Queens-Nassau County interconnections.

Over the next decade, New York State Department of Environmental Conservation and Connecticut Department of Energy and Environmental Protection should identify opportunities for water-supply interconnection, similar to the 2007 NJDEP study. States should implement regional water-management plans, while states and land trusts could partner to identify land-acquisition priorities that conserve the region's drinking water supply.

OUTCOMES

By 2040, the completion of bidirectional interties between the region's major water systems—for example, between Long Island and New York City, and New York City and Northern New Jersey—would ensure all parts of the region have access to clean water in the event one system is under stress, thereby reducing risks to public health.

PAYING FOR IT

Water infrastructure funding typically comes from rate payers, federal or state grants or loans, or tax-exempt municipal bonds, while utilities themselves (whether public or private) implement the projects. Utilities may be able to generate revenue through interconnection agreements by negotiating fees with the purchasing utility.

It is difficult to estimate costs for all the strategies mentioned. A similar, single water-supply interconnection project in California cost between $5 million and $10.5 million, though even the cost of that type of project could vary greatly depending on various factors such as distance and whether additional facilities are required.

CREATE A GREENER ENERGY SYSTEM, WITH MORE CAPACITY

The projected growth in population and jobs in the region, along with increased demand for electricity to power electric vehicles and the digital economy, will put strains on the electrical grid to increase power generation, despite ongoing improvements in energy efficiency. Without more coordinated planning and targeted investments, the energy system will not be able to meet growing energy demand, or reduce the region's reliance on sources of power that contribute to climate change and pollute the air of disproportionately low-income communities of color.

Local and state governments have taken steps to reduce greenhouse gas (GHG) emissions, focusing on renewables and greater efficiency. But this will not be enough for all three states, which have each committed to reducing regional GHG emissions by 80 percent by 2050, to reach this ambitious goal. Achieving that reduction level as the region grows will require a multipronged approach to dramatically scale up renewable energy, improve energy efficiency, manage demand with variable pricing, electrify vehicles, and convert the heat and hot water systems of large buildings to electric, while at the same time upgrading the power grid to support all of these changes.

42 Modernize the electric grid

The region's electrical grid has not kept pace with advances in energy technology and will require greater investment and coordination among energy providers and regulators across the three states to become a lower-emitting, reliable, and flexible system. Long-term planning for electricity demand should be focused in the region through a Tri-State Energy Policy Task Force. With a clearer sense of demand and a cohesive approach to incorporating emerging renewables such as wind and solar and storage technology, the grid can be updated to become more intelligent, with two-way communications, integration of distributed generation, and greater use of products that help consumers manage their energy use. As cleaner fuels generate more power, existing electricity-supply facilities—including fast-ramping plants necessary for rapid changes—can be updated and used more effectively.

Today's grid is outdated and ill-equipped for the cleaner, distributed, and digitized power system of the future.

The system of power generators and transmission and distribution infrastructure that comprises the grid supports our economy and, indeed, our entire society. But despite significant innovations in energy science and technology over the last few decades, our grid has not kept pace. Built to convey power in one direction from large, centralized plants burning fossil fuels, the grid is not properly equipped to integrate new and intermittent, renewable supply, small-scale distributed resources. The grid is also not prepared for smart homes, buildings, and devices, or to meet the demand for additional electrification of all sectors of the economy. The vast majority of ratepayers know little about their energy, and thus have few reasons to change their behavior and become more efficient.

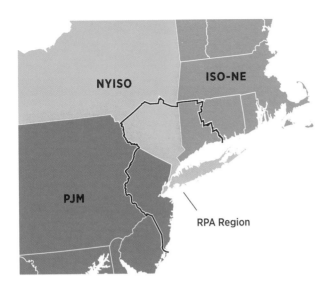

RPA Region

The tri-state region is divided among three different transmission planning entities that don't collaborate.

The PJM Interconnection, the Independent System Operator (ISO) New England, and, and the New York Independent System Operator are federally regulated, nonprofit corporations, created to coordinate transmission and ensure the safety and reliability of the electric system. A Tri-State Energy Policy Task Force would bring together these entities, along with other stakeholders, to promote coordinated networks to support new energy technologies.

Responsibility for modernizing the grid is divided among private utilities and regulators located within a complex network of regional transmission organizations and independent system operators, each with their own guidelines and territorial responsibilities. Energy suppliers and local governments, with their authority over siting and land use, also have a stake in how the grid is transformed. Without significant changes to regulatory structures and policies, and without substantial new investment, our region will remain bound to a grid that pollutes and warms the planet, misses opportunities to innovate, and fails to meet growing demand.

Plan for a more electrified, renewable region

With an expected increase of as four million people and two million jobs in the region over the next 25 years, more electricity will be needed. And as buildings and vehicles move toward greater electrification, that demand will grow even more. Unfortunately, too little transportation and land-use planning takes energy consumption into consideration. And if we continue down our current path, greater demand will be met through the burning of fossil fuels rather than by renewable energy.

Form a Tri-State Energy Policy Task Force

A regional task force bringing together regulators, public officials, utility executives, generators, and other stakeholders and advocates could plan more effectively for the future of energy production. The Task Force should assess jurisdictional barriers to renewable energy and grid modernization, and foster the development of a comprehensive,

regional assessment of future electricity demand. The effort would require cooperation among entities that rarely interact, including the metropolitan planning organizations, state transportation and planning divisions, Regional Transmission Operators/Independent System Operators (RTO/ISO), and utilities.

The Task Force should be guided by the competitive market designs and principles that govern the wholesale markets in each of the RTO/ISO jurisdictions, which seek to maximize the use of market forces to produce the lowest-cost outcomes and shield electricity consumers from the cost of bad investments and poor performance. This group should be established at the direction of the states' governors and consider, among other things, new technologies such as offshore wind, energy storage, alternative-fuel vehicles, and the potential implementation of coordinated networks to support these new technologies in response to market needs.

Adapt the grid for the greater variability of cleaner, renewable energy

As recent innovations in technology make wind and solar energy economically competitive, states and power-generation companies must continue to promote their adoption. But the growth of these renewable sources of energy will require modifications to the electrical grid. Compared with nuclear or natural-gas-fueled power plants, the output of renewable energy generators is highly variable, with intermittent peaks and valleys of supply over the course of days and seasons, and moment-to-moment shifts in conditions such as cloud cover and wind. In order to successfully harness the potential of these low-emission fuels while ensuring there is adequate power supply, providers and regulators will need to take the following actions:

Use pricing and technology to smooth out peaks in energy demand

Pricing is an effective strategy to influence consumers' demand for energy. Customers respond to energy rates that vary based on the time of day and season, especially critical peak pricing. Service providers in our region offer optional time-of-use rate plans, but few customers have signed up for them. California already offers customers who use distributed solar power a time-of-use rate—which will become the default rate for all customers in 2019. Energy regulators in the region should require all customers be transitioned to time-of-use rate plans.

As the grid becomes "smart," users will know in real time how much power they are consuming and what the overall demand on the grid is—perhaps even predicting power spikes. Smart home systems could adjust accordingly, taking actions to delay usage or turning off nonessential appliances—some of these systems are, in fact, already available. Utility companies should accelerate the widespread adoption of smart devices connected to the grid by promoting, or even incentivizing, their purchase.

Enhance energy storage

Peak time for energy production from renewables does not always align with peak demand. Solar panels produce maximum energy in the afternoon, for example, but peak demand for electricity typically occurs in the evening. The timing and "shape" of electricity use throughout the day will continue to change as a result of more efficient and smarter end-use devices, consumer behavioral changes, and the increased electrification of transportation and space-heating applications. Storing the power created for later use is critical to the widespread adoption of renewable energy, and the federal government and states need to further invest into R&D of new and cost-effective storage technologies. At the regulatory level, states in the region's three different transmission planning entities (ISO-NE, NYISO, and PJM) should initiate market rule changes to facilitate the participation and full valuation of energy storage in their wholesale markets, and support the commercial deployment of energy storage as an integral part of a flexible, sustainable, low-carbon grid.

Create a resilient grid with clean, stable energy sources and supply that can quickly come online to fill gaps

A modern and efficient energy grid has diversified sources of power and the ability to cycle energy into and out of the grid. Renewables should make up at least 50 percent of our region's electricity generation over the coming decades. But because sources such as solar and wind can be highly variable, other sources will be needed until advances in storage are made. Existing nuclear power can also play an important role in a low-carbon energy system, providing a steady and inexpensive base load of power without emitting greenhouse gases. Nuclear power plants that pose the greatest safety risks, such as Indian Point, should be closed, while others should continue to operate, provided they meet the most stringent safety and operating standards. Natural gas has allowed the region to shift away from the dirtiest sources of fuel, including coal and oil, and will continue to play an important role for the near term. The need for fast-ramping "peaker plants" will also remain for the foreseeable future, but their use and footprint should decline over time. As the rest of the electrical system modernizes and transforms, existing peaker plants in the metropolitan area should be modernized and, where possible, reduced in size to meet the highest standards of flexible performance and emissions control, while opening up the potential for new land uses around them.

Make the grid flexible and efficient with distributed generation

The electrical grid has traditionally been considered a "one-way" network to transport energy from large-scale centralized power plants, through wires for ultimate delivery to electricity consumers. More recently, with the improved technology and economics of small-scale power production such as rooftop solar panels, microgrids, and other technologies, distributed generation has been gaining traction, paving the way for a more intelligent "two-way" grid. Distributed generation allows consumers to generate power onsite for direct consumption, and for small-scale grid-connected generation sources to support grid operations more cost-effectively than traditional "wired" solutions.

Increasingly, distributed-resource owners, utilities, and regional grid operators are establishing effective mechanisms for selling excess power to the utilities or other customers through the wholesale markets. This, as well as advances in metering and communications technologies, is enabling utilities and regional grid operators to be more comfortable with distributed generation as part of their reliability planning and operations. The increased deployment of distributed generation could lead to greater resiliency, reliability, and flexibility, with reduced demand and load on the grid.

States should help accelerate and leverage these trends to create a robust grid that integrates significant amounts of distributed generation, supports the ability for two-way power flows, and has open and flexible communication channels between utility companies, regional grid operators, and electricity consumers. New technologies for sensing system conditions at more points on the transmission and distribution system, improved communications, data-processing

capabilities to capture and organize the data, and more interactive consumers and devices will create opportunities for better management of the grid by the utility and regional grid operator. It will also enable more engagement by consumers and their devices to balance the system moment by moment. New York's Reforming the Energy Vision (REV) plan is a model for the region in advancing this more intelligent and flexible grid. Similar approaches should be taken in New Jersey and Connecticut.

OUTCOMES

A 21st century grid would lead to a cleaner and more reliable energy system. As older power plants are used less and ultimately retire, air pollution will decrease, improving the quality of life for all residents, including those burdened by their location. Fewer greenhouse gases would be emitted, slowing and/or minimizing the consequences of climate change. The grid itself would become a more democratized system, allowing for increased knowledge and participation by users in decision-making around energy. Innovative technologies would find more equal footing with traditional energy technology, allowing the opportunity for increased economic development. New green jobs could be created. And finally, a comprehensive energy vision would help both residents and energy suppliers determine where investments are needed for the future.

PAYING FOR IT

Many of the improvements discussed above will require considerable public and private investment into new technologies and added infrastructure. Some of these costs—particularly those that align with relevant criteria—could be covered by the proceeds generated from an expanded greenhouse gas market. Other measures will require private investments, which should rely primarily on the wholesale competitive markets and potential distribution markets, such as those advanced by New York's REV plan. In other cases, such private investment may need to be helped along by public incentives. Connecticut's and New York's Green Banks maximize public funds by working with private sector investors to create low-cost, sustainable financing for clean-energy investments. Infrastructure to facilitate expanded customer and investor engagement in the distributed grid may best be supported by investment from utilities backed by ratepayers, who will ultimately pay more stable and even lower rates as a result of expanded choices and greater system efficiencies.

43 Scale up renewables

Photo: Urk Noordoostpolder

By 2030, the tri-state region should be producing half of all its electricity from renewable, clean power sources such as solar and offshore wind to keep us on a path to sustainability. While rooftop solar panels are increasingly popular, large-scale solar and offshore wind projects remain largely conceptual. States and energy companies should take aggressive steps to make the region both a leading user and supplier of renewable energy. The region can sharply reduce greenhouse gas emissions by expanding state renewable portfolio standards, restructuring energy markets to factor in renewables, planning for land use and economic development opportunities and using the purchasing power of large cities.

Without significantly scaling up renewable energy projects, the region will fail to meet its goal of reducing GHG emissions by 80 percent by 2050.

Innovations in battery storage and other energy technology are making renewable energy increasingly competitive. Rebates and policies allowing homeowners to sell power back out to the grid have helped to expand distributed solar generation. But no large-scale solar and offshore wind farms exist today in the region. In 2017, the Long Island Power Authority approved the nation's largest offshore wind farm: 15 turbines capable of powering 50,000 homes.

The electricity grid in its current form isn't designed to efficiently integrate renewables, which generate power intermittently, with existing power sources. At the same time, New Jersey and Connecticut haven't taken aggressive steps to signal market changes, such as restructuring how non-utility distributors are paid for power generation. All three states have not made nearly enough direct investments into renewable energy project planning nor have they helped municipalities to coordinate land use and economic development opportunities for renewable generation.

230   Actions / Rise to the challenge of climate change

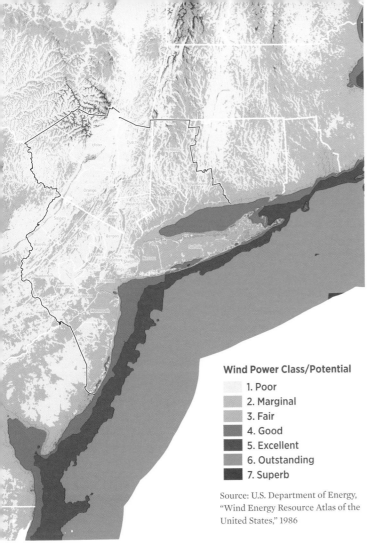

Wind Power Class/Potential

  1. Poor
  2. Marginal
  3. Fair
  4. Good
  5. Excellent
  6. Outstanding
  7. Superb

Source: U.S. Department of Energy, "Wind Energy Resource Atlas of the United States," 1986

Offshore wind could become a major source of affordable, renewable energy for the region, especially off the coast of New Jersey and Long Island.

Scaling up renewable energy will require proactively increasing both the supply and the demand.

With new policies and investment to promote the production of renewable energy and consumer demand, the region can reduce greenhouse gas emissions and take advantage of opportunities to create new energy-related jobs.

Catalyze local renewable energy industries through land use planning and organization

Large arrays of solar panels or farms of offshore wind turbines hold tremendous potential for economic growth. The three states, New York City, regional entities such as the Port Authority and coastal municipalities should collaborate to bolster a home-grown offshore wind industry, by determining ideal sites for offshore wind turbine construction, partnering with manufacturers to build local supply chains and encouraging institutions of higher education to focus on this important resource.

The three states should also work closely with local communities to determine the land use opportunities and implications for large solar farms, by collaborating with grassroots organizations on education and economic development to develop long term plans for how land could be used to host solar arrays.

Require 50 percent of all energy produced and consumed in the region to come from renewable sources

New York, New Jersey and Connecticut each require electricity suppliers to generate and sell a minimum amount of their electricity from eligible renewable energy sources, including solar, wind, fuel cells, geothermal, and others. These so-called Renewable Portfolio Standard policies have been central to increasing the production of renewable energy in the region and nationwide.[66]

In 2016, New York State updated its Renewable Portfolio Standard (RPS) from 29 percent to a 50 percent Clean Energy Standard for renewable energy by 2030 along with

- New York State has been leading the region, most notably through its renewable energy goals and its Reforming the Energy Vision strategy. About 23 percent of its energy comes from renewable sources, primarily hydropower. In 2016, New York State established nation-leading goals for clean energy (50 percent by 2030) and offshore wind (2,400 MW by 2030), though the path to implementation is unclear. New York City, similarly, has established an ambitious 100 percent renewable energy target, but has taken few steps toward implementation.

- New Jersey, which gets about 5 percent of its energy from renewable sources (mostly solar), adopted ambitious legislation a decade ago and successfully established the state as a solar leader. It has languished since then, losing opportunities to lead in other areas, such as offshore wind. Nearly half of New Jersey's energy comes from nuclear energy, which emits nearly zero greenhouse gases but has other environmental impacts.

- Connecticut, which gets less than 5 percent of its energy from renewable sources and more than a third from nuclear, has been successful at advancing some small- to mid-sized renewable energy projects through its Green Bank, but is not a renewable energy leader.

the multiyear collaborative process called Reforming the Energy Vision (REV) that aims to modernize the grid and create more competitive markets for renewable energy.

New Jersey and Connecticut should follow suit and raise their standards to 50 percent by 2030. Currently, New Jersey's Board of Public Utilities currently has an RPS of just over 20 percent by 2021, with an additional solar requirement of 4 percent by 2028. Connecticut's Public Utilities Regulatory Authority has RPS of 27 percent by 2020. Both states should look at lessons learned from REV to date, and develop a process tailored for their own needs and aspirations to enable and facilitate the increased deployment of distributed renewable energy.

Cities and public authorities should procure renewable energy to power their operations and influence the market

As some of the largest energy purchasers, the region's cities have the ability to influence the energy supply mix through what they buy. In 2015, New York City, which spends upwards of $650 million per year on electricity, requested proposals for ways that city operations could be run on 100 percent renewable resources from new power generation. While none of the proposals has moved forward to date, the concept should be acted on in New York City and pursued in other large cities.

The MTA is also a major consumer of power, spending $400 million a year on electricity. The agency's focus has been on finding ways to conserve power, but could use its leverage as a big customer to promote renewable energy.

OUTCOMES

Scaling up renewable energy in the region would have many benefits, including reducing greenhouse gas emissions and helping states reach their emissions targets. Renewables, which contribute little or no air pollution, would also help meet energy demand while also improving air quality. Renewable energy could boost economic development through the manufacture and construction of solar panels, wind turbines and other equipment, and provide green-collar jobs in the region. Contracting opportunities generated by the transition itself could be geared toward including advocacy and grassroots perspectives, such that green jobs are created and aid historically burdened community residents. Creating more renewable energy sources would require trade-offs that balance competing land uses, in particular for large solar arrays and storage facilities that would affect communities. States, local municipalities and energy companies should engage residents and stakeholders in assessing costs and benefits.

PAYING FOR IT

Investments in new infrastructure will be needed from both the private and public sectors. More importantly, increasing renewables will require government to change the way the economy recognizes the value of these resources in terms of sustainability, operational flexibility and resiliency. New York's REV initiative is one example of an effort to create a new framework in which renewable energy and distributed generation are the norm and derive from customer and investor actions, rather than ad hoc, short-term government subsidies. Broader-based pricing of carbon, and added valuation of flexibility and responsiveness in wholesale markets—of storage, for example—are additional initiatives that will facilitate and encourage investment in renewables. In addition, underlying investments in a smarter and more flexible grid funded through regulated utility investment, as well as other enabling infrastructure funded through other public support, would be necessary to enable the maximum deployment and efficiency of new renewables and distributed generation.

Federal credits, such as the solar tax credit, in combination with state net-metering policies have helped solar to gain a foothold, particularly at the residential level. Continued credits, combined with additional state incentives and policies, will be needed to advance large-scale solar and offshore wind projects. Proceeds from an expanded greenhouse gas market, would help build a growing reserve of capital to invest into such projects. Private renewable energy companies are already investing in projects on the leading edge of a new economic success story, and should continue to lead the way.

44 Manage demand with energy-efficient buildings and variable pricing

Photo: Lucas Braun

Energy conservation through efficiency measures is the best way to reduce greenhouse gas emissions in the short term. While energy efficiency upgrades to older buildings are complicated and expensive, new buildings can be constructed according to stronger and more consistent energy efficiency codes. At the same time, we can improve the monitoring and comparison of building energy data to ensure improvements are taking place. Further efficiencies could be achieved with a more intelligent electrical grid, providing opportunities for users to pay variable rates and modify their energy use accordingly.

The adoption of energy-efficiency measures is hampered by institutional barriers.

The energy required to power, heat, and cool buildings accounts for a significant share of the region's greenhouse gas (GHG) emissions. Improving the efficiency of buildings, especially in large cities, is a low-cost, high-impact strategy to reduce emissions. Yet implementing energy-efficiency measures is often slowed by institutional barriers.

Building codes are the best tools states and municipalities have to reduce greenhouse gas emissions from new construction and major renovations. Greening these codes, however, is complicated because so many of them regulate construction, electricity, mechanicals, health, and maintenance, among others. Only the largest of municipalities have the capacity to evaluate these codes, and thus propose changes.

Measuring the energy performance is key to improving a building over time, and technology now allows building owners and the cities and states that regulate them to monitor and compare the energy performance of buildings. With legislation, however, building owners are less likely to do this on a voluntary basis, thereby eliminating an opportunity to benchmark building efficiency.

Strengthen building energy-efficiency codes and compliance

Instead of devising their own, cities can use off-the-shelf codes, such as the International Green Construction Code (IGCC), which emphasizes site development and building performance such as indoor air quality, energy efficiency, renewable energy systems, and water conservation. Every city in the region should at least adopt the IGCC standards.

Cities should also undertake the more complex task of comprehensively evaluating existing construction codes. A multidisciplinary task force of public, business, and civic-sector experts should determine which new requirements are adopted to promote sustainability in buildings, and which should be removed. New York City's Green Codes Task Force is a good model of this type of initiative, while Energy Code Collaboratives are a model for an ongoing task force focused on code compliance.

Cities should also incorporate energy- and health-related improvements into the Integrated Physical Needs Assessment tools they use to ensure affordable multifamily buildings are safe and healthy.

Establish benchmarking programs for buildings

Benchmarking is the process of comparing a building's energy performance from one year to the next, or to another building similar in size and use. It allows building owners—and the cities and states that regulate them—to identify large energy users and target them for improvement. It can also identify the most energy efficient buildings as well as best practices and investment opportunities. With benchmarking, building owners are motivated to compare energy-efficiency data and compete for better performance.

New York City has led the way with both mandated and voluntary benchmarking programs. All three state governments, as well as city governments, should advance similar initiatives across the region, particularly in urban centers where building emissions levels are highest.

Use pricing and smart technology to manage demand

Energy production is highest—and the most polluting—during peak demand times, such as hot summer days. Unless consumers are given pricing queues, it will be difficult to change their behavior—like turning down the air conditioning. Variable billing rates can encourage consumers to either shift or reduce their energy usage in peak periods. Additionally, "smart" home systems and individual appliances that can communicate with the grid and know current demand and current rates could further improve efficiency. Utility companies, states and local governments, and building developers and owners should all work to expand the use of these smart systems and appliances through incentive programs, rebates, and investments.

OUTCOMES

Adopting energy-efficiency measures, encouraging building owners and consumers to reduce energy use by changing behavior patterns, and using up-to-date technology for pricing and regulating demand, would reduce GHG emissions. Taking steps to use existing energy sources more efficiently would allow time for renewable energy sources to come online, and reduce energy production during peak usage, thereby improving air quality.

PAYING FOR IT

Making existing buildings more energy efficient would mean more upfront costs for building owners. Some of that investment would be recouped over time through lower energy bills, but upfront capital could be made available through low-interest loans, as New York City has proposed for its mandated efficiency upgrades. New York City also announced that it will establish a Property Assessed Clean Energy program for commercial buildings to offer financing for property owners to fund energy efficiency and renewable energy projects on existing commercial structures. The property owner repays the financing through a special assessment or tax charge placed on their annual property tax bill. This provides financing for improvements over time without requiring the property owner to make a large upfront investment.[67] Other existing programs could be expanded or strengthened, including Connecticut's Green Bank program and other commercial and residential programs being developed through New York State's Reforming the Energy Vision (REV). States that participate in an expanded greenhouse gas market could dedicate some of the proceeds toward building upgrades.

45 Electrify buildings and vehicles

Photo: Ross Helen

The electrification of vehicles and buildings represents a tremendous opportunity to reduce our reliance on greenhouse gas emissions, in combination with a cleaner, modernized grid. Unfortunately, change has been slow. Upfront investment costs are high, and payback periods uncertain. A combination of financial incentives, policy mandates, and direct investments can help electric buildings and vehicles gain more widespread adoption.

Buildings and vehicles are the region's greatest sources of greenhouse gas emissions.

Buildings and vehicles account for the vast majority of greenhouse gas emissions in our region. Centralized electric-power generation is on a clear path toward cleaner and renewable fuels, but our homes and vehicles are stuck in the fossil fuel era. Nearly all vehicles burn gasoline, and nearly all homes and businesses are heated with either natural gas or heating oil.

Photo: paul bica

Energy standards for new buildings are high, but many buildings in our region are old—70 percent of all homes, for example, are more than 50 years old. Unless the buildings have been retrofitted, they are energy inefficient, and many burn heating oil, a more polluting source of heat than natural gas. The widespread adoption of electric furnaces and electric heat pumps has been hampered by high upfront costs and uncertain payoff periods.

Consumers have been slow to transition to electric cars because of higher upfront costs, different maintenance needs, and "range anxiety"—the concern drivers have about running out of power before reaching their destination. The upfront costs and logistics of building a comprehensive network of charging stations represents an additional hurdle. Sales are increasing, but the vehicles remain just a very small fraction of cars driven in the region.

Electrify the largest emitters of greenhouse gases: buildings and vehicles

Major policy shifts and investments are needed to reduce our region's greenhouse gas emissions from buildings and vehicles. In our region's cities, where residents drive less and live in older buildings, the focus should be on retrofitting and electrifying buildings, as the grid becomes cleaner and modernized. In the suburbs, where transportation represents a larger share of GHG emissions, the focus should be on promoting the wider adoption of electric vehicles.

To accelerate the pace and extent of electrification, state and city energy offices and regional transmission organizations should establish performance targets and track progress against them. States will also need to support the expansion of the electric systems needed to meet the energy needs of a more electrified future.

Cap greenhouse gas emissions on large, urban buildings

Sixty-seven percent of greenhouse gas emissions in New York City come from buildings, and about one-third of those building emissions are from burning fossil fuels for heat and hot water. Conserving energy by requiring more energy efficient building systems is important, but dramatic reductions in carbon emissions in the city will be possible only if we take steps to electrify buildings.

Transitioning heat and hot water systems to be powered by electricity instead of fossil fuels will evolve over a decade or more, as building systems age and need replacement. The public sector can help accelerate that transition.

The region's cities should measure the energy use and GHG emissions of every large building, and make the data publicly available, as New York City does already. A combination of tax credits, tax rebates, low-interest loans, and voluntary building-by-building targets for energy consumption and GHG emissions would encourage property owners to invest in retrofits. Ultimately, cities should be prepared to set and enforce hard caps on emissions.

Promote electric vehicles

Outside the region's cities, where residents typically drive to get around, and where homes are owned by individuals, not institutional entities, the key to GHG reductions lies in converting vehicles to cleaner fuels. Electric vehicles currently offer the greatest opportunity for that transition. Rapid innovations in batteries are making electric vehicles increasingly competitive, and sales are rising.

To address the higher purchase costs of electric vehicles, New York, New Jersey, and Connecticut should expand existing incentive programs, including purchase or lease rebates, exemption from sales and use taxes, access to carpool lanes, preferential parking, and lower rates on toll roads. States should provide incentives for the transportation industry, especially goods movement, to transition to electric vehicles as the technologies evolve. Public sector agencies with car fleets should convert them to EVs and invest in vehicle-charging infrastructure.

To make the use of electric vehicles more geographically flexible, public utilities commissions should partner with states, municipalities, utilities, and EV and charging infrastructure companies to plan for an extensive, cohesive, and competitive network of charging stations across the region. Planning should anticipate the emergence of fast-charging technology, and consider land-use opportunities and conflicts.

OUTCOMES

Electrifying vehicles and the heating systems of buildings as the grid becomes cleaner would lead to significant declines in greenhouse gas emissions, which would help to limit the consequences of climate change. It would also lead to greater demand for electricity from the grid and the need for additional energy supplies. Some of this could be offset through energy efficiency improvements. Energy planning should take this fuel switch into account, as investments into power supply are made. A more robust electric-vehicle charging network could help energy operators manage the load of the grid, as renewable energy could be stored in EV batteries.

PAYING FOR IT

Switching from combustion fuels to electricity would require significant investments in equipment and infrastructure. Mandated changes—such as building upgrades—would require upfront investments by building owners, which could see paybacks over time in lower energy bills. But it's possible that costs could be passed on to tenants. Governments can help to offset these costs through low-interest loans, as New York City has proposed with its announced efficiency mandates. Government would also need to dedicate funding to pay for incentive programs for electric vehicles, while—along with private companies—investing in the infrastructure to support the vehicles. Funds from an expanded greenhouse gas emissions market would help pay for some of these investments.

Make the region affordable for everyone

Wherever they choose to live in the region, people seek many of the same things: an affordable home, a good job within commuting distance, safe streets, a healthy environment, and good schools. Yet rising housing costs and stagnant incomes are making these qualities increasingly hard to find in one place. More and more, residents must make difficult decisions between an affordable home and a good school; a better job or a safe environment; a community they value or one from which they may get displaced.

We need complete communities that are healthy, welcoming, and enjoyable places to live—as well as affordable. Constructing more new homes, especially near transit stations, is only the first step to make the housing market more stable and affordable. We should also make sure all neighborhoods include homes that are affordable for low-income households, and that fair housing regulations are enforced. We must also encourage diversified job growth in cities and downtowns throughout the region, while maintaining New York City's position as a leading global city and economic powerhouse that offers opportunities for all.

PROVIDE AFFORDABLE HOUSING FOR ALL INCOMES, AGES, RACES, AND ETHNICITIES

The tri-state region suffers from a severe and growing housing crisis, due in part to stagnant earnings and rising housing costs. This has squeezed out middle-income families, while those with low incomes can face overcrowding, displacement, and homelessness. The region's legacy of discrimination and segregation has limited housing opportunities, especially for communities of color.

At the regional level, demand for housing far exceeds supply. The region needs more multifamily, affordable housing in every community, particularly near transit. A stable and rational housing market will require reforming zoning and financing rules to facilitate more transit-oriented and mixed-use development; allowing more two-family houses and accessory dwellings, and providing incentives for primary residences over secondary ones.

We must invest in public housing and increase subsidies to low-income people who cannot find homes in the private market. And we need to maintain diverse and mixed-income neighborhoods in all communities by requiring inclusionary zoning in every community, expanding and enforcing fair housing laws, and protecting people from unaffordable rent increases and displacement.

46 Protect low-income residents from displacement

The region's housing affordability crisis has put more than one million households at risk of being displaced from their homes. Cities and states must be more proactive in protecting economically vulnerable residents who have few options for affordable housing due to increasing housing costs. Policies to generate more permanently affordable and resident-controlled housing can increase wealth in lower-income communities. More supportive housing and better public housing, rent regulations, and legal aid for low-income renters would help protect people from unreasonable housing cost increases, displacement, and homelessness. Together, these policies would allow diverse, mixed-income communities to thrive.

Housing displacement is the most disruptive consequence of the region's affordability crisis.

In the metropolitan region, more than one million low- to moderate-income households are vulnerable to displacement. Most at risk are residents of pedestrian-friendly urban communities with good access to jobs and services.[68] As demand for homes in cities like New York, Jersey City, and Stamford push rents and sale prices upward, lower-income households are pushed outward. Even in cities with weaker housing markets—such as Trenton and Newburgh—where many live in substandard or even unhealthy homes, new investment is sometimes resisted by residents who fear gentrification and eventual displacement.

The result is low- to moderate-income households, 70 percent of them Black or Hispanic, are at risk from displacement. The current situation is largely the result of discriminatory policies over decades, such as unequal access to financing, restrictive covenants, and redlining that prohibited people of color from living in the region's new and desirable communities in the suburbs. Black and Hispanic families were largely confined to many of the urban areas that today are experiencing growth and reinvestment, and were also often prevented from owning homes and building equity and stability, thus making them vulnerable to the shifting forces of the housing market.

There is a clear link between increasing rents, displacement, and homelessness. In New York City, a 5 percent rent increase has been associated with an additional 3,000 residents becoming homeless.[69] The number of people experiencing homelessness in New York City—over 60,000—is among the highest in the country, having tripled over the last 20 years.

To reduce displacement and homelessness, build community wealth, produce and protect more affordable homes, and strengthen tenant protections

Ending the region's affordability crisis will ultimately require creating enough homes for all income levels. But a robust housing-construction strategy will take many years to achieve and could potentially increase rents in particular neighborhoods. To stabilize communities, we must preserve existing affordable housing, strengthen tenant and rent protections, and enable existing residents to capture more of the wealth created from rising property values.

Use government-owned land to create permanently affordable homes and build community wealth and stability

Community land trusts and limited-equity cooperatives are effective tools for producing healthy, affordable homes and stable neighborhoods. The Dudley Street Housing Development in Boston and the Cooper Square Mutual Housing Association in Manhattan are two successful examples of such shared-equity ownership structures.[70]

Municipalities at risk of rapid neighborhood change should conduct an inventory of publicly owned land and transfer the underused parcels to shared-equity ownership models, including community land trusts, community-owned limited equity cooperatives, community development corporations, and mutual housing asso-

ciations. When ownership opportunities are being created for lower-income residents, they should be accompanied by technical assistance from the municipality.

Collective ownership of housing provides an alternative to conventional home ownership and limits price increases due to speculation by making housing less of a commodity and taking profit out of the equation. Furthermore, by dividing the rights to the property between the homeowner and the community at large, shared-equity ownership models give households access to affordable home ownership and the ability to build wealth through real estate.

Community land trusts and limited-equity cooperatives also give communities—via a nonprofit steward—the ability to retain a long-term financial stake in the land, maintaining permanent affordability through land leases and deed restrictions that require it, and mitigating speculative market forces.

Invest in public housing as a critical element of public infrastructure

Public housing and other government-owned or controlled housing provide a stable source of permanent and deeply affordable homes for more than half a million people in the region. These homes are not only the best housing available for many of the region's poorest residents, they support complete communities with a range of incomes, backgrounds, jobs, and skills.

In many neighborhoods, public housing is often the only option for truly affordable housing. But this essential part of the region's housing market is at serious risk. Public housing authorities have been severely underfunded for decades, with declining support from both federal and state sources. Today, the region's public housing faces a capital budget shortfall of over $20 billion. The federal government, all three state governments, and their municipalities must recognize the lack of adequate public housing as a critical public infrastructure issue. They should dramatically increase the maintenance budgets for these valuable assets, and invest in the upgrades needed to raise public housing to modern standards and improve resilience to climate change.

Enable rent regulation to prevent sudden, sharp rent increases, and keep homes safe and healthy

Rent regulation is the most effective policy to mitigate unexpected increases in rents, especially for low-income residents, many of whom are unable to obtain housing stability through other means.

New Jersey and New York are two of only four states in the U.S. where at least some localities are able to regulate and limit rent increases. While some jurisdictions—most

Areas with residents at risk of displacement are geographically distributed across the region. But by and large, these areas are walkable neighborhoods with good access to jobs, with large concentrations of lower-income, Black, and Hispanic households.

Areas with residents at risk of displacement

Areas with residents at risk of displacement, with recent changes in pricing

Source: 2011-2015 American Community Survey; RPA & Conveyal Access to Jobs Analysis from Fragile Success, 2014; Walk Score®, 2014

Population by race and ethnicity by level of risk, 2015

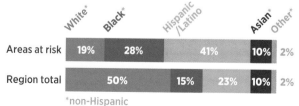

	White*	Black*	Hispanic /Latino	Asian*	Other*
Areas at risk	19%	28%	41%	10%	2%
Region total	50%		15%	23%	10%	2%

*non-Hispanic

Source: 2011-2015 American Community Survey; RPA Analysis

Burnside Avenue, Bronx NY

notably New York City, through its rent stabilization system—take advantage of this, many do not: Only 38 municipalities in New York and 90 municipalities in New Jersey have some form of rent regulations. States should be more proactive in strengthening—or in the case of Connecticut, enabling—rent regulations at the municipal level to cover all municipalities where displacement is a concern. These should include some limits on the amount, frequency, and timing of rent increases. They should also allow for the right to a renewal lease, require minimum services for tenants, limit the grounds under which tenants can be evicted to nonpayment of rent or violation of an existing lease, and protect tenants from harassment, as New York City has done.[71] At minimum, rental properties that receive any government subsidy should automatically be subject to rent regulations.

Strict enforcement of the housing maintenance code should accompany rent regulations in order to prevent landlords from displacing low-income tenants through lack of upkeep and proper maintenance. And when fines are not effective, municipalities should conduct the repairs proactively, with a foreclosable lien filed against the property. Funding for enforcement of the rent regulations and housing maintenance code is also critical.

Provide free legal counsel to those most at risk

Approximately 400,000 eviction actions take place each year southern New York State and central/northern New Jersey counties, with more than three-fourths in New York City and New Jersey's Essex, Hudson, and Middlesex counties. Even when tenants win in court, legal fees and lost wages from attending court often create a downward financial spiral, leading to more financial struggle, evictions, and often, homelessness.

Cities and counties, with state support, should provide free legal counsel to all economically vulnerable residents facing eviction. The cost of providing counsel would be at least partly offset by future savings from preventing homelessness and associated shelter costs, and from not needing to replace affordable housing that may be lost when a tenant is evicted. Free legal counsel would also help to enforce anti-harassment policies, such as those passed in New York City in 2017,[72] and prevent landlords from coercing tenants into leaving their home due to negligence or intimidation.

End homelessness

Homelessness in New York City has tripled over the last 20 years. On a per-capita basis, it trails only Washington, D.C., and Boston among major U.S. cities. But other parts of the

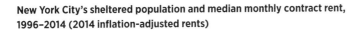

New York City's sheltered population and median monthly contract rent, 1996–2014 (2014 inflation-adjusted rents)

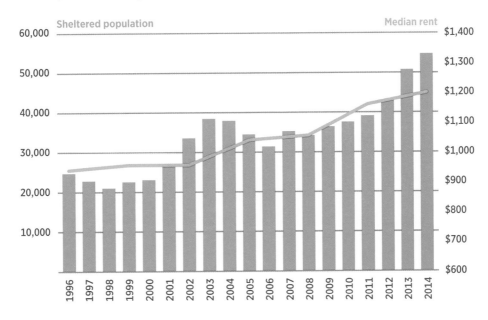

Source: U.S. Census American Community Survey and New York City Department of Homeless Services

region have made great progress in reducing, or even ending, homelessness. In 2017, Bergen County, NJ, became the first in the nation to end chronic homelessness, and the state of Connecticut has the lowest number of people experiencing homelessness on record.

We can end homelessness in the region with the right level of commitment and funding. Although the magnitude of the problem in New York City makes it more challenging, the following strategies can apply to the entire region.

Prevent people from losing their homes, and rapidly rehouse those who do

The leading causes of homelessness in both New York and New Jersey is eviction due to rising housing costs, overcrowding, and loss of a job.[73],[74] The most important intervention cities can take, therefore, is to prevent evictions, especially among working-poor households, and provide immediate help and rehousing when they do. Instituting better rent protections, providing free legal counsel to families facing eviction in court, and directing subsidies and housing assistance programs to low-income families who need it most are three strategies that could both help prevent people from losing their homes, and rapidly rehouse those who do.

As rents increase, so does the population in shelters.

Invest in supportive housing

Supportive housing, which combines deeply affordable housing with individualized social services to help support resident health and well-being should be provided to individuals and families who are coping with mental illness, trauma/abuse, substance abuse, chronic illness including HIV/AIDS, or otherwise may need additional support. Supportive housing programs significantly reduce the need for emergency medical services, police, jails, homeless shelters, and other publicly funded services.[75]

New York State has made progress on this front, building more than 50,000 units of supportive housing and recently committed to building another 35,000—but more is needed. All three states should expand or institute long-term agreements on funding and siting for supportive housing units, and should codify these into housing-agency budgets. Municipalities should adopt the "housing first" approach, which prioritizes providing people with permanent housing.

Both Bergen County and Connecticut run coordinated programs that are targeted at the community level. In Connecticut, the statewide Reaching Home Campaign includes representatives from the civic and public sectors focused on housing, health, education, job training, and food insecurity. By promoting the following policies, the campaign has significantly reduced homelessness throughout the state:

- Strengthening the state's housing delivery system through the expansion of affordable and supportive housing

- Retooling the crisis-response system

- Improving economic security through income growth and employment

- Coordinating healthcare and housing stability

They agree on three core values, modeled after the federal Opening Doors plan to end homelessness.

- Homelessness is unacceptable because it is solvable and preventable.

- There are no "homeless people," rather there are people who have lost their homes who deserve to be treated with dignity and respect.

- Homelessness is expensive for governments, and it is much more cost effective to invest in preventative and long-term solutions.

OUTCOMES

These actions will help maintain the current number of existing affordable housing units, which is the first priority in reducing displacement and homelessness. Creating more collectively owned and controlled, permanently affordable housing would provide an important source of housing at a much lower long-term cost to the public, while also generating wealth in low-income communities. Strengthened rent regulation would stabilize a significant percentage of the region's housing stock and help low- to middle-income renters manage their finances. Free legal counsel would protect those facing evictions due to price escalation, and promote income and racial diversity. Expanding supportive housing would result in higher-quality housing conditions, especially for the region's most vulnerable residents. Treating public housing as public infrastructure with sufficient funds for upgrades and proper maintenance would help preserve existing, deeply affordable housing.

PAYING FOR IT

The actions with the highest direct public costs would be investments to maintain public housing and expand supportive housing. In New York City alone, the cost of returning the public housing stock to a state of good repair is estimated to be $17 billion,[76] and the annual cost of managing and maintaining it at least $2.2 billion.[77] Consistent with funding streams for other needed public infrastructure, federal funding should remain the largest source of revenue for public housing—and it is imperative that the region's congressional representatives continue working to reverse the trend of declining federal support. States and cities will need to provide new revenue as well. New York City, for instance, is evaluating parking lots and other housing-authority property for mixed-use, mixed-income development that could both generate revenue to fix and maintain existing public housing and bring needed affordable housing, new jobs, and other services. The cost of expanded supportive housing would also be high, but would better serve this population while offsetting many other more expensive public services.

Creating permanent affordable housing on government land could be accomplished at a relatively low cost in places where local, county, or state governments own significant assets. But it would be higher in places where local governments and community organizations need to acquire public land, and where housing market demand is strong. The most cost-effective strategies should focus on neighborhoods where trusts can be established before prices escalate.

The cost of expanding rent regulation could range from very low (administrative costs of the expanded regulation plus enforcement) to moderate depending on structure (e.g., more expensive if additional subsidies are provided for new rent regulated apartments). Housing agencies will also need additional funding for enforcement. The main trade-off is rent regulation reduces turnover, making it more difficult to find an available apartment, and can subsidize higher-income residents; however, well-structured regulations can minimize these effects.

Free legal counsel could be fiscally neutral or positive when accounting for savings incurred from other government costs related to eviction, especially emergency shelter costs. In New York City, studies of the costs of providing free legal counsel for evictions have estimated municipal budget impacts from a $320 million surplus to a $203 million deficit.[78]

47 Strengthen and enforce fair housing laws

Although the tri-state region as a whole continues to be increasingly diverse, our communities are still some of the most segregated in America. Eradicating our legacy of racial and economic segregation will require both correcting the wrongs of the past and proactively protecting people of color from discrimination today. Expanding and enforcing fair housing policies, and encouraging multi-jurisdictional strategies to affirmatively further fair housing, will give all residents more housing opportunities and put the region on the path to success.

Fifty years after the Fair Housing Act, segregation in the region persists.

Even though housing discrimination and the mechanisms used to enforce it—including redlining, restrictive covenants, racial steering, and exclusionary zoning—have been outlawed since the 1960s, its legacy persists. Today, the New York region continues to rank as one of the most racially and economically segregated metropolitan areas in the United States. While racial and ethnic segregation in the region has decreased in the last two decades, segregation by income has increased.[79]

The federal Fair Housing Act makes it unlawful to refuse to sell or rent to someone on the basis of race, color, religion, sex, familial status, or national origin. Many communities in the tri-state region have adopted fair housing protections that go beyond those set by the federal government. New York, New Jersey, and Connecticut, for instance, extend fair housing protections to people based on sexual orientation and marital status. But other types of discrimination exist that are not protected by the rule of law.

Efforts to uncover housing discrimination—primarily through testing, where two people with identical financial profiles but of different races or other protected statuses attempt to rent the same apartment—have been inconsistent. Enforcement deters future discrimination, but the financial resources haven't been made available for consistent enforcement.

Strengthen, enforce, and build on fair housing laws

Racially, ethnically, and economically integrated regions lead to stronger economic growth, greater economic opportunity, better education outcomes, and more efficient housing markets.[80] Creating more affordable homes in all communities, especially those that currently have predominantly high-income households, is essential to promoting racially and economically diverse communities. But affordable housing policies won't end discrimination. We must also ensure that everyone regardless of race, ethnicity, source of income, and other characteristics, has access to housing choices.

Expand fair housing laws to prevent more types of discrimination

Even though the tri-state area generally has robust and expansive fair housing protections, gaps remain. New York State, for instance, should ban discrimination by source of income—currently, landlords can refuse to rent to families who rely on Section 8 and other housing vouchers. New York State should also ban discrimination on the basis of gender identity. New Jersey, Connecticut, and New York City have already adopted both of these protections.

New Jersey and Connecticut should institute protections against discrimination due to military service, as New York State has already done. Protections based on citizenship status, lawful occupation, and status as a victim of domestic violence have all been instituted by at least one of the region's states or major municipalities, and should be expanded throughout the region.

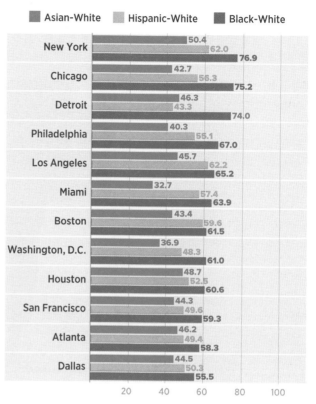

Index of dissimilarity, 2010
A higher number indicates higher segregation

The New York region is the most highly segregated major metropolitan area in the country.

Provide more resources for housing discrimination testing and fair lending practices

Housing discrimination testing is the single most effective way to prove housing discrimination and deter future discrimination by sellers and landlords. But it requires funding. States should dedicate appropriate resources for both testing and the necessary legal support. One source of funding could be the fines imposed on landlords and banks found guilty of discrimination.

Discrimination testing and enforcement should also be extended to include mortgage lenders. While redlining officially ended decades ago, redlining of a different sort takes place when lenders offer predatory financing to vulnerable people, leading to unsustainable debt and increased rates of foreclosure.

Source: New York State, New York City, Connecticut, and New Jersey legal code

Categories protected by city, state, and federal fair housing laws	Connecticut	New Jersey	New York City	New York State	Federal Law
Age	✓	✓	✓	✓	✓
Ancestry, nationality, or national origin	✓	✓	✓	✓	✓
Arrest or conviction history	✗	✗	✗	✗	✗
Citizenship status	✗	✗	✓	✗	✗
Color	✓	✓	✓	✓	✓
Creed/religion	✓	✓	✓	✓	✓
Disability	✓	✓	✓	✓	✓
Domestic status	✗	✓	✓	✗	✗
Family status	✓	✓	✓	✓	✓
Gender identity/expression	✓	✓	✓	✗	✗
Lawful occupation or source of income	✓	✓	✓	✗	✗
Marital status	✓	✓	✓	✓	✗
Military service	✗	✗	✗	✓	✗
Race	✓	✓	✓	✓	✓
Sex	✓	✓	✓	✓	✓
Sexual orientation	✓	✓	✓	✓	✗
Status as a victim of domestic violence, sexual assault, or stalking	✗	✗	✓	✗	✗

Fair housing protections vary by state and locality—and several gaps remain.

Assist cities, towns, and villages in meeting Affirmatively Furthering Fair Housing goals and obligations

In 2015, the Supreme Court found that fair housing laws apply when policies result in disparate impacts, even when there was no explicit discriminatory intent. For example, if town zoning makes it unreasonably difficult to build housing that low-income renters can afford, it could be in violation of the fair housing law even if it cannot be proven that it was intended to discriminate.

Municipalities are required to abide by this legal ruling, but implementation would be far more effective if regional entities provided resources, technical expertise, and leadership. Coordinating land-use policies across municipal boundaries, supporting affordable housing with transportation and other investments, and ensuring police, schools, and other services support fair housing goals are all important, but cannot be implemented by individual towns and villages. Counties, regional councils of government, and metropolitan planning organizations are positioned to lead these efforts and help use the growing number of tools and best practices available to municipalities. States should also provide incentives for municipalities to implement these plans through grants and aid that prioritize inter-municipal collaboration and require meeting federal AFFH obligations.

Incentivize housing that leads to economic and racial integration

Moving forward, homes in the region need to be affordable to a range of residents, and built in a range of communities. In places with high real estate values, inclusionary zoning is the most effective tool to promote the construction of affordable housing.

In fact, states should prioritize inclusionary zoning provisions and fair housing enforcement in the upper-income neighborhoods and places with a history of exclusionary practices. Any available affordable homes in those communities should be marketed to a wide range of potential homebuyers to ensure a diverse applicant pool and promote more diversity in the community.

OUTCOMES

By 2040, the tri-state region should be one of the least, rather than most, segregated metropolitan areas in the nation. Every city, town, village, and county in the region would have an effective plan in place to affirmatively further fair housing. Greater racial and economic integration should lead to stronger economic growth as education and labor market outcomes improve in a region that fulfills its promise of equal opportunity and upward mobility.

PAYING FOR IT

Strengthening fair housing laws would cost the public little. Better enforcement through testing and oversight would incur costs, although they can be at least partially funded by landlords and financiers who have been found guilty of discrimination. While directing housing subsidies toward wealthier areas with higher land costs can add expense, land-use policies that leverage affordable housing, such as inclusionary zoning, generally receive less from subsidies in higher-market areas than in lower-market ones.

④⑧ Remove barriers to transit-oriented and mixed-use development

Photo: ORG Permanent Modernity

Land-use, tax, and financing restrictions are preventing construction of the types of housing the region needs in order to bring down the high cost of living. To expand the number of affordable homes while creating healthier, more attractive, and energy-efficient neighborhoods, we need to lift arbitrary density limits in the urban core, allow multifamily homes in more suburban downtowns, end the warehousing of vacant land that could be used for development, and reform federal rules that inhibit mixed-use development.

Outdated policies restrict home building in the right places.

Property tax policy and zoning and financing restrictions often make it difficult to build more homes where it makes sense—for instance, in walkable or potentially walkable neighborhoods near mass transit. Instead, locations with easy transit connections to job centers are used for part-time parking. Places that could become vibrant mixed-use districts that provide jobs and urban amenities are limited to residential uses, with any kind of shopping or other excursions requiring car trips. And in our region's core, artificial restrictions limit both housing and commercial space in places where they are needed and the market could support them.

Lift restrictions to encourage new homes and mixed-use development with good access to jobs

All levels of government need to be part of the solution. Municipal, state, and federal regulations need to encourage multifamily and mixed-use development in places with transit and other infrastructure to support it.

Allow for multifamily and mixed-used development in proximity to all train stations, especially on sites currently used for parking

Local zoning regulations often restrict multifamily development in places it would make the most sense—near mass transit, and where less parking would be needed for the new homes. By proactively zoning for multifamily, mixed-use development near rail stations, we can create the sort of walkable, transit-oriented communities that are in demand today and needed for the future. Throughout the region, an estimated 263,000 new homes could be built with well-designed, appropriately scaled housing on unbuilt land within a half mile of commuter rail stations. While this is primarily the responsibility of the region's 782 municipalities, states should provide planning assistance to encourage municipalities to allow more multifamily and mixed-use development near stations.

Reform federal financing mechanisms to allow for easier mixed-use development

Federal insurance and financing programs through the Department of Housing and Urban Development, the Federal Housing Administration, Fannie Mae, and Freddie Mac are used in the vast majority of new housing development. But restrictions on the proportion of commercial space and income allowed in these developments often don't allow for the type of two- or three-story mixed-use development that is common to the region's smaller downtowns—and needed in commercial strips and near transit. Federal regulations should be changed to allow for this type of mixed-use development.

Allow for more homes to be built in the region's core by lifting the arbitrary state cap on residential development

New York State law currently does not allow residential floor area on any site in the state to exceed 12 times the lot area, despite new commercial buildings and residential development in converted New York City office buildings often being twice this density or more. This restriction keeps New York City from growing its housing stock in denser areas near transit and amenities. It also precludes the city from creating more affordable homes and economically integrated neighborhoods through the city's Inclusionary Housing program, which requires low- and medium-income homes in new housing developments on upzoned parcels.

Allow more storefront-retail and community-facility uses on major thoroughfares, and make it easier to convert ground floor space to commercial or community-facility usage

Storefront commercial and community usage brings jobs, amenities, and street vitality to a neighborhood. On many main thoroughfares, however, storefront commercial usage is prohibited, leading to dead streets, fewer shopping options for residents, and higher rents for commercial space overall. Storefronts should be allowed wherever the market will support it and sufficient street space exists, and where surrounding density can ensure a walkable community without adding to traffic or parking. Other structures that abut sidewalks on major thoroughfares, such as garages, should be allowed to convert to commercial usage as well.

Change tax policy for vacant land, with a phased-in rate based on potential valuation instead of current use

It can be more lucrative for landowners to warehouse vacant land, waiting for rising prices in hot neighborhoods to peak, while still paying very little in property taxes. This means residents must live next to eyesores instead of homes, shops, or community spaces. And it reduces the number of available sites to develop in rising markets, which in turn constricts housing supply and further drives up land prices. States should allow cities to innovate with phased-in revaluations of property taxes on vacant land to reflect their potential value if developed. This would encourage home construction and job creation, and help solve our housing crisis by turning civic liabilities into assets.

OUTCOMES

Removing these restrictions would lead to hundreds of thousands of new homes over the next two decades in walkable neighborhoods with access to jobs, schools, stores, and other necessities. This would not only bring down the cost of housing, but would also reduce the cost of transportation by letting more people walk or take the train or bus to their destinations. Expanding housing choices and creating new commercial space would help accommodate a growing and changing population, and attract the workforce needed for a vibrant economy. Since this construction will either take place in, or lead to, walkable neighborhoods, it will reduce automobile usage and improve the environment and health of millions of people in the region.

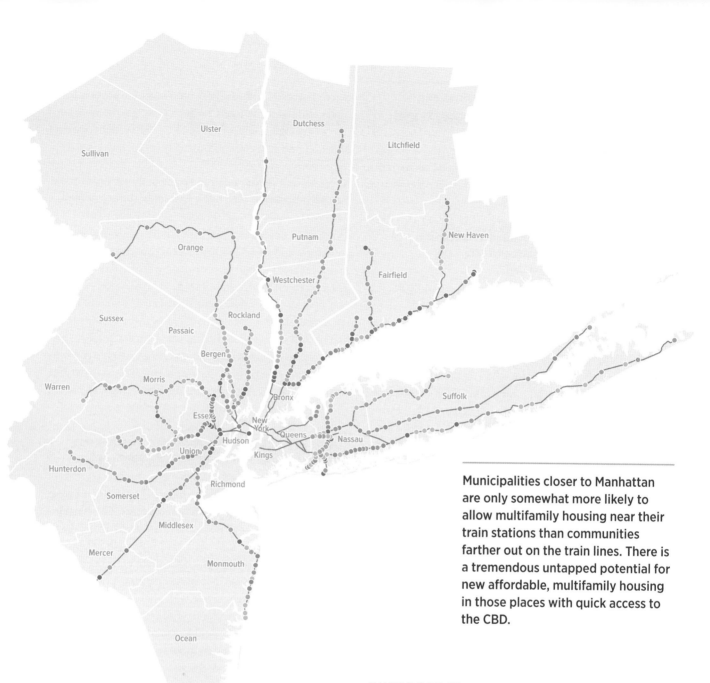

Municipalities closer to Manhattan are only somewhat more likely to allow multifamily housing near their train stations than communities farther out on the train lines. There is a tremendous untapped potential for new affordable, multifamily housing in those places with quick access to the CBD.

PAYING FOR IT

Implementing these recommendations would produce significantly more revenue than costs for the cities, towns, and villages that enact them. By allowing and encouraging development in places where the market can support it, development costs would mainly be incurred by the private sector. This would lead to increased public revenue through property taxes, and to a lesser extent, local sales taxes through added economic activity and commercial space. Job growth through more construction and commercial activity would also mean increased wages, which adds to revenue and economic activity.

Allowing for significantly more development throughout the region, especially small- and medium-construction projects should also encourage more business development among contractors and subcontractors, thereby increasing competition and ultimately lowering construction costs. The vacant land tax would also lower land costs.

Commuter-rail station areas with:

- Multifamily not allowed
- Minimal multifamily allowed
- Moderately multifamily friendly
- Mostly multifamily friendly
- Data not available

Source: RPA

Photo: ORG Permanent Modernity

49 Increase housing supply without constructing new buildings

Demand for housing far outstrips supply, but local regulations and the high cost of construction limit the production of new housing. What few people realize, however, is that half a million homes could be added to our housing supply without laying one new brick. Revising zoning regulations to legalize two-family homes and other accessory dwelling units, incentivizing the subdivision of overly large housing units, and encouraging the year-round use of units could make a significant dent in the region's housing crisis at low cost.

Archaic regulations prevent the creation of new homes, even when they don't require new construction.

The region faces a severe housing shortage, yet many communities continue to oppose the creation of new homes. Even simple measures to allow more people to live in the housing structures that already exist can be unpopular. Zoning codes prevent single-family homes—even large ones—to be converted to two- or three-family homes. Spaces above garages, on ground floors, or in attics of houses could be converted to small apartments—for an elderly parent, a care provider, or a renter—but that is not allowed. Regulations also fail to encourage vacant apartments from being rented in urban neighborhoods. In Manhattan, where demand for housing is the highest, many homes go unoccupied most of the year as their owners have primary residences elsewhere.

The region needs to create more than two million homes over the next 25 years to relieve our housing shortage and accommodate new residents. Yet we do not allow new homes to be created, even when they don't require new construction.

Add half a million new homes to the region's housing supply without constructing one new building

Regulations should be revised to allow more homes to be created in each housing structure, particularly in single family homes. New incentives can be used to discourage using real estate as investment vehicles and leaving apartments empty in the midst of a severe housing shortage. With these changes in place, there is potential to house more than a million new residents without building a single new house or apartment. What's more, these new homes could provide some diversity to the housing mix—creating housing that is more affordable in otherwise expensive communities. They could also be helpful in providing a convenient place to live for the growing elderly population who want to stay near family, and to low-income families and young adults looking to be first-time home buyers.

Make it easy and cost-efficient to convert single-family homes to two-family homes, and legalize accessory dwelling units

Zoning should be reformed such that every single-family dwelling is allowed a second dwelling unit if it meets appropriate fire and building codes. Other accessory dwelling units should be allowed by reforming rules related to light, air, relation to ground level, and other laws and regulations that do not affect safety, while retaining strict safety and housing quality measures appropriate for modern life. Approximately 100,000 new homes could be added in New York City alone by instituting these reforms, and potentially up to 300,000 throughout the region.

Institute a pied-à-terre tax in municipalities with a low vacancy rate

In counties with rental vacancy rates under 5 percent— where there is a housing emergency—a property tax surcharge should be implemented on all residences that are not a primary residence of a household paying local income tax, in order to incentivize primary use of housing.

In these counties alone, there are approximately 125,000 houses or apartments that are vacant and habitable, but kept

Potential number of new homes

Allowing single-family houses to have second dwellings would greatly help our housing shortage. If 10 percent of single- and two-family houses had another dwelling, it would add over 300,000 homes across the region, including in places with significant housing shortages like Long Island.

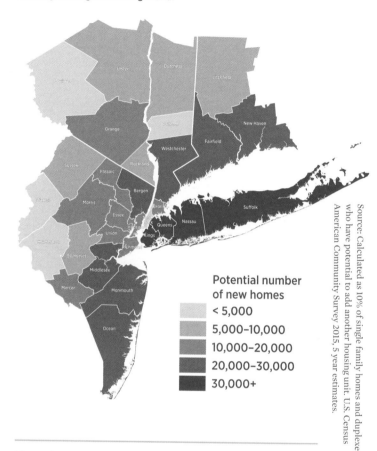

Potential number of new homes
- < 5,000
- 5,000–10,000
- 10,000–20,000
- 20,000–30,000
- 30,000+

Source: Calculated as 10% of single family homes and duplexes who have potential to add another housing unit. U.S. Census American Community Survey 2015, 5 year estimates.

More than 60,000 apartments in New York City alone are vacant but not on the housing market because they are second homes, pied-a-terres, or used for short-term rentals. The more of these units that are put back on the market, the more it will help our housing crunch, especially in Manhattan.

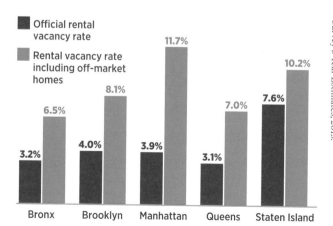

- Official rental vacancy rate
- Rental vacancy rate including off-market homes

	Bronx	Brooklyn	Manhattan	Queens	Staten Island
Official	3.2%	4.0%	3.9%	3.1%	7.6%
Including off-market	6.5%	8.1%	11.7%	7.0%	10.2%

Source: U.S. Census American Community Survey 5 Year Estimates, 2015.

Image: ORG Permanent Modernity for the Fourth Regional Plan

Reforming the zoning regulations that prevent owners from renting out part of their home could generate hundreds of thousands of new, affordable homes—with little new construction. Local suburban streets could also be transformed to prioritize neighborhood activities instead of cars.

off the market for occasional use as pied-a-terres or second homes. (About half of those are in New York City and half in other counties.) Another 140,000 units are habitable but kept off the market for other reasons. If just half of all these empty units were put back on the market, it would add as much new housing as is built in two years regionwide.

Disincentivize overly large residences near train stations and in the urban core through zoning, tax, and building code reform

Multifamily housing is most needed in areas within walking distance of mass transit in the urban core. Yet we have over six square miles of land near transit where zoning rules only allow single-family homes. These regulations should be changed to allow for multifamily housing in both new and existing homes. Homes in these districts in excess of 2,500 square feet should also be treated as more than one unit for property tax purposes (e.g., a 10,000 square-foot home should be treated as four 2,500 square-foot homes). Building codes could also require large units to install kitchen and bathroom fixtures as if they were several smaller units, to enable easier subdivision when market conditions allow. Co-op- and condo-law reform should also be explored in order to legalize and ease conversions to several smaller apartments. Reforms to building codes to allow smaller units and co-housing situations should continue and be expanded.

Reform short-term letting policy

Short-term letting, meaning renting or subletting out apartments for short periods of time generally utilizing platforms such as Airbnb, should be regulated with a policy of one apartment allowed per host, which would have to be at an address where the host has their primary residence and pays local income tax (if applicable). This would include two- and three-family homes, where a landlord would not be allowed to rent out units that are not their primary residence on a short-term basis. In addition, the amount of time people can rent out apartments should be limited.

These reforms would have the effect of largely limiting short-term rentals to times when an apartment would have otherwise been vacant, as opposed to taking potential permanent housing off the market for the sole purpose of generating income through hotel-like short-term rentals. More specific rules should be established for public housing, other subsidized housing, rent-stabilized apartments,

and cooperative and condominium housing. New York City, in conjunction with either the region or other large destination cities, could also explore establishing its own platform to more efficiently regulate short-term letting, and lower costs for hosts.

OUTCOMES

Hidden housing can make more homes available at little cost, provide income for homeowners, and allow residents to stay in their communities. Approximately 500,000 homes could be added to the housing inventory without any additional major construction. These homes would likely be more affordable than newly built housing. For the most part, accessory dwellings are less expensive than main housing units, and smaller units are less expensive than larger units.

In addition, many of these homes would be produced in desirable, walkable urban areas that have good urban infrastructure and few opportunities for newly constructed affordable housing. Both pied-à-terre units converted to permanent housing and units used for short-term rentals converted to residential usage are likely to be in denser, more desirable urban areas.

PAYING FOR IT

These policies would increase tax revenues with few direct public costs. Allowing accessory dwelling units would have a cost of added regulation and enforcement, but increased property tax revenue from the additional value they provide would more than offset this cost. A tax on non-primary residences would generate revenue for the city. Reforms to disincentivize overly large units in favor of smaller units would also allow for more property tax revenue. Reforming short-term letting would have a cost on existing owner/renters who benefit from the practice, as well as a small municipal cost in added enforcement. All of these policies would allow for more densification of areas with existing infrastructure, which lowers costs of infrastructure improvements overall throughout the region. There would, however, need to be targeted infrastructure investment in the areas that would add a large amount of population through these reforms.

Build affordable housing in all communities across the region

Photo: David Sundberg

Many towns and villages in the region do not allow the construction of sorely needed affordable, multifamily housing in locations with access to good schools and jobs. A requirement that a share of all units in new multifamily developments be affordable is a key part of an overall strategy to address poverty, expand economic opportunity and reduce segregation. New York, New Jersey and Connecticut should approve legislation mandating inclusionary zoning in all municipalities, provide strong incentives for municipalities to jettison outmoded rules that prohibit the development of multifamily housing in certain areas, and enforce overall targets for affordable housing in municipalities.

The tri-state region is one of the least affordable and most segregated metropolitan areas in the U.S.

More than one out of every five households in the region pays more than half of their income for housing, and most of these households have low or very moderate incomes. With rents rising virtually everywhere across the tri-state area, there are fewer places where these families and individuals can afford to live. It is particularly difficult, and often virtually impossible, to find an affordable home where the schools are good, the streets are safe, and jobs are accessible by public transit.

This affordability crisis accentuates the deep divides by income and race that stymie opportunities for many poor, especially Black and Hispanic residents, to get ahead, and limits the economic potential of the region as a whole. In spite of our diversity, the region is one of the most segregated metropolitan areas in the United States.[81] A contributing factor is that many places still restrict the creation of apartments and townhouses—home types that are generally more affordable than single-family houses. Even when these are permitted, development that includes subsidized housing is often fiercely resisted by existing residents. These regulations exclude poor and even moderate-income residents. Since lower-income residents are disproportionately people of color, and because of previous policies like redlining and restrictive covenants, limited zoning regulations that allow only single-family houses or make no provisions for affordable housing also perpetuate racial and ethnic segregation.

Use inclusionary zoning to address segregation while creating more affordable homes

Inclusionary zoning is a policy that requires new multifamily housing construction to include some low- and moderate-income homes. An effective way to create more affordable homes, inclusionary zoning plays a critical role in creating more mixed-income housing and neighborhoods. New York City now requires affordable homes as part of every new housing development, but only in a few parts of the city—specifically, areas that have in recent times been rezoned to create more housing.

Outside of New York City, almost 100 municipalities in our region, and hundreds more across the country, have adopted some type of inclusionary zoning, but these vary widely and have no clear or consistent definitions or minimum standards across jurisdictions. On average, municipalities which have these policies in the region are lower-income, and therefore offer fewer opportunities for affordable housing in communities where there are resources to support high-quality schools, parks, transportation and other sources of well-being and opportunity.

To be fair and effective, inclusionary zoning needs to be applied throughout the region

To promote mixed-income, diverse communities, inclusionary zoning needs to apply in affluent as well as low and middle-income jurisdictions. Regulations can and should be flexible enough to apply to the needs of each community, existing neighborhood characteristics, incomes and market conditions. It does mean, however, that New York, New Jersey and Connecticut will need to enact legislation to:

- Allow multifamily housing near all train stations as-of-right, making it easier, faster and more cost-effective to build this type of housing.

- Develop and enforce minimum thresholds for affordable housing for every municipality (or sub-municipality in the case of larger cities), with enforcement policies

such as local zoning overrides for affordable housing or mixed-income developments.

- Ensure that new housing construction in every municipality provides specified shares of low- and moderate-income housing that is affordable to households that would otherwise be excluded from the neighborhood; that minimum acceptable standards be applied; and that similar definitions of terms and enforcement mechanisms be used.

These three components will encourage substantially greater production of new homes, especially mixed-income housing, thereby increasing development opportunities while reducing racial and economic neighborhood segregation.

To maximize the amount of affordable housing, prioritize its location in higher-income areas, and respond to local conditions, municipalities and states should adopt these policies:

- **Give developers options to make projects financially feasible across a range of market conditions.** These options should be structured to encourage more market and moderately priced homes in low-income neighborhoods needing investment, and build more low-income homes in high-income neighborhoods. This structure also enables more growth across the board, by leveraging the market in high-income areas while not overly depressing it in lower-market areas.

- **Set minimum thresholds for the share of low-to-moderate income homes at 15 percent to 30 percent.** While specifics should vary depending on the local market, lower minimums should generally be set for projects providing homes for low- and very low-income households, and higher thresholds for projects providing homes for moderate income households.

- **Encourage homeownership for moderate-to-middle income households by prioritizing owner-occupied units when developing middle- income homes pursuant to inclusionary zoning laws.** This can be especially important to help stabilize neighborhoods and give existing residents a means to benefit from rising property values.

- **Limit options for building affordable homes off-site, or paying into a fund that supports affordable units at off-site locations.** Allowing developers to buy out of their requirement to build affordable units within their proposed development perpetuates segregation and often leads to poorer quality, poorly maintained affordable units. However, if offsite land is cheaper it may result in the ability to build more affordable homes while main-

Require mixed-income development

Allow multifamily development as-of-right

Affordable housing in all communities

Set affordability targets by municipality

OUTCOMES

The success of new policies requiring low- and moderate-income homes will be measured by the number of affordable homes that are created and the degree to which it reduces segregation by creating mixed-income communities. Combined with other strategies to increase the construction of multifamily homes and preserve existing affordable housing, the region could produce more than half a million new affordable homes in high-income neighborhoods by 2040.[83] This would increase the share of homes affordable to low-income households, help stabilize gentrifying neighborhoods and expand opportunities to live in neighborhoods with good schools and healthy environments.

PAYING FOR IT

Inclusionary zoning can be implemented without government funds beyond the cost of administering and enforcing the program. Rather, it cross-subsidizes homes at below market rents and prices with a portion of the market value of a development project. New rules to allow larger multifamily developments and reduce time and costs of construction would help offset the added costs of providing the affordable homes. In cases where it does not, the cost of subsidizing the below market housing will be borne either in reduced profits to the developer or by delaying construction until the market improves. Government subsidies can also be utilized if the regulation requires more affordable units or lower rents than the market units can support. Ideally, inclusionary zoning should be combined with an effective subsidy policy. Long term, the added costs from the required affordability will result in lower land costs than would have been in place without these requirements.

The major risks are that requirements will be either too weak, and result in little affordable housing and neighborhood desegregation, or so stringent and inflexible that it depresses the housing market long-term. The major limitation is that it is difficult to provide significant and deep housing affordability without government subsidy. Even in strong housing markets, there is a limit to how much projects can internally subsidize low-income housing. Inclusionary zoning cannot solve the problem of housing affordability on its own, but it is an effective strategy for creating mixed-income housing in affluent communities, and expanding housing options for existing residents in gentrifying neighborhoods.

taining a financially feasible development. The cost of buying out of onsite affordability through a cash payment or constructing off-site housing should be set significantly higher than it is currently, in order to make sure that the number of new affordable homes created outweighs the benefits of creating mixed-income, onsite housing developments.

- **Implement inclusionary zoning in tandem with stronger state incentives and assistance for municipalities to develop multifamily homes in appropriate locations.** These homes can range from accessory apartments in one and two-family homes to large apartment buildings near transit hubs. Planning grants and technical assistance should be provided to assist municipalities, and state infrastructure funding should be contingent on municipalities enacting zoning to allow multifamily housing in appropriate locations.[82]

Each state has different contexts to build on:

- In New Jersey, statewide inclusionary zoning would complement a state housing plan that sets affordable housing targets for each municipality.

- Connecticut requires towns and cities to allow developments with affordable housing if the municipality currently has less than 10 percent low-income housing. Inclusionary zoning would reduce litigation, speed approvals and expand the number of mixed-income projects.

- Inclusionary zoning would be a major step forward in New York State, and needs to include affordable housing goals for municipalities and a provision that requires municipalities to accept new development that makes progress toward these affordability goals.

51 Make all housing healthy housing

Photo: Adam Weiss

The region's aging housing stock and housing-affordability crisis means that many families, especially low-income families, live in substandard housing that can cause or exacerbate poor health. Policy makers struggle to respond to these problems, as enforcement of building codes is spotty and funding streams are minimal and highly fragmented. To improve the health of residents regardless of income, cities and counties in the region need to invest in their building data systems, conduct more proactive inspections, and look for ways to pool funding in order to make our region's housing stock healthier.

Many low-income people in the region live in homes that are detrimental to their health.

The tri-state area has the oldest housing stock in the nation, with more than half of all homes built before 1960. While some older homes are still in good condition, a combination of disinvestment, absentee landlords, the deterioration of facilities, and lax housing code enforcement have led to high levels of indoor air pollutants, heavy metals, and mold. These conditions can contribute to diseases, such as asthma and lead poisoning—one in 50 children tested in the region suffer from high lead levels—which are more prevalent in low income communities.

Unfortunately, addressing health hazards in homes is done reactively. Remediation often occurs only after an individual health condition has been identified—that is, after renters have complained or gotten sick. Even worse is when renters fail to complain, despite a hazardous condition, because of a language barrier, or because they fear angering their landlord and compromising their housing situation.

Areas with high poverty rates and old buildings

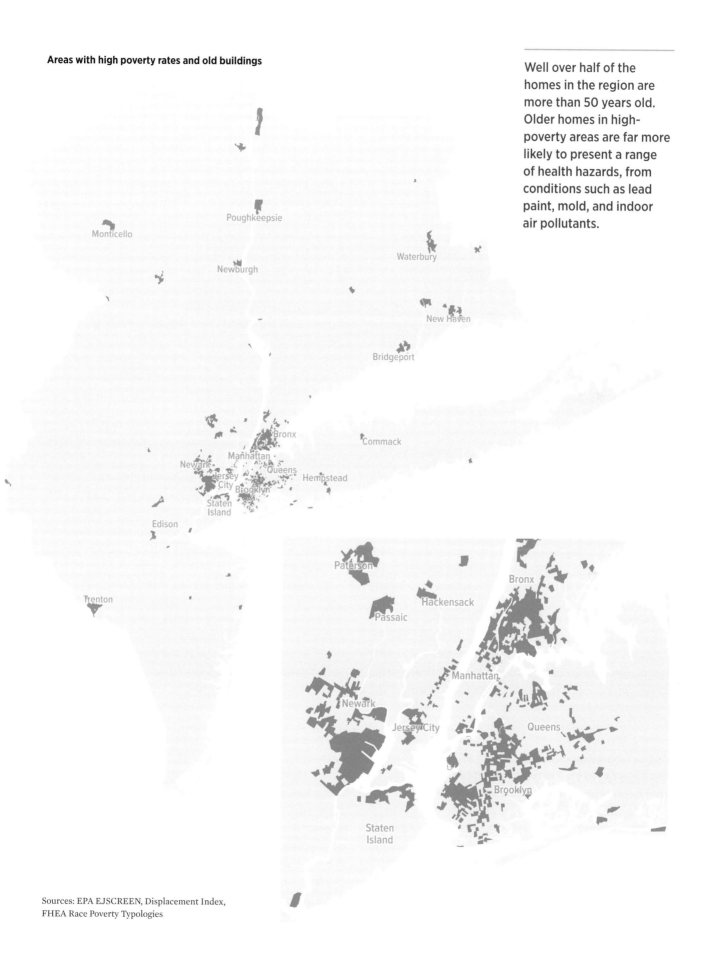

Well over half of the homes in the region are more than 50 years old. Older homes in high-poverty areas are far more likely to present a range of health hazards, from conditions such as lead paint, mold, and indoor air pollutants.

Sources: EPA EJSCREEN, Displacement Index,
FHEA Race Poverty Typologies

Addressing health hazards in the home is also hampered by the fact that responsibility for housing issues and funding are divided among agencies. Buildings departments are typically responsible for overall building conditions. Tracking health data like blood lead levels is the responsibility of public health agencies. And energy efficiency programs, which can improve health conditions, are frequently led by state energy agencies.

Improve people's health and reduce costs with proactive monitoring of hazards

Improving housing quality can bring enormous benefits to residents health as well as the economy. One study estimates that replacing lead-paint windows in the estimated one million U.S. homes that need it would cost between $1.2 billion and $11 billion. But the avoided health impacts would save the overall economy between $181 billion and $269 billion.[84] For that to happen, however, requires moving from haphazard to regular and more frequent monitoring.

Routinely inspect homes in at-risk neighborhoods

States or counties should provide the tools and technical assistance for localities to implement Proactive Rental Inspection (PRI) programs in at-risk neighborhoods—neighborhoods with older housing stock and low market rents, where landlords may not have many incentives to keep their properties in good upkeep. By periodically inspecting all rental properties, PRI programs relieve renters from initiating complaints, and avoid problems with absentee landlords. PRIs can also make inspections more efficient by combining inspection types, and collecting data on housing stock. In New York State, the Integrated Property Needs Assessment provides a model for integrating inspections for energy efficiency improvements and health hazards. Establishing a PRI program should involve renter organizations and landlords to make sure all needs are being accommodated.

Update technology and sensors to alert health departments and maintain up-to-date information

Health inspectors should follow a standard format for documenting the health and safety history of housing units in order to facilitate comparison over time and across city boundaries, and data should be published online. Sensors installed in homes can make inspections more accurate by continually monitoring air and water quality, and ensuring that problems are addressed before a health problem arises. Investment in sensor technology is crucial to develop low-cost, accurate models to monitor hazards such as mold, for which no technology now exists.

Build health requirements into city, state and federal housing grants and streamline the application process for remediating health hazards

Healthy home standards should be built into requirements for low income housing tax credits, tax exemptions for residential developments, and other housing grants and subsidies. Hospitals submitting community benefit plans under the Affordable Care Act should also be evaluated for how these plans improve housing quality. In addition, application requirements for remediation should be made more flexible to make it easier for landlords and tenants to apply for funding to remediate hazards. Standardized requirements for healthy homes will help establish codes and inspections that cover all key health components rather than singular hazards.

OUTCOMES

In the short term, streamlined inspection processes will produce better data that will enable more effective identification of the most burdened households, and as a result, more housing improvements. In the longer term, up to date inspection systems will make it easier to identify hazards and quickly reduce exposure to unhealthy conditions.

By 2040, lead and other leading health hazards should be eliminated from the region's housing stock, with priority placed on the neighborhoods with the highest rates of related disease and health conditions. Just as states and municipalities set goals for carbon emissions, traffic deaths and other environmental and health conditions, they should set and meet targets for the eliminating residential health hazards.

PAYING FOR IT

Streamlining inspection processes can result in better use of existing funding, but routine inspections will likely require some additional funding. Upfront investments in sensors and technology could reduce long-term remediation needs. A more holistic approach to housing quality can also create a better business case for increasing funding, whether from municipal budgets, hospital community benefits or energy efficiency grants.

52 Reform housing subsidies

The tri-state region, and especially New York City, produces a considerable amount of affordable housing through the use of public money, such as tax-exempt bonds, tax exemptions, and direct subsidy. But they are not always used in the most efficient way. These subsidies should be targeted toward meeting the greatest housing needs, such as very low-income rental housing, first-time homeownership, and affordable homes in high-opportunity neighborhoods. In many cases, a bidding process should be created to prioritize subsidizing developments that create the most high-need housing for the least amount of subsidy.

Existing subsidy programs can be used far more effectively than they are today.

The key to creating enough affordable housing to sustain a broad middle-class is to build enough homes to create a rational housing market, although the main housing needs of the region are at the extremely low income levels, for whom the market alone has no history and no expectation of providing affordable housing. There are over a million renting households in the region making under $20,000 a year—an income too low not only to find housing on the open market, but also to be eligible for government workforce housing programs such as the Low Income Housing Tax Credit. But there are only about 670,000 apartments that are part of programs where tenants are guaranteed to pay only what they can afford, and can be expected to be affordable to very low-income households, such as Public Housing, Housing Choice Vouchers, and HUD 202 Senior Housing.

There is, however, a robust government sector dedicated to subsidizing new and existing homes. In New York City, there has been an explicit municipal commitment to building 5,000 to 8,000 government-subsidized homes every year for nearly three decades, and almost all new rental housing has used tax exemptions as a partial financing tool. Elsewhere in the region, tax-exempt bonds and low-income housing and historic tax credits account for a significant amount of new housing—up to 40 percent of all construction in some counties. Even more money is spent to preserve affordable homes, provide emergency shelter for the homeless, and support low-income people with housing subsidies through public housing or vouchers. Because so many homes require large subsidies, this government-sponsored housing is a de facto part of our housing market.

While additional funding is needed, particularly from the federal government, existing subsidies can be used far more effectively than they are today.

Subsidies should target housing that cannot be produced by the private market.

Government money should be used to create the type of housing not created by the market instead of for uses the market can or should do unsubsidized. This includes all types of subsidy, whether it comes from tax exemptions, capital dollars, or other sources. Every form of subsidy should be more fair and transparent, and support greater efficiency in both the public and private sectors.

Move subsidies toward preventing homelessness and housing the lowest-income New Yorkers

Capital dollars should be channeled toward low-income rental subsidies, housing-court help, senior and supportive housing, and permanently affordable housing for people who have the least amount of market choice. Rental subsidies have consistently been shown to be the most effective means of housing low-income households and

preventing homelessness.[85] Construction overall should be stimulated by loosening the zoning envelope and allowing for more development opportunities, not by using government subsidy to attempt to outbid the private market for a constrained amount of housing construction opportunities. Numeric goals for building and preserving affordable housing units should be ended in favor of a qualitative, not quantitative, approach that focuses on reducing overall rent burdens and housing expenses across the board. A health impact assessment on housing subsidies could help identify the highest priority investments.

Put all subsidies through a competitive process

The most efficient housing subsidies, such as 9 percent tax credits, are put through a competitive process for a limited pool of money. However, most tax subsidies and some capital subsidies are as-of-right, with no ability to funnel money to the most deserving projects, and in the case of tax exemptions, no ability to ultimately cap the cost of the subsidy. Bidding on subsidies would both provide budget stability for states and municipalities, and ensure government dollars are used most efficiently. This could also be expanded to tax subsidies for economic-development projects.

Target middle-income housing programs to home ownership, not rental housing

Although subsidies should be targeted at those most in need, there are cases when it may make sense to spend a limited about of money to incentivize middle-income housing as well. The lack of supply at middle-income ranges is, however, for home ownership, not rental housing, and incentives should be targeted accordingly. Not having middle-income homeownership also leads middle-income households into entering the rental market, where they are often able to outbid lower-income households for the available rental housing, therefore reducing the affordable rental stock. And in areas needing revitalization, the stability provided by homeownership is of more value in this effort, as is the likelihood these programs will attract middle-income buyers.

Five largest FY2017 New York City real property tax expenditure programs (millions)

421-a New Multiple Dwellings	$1,319
Industrial & Commercial Incentive Program	$653
New York City Housing Authority	$649
Co-op/Condo Abatement	$487
Urban Development Corporation	$318

Source: New York City Department of Finance, "Annual Report on Tax Expenditures," 2017

Households that can afford most rentals in the region find buying a home far more difficult.

Percentage of rentals vs. homeownership affordable to households making $100,000 annually

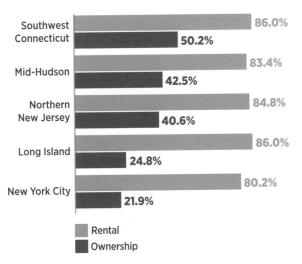

Southwest Connecticut — 86.0% / 50.2%
Mid-Hudson — 83.4% / 42.5%
Northern New Jersey — 84.8% / 40.6%
Long Island — 86.0% / 24.8%
New York City — 80.2% / 21.9%

Rental
Ownership

Source: U.S. Census American Community Survey 5 Year Estimates 2015 and RPA Analysis

Treat publicly owned land as an asset, not a liability

Instead of selling land to developers, municipalities and states should treat public land as a significant and irreplaceable public asset. The government should retain ownership, either directly or through mechanisms such as community land trusts, mutual housing associations, or other entities. This would still allow municipalities to lease the land to developers to build affordable housing or for economic development projects. In addition, steady lease payments, as opposed to fluctuating property taxes, would help bring stability to the underwriting and financing of development.

Use government programs to create more competition in the housing industry and jump-start new technologies

Many of the recent innovations in construction technology in the New York region—such as multifamily modular housing and passive housing technology, which uses construction techniques to reduce heating and cooling needs and greatly reduce energy costs—have taken root largely because government programs have either directly or indirectly encouraged their initial development. Government also has the ability to give an edge to smaller businesses and industry sectors, such as minority- and women-owned businesses and the nonprofit sectors, which can provide more competition in the industry and bring down housing costs overall. Whenever possible, government subsidies should give preferences to these sectors and provide requirements and incentives to use new technologies that can bring down the cost of construction.

Consolidate marketing and make tenanting fairer

Most cities around the world with significant amounts of government sponsored or social housing have an easy and rational system for obtaining this housing, rather than a series of lotteries and individualized waiting lists, each with their own process and requirements. Every county and large municipality should move toward a single application system where all subsidized housing would be available on a waitlist basis, with a single government agency overseeing the process and developing a comprehensive inventory of social housing.

The number of households that need subsidized rents is far greater than the number of homes with subsidized rents. In the region, there are 1.6 million households who rent with incomes of less than $35,000, but only 620,000 homes guaranteed to be affordable to them, because rent is determined by occupant's income.

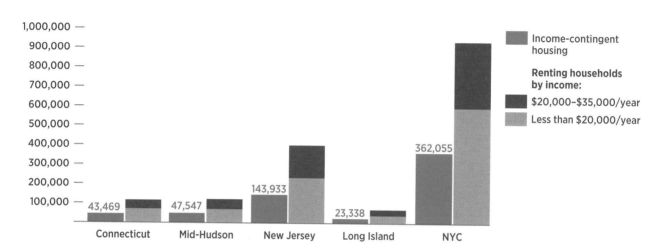

Source: HUD Picture of Affordable Housing 2015 , U.S. Census, American Community Survey 5-year estimates, 2015

OUTCOMES

Reforming our housing subsidy policy would directly lead to housing relief for significant numbers of low-income households throughout the region, resolving a major source of stress and instability for hundreds of thousands of residents and unlocking a path to upward mobility. These changes would not affect overall housing production if complemented by significantly growing the overall number of homes through upzonings and other market actions in order to provide more options for middle-class residents. Bringing rationality to the tenanting process and retaining land in the public interest would also help create more public trust in government.

Ultimately, providing housing affordability and stability for low-income households; investing in middle-class homeownership; targeting more development opportunities to small businesses, M/WBE developers and contractors, and nonprofits; and retaining land in the public interest would help build wealth and opportunity for low- and middle-income people and communities.

PAYING FOR IT

In the short term, reforming our housing subsidy system would not necessarily cost more or less than it does now, but would use existing funds more efficiently—although in order to be most effective it would need to be coupled with additional federal investments in housing. In the long term, reforming our housing subsidy system saves money through retaining control over land; allowing government to leverage better terms from any affordable housing renewal; providing more competition and lower building costs through government incentive programs; and ending uncapped subsidies that can cost unforeseen amounts.

EXPAND ACCESS TO MORE WELL-PAYING JOBS

The economy of the tri-state region has grown dramatically over the past two decades, and today is currently one of the world's largest. Yet even in this thriving economy, income inequality and a lack of upward mobility persist. Wages have stagnated, even as living costs have risen. And although there is strong job growth in New York City, the number of jobs outside the core of the region has hardly increased over the last 15 years.

Fostering a diverse economy with good jobs for people with a variety of skills requires investing in places that can support a broad range of industries and opportunities, from downtowns with large concentrations of office and service jobs to neighborhoods where residents can build careers in health, education, trades and the arts. Concentrating these jobs in the most transit-accessible places lets employers access a larger workforce and allows residents to reach a greater number of employment opportunities.

While it is crucial to maintain a strong Central Business District in Manhattan, we must also expand a network of mixed-use districts outside of Manhattan that can support a wider range of jobs and strengthen the economies of poorer cities. Cities and states should retain space for essential industrial activities while supporting new businesses pursuing innovative production methods. Cities should develop partnerships with local anchor institutions, such as schools and hospitals, that generate jobs and skills for community residents.

53 Maintain a globally competitive regional business district

Photo: RPA

Jobs and incomes throughout New York, New Jersey and Connecticut depend on a dynamic, globally competitive central business district. But without proper investment and expansion, Manhattan could easily decline in favor of both traditional centers of commerce such as Tokyo and London, and newer global centers such as Shanghai and Dubai. To support an expanding regional economy, the Central Business District will need to maintain a diverse mix of office and entertainment districts, improve transit and pedestrian access into and within the commercial core, and expand across the Hudson and East rivers.

Demand for new office space in the core is outpacing supply, limiting the economic growth of the entire region.

While Midtown and Downtown Manhattan have come a long way since the 1970s, regaining their standing as business centers on the world stage, other cities today are surpassing New York, with more investments in new office space and infrastructure. In the next 25 years, the region has the potential to add 1.9 million jobs, with nearly a million of these in office industries ranging from finance to technology. While many of these jobs can and should locate in commercial and business centers throughout the region, the core central business district (CBD) will need to accommodate more workers even as it deals with growing congestion and a shortage of room for expansion.

A CBD that attracts more high-value jobs and businesses is essential to meeting the goals for a successful region. The income of workers in the core flows throughout the boroughs and counties outside of Manhattan, supporting jobs in industries ranging from technology to retail, that expand economic opportunity. This revenue and economic activity create the demand needed to strengthen the economies and tax base of cities, towns and villages. And attracting jobs to the urban core where transit access is the greatest can make the region even more energy-efficient and sustainable.

To support this growing regional economy, the urban core should be able to absorb over 800,000 jobs by 2040, with over 300,000 of these in the Manhattan CBD. The barriers to achieving this potential are limited space for expansion, congested access into the core, and the need to improve the public realm.

- Once the development of Hudson Yards on Manhattan's Far West Side is completed, there will be no more large areas where commercial development can expand within Manhattan. In addition, many older commercial buildings are being converted to residential use. Any additional job growth south of 59th Street will need to be accommodated either by adding more workers to current office space, or building new and taller buildings in existing office districts.

- Transit capacity into Manhattan, whether from subways, buses or commuter trains, is already straining to meet demand. Projects planned or under construction, chiefly the East Side Access project bringing the Long Island Rail Road into Grand Central Terminal and the Gateway project that would build two new tunnels under the Hudson River, are essential but will not provide all the transit capacity needed.

- Streets and public spaces need to be less congested while adapting to changing technologies, new businesses and evolving worker needs.

Expand Manhattan's main Midtown business district south, east and west

While Manhattan is heavily built up and difficult to redevelop, with high-density residential districts surrounding most of the Central Business Districts, there are some opportunities for expansion:

- A redeveloped Penn Station should allow for air rights to be unlocked, and a modern office district developed in conjunction with a transformed West Side.

- The newly rezoned East Midtown office district could be further extended to the Second Avenue corridor in East Midtown, as well as possibly south along Madison Avenue, Park Avenue, and Lexington Avenue. This would also allow businesses to fully take advantage of RPA's proposed regional rail hub on 31st Street and Third Avenue.

- South of 34th Street, older office buildings should be allowed to build additions or take other opportunities to add usable space in return for preserving office, commercial, or light industrial uses. The Garment District should be a vibrant place anchored by the next generation of manufacturing activities.

- In the longer term, an extension of the #7 train south with a new stop on 23rd Street would allow for rezoning for more office development west of Ninth Avenue, as well as transit access to Chelsea Piers and the 23rd Street ferry terminal.

Preserve the CBD's older office space

One of the keys to the region's strength is the synergy which allows both emerging and established businesses to coexist in desirable commercial areas which have proximity and access to a talented workforce. Our older class B & C office space, with their less expensive rents, help provide this.

Class B & C office space is often under pressure to either renovate into more expensive class A office space, or convert to residential use. Conversions to residential use are most prevalent in older buildings with smaller floor plates, which are difficult or impossible to renovate to modern standards. This is especially true of buildings outside of core Midtown Manhattan.

Iconic buildings define our city's history—and our future ambitions.

Woolworth Building
1913, New Gothic

Chrysler Building
1930, Art Deco

UN Secretariat Building
1952, International Style

Citigroup Building
1977, Modern

One World Trade Center
2013, Contemporary

However, zoning regulations can limit the amount of residential conversions and preserve much of this cheaper office space, while still allowing for other uses which can help the finances of the building. These regulations are already in place in some areas of Midtown South and Chelsea, and can be extended both geographically and in the types of buildings they cover. In districts where older office space is underbuilt, these can be combined with regulations to allow for expansion of the building envelopes if office space is preserved.

Create an inner ring of mixed-commercial/residential neighborhoods in New Jersey, Brooklyn and Queens

One of the successes of Downtown Manhattan and Downtown Brooklyn, and East Midtown is how they have developed into mixed residential/office districts, providing vibrant 24-hour neighborhoods with jobs, housing, retail, and attractions. Other areas proximate to the CBD, such as West Midtown, Jersey City, Downtown Newark, and Long Island City, should follow this model and balance office, residential, and amenities growth in a similar way.

In addition to providing more office space, as well as more options for business locations and worker commutes, this also allows for an easier transition between the CBD and residential neighborhoods. This 24-hour nature also allows for more off-peak work hours, as well as shopping and other excursions before or after work, which helps reduce peak-hour commutes and overcrowding.

It only takes a small amount of housing to balance a Central Business District neighborhood. In Downtown Manhattan and East Midtown, there is about 3 square feet of residential space for every 10 square feet of office space. Downtown Brooklyn, Jersey City, Hoboken, Long Island City, and other inner-ring areas with good transportation and the potential to become mixed commercial/residential neighborhoods should attempt to increase commercial space to achieve a similar balance.

It is also vital that the type of housing in these neighborhoods consist of mixed-income, primary-residence apartments whose residents will contribute to the everyday vitality of the neighborhoods. In New York City, this can be done through lifting the 12.0 residential zoning cap and upzoning for Inclusionary Housing to require mixed-income developments, and instituting a pied-a-terre tax to encourage primary occupancy.

Expand exclusive commercial zoning and protections

Areas that were recently rezoned largely for commercial development, such as Downtown Brooklyn and Long Island City, have instead become predominantly residential districts. Hotel use can also take the place of intended office development in some of Manhattan's zoning districts in Midtown South and the West Side.

Many different zoning protections can allow for the preservation of office space, either alone or in tandem with other uses, in addition to special districts such as Hudson Yards which can guide its creation, and these should be utilized and expanded.

This type of zoning is especially important if the 12.0 FAR limit on residential is raised or lifted. This would encourage the type of large, mixed-use, mixed income developments in the urban core which can add significant amounts of both mixed-income housing and needed office space.

Implement a phased expansion of subway and commuter rail access into the Central Business District

A premier central business district needs to be able to draw on a large and varied labor pool, over a wide geography. Mass transit access has driven Midtown's primacy as the region's main business district for decades. RPA's proposed regional rail system and subway improvements to modernize and expand this infrastructure will allow the central business district to not only thrive, but also improve connections to other CBDs throughout the region. In the next decade, the most critical improvements include:

- Build new rail tunnels under both the Hudson and East rivers ("Gateway East") creating a new crosstown line and through service at Penn Station

- Construct a second bus terminal under the Javits Convention Center

- Reconstruct the L train with radically improved service

- Extend the Second Avenue subway to 125th Street

Encourage innovative buildings, signature design, and a sense of place and openness

One of the major strengths of New York's Central Business District is its iconic skyscraper architecture, from pre-war to Art Deco and International Style buildings, which contribute to the identity of Manhattan. We need to continue this tradition of pioneering urban design and diverse building types. There should be more flexibility and incentives in the zoning and building code for innovative architecture in Central Business District. We should encourage buildings with amenities such as observation decks and restaurants, or those with greater public access and interaction with the streetscape.

In addition, both Downtown and Midtown have several distinct subdistricts, each with their own character, which should be nurtured through BIDs, protective zoning, Special Districts, and other mechanisms. Some, such as Stone Street, are only a few blocks while others, such as the Theatre District, are the size of small neighborhoods. This diversity of subdistricts leads both to a variety of location choices for businesses, and helps make the city a leading global tourist attraction.

OUTCOMES

By creating the ability and conditions for the CBD to grow and remain diverse, we will build on the recent successes that have made Manhattan and the region a premier global business and tourism destination. Jobs, wages, and investment will all continue to grow, providing opportunity and growth throughout the region. This vibrancy will continue to serve the people of the region through maintaining and building on the world-class public and cultural amenities that are used by all people in the region— the museums, parks, libraries, theatres, historical sites, and everything else that makes Manhattan what it is.

These recommendations will allow the urban core to add over 800,000 jobs over the next 25 years, almost twice as many compared with current trends. At current salaries, these added jobs represent an additional $75 billion in wages annually that will boost economic growth and opportunity throughout the region.

PAYING FOR IT

Making sure we keep a competitive CBD will greatly impact the finances of the city and the region in a positive way. The highest government costs will be investments in transportation and streets. These multibillion dollar investments will serve the entire region and could be paid for through a combination of federal funding and new state and local sources, including congestion pricing, carbon fees and revenue from increased real estate value. Over time, these will generate tax revenue and economic activity that will more than pay for the investments. Zoning protections for commercial development will allow for more value-added jobs, although it may somewhat repress residential development by disallowing the highest current economic use.

54 **Restore regional job centers**

Photo: Denis Tangney Jr

The urban revival that has led to an economic resurgence in New York City has bypassed many of our smaller cities. These centers—places like Paterson, Poughkeepsie, and Bridgeport—have continued to struggle in the post-industrial era to build and attract businesses, and achieve the prosperity that comes with them. But these older job centers are positioned to once again become significant providers of employment and homes for local residents, and help generate an era of sustainable economic growth in the region. States and regional authorities should focus resources in these cities and reform programs that inhibit private investment. Local leadership should implement comprehensive economic-development strategies to ensure existing residents benefit from job growth and new development.

Smaller cities have languished, even as the region has prospered.

In the second half of the 20th century, the suburbs attracted nearly all of the region's job growth, in the form of office parks and malls. More recently, nearly all the job growth has taken place in New York City. Neither cycle benefited most of region's small and mid-sized cities. Many poorer villages with sizable downtowns, such as Hempstead, NY, have similarly been been left out. These centers have been left without the tax base needed to provide robust municipal services and upgrade infrastructure—and their residents have seen their incomes stagnate for more than 30 years.

Declining downtowns and fewer industrial jobs contribute to a vicious cycle that also includes population loss and more concentrated poverty. Despite the region's population having grown by more than 20 percent over the past 50 years, including New York City gaining over 650,000 people, the next 10 largest cities have actually seen their combined population fall by more than 100,000.

Build on emerging trends to create a network of thriving cities and job centers

In many ways, these older job centers are extraordinarily well positioned to rebound. Despite their relatively dense environments, many are well below their peak historical population and have the space and infrastructure to handle substantial population and job growth. Many have vacant or underutilized land and buildings that could become home to new, green industries and businesses. Their older street grid patterns and neighborhood character offer the potential for the type of walkable neighborhoods that are critical for future growth—and that are in such popular demand today. They already have the water and sewer systems, the roads, the schools, and the other basic infrastructure necessary for dense communities. Many are served by commuter rail, giving them good access to the Manhattan jobs engine. And new transit infrastructure, such as better regional rail and on-street transit, can provide the connectivity necessary to thrive. With the right investments and policies, these older centers could add 360,000 jobs and grow faster than the region's economy as a whole.[86]

Several cities in the region have already benefited from these physical assets and intentional revitalization efforts pursued by local governments, businesses, and civic leaders. Stamford, Jersey City, and White Plains have experienced both job and population growth, led by mixed-use downtown development near busy transit hubs. Others, like Newark, are seeing their downtowns finally turn around after years of strategic planning and major investments. In nearly every instance, these places have benefited from easy transit access to a growing New York City economy, and significant support from state-government and regional transportation agencies.

One challenge is bringing this prosperity to all the residents of the cities where new development takes place. Too often, the redevelopment of a downtown fails to improve conditions or economic opportunities for people living there or in the surrounding neighborhoods.

Another challenge is bringing this prosperity to a larger number of places—particularly the smaller, isolated cities, and places where public safety, schools, and housing quality are seriously deficient after decades of disinvestment.

Half of the ten largest cities (other than New York City) in the region in 1970 have a lower population today than they did nearly half a century ago—and none have grown as fast as the region as a whole.

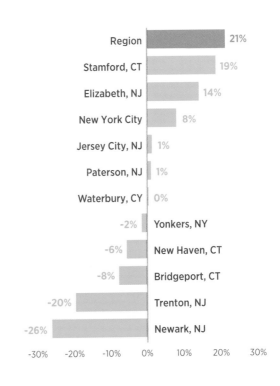

Source: U.S. Census 1970, American Community Survey 2015

Each city requires its own unique strategy—and effective leadership based on a shared vision is critical.[87] These strategies would have the greatest success when the cities use their existing urban form to create vibrant downtowns and districts; build on the strengths of neighborhoods and not just downtowns: and partner with private and nonprofit institutions to give residents the skills and access they need for stable employment and well-paying careers.

But restoring and strengthening these places would not be the job of the municipalities alone. Although state and federal policies were primary causes for the decline of cities and older suburbs, they would need to take a lead role in providing the infrastructure, rules, and support for their cities' revival. Counties would also have a major stake in the success of their cities, and collaboration would help both take advantage of the rising opportunities for regions with thriving downtowns.

Use the existing urban form to create vibrant downtowns and neighborhoods

Walkable neighborhoods produce more jobs and economic output, expand opportunity, and reduce combined housing-transportation costs for their residents.[88]

The cities in the region with the most potential to become job centers are typically older cities with the compact street grids and mixed-use character that can, with some attention and investment, become safe, active, and walkable neighborhoods. But for these neighborhoods to reach their full potential, local leaders need to promote the rehabilitation of smaller mixed-use buildings, encourage population growth to support new businesses, and make the streets safer. Street design improvements should include protected bike lanes and sidewalk expansions, while successful green streets programs should be expanded to cool city streets. Most of all, local leaders must resist large-scale urban redevelopment projects, which can destroy the walkable character of a community and displace existing businesses.

State historic tax credits make it easier to leverage federal and private funds for the rehabilitation of properties in several historic downtown neighborhoods. New Jersey should institute such a program, and New York and Connecticut should expand theirs. Federal financing regulations that prevent many types of mixed-use development and rehabilitation should be reformed. Lastly, the three states, industrial-development authorities, and redevelopment authorities should adopt or expand loan-guarantee programs for both local business development and housing.

Invest in economic development, not economic upgrading

Older cities have a diverse array of neighborhoods and communities. Some areas suffer greatly from disinvestment and abandoned and deteriorating buildings, while others have low retail-vacancy rates, healthy local economies, and active communities, even when the population is predominantly low-income. These types of neighborhoods already provide jobs, business opportunities, and community for existing residents. While better municipal services, economic opportunities, and protection from displacement are needed in virtually all low-income neighborhoods, municipalities should focus redevelopment on places where it can have the most impact—the truly blighted areas that are most in need of change—especially as this type of investment is more likely to lead to increased job opportunities for the local population.[89]

In areas where there is already an existing job base, the public sector should focus on supporting existing economies and growing local business. For example, Pat-

erson, NJ, has demonstrated the possibilities of building on existing assets such as arts, recreation, and small immigrant-owned businesses.

Help residents get better-paying jobs and careers

The physical redevelopment of regional centers should be undertaken, when at all possible, by smaller local contractors and developers in order to grow and build a base of local employers. Cities could adopt policies that give limited tax incentives to companies that commit to specific job and wage targets, preference to local university graduates, or incentives to workers who live in these cities. The cities that are home to large universities, hospitals, and other anchor institutions should collaborate with businesses to improve neighborhood conditions and help train and place workers neighborhood residents in a growing job base.

Provide the infrastructure necessary for more growth

Improving commuter rail and other forms of suburban transit is critical to revitalizing these cities and turning them into job centers. In the short term, this means funding the transit agencies adequately and improving the level of service. In the longer term, turning the region's fragmented commuter rail system into a regional rail network that is better able to help workers commute into regional job centers, and not just into Manhattan, would also make these centers far more competitive.

RPA's proposed Trans-Regional Express would drastically cut commute times to many of these centers from anywhere in the region—dramatically increasing their potential as job hubs. Places that do not have easy access to Manhattan, such as Newburgh or Danbury, should invest in bus and other on-demand connections to the commuter rail network.

Reform the institutional and regulatory hurdles to creating more affordable housing, good jobs, and better schools

Sometimes, it's the government's own regulations and institutional structures that hamper the growth of these cities. Although developers could build more affordable and middle-income homes, create active commercial districts, and support competitive industrial jobs, such development is simply too expensive. State-level actions that could help bring development costs in-line with demand include reforming the development approvals process to make it more predictable, giving cities the ability to reduce property taxes and raise revenue from other sources, reducing municipal school costs by creating regional school districts, coordinating or consolidating services with other municipalities, and providing more funding for brownfield remediation.

Promote equity, not just development

As cities grow, they need to make sure they put in place policies that ensure everyone benefits, especially existing residents. Wage growth should not be taken up or exceeded by cost-of-living increases in the form of higher rents or more expensive goods and services—and new housing should be for more than just the highest earners. Newark is an example of a municipality that has adopted strong inclusionary zoning policies while also encouraging more growth. Worker- and community-owned business cooperatives, which have operated successfully in Minnesota and other states, and are under consideration in places like the Bronx and Newburgh, can be an effective way to capitalize on local expertise and resources to build and keep wealth within an existing community while reviving the city as a whole.

OUTCOMES

Creating a network of growing job centers that increase incomes and opportunity for those who live in them would be a game changer for the region. It would decrease inequality and generate tax revenue that could be reinvested in schools and services. Encouraging job growth outside the urban core means reducing commute times and improving quality of life for nearby residents. The dense and walkable infrastructure and lower market and construction costs would lead to more affordable homes near jobs and amenities, saving people significant time and stress. And by making sure this growth is equitable, and targeted to places that truly need investment and development, both new and existing businesses can thrive and build off of each other.

PAYING FOR IT

Restoring our regional job centers would have up-front costs but large returns. Investments in infrastructure are needed in these centers for commuter rail, bus, streetscapes, and other municipal improvements. Especially in the poorest municipalities, county, and state funding should provide for the initial investment. Some incentives to attract new businesses would likely be necessary as well, although they should be limited and targeted toward local-job and wage growth directly.

In the long run, these initial public investments would leverage much larger investments by private businesses, and create exponential returns. Overall, restoring our regional job centers would result in significant revenue for municipalities, workers, businesses, and the region at large.

55 Make room for the next generation of industry

More and more, housing and office development is encroaching on areas formerly reserved for industrial uses. To maintain industrial activities of all kinds—from essential services such as power plants, waste-transfer stations, and goods-distribution centers to more diverse manufacturing opportunities that support the larger creative economy—they must be modernized, made environmentally sound, and provide the amenities high-value businesses need. This requires new policies concerning workforce development, real estate, and urban design that are uniquely tailored to local contexts and the needs of residents and the economy.

Industrial land is both underutilized and in danger of disappearing where it is needed most.

Less than 2 percent of the region's land is devoted to industrial uses, but that number is steadily decreasing. In high-value areas in Manhattan, Brooklyn, Queens, and Hudson County, the main reason for industrial job losses is the land zoned for industrial uses is steadily being converted to housing, offices, stores, and institutions. Even where manufacturing is thriving or facilities are serving important functions, industrial land values are no match for the high prices residential and commercial uses can command.

This loss of industry in the core of the region has important repercussions. Having warehouses, waste management, and electricity generators located at the periphery of the region increases truck traffic, pollution, and transportation costs. It also exacerbates the decline in manufacturing employment, thus reducing economic diversity and limiting access to living-wage jobs. While automation and national economic shifts are partly responsible for the decline of manufacturing in the core of the region, high rents and a shortage of suitable space also constrain its growth.

In smaller, formerly industrial cities, the problem is different. There, many industrial areas have been abandoned as the kinds of spaces needed for manufacturing processes have changed. Because land values don't justify the costs of environmental remediation, post-industrial lands become brownfields that disproportionately burden poor communities and communities of color.

Across the region, a further challenge to industrial lands is climate change and sea-level rise, as they are so often located at the water's edge.

Recognize the importance of a thriving industrial sector to a resilient regional economy

The region could retain a million industrial jobs over the next 25 years if the land and infrastructure is made available, and with the right investments in workforce development.[90] A thriving industrial sector provides the essential services that make our homes, offices, stores, schools, and hospitals run, in addition to well-paying jobs that don't require a college degree.

Maintaining a healthy industrial sector requires a range of strategies to reflect the needs and opportunities of the region's diverse places of production, from urban manufacturing districts to suburban industrial parks, as well as exurban warehouses, distribution centers, and food hubs. Each requires a different approach to improve their functionality and competitiveness, and to regulate redevelopment from competing non-production uses such as mixed-use redevelopment, open spaces, and flood protection.

Preserve industrial land in the region's urban core

Industrial land is under the greatest pressure in the region's urban core—including most of Manhattan, Brooklyn, Queens, and the Bronx, and large portions of Hudson and Essex counties in New Jersey. About 35 percent of the region's industrial employment is in the core, where industrial job densities of 87 jobs/acre are several orders of magnitude higher than elsewhere in the region. Active industrial districts, such as the Industrial Business Zones in New York City and urban industrial parks elsewhere in the core should be protected from displacement. Essential improvements should be made to infrastructure and open spaces that affect the quality of the working environment. At the edges of these districts, design guidelines can manage the transition in scale and activity to the adjacent neighborhoods.

Traditional manufacturing neighborhoods present an opportunity to combine policies that protect industrial uses with new forms of live-work mixed-use development. This can support naturally occurring "innovation districts"—places where product innovation is supported by institution-sponsored research, allied design professions, and high-value-added manufacturing such as medical equipment or electronic components. These places need to be supported by flexible but targeted regulations that preserve industrial employment, high-speed internet, and ongoing support for local partnerships between research institutions, government, and industry.

Most of the major concentrations of warehousing and distribution are within 10 miles of New York City, which is a reflection of the value of having these facilities close to ports, airports, and the large population in the core. These locational advantages should be protected, even as new technologies make these sprawling facilities more compact and responsive to environmental priorities in places like the Meadowlands.

Finally, lands currently used for energy production should be evaluated in consideration of long-term changes in energy production and transmission. Waste-management facilities should be equitably distributed across the city and upgraded or adapted with technologies that reduce noise, odor, and other externalities.

New and existing urban manufacturing districts are challenging to manage, but are a vital source of employment and economic value.

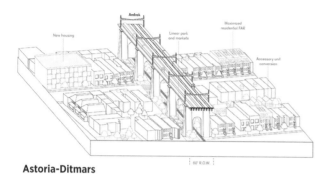

Astoria-Ditmars

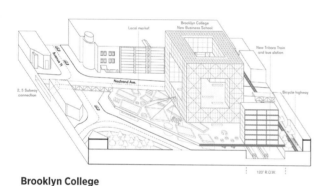

Brooklyn College

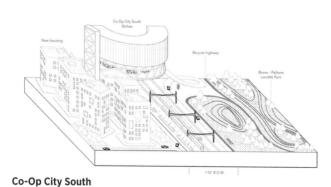

Co-Op City South

Image: Only If + One Architecture for RPA's 4C Initiative

Incorporate production into economic-development strategies for the region's downtowns and centers

Almost half of the region's industrial jobs are in commercial and mixed-use areas around downtowns and centers outside of the urban core—places like Trenton, Poughkeepsie, and New Haven—that have a strong industrial legacy. These industrial districts share some of the same issues and opportunities as those in the region's core, although at a very different scale and under less displacement pressure.

Yet they also have the potential to anchor much of the region's future economic growth, and to accommodate new homes that will help relieve the region's housing shortage. Developing balanced growth strategies that attract new businesses and population while improving opportunities and quality of life for existing residents is a major challenge. Retaining and growing manufacturing and distribution jobs, and giving residents the skills to advance their careers in these sectors, should be key elements of these strategies. Future use for production-related activities should be based on access to existing labor and skill sets, as well as the capacity to link to other institutional partners. Many of the strategies are the same as those described for the urban core: allow new mixed-use building types, connect the sites to the rest of the downtown, and create guidelines designed to manage the transitions in scale and use at the edge.

Ensure that production places in suburban areas have the right infrastructure to support high-value industries

Places of production in suburban areas include industrial parks and manufacturing "campuses" such as those found in the corridor of pharmaceutical industries in Somerset County, NJ, and the Hauppauge Industrial Park in Suffolk County. Many of these places are attractive to businesses looking for less-expensive office space, and therefore have low vacancies. However, many do not have the digital infrastructure and services needed by an increasing number of companies, and also lack the transportation, amenities, and mixed-use character sought by many high-value industries.

In evaluating these places for possible investment, priority should be given to local employment impacts, the capacity of the facility to adapt to changing industry trends, and the ease of connection to local neighborhoods and open spaces. Regulations must encourage mixed-use development and flexible adaptation of the typical one-story industrial shed to create more flexible space, such as carving into and clipping onto it as demonstrated at the Bayer facility in Berkeley, California.

Image: ORG Permanent Modernity for the Fourth Regional Plan

Reintegrate large industrial landscapes into the region's open-space systems

Some industrial areas are in less-developed parts of the region, such as between the New Jersey Highlands and the first ring of suburban communities. Sometimes, these sites encroach on natural open spaces—and would encroach on the tri-state trail network proposed in this plan. But large industrial sites, particularly those that are underused, should be reintegrated into nature.

Several larger-scale industrial landscapes, such as major landfills and large-scale fuel-storage facilities, need district-wide plans that address their scale and complexity. This scale makes it possible to explore innovative models for industrial landscape design. These are places, such as the Meadowlands in New Jersey, where large-scale natural systems and large-scale infrastructure systems intersect, requiring a more comprehensive approach that addresses environmental and land-use issues. The cost of environmental remediation, the potential contribution to the larger open-space system, and the impact on resilience to sea-level

Places of production can be built at a scale that fits in with neighboring residential communities.

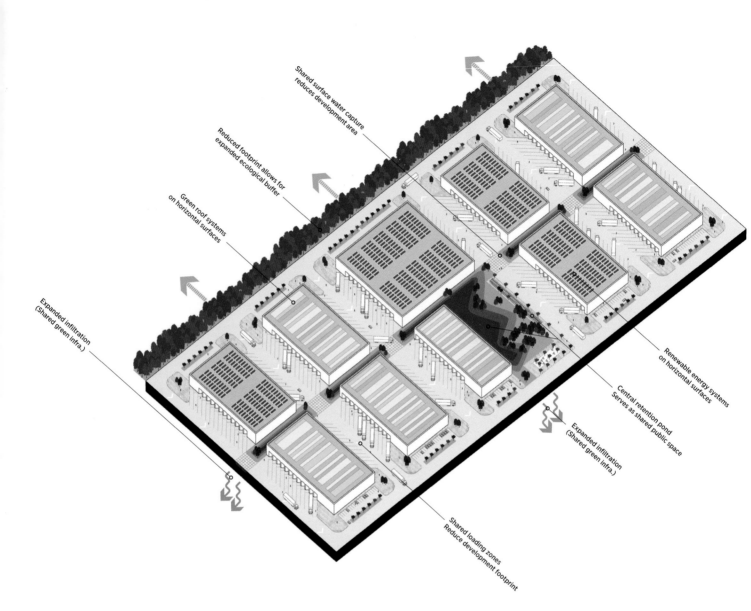

Shared surface water capture
reduces development area

Reduced footprint allows for
expanded ecological buffer

Green roof systems
on horizontal surfaces

Expanded infiltration
(Shared green infra.)

Renewable energy systems
on horizontal surfaces

Central retention pond
Serves as shared public space

Expanded infiltration
(Shared green infra.)

Shared loading zones
Reduce development footprint

Green infrastructure elements can be
incorporated into suburban and exurban
industrial areas to reduce stormwater
runoff, lower ambient temperatures, and
create a nicer pedestrian environment.

Image: PORT + Range for RPA's 4C Initiative.

rise, storm surges, and other effects of climate change should be considered along with the economic benefits of maintaining industrial functions. Examples of places that are attempting to balance these objectives include Freshkills Park on Staten Island, the Menomonee Valley redevelopment project in Milwaukee, and Emscher Park in Germany.

For all types of places, enact zoning regulations that detail the conditions for different forms of production

Most industrial zoning relies on outdated and oversimplified definitions of manufacturing. Cities that are known for proactive and progressive efforts to grow their manufacturing economies, such as Portland, OR, and Berkeley, CA, manage the complexity of urban production in several ways. The lists of defined uses are extremely detailed and are updated on a regular basis. The scale of the zoning districts is small, enabling the regulations to be calibrated to particular conditions. The review process enables a certain amount of discretionary review based on how the use performs in terms of impacts such as noise, dust, odor, and the role of that use in the overall economy of the district. As sensors measuring noise and other pollution become more affordable, data-driven approaches can support more flexible zoning models that allow for mixed-use manufacturing.

Implement district-wide strategies for environmental remediation in industrial areas

State funding for environmental remediation needs to support a more comprehensive approach that links remediation to overall objectives for health, open space, and job creation. The overall environmental process should be reformed to combine environmental review with comprehensive planning, and to expedite redevelopment of land for specific uses and aid in the reclamation of industrial sites and buildings.

Realign federal industrial revitalization policies to support local place-based organizations

Production is for the most part locally based, and depends on the specific resources, geography, labor force skills, and industrial legacy of the specific place. But federal industrial policy largely focuses on integration and the uptake—most commonly by multinational firms—of cutting-edge technologies, as well as on commercialization and productivity increases. While there are a few national initiatives aimed at being more place-based, such as the Investing in Manufacturing Communities Partnership, these do not receive sufficient funding. Realignment of federal policy would mean place-based, mission-driven organizations would be recipients of federal funding, and other support programs would be more narrowly calibrated to the local production ecology.

OUTCOMES

Implementation of these actions would allow the region to balance the need for industrial space and industrial jobs with the demand for more housing, open spaces, commercial development, and climate adaptation. There would be no net loss of industrial space in the region's core, although much of the existing space would be converted to more flexible, mixed-use activity. Both New York City and the region's other downtowns would retain a vital production sector that successfully coexists with residential neighborhoods and service industries. The region as a whole would retain a million industrial jobs, and high-value sectors would likely grow. More residents without college degrees would be able to pursue successful, living-wage careers. The reliability of the transportation and energy systems would be maintained at a reasonable cost, because there would be sufficient space available at the right locations. And fewer communities would be burdened with environmental hazards from outmoded or abandoned industrial properties.

PAYING FOR IT

Of all these actions, the highest cost will be for brownfield remediation, with state programs and tax credits providing the largest source of public funding to expedite cleanups. Brownfield remediation costs vary widely, from several hundred thousand dollars for a straightforward gas station cleanup to multimillion-dollar cleanups for large facilities. But a federal study found that each dollar of brownfield funding leveraged $18 of economic benefit. Studies of New York City and state programs have found comparable benefits. Infrastructure upgrades would require a combination of state and local funding, depending on the site and objective. Workforce-development funds could come from a variety of federal, state, and local sources, and could leverage private-sector training resources.

Most of these infrastructure and cleanup expenditures would be needed for any type of redevelopment of industrial properties. Still, the long-term benefits of job creation, tax revenues, and health and environmental improvements are substantial. There would, however, be some trade-offs from forgoing residential and office values, which would pay higher land prices and taxes on some industrial land, that need to be weighed against the benefits of better-functioning infrastructure and a more balanced economy.

56 Promote partnerships between anchor institutions

Image: Gamble Associates

Leveraging the capital, human resources, and economic output of anchor institutions presents a significant opportunity to address some of the most persistent socioeconomic challenges that perpetuate poverty and inequality across our region: access to jobs, quality housing, and healthy neighborhoods. Promoting meaningful dialogue and institutionalizing collaboration between anchor institutions, municipalities, and local neighborhoods connects the people, knowledge, physical spaces, and economic power of these partners to create healthy communities and mutually beneficial, sustainable local ecosystems.

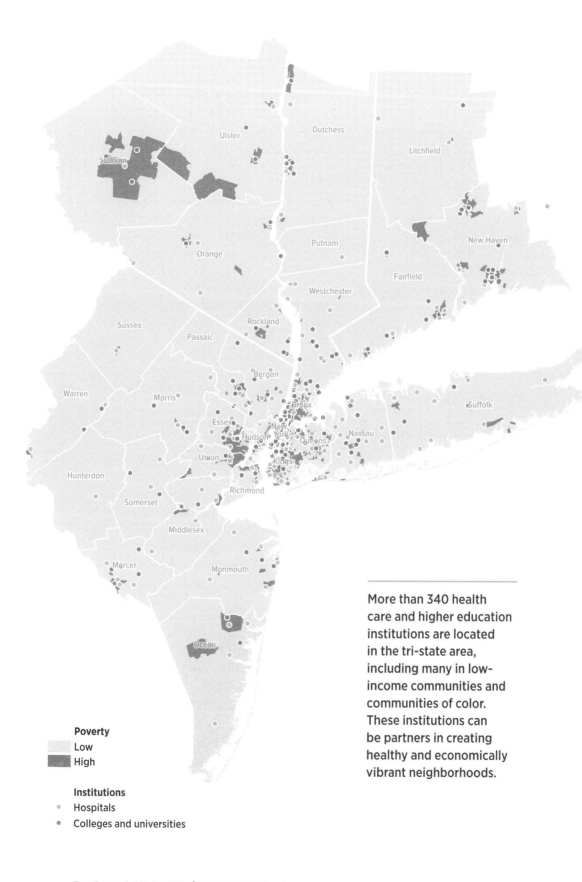

More than 340 health care and higher education institutions are located in the tri-state area, including many in low-income communities and communities of color. These institutions can be partners in creating healthy and economically vibrant neighborhoods.

Poverty
Low
High

Institutions
Hospitals
Colleges and universities

Data Source: HRSA Data Warehouse, 2010-2014 American Community Survey 5-year estimates.

Educational, medical, and other institutions represent critical and often untapped assets for local economies.

Universities, hospitals, and other large nonprofit and public institutions are often a community's largest local employer and a dominating presence in the neighborhood. These "anchor institutions" are rooted in place, and because of their ownership, customer base, and mission, are unlikely to move to another location. They have a vested interest in the local community by virtue of their land holdings, capital, and physical structures—as well as historic ties—and as a result have substantial economic impact in terms of hiring and purchasing power.

Despite this relationship, many institutions have historically been inward-facing: physically and operationally disconnected from their neighbors. They have often thought of their business functions as separate from their missions rather than as assets to be leveraged for their own benefit and the benefit of their surrounding community. In many cases, residents and businesses have limited relationships with their local institutions and struggle with physical, economic, and social disinvestment. This disconnect is a missed opportunity for both anchors and neighborhoods.

Collaboration helps stabilize and revitalize neighborhoods while creating tangible benefits for anchor institutions.

Connecting the people, knowledge, physical spaces, and economies of these powerful institutions to their surrounding communities—particularly when they are low-income with limited opportunities—leads to mutually beneficial and self-sustaining local ecosystems. Forging stronger ties between institutions and communities improves economic, physical, and social conditions in low-income communities and communities of color in six key areas:

- **Hiring and workforce development:** Partnering with existing community-based organizations to train local residents for existing employment opportunities benefits institutions by allowing them to leverage existing public resources to create a diverse local workforce that exhibits less tardiness than those with longer commutes. Further, local partnerships and investments in employees help improve staff morale and employee retention.

- **Inclusive, local purchasing:** Healthcare and higher-education institutions have tremendous purchasing power, which can provide critical support for diverse and local businesses, and to incubate new enterprises in local neighborhoods to fill supply-chain gaps.

- **Place-based impact investing:** Institutions can earn a financial return on their investments while producing a positive social, economic, and/or environmental impact within their geographical service areas. These can be as simple as shifting cash deposits to local banks and credit unions, or investing in low-risk fixed-income products offered by community-development financial intermediaries that provide services and resources to underserved communities.

- **Coordinated capital investments:** Coordination of anchor and municipal capital investments in streetscapes and public spaces can make communities safer and more attractive for residents, and also help anchors retain and attract talent. In particular, these investments can benefit those who have traditionally been underserved, reversing patterns of disinvestment and disparities between communities.

- **Increased access to quality housing:** Investments in a quality, mixed-income housing stock create a healthy and socially diverse neighborhood where people at multiple income and skill levels can live and work. Quality housing improves health outcomes for children, families, and individuals, while well-maintained homes and streets have the added benefit of improving neighborhood safety and security.

- **Mission alignment:** Nonprofit and public institutions bring expertise to local communities in areas such as healthcare, education, and arts and culture, and can work with local residents to tackle persistent community challenges in these fields. This helps institutions advance their missions while also improving community well-being.

Support a growing number of partnerships across the region

Growing partnerships among anchor institutions, community-based organizations, and other intermediaries already exist in the Bronx, Newark, and Stamford, to the benefit of local residents. With over 340 anchor institutions in the tri-state region, there is even greater potential for new investment as part of an anchor strategy.

For more of these partnerships to take place, incentives are needed for anchors, municipalities, and local neighborhoods to collaborate. These could come from government, nonprofit foundations, or industry associations, in the form of learning networks, competitive grants, or technical support that facilitates collaborative partnerships.

Creating these partnerships would require dialogue and engagement between local municipalities, neighborhoods, and anchor institutions, while effectively communicating the benefits to these partners as follows:

Foster a culture of collaboration

While collaboration begins with an agreement to share information and coordinate projects and planning, the true work begins when anchor institutions and local governments agree to learn about and implement best practices to advance community economic-development strategies. Given that this strategy is not yet commonplace, it necessitates openness to creativity and new methods of problem solving. This approach requires both institutions and municipal governments to commit to advancing a culture of collaboration and developing a structure that facilitates interdisciplinary and interdepartmental collaboration.

Establish a clear line of communication

A clear, direct, and regular line of communication between municipal and institutional leadership is vital to establishing the relationships and trust necessary to advance an anchor strategy and uncover the joint benefits of collaboration. Regular leadership meetings provide an opportunity to explore common interests and shared goals, as well as opportunities for joint projects and partnerships on many levels. They also help establish the leadership buy-in that is critical to success.

Initiate joint projects and planning efforts

Joint projects and planning efforts between anchor institutions, municipal government, and local communities can provide important opportunities to establish and grow partnerships, and determine points of common interest and benefit. New York, New Jersey, and Connecticut can incentivize this type of collaboration by providing grant funds to support joint projects and joint planning efforts; and prioritizing infrastructure investment, housing subsidies, and economic development funds for implementation of such efforts.

The states should also explore leveraging federal programs, such as the Affordable Care Act's community-benefit requirement, to encourage healthcare and other institutions to implement joint projects and planning efforts in partnership with their local community and municipal government.

OUTCOMES

By 2030, collaboration between anchor institutions, municipalities, and local communities should be standard practice and imbedded into the fabric of government and anchor institution operations throughout the region. Anchor strategies and community partnerships should be included in local comprehensive plans, and partnerships with municipalities and local neighborhoods should be included in anchor institutions' strategic planning documents. The outcome of this cultural shift should include:

- Collaborations between anchors and public schools, community colleges, vocational training centers, workforce intermediaries, and other community-based organizations to connect residents with jobs at the anchor institutions that have clear career pathways.

- Mechanisms to facilitate anchor purchasing from local businesses, including minority-, women-, and employee-owned firms, by establishing targets and incentives for procurement, creating systems that allow multiple small businesses to provide bundled services to anchors, helping small businesses scale by connecting them to technical assistances and subcontracting opportunities, and addressing procurement barriers such as access to online hubs and contracting insurance and bonding requirements.

- Anchor investment in quality affordable and mixed-income housing that can include partnering with or creating a subsidiary community development corporation, providing employer-assisted housing programs, or repurposing unused space or buildings for affordable and/or supportive housing.

- Capital investments that can include removing walls, fences, and other physical barriers that separate institutions from their communities, intentionally connecting campuses to local streets with signage and uniform streetscapes, creating an accessible broadband network that spans both the anchor and the local neighborhood, and expanding transit access for both residents and employees.

- Alignment of anchor core missions with local community needs and local expertise to sustain meaningful partnerships over the long term.

PAYING FOR IT

Establishing effective anchor strategies requires a commitment of staff resources necessary for developing relationships and growing sustainable collaborative institutional structures within government, institutions, and neighborhoods. Some new capital or programmatic investments may be needed from either the institution or municipality, but most investments would involve reprogramming or prioritization of existing resources.

SUPPORT HEALTHY AND LIVABLE COMMUNITIES

Thriving communities are about more than just housing and jobs. Residents also want and deserve a safe and welcoming neighborhood, access to good food, a healthy environment, and the opportunity to enjoy arts, culture, and recreation. Thriving communities are places where people come together to live and work, and also to build community.

Yet throughout the region many residents live in places burdened by pollution from airports, factories, solid-waste-transfer facilities, and brownfields. A disproportionate number of residents in these communities are people of color.

As the region grows, we have a particular opportunity to address these needs and create places that improve the health and well-being of residents. We can transform underutilized commercial and industrial strips in the suburbs into walkable, complete communities, and mitigate the impact of pollution and fossil-fuel-burning power plants. And with the support of municipal and state government, communities can promote healthy food, local arts, and culture—and lively public spaces that contribute to the enjoyment of everyday life.

57 Remake underutilized auto-dependent landscapes

Underused commercial strips, industrial parks, and old shopping centers are lost opportunities for the region. Despite their sprawling appearance, many of these places house large numbers of people and jobs. If designed properly and supported by new land-use regulations and roadway-design standards, these places could be transformed into sustainable developments that support their surrounding communities. Elsewhere, underutilized commercial properties could become part of the region's open-space system.

The region has inherited a legacy of disconnected, auto-dependent developments.

The growing demand for walkable, urban living has left car-dependent communities behind. Vacancy rates are on the rise in suburban commercial strips, industrial parks, office parks, shopping centers, and institutional campuses. Demand is also falling for single-family homes in low-density communities. A number of national studies estimate the current supply of single-family homes will meet demand for decades to come, and that demand for walkable urban places in the New York Region is 150 percent higher than for auto-oriented suburban strips, retail centers, and commercial campuses.[91]

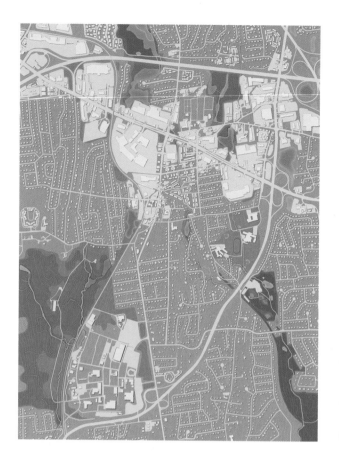
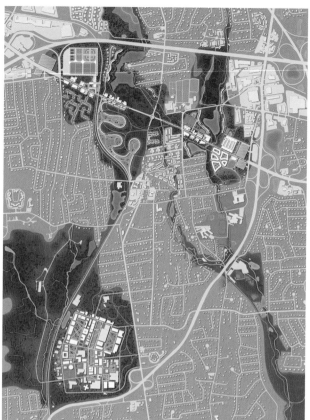

Image: WorkAC for RPA's 4C Initiative

Car-dependent landscapes, such as suburban and exurban commercial strips, can be transformed into walkable streetscapes that Integrate living and working.

These underused or even abandoned car-dependent places are visual scars for their surrounding communities. They drag down the local economy and pose environmental challenges. But their revitalization into new, sustainable communities is often impeded by the difficulty of developing a vision and consensus among multiple municipalities, overcoming the regulations and practices that were designed to promote auto-oriented growth, and obtaining financing for infrastructure design and development.

Redeveloping these underused places would be of tremendous benefit, both to the communities around them and to the region as a whole.

Many of these areas are spread out and remote and therefore difficult to make into complete communities. Yet some of them—those that already have concentrations of population and jobs nearby, as well as access to existing or new transit services—could be adapted for a new generation of suburban residents.

Some of these places are corridors that are organized around major arterials. Others are sometimes called "edge cities," loose agglomerations of stand-alone, auto-dependent developments that could be stitched together to make complete transit-enabled centers if new infill development and public spaces were properly configured.

The capacity for new jobs and homes in these places is huge. Route 110, already home to 30 percent of all jobs in Suffolk County, could be redeveloped to easily accommodate close to another five million square feet of office space and almost one million square feet of industrial space.[92] Nanuet in Rockland County, NY; Route 7 in Fairfield County, CT; and the Hoffman-LaRoche campus in Nutley, NJ, are all examples of places with large amounts of fallow or underutilized land that, with the right policy and planning actions, could be transformed into productive, community-oriented places.

Revise and disseminate model land-use regulations to encourage transformation

Many existing land-use regulations were written at a time when the goal was to promote large, single-purpose precincts. Using well-established models of best practice, zoning regulations should be updated to reduce parking requirements, allow shared parking, and promote increased use of walking, biking, shuttles, and on-demand services. Building-design guidelines should be written to create transitions in scale between new and proposed buildings, and between redevelopment areas and their surrounding neighborhoods. Finally, site-planning-design guidelines should require more street connectivity within large-development parcels and with surrounding areas, and organize buildings in ways that create public spaces and well-defined streets.

States should encourage municipalities to update their land-use regulations by providing free audits and trainings; and applications for state and county grants should include these objectives in selection criteria.

Introduce new transit options to reduce auto dependence

Connecting lower-density environments to the region's commuter rail and bus network is essential to reducing auto-dependence. Providing a range of fully integrated mobility options to complement public transportation with bicycling, walking, buses, taxis, carsharing, car rentals, on-demand vehicles, and in the future, autonomous vehicles, is an approach called "combined mobility."

To implement this innovative transportation strategy, transit agencies will need to collaborate to implement an integrated payment system across the region, allowing customers to use a single card or smart-device application across all modes, including carsharing and bike rentals. State transportation departments and regional transit agencies will all need to construct new infrastructure that includes convenient transfer points between modes.

Revise road-design standards

Turning auto-dependent landscapes into communities will require transforming the major roads around which they are organized. While departments of transportation have paid lip service to "context-sensitive design," too little has been done to redesign roads to support the needs of the local community. Traffic planners should evaluate and prioritize a number of interventions, such as narrowing roads, reducing the required turning radii to slow down drivers as they turn, providing mountable curbs at intersections to reduce pedestrian crossing distances, decreasing lane widths to reduce vehicle speeds, creating well-designed bus stops and dedicate lanes to improve transit service, and requiring shared driveways to reduce the number of locations where vehicles interrupt pedestrian sidewalks.

When commercial corridors pass through multiple jurisdictions, which is typically the case, states and counties should help establish and fund multijurisdictional partnerships to implement coordinated planning. One model is the I-35W Corridor Coalition in Minneapolis, which was established in 1996 as a civic organization through which individual municipalities along the corridor could share information, and identify and lobby for investments with shared benefits.

Reclaim impervious surfaces for storm-water management and other environmental objectives

The large expanses of pavement that come with auto-dependent landscapes, such as roads and parking lots, generate heat in the summer, and polluted storm-water runoff when it rains. The redevelopment of these places into real communities is an opportunity to replace pavement with more natural landscaping.

Sprawl can be retrofitted to create
new kinds of communities and support
connected open-space systems.

Credit: Work AC for the RPA Design Initiative

Large expanses of pavement originally designed for automobiles can be reclaimed to promote walking, biking, and green infrastructure.

Photo: Chesapeake Bay Program

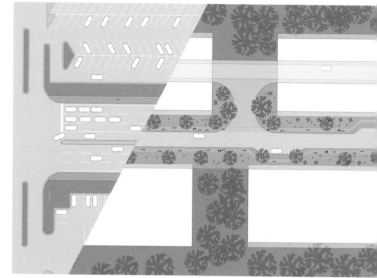

Credit: Work AC for the RPA Design Initiative

OUTCOMES

In the targeted edge cities and corridors alone, more than 13,000 acres of marginal, low-density land could be redeveloped into higher revenue-producing, compact mixed-use development. RPA's experience with redesigning arterial corridors shows it is possible to double the amount of commercial development in selected sections to generate twice the tax revenue for the municipality. Overall, these targeted corridors and edge cities could add 100,000 jobs and 110,000 people.[93]

There are additional important positive outcomes that are more difficult to quantify. More families could live in higher performing school districts and closer to better paying jobs. As paved areas are reclaimed for green infrastructure, storm-water quality would increase, thereby decreasing the urban heat island effect. Moreover, these new places, with their own unique identities, could reinforce a sense of community.

PAYING FOR IT

These proposals are less capital-intensive than process-intensive. The identified auto-dependent landscapes already have water and sewer services, as well as transit connections, but will require revisions to state and county roadway design and access standards and, even more importantly, revisions to local zoning codes and regulations. Municipalities can require that new development projects implement design improvements such as sidewalks, lighting, and green infrastructure elements. However, some capital investment will be required to build new transportation infrastructure and reconfigure a select number of roadway segments. An estimated 40 miles of corridor would cost approximately $400 million. This represents only a very small fraction of DOTs' annual budgets and can be accomplished by prioritizing within existing budgets.

58 Turn environmentally burdened neighborhoods into healthy communities

Photo: Richard Levine

The region's infrastructure has taken a heavy toll on low-income communities and communities of color. Highways, industrial facilities, and other sources of pollution are disproportionately located in these communities, causing serious health impacts and damaging neighborhood economies. Infrastructure agencies as well as states and municipalities need to prioritize the health of these communities by removing sources of pollution wherever possible and providing new sources of revenue for neighborhood investment.

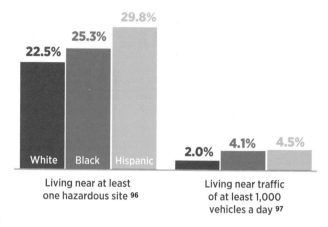

Living near at least
one hazardous site [96]

22.5% White
25.3% Black
29.8% Hispanic

Living near traffic
of at least 1,000
vehicles a day [97]

2.0%
4.1%
4.5%

Source: Environmental Justice Screen, Environmental Protection Agency, 2015

Hispanic and Black residents of the region are far more likely to live near a hazardous site or in a district with high vehicular traffic.

The health impacts of pollution are unequally distributed.

Many residential communities in the tri-state region are located near sources of pollution, including current and former industrial sites, highways, seaports, and airports. Residents can be exposed to noxious emissions from fumes, contaminated soil, or water, and in some instances, disruptive levels of light and noise that can cause stress.

The communities with the most exposure to these negative environmental conditions are disproportionately low-income communities of color, resulting from a history of government housing and infrastructure policies that paid little regard to the health and environmental impacts on these communities. Hispanics in the region are 30 percent more likely to live near hazardous sites, and Blacks and Hispanics are twice as likely to live near heavy traffic. These are communities that often already face many health challenges, such as limited access to health care, lack of access to healthy food, and unhealthy housing conditions because of poverty and other socioeconomic stressors.

East Harlem and Hunts Point residents, who are predominantly Black and Hispanic, are three to four times more likely to die from exposure to air pollution than residents of other New York City neighborhoods.[94] Asthma rates in Newark are 80 percent higher than those in neighboring Jersey City.[95]

Prioritize the health of all communities

Addressing this public health crisis is particularly urgent as climate change is likely to intensify the impacts of these sources of pollution. As heat waves worsen the impact of air pollution, and as sea-level rise and storms cause flooding in low-lying industrial areas, releasing contaminants into the water, we must remedy the environmental injustices of the past, and give everyone the chance to live in healthy communities in the future.

Collect better data to focus efforts on the communities that need the most attention

Departments of Health should expand their monitoring of ambient air quality regularly, with a particular emphasis on communities with poor air quality. The more specific the monitoring can be (location, time, type of pollutant), the easier it will be to identify the communities at risk, pinpoint specific sources of pollution, and drive political action. Better data can also enable a more effective distribution of resources to address the problem. As technologies develop, health and transportation departments should explore limiting vehicle traffic on poor air quality days. Converting tolling at crossings to charging drivers by the number of miles traveled, for example, could provide a valuable data source on vehicle movements and emissions.

Reduce pollution from ports, airports, and trucks

Ports and airports, and the truck traffic they generate, are terrible sources of air, light, and noise pollution for the people who live near them—particularly the residents of Newark and Elizabeth, who have both facilities in their backyard; Bayonne and Jersey City residents near the New Jersey ports; and Queens residents near LaGuardia and Kennedy airports. At the region's seaports, the Port Authority should set a target of zero emissions from cargo-handling equipment by 2030, and zero emissions from trucks by 2035, as the Port of Long Beach, CA—the only U.S. port bigger than New York's—recently adopted. In addition, ships at berth should plug into the electric grid instead of burning highly polluting bunker fuel (so-called "cold ironing"). Light- and noise-abatement programs should also be expanded to buffer nearby communities from their impacts.

At the airports, the worst local air pollution emitters are not airplanes, but ground vehicles. The best strategies for improving air quality are better access to the airports, and requiring all on-airport vehicles (baggage haulers, aircraft tugs, etc.) to be electrically powered. Aircraft could also be required to be plugged into the electric grid when stationary.

Retire the dirtiest power plants and ensure future infrastructure is equitably distributed

The tri-state area's last highly polluting coal-fired power plants are scheduled to close in the next few years. But combined gas/coal power plants remain. As more renewable energy comes online in the next decade and fossil-fuel plants are retired, the dirtiest facilities should be retired first. New infrastructure, particularly polluting facilities, should not be sited in communities that are already overburdened by pollution and poor health outcomes.

Remove, bury, or deck over highways

Many urban highways blight and divide neighborhoods, exposing them to dangerous levels of air pollution. High volumes of traffic also cause noise and dangerous pedestrian conditions. State departments of transportation should prioritize improving the highway segments that cause the most harm to neighborhood health, prosperity, and cohesion, and work with communities and municipalities to remove or transform them into community assets.

Invest in neighborhood improvements

From South Bronx to Newark and beyond, neighborhoods that have been damaged by these policies should receive preference for funding neighborhood improvements. This is especially true for new sources intended to address environmental challenges. One potential source would be revenue from an expanded cap-and-trade market, a portion of which could support energy rebates and community investment. Some of the this support should be directed to nongovernmental organizations that have been vital to successful clean-up and revitalization efforts in environmental-justice neighborhoods.

OUTCOMES

These proposals would result in reduced vehicle pollution near vulnerable communities, especially around ports and certain highway areas. Eventually, coupled with greater investments in these communities, health outcomes should improve. The governance mechanisms proposed would help prevent new environmental health disparities from emerging as a result of climate change.

PAYING FOR IT

The Fourth Regional Plan proposes several new revenue sources, such as expanded carbon pricing and vehicle miles tolling. A portion of these revenues should go to communities most overburdened by our energy and transportation infrastructure, for planning and capital investment purposes. The costs of highway decking could partially be covered by redevelopment and increased property tax revenues. Depending on the specific impact, developers and other private companies should carry some of the costs.

59 Support and expand community-centered arts and culture

WEPA! Festival in South Williamsburg Brooklyn. Photo: El Puente

One of the tri-state area's greatest strengths is its creative and cultural diversity—from our major art institutions to community cultural spaces across the region. But as neighborhoods change, local artists and cultural groups may be forced to move out of the communities where they are rooted, leading to cultural displacement. Supporting arts and culture in the region's communities requires investment and policies at the local and state level. To preserve the region's naturally occurring cultural districts and encourage more creative activity in all communities, the region needs more funding for the arts, more affordable housing and flexible creative spaces, more equitable access to arts and culture activities, and more opportunities for the emerging practice of creative placemaking.

Neighborhood-based arts and culture are a critical but undervalued part of the region's creative sector.

The tri-state region is a global leader in creativity. Its world-class art institutions are essential to the region's identity and vitality, and drive major economic benefits through tourism, film production, fashion, and other supporting industries. Yet creativity on the neighborhood level is often overlooked and receives less support. While large, traditional institutions are financed by foundation donations and government grants, many smaller organizations and spaces across the region struggle to find adequate funding and other resources, making it difficult to make long-term plans. There is a lack of diversity among the groups that do receive funding, less support for art spaces in communities of color, and a lack of diverse representation in the programming of larger cultural institutions.[98]

Another major challenge for local arts and culture is a lack of space to create and enjoy art. Many local zoning and building regulations make it difficult or expensive to establish the flexible spaces artists need to create and share their work. In many communities, real estate prices are beyond what local artists can afford; and when the less affluent neighborhoods artists settle into becoming more desirable, they can find themselves at risk of being displaced by wealthier newcomers.

Create the space for naturally occurring arts and cultural districts to flourish

Arts and culture are often treated as luxuries, and defined in the limited terms of traditional arts such as theater and museums. But a broad range of local creative and cultural activities, from libraries to street festivals to small galleries, provide compounding benefits to all communities. There are documented social, economic, and health benefits from local arts and culture activity in low-income neighborhoods.[99] Local artists, cultural spaces, and institutions should be supported in all neighborhoods through initiatives at both the local and state level through zoning, funding initiatives, and comprehensive creative placemaking efforts. Cultural events can help communities bridge divides, increase citizen participation, build trust in government processes, create safer and healthier communities, and preserve neighborhood history while elevating the narratives of traditionally marginalized communities.

Invest in arts and culture
While most communities consider arts and culture projects to be important, that often doesn't necessarily translate to monetary support from private and governmental sectors. Planners should see arts and culture as a fundamental part of a community's infrastructure. Joint ventures between local governments, community groups, and cultural institutions can encourage a more equitable investment in arts and cultural activities.

All publicly funded projects should build in a budget for art. New York City's Percent for Art and the MTA's Arts & Design are innovative programs that have, in the 30 years since their inception, promoted local artists and local art, increased civic pride, and demonstrated that city government and transit authorities are effective custodians of public space. Other communities and state agencies should follow their lead. New Jersey has adopted a different but equally effective strategy of dedicating funds from the state's hotel tax to the arts. Both Connecticut and New York should explore leveraging a similar tax or developing new funding streams to bolster arts and culture in local communities.

Lastly, municipalities can engage more residents in creative activities by providing more arts programs in public schools and continuing education opportunities through local universities, community colleges, or other educational institutions for adults and seniors. This could be accomplished through partnerships with anchor institutions or through public planning processes, like Participatory Budgeting.[100]

Build and preserve flexible and affordable space for living and producing art

Municipalities can support local artists by creating more flexibility in the zoning code to include provisions for live-work artist housing and workspaces, zoning bonuses for cultural uses, temporary occupancy permits, allowing rooftop cultural spaces, and giving special considerations to development projects that include arts—as Seattle has done.[101]

Promoting arts and culture can be an effective way to invest in the future of historic neighborhoods, including historically underinvested low-income communities of color. In addition to the zoning provisions specified above, municipalities can promote the preservation and reuse of historic buildings into community facilities or live-work situations by assisting owners with national register designation, historic tax credits, and other preservation opportunities. The CreateHereNowCT project has partnered with twenty cities in Connecticut to use vacant buildings as spaces for creating art. But local leaders also need to take steps to ensure investment is sustainable and equitable by protecting existing low-income tenants from displacement. In communities with expensive real estate, municipalities can promote community preservation by strengthening their affordable housing regulations.

Expand access to arts and culture opportunities
While the region has unmatched arts venues and events, art can also be experienced in a wider range of places, including the public spaces that tie communities together.

Local leaders should leverage streets, plazas, transit, community centers, and schools as places to create and enjoy arts and culture. New York City runs several city-wide and neighborhood-led street-closure events that are a simple and inexpensive way to program public space and engage hundreds of thousands of visitors in creative activities. Smaller cities and towns have similar car-free days, which should be expanded and made permanent when possible.

Space for arts and culture provides multiple benefits to the region's communities beyond beautification and economic development.

Photos: Safe Harbors of the Hudson, Van Alen Institute, NYC Department of Health and Mental Hygiene, and Christian Abraham, Hearst Connecticut Media.

Preservation
Safe Harbors of the Hudson
Newburgh, NY

Community building
Rebuild One City Parade
Asbury Park, NJ

Health
Health Dept. Mural Arts Project
New York City, NY

Economic development
Bridgeport Arts Trail
Bridgeport, CT

States, municipalities, and private funders should increase support for innovative neighborhood arts initiatives spearheaded by local organizations. Arts East New York, Newark Arts, open studios in Newburgh, and the Wassaic Project are just three of the many initiatives across the region that have grown local cultural offerings and helped to sustain communities through partnerships with local artists, schools, and government officials. Connecticut's Office of the Arts has also provided numerous grants for arts education in an effort to grow future arts audiences statewide.

Use creative placemaking to engage residents and other key stakeholders in planning for their community's future

Communities throughout the region are struggling with low local participation in political and planning processes. Creative placemaking emphasizes fostering more meaningful and inclusive community dialogues by investing in a community's existing cultural strengths while promoting equity, justice, and inclusion.[102] Rather than revitalizing communities by attracting artists from outside the community, creative placemaking promotes comprehensive planning with a central focus on art from the community up.[103,104] Creatively rethinking how we plan our communities can result in innovative solutions to some of our most pervasive problems.

Communities looking to pursue creative placemaking can apply for grants from the National Endowment for the Arts' Our Town project and ArtPlace America. New York's Naturally Occurring Cultural Districts Council and the National Consortium for Creative Placemaking based in New Jersey, can also serve as a technical resource for communities hoping to engage in the process.

OUTCOMES

Supporting existing creative and cultural assets in an equitable way would lead to more engaged communities with more active street life, civic pride, and economic activity. Children who have more access to the arts in school have better education (and therefore health) outcomes. Other vulnerable populations, such as seniors, who engage in social and creative activities, feel more connected to society. By embracing a wider range of the region's already rich cultural network, the region would see a rise in arts and culture tourism in other parts of the region, while boosting distressed communities and preserving their history. And through creative placemaking, neighborhoods would be better able to plan for and, with their cultural assets, ensure their success in the future.

PAYING FOR IT

Greater investment in neighborhood arts and culture could come from reallocation or incremental expansion from existing programs and funding streams. But creative ways for incorporating arts in both public and private initiatives should be explored, including tourism taxes, as the arts are a driving force of the region's tourism economy. Participatory budgeting should be considered as a way for residents to drive creative programming in their neighborhoods. Partnerships with institutions, such as hospitals, universities, and museums, could bring additional resources. And, in order for communities to engage in creative placemaking themselves, they should consider grants from the National Endowment for the Arts or ArtPlace America.

60 Expand access to healthy, affordable food

Photo: Rob Nguyen

Chronic health conditions related to a lack of healthy food are on the rise in the New York region, particularly in communities of color, despite the availability of restaurants and many types of grocery stores. Municipalities across the region must ensure all communities have access to healthy, affordable, and culturally appropriate food. This can be done by supporting wholesale and retail markets, preserving the region's farmland, and including food availability in all local planning.

Too many communities lack access to healthy and affordable food.

Access to healthy and affordable food is a challenge for many communities in this region. Nearly half a million people live in food deserts without access to affordable, healthy food options. And although residents may have access to fresh fruit and vegetables, it may not be culturally appropriate or affordable. One million households in the region receive food stamps to help pay for groceries.

Lack of access to healthy food is a critical challenge because a poor diet is related to chronic health conditions such as diabetes and obesity.

Prevalence of diabetes in adults

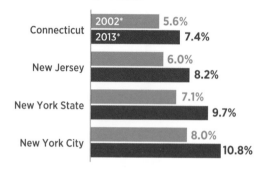

Connecticut	2002*	5.6%
	2013*	7.4%
New Jersey		6.0%
		8.2%
New York State		7.1%
		9.7%
New York City		8.0%
		10.8%

*For NYC, earliest year is 1999–2001 and latest is 2011–2013

Sources: Centers for Disease Control and Prevention, New York City Department of Health and Mental Hygiene

Lack of access to healthy food is a critical challenge because a poor diet is related to chronic health conditions such as diabetes and obesity. In the tri-state area, one in three adults is obese and about one in ten adults has diabetes, both of which have grown dramatically over the past two decades, and disproportionately affect people of color.

The food that is available in neighborhoods depends on several factors, including whether a community is designed to include retail, the proximity of wholesale food markets, the cost of commercial rents, and the efficiency of goods movement. Even in an area with good food options, food needs to be affordable, healthy, and varied.[105] The region's high transportation and real estate costs make it harder for smaller food shops to stay in business. Immigrant food businesses are essential to providing culturally appropriate food to the New York region, where so many immigrants reside. Many of these businesses, however, rely on more informal supply chains that are more vulnerable to disruption and displacement.[106]

Create healthy food options in all communities with comprehensive improvements to supply and distribution systems

Improving access to healthy and affordable food starts with understanding the food supply chain, from farm to wholesale and retail distribution. In places that need greater access to healthy food, community needs should drive planning decisions, as barriers to access to food can be highly individual. Municipalities must support different types of food businesses, while economic-development agencies should partner with planning agencies to preserve and create new space for food distribution.

Conduct local food-needs assessments

National studies have helped public-health and community-development experts understand how to improve access to food, but as every neighborhood is different, we must assess food availability and specific health, cultural, and food needs at a local level. States and cities should provide more resources for neighborhood food- needs assessments. Once the needs have been identified, they should be included in planning initiatives and used to inform public policy and investments. Communities with a higher rate of food-related health conditions and poor access to food should be prioritized.

Support vendor networks providing affordable food

Food is a high-cost, low-margin business, especially in this expensive region. It also requires a complicated network of physical assets, such as large wholesale warehouses, small retail stores, and an efficient transportation network. Local governments can help large and small food businesses thrive in all communities by taking the following actions:

- **Create more permanent public markets.** Typically located indoors in spaces with subsidized rents, public markets sell a wide range of foods produced locally and elsewhere. Lower operating costs mean cheaper prices for consumers, and markets located in the urban core can help revitalize downtowns. Cities can promote the creation of permanent food markets by allocating land and subsidizing rental rates for business owners.

- **Adopt mobile vending programs.** New York City's Green Cart program has increased access to fruits and vegetables in food deserts by both making it easier for mobile produce carts to operate and providing incentives such as food storage space.

- **Support new and existing small-scale retailers.** Bodegas and small supermarkets, often owned by immigrants, can be sources of healthy, affordable, culturally appropriate food. Local governments can help support them with funding and streamlined administrative procedures for licensing. Any neighborhood anti-displacement plans should include businesses that face displacement pressures.

- **Support food cooperatives.** Food cooperatives have been in the tri-state region since the 1970s, offering healthy food at affordable prices. Incentives to create food cooperatives and offer technical assistance will make it easier to start and run these suppliers.

Create regional food warehousing, wholesale, and manufacturing, at different scales, to improve the efficiency of food distribution

The Hunts Point Food Distribution Center, the region's single largest food wholesaler, supplies about 12 percent of New York City's food. In New Jersey, there are many national food service distribution centers that move large volumes of food, while most other food wholesalers are scattered all across the region. These wholesalers often struggle with deteriorating infrastructure and high costs, but are essential to smaller suppliers by keeping costs low for them to remain competitive. Some initiatives are already underway to create local food hubs to help farmers get their goods to market, and could be expanded to include other types of food businesses. Funding can come from from federal sources and industrial development agencies.[107]

Preserve farmland and better connect the region's farmers to markets

Green markets and small retailers play an important role in supplying locally produced food to residents. Better farmland-protection policies can help expand green markets, while also contributing to cleaner air and water, and thereby preserving the region's environment.

Include food-supply strategies in the budgets of planning, transportation, and economic-development agencies

Industrial policy and goods movement in the metropolitan area are fragmented by state and municipality, and food is infrequently considered by responsible agencies. To integrate food policy, regional economic-development councils and major economic and industrial-development agencies need to develop expertise in all aspects of the local food industry.

The region needs a comprehensive goods-movement strategy supported by the Port Authority and transportation departments. A regional food council, comprising food advocates and policymakers from across the region, could coordinate these efforts. The model for such a food council has worked in places such as Puget Sound, Washington, and in central Ohio, in which various stakeholders including food-justice activists and economic-development agencies establish shared policies to improve the food supply.

OUTCOMES

The outcomes of these policies would be reduced costs for food suppliers of all scales. This would be particularly important for smaller food chains, leading to more food businesses, and more affordable and diverse food options in more locations. The result would be greater access to healthy food, especially in low-income neighborhoods.

PAYING FOR IT

As the food system is embedded at all levels of the region, paying for these investments would be the responsibility of the agency or municipality in every geography and sector. Investments in regional infrastructure such as food hubs could come from federal sources and state economic-development councils. State and local economic-development councils and agencies that support small businesses could help businesses launch. Depending on the location, anchor institutions could support a variety of activities. Additionally, local health departments would receive more funding to promote food access.

61 Expand and improve public space in the urban core

Photo: RPA

Streets and parks in the core of the region are crowded with people who live, work, and visit. Yet there are underused spaces—such as parking lots, long-closed streets and underground passageways, office lobbies, rooftops, and underused public buildings—that could be opened to the public to relieve congestion. This would also provide new places for people to gather, create a more enjoyable urban experience, boost civic pride and encourage community involvement.

More public spaces are hidden in plain sight.

The core of the region is crowded and getting more so every day. Streets and public plazas are filled to the breaking point. And yet, there are a number of places that could or should be a part of the public domain: streets and underground passageways that have been closed, underused public structures, hidden privately owned public spaces, rooftops, building lobbies, and architectural treasures that are largely inaccessible to the public.

These places could provide a range of urban environments to enjoy, infuse vitality into civic life and give residents a sense of ownership, civic pride, and connection with their city. But zoning regulations, insurance policies, and a culture of not prioritizing public access have prevented us from making full use of these places.

Open more spaces to the public and transform our experience of the city

The success of the High Line, proposals like the Queensway and Low Line, and popularity of events like Open House New York show the demand for more public access to all parts of the urban environment, from tunnels to streets and rooftops. The more this demand can be fulfilled, the more people will be interested in and involved with their city, and the stronger our civic life will be be.

Empower communities to run pavement-to-playgrounds programs

Existing streets, parking spaces, vacant lots, and sidewalks could be reimagined as areas to play, both for permanent and temporary installations—particularly in neighborhoods with few playgrounds. Larger areas like parking lots could be permanently transformed, while smaller-scale on-street parking spots or underutilized sidewalk space in residential neighborhoods could be used as spaces to play on a temporary basis.

New York City already has a number of successful programs that should be expanded, streamlined, and coordinated, such as Schoolyards to Playgrounds, which is responsible for the renovation of hundreds of schoolyards and opening up access to them outside of school hours; the Play Street program, which allows communities to open up their streets to pedestrians for play on a recurring basis; and the Neighborhood Plaza Partnership initiative, which works with communities to turn parts of streets into public plazas.

Better manage privately owned public spaces

More than 500 privately owned public spaces (POPS) have been created in New York City in the 50 years since zoning regulations started to provide concessions to developers in exchange for giving public access to spaces within their property. But rather than requiring the POPS properties to remain in private ownership, the Department of City Planning should follow its waterfront development model and allow property owners to transfer title directly to the city. Other ownership and management options, such as easements, could also be explored. These alternative ownership structures should be prioritized for POPS with a history of access and maintenance problems.

"Access and openness—to the City and each other—are fundamental to a healthy civic life and an empowered citizenry."

—Open House New York Executive Director Greg Wessner

Once in public ownership, these spaces could be managed directly by a city agency, likely the Parks Department. Local Business Improvement Districts could also extend their jurisdiction past sidewalks and streets to improving POPS. The city could also explore using the space for more public amenities such as playgrounds, bathrooms, public art, and community events.

Where possible, POPS should be built to provide a continuous pedestrian area, with multiple entrances and exists. POPS that provide these connections between streets should be treated just like city streets, with matching signage and active incorporation into navigation apps and websites.

Reopen unused passageways and rights-of-way for public use

Several unused underground passageways in Manhattan could be reopened to relieve overcrowded streets and provide alternative pedestrian paths in inclement weather, such as the Gimbels Passageway between Penn Station and Herald Square, the Sixth Avenue passageway between Herald Square and Times Square, or the the 14th Street passageway between Seventh Avenue and Eighth Avenue. These passageways, as well as currently open ones, could also serve as retail corridors similar to the underground concourses in Columbus Circles or Rockefeller Center. Similarly, streets that have been closed to traffic for security reasons, such as Park Row in Manhattan, should be redesigned to be open, welcoming, safe, and accessible to bicyclists and pedestrians.

Connect office lobbies with the streetscape and allow more retail uses and openness

Office-building lobbies, although privately owned space, could be designed and programmed to be open extensions of the retail streetscape. Shops, cafes, and other commercial and community uses should be easily allowed inside building lobbies. Lobbies can also offer mid-block passageways— a valuable amenity in a city with long distances between avenues. Some New York City buildings already do this voluntarily or through the POPS program, and allowing retail uses or other incentives could encourage this to become standard practice.

Heavy security controls, minimal in other major cities but increasingly a standard part of the Manhattan landscape, are detrimental to a welcoming environment and often lead to significant delays, affecting business productivity. If these controls are necessary, they should not impede pedestrian flow through the building lobby. Many lobbies, most notably inside the Empire State Building, arrange security desks in a way that's friendlier to pedestrian flow, and can serve as a template for best practices. In particular, the city should create a program to encourage public access to the more than 100 lobbies that are designated as historic landmarks.

Rethink roofs as public spaces

Roofs are one of our greatest untapped public-space resources. Although some building systems need to be located on roofs (particularly in flood zones), this does not preclude roofs from also being used for other purposes— such as playgrounds, rooftop parks, farming and horticulture, next-generation digital and wireless networking infrastructure, or even goods delivery via drones.

Insurance requirements and building codes should be reformed to allow for more open and flexible use of roof space and give the public access to it. The Department of City Planning should reform zoning to allow POPS spaces to be located on publicly accessible roofs or terraces, or offer different concessions, as San Francisco has done. Zoning codes should also be changed to more easily allow commercial uses such as restaurants on roofs and upper floors of buildings.

Public buildings should take the lead in this transformation. The Bronx Borough Courthouse, which has a publicly accessible green roof, could serve as a model for other government-owned buildings.

Reserve more space for facilities-use through zoning

As the city's population grows, so does the need for public facilities such as schools, libraries, hospitals and clinics, houses of worship, and senior centers. In central areas where land values are high, these facilities find it difficult to compete with stores, offices, and other commercial uses that are able to pay more. The city's zoning code should be more proactive in setting aside land for community facilities to ensure they are part of the neighborhood fabric.

Give the public better access to public buildings

Many publicly owned buildings could be made more welcoming and useful to visitors and neighbors. Dozens of small Parks-Department structures, schools, libraries, and administrative office buildings are scattered throughout the five boroughs and could be made more accessible to the public— letting civic organizations and residents use meeting spaces, for example.

New York City's GreenThumb program, which has allowed many neighborhoods to create community gardens out of vacant lots, could be the model for a new program allowing community groups to access and use underused public structures, or even renovate them in exchange for long-term lease agreements.

Let people experience more of the city

Many public buildings and structures could be world-class attractions. Creating permanent spaces or even allowing special events in these structures would attract tourists and help locals celebrate their city's architectural heritage. Cities such as Los Angeles, Philadelphia and Tokyo have public observation decks on top of city government buildings. In New York, one could be opened on the Municipal Building or another city- or state-owned skyscraper.

BridgeClimb is an attraction in Sydney, Australia, that allows visitors to climb up the Sydney Harbor Bridge. Similar climbs could occur on the Brooklyn Bridge or another landmark bridge, giving tourists and New Yorkers a new experience of their city. In previous decades, spectacular spaces such as the Brooklyn Bridge anchorages have been used for special events, which could be revived, and others spaces could also be opened for events or tours, following in the footsteps of the Transit Museum tours of places like the abandoned City Hall Subway Station and Williamsburg Trolley Terminal. These types of experiences don't have to just be reserved for New York. All municipalities in the region have their own heritage and signature places, and could also institute their own "Open House" days.

OUTCOMES

Creating more space and places for people to enjoy in the urban core would make for an area in which living, working, and visiting is pleasant instead of stressful and overcrowded. A sense of civic pride and ownership would be created. Playgrounds, parks, and community facilities could be provided in areas where it would be much too expensive to find traditional sites to build them. New tourism opportunities would bring in more revenue and continue New York's relevance as a global center and primary destination for visitors around the world. Allowing new retail spaces in lobbies and passageways would create more business opportunities, particularly for small local businesses who may not be able to afford store fronts in the expensive thoroughfares of Manhattan.

PAYING FOR IT

There would be some implementation costs for wayfinding, street redesigns, and building retrofits which would likely be paid for by municipal governments or Business Improvement Districts. However, these costs would generally be minimal. Some costs for landowners and developers could be absorbed through zoning or other development bonuses. Public buildings could also increase revenue through fees for usage, and more signature tourism opportunities have the potential for significant revenue—the Sydney Harbour Bridge Climb brings in over $50 million a year in direct income. A more pleasant and open urban core is also a necessary investment in retaining and encouraging business and tourism, and the significant economic impact they bring.

Places

The policy recommendations of the Fourth Regional Plan will transform communities across the region. But different places have different needs and different aspirations—and some places represent particular opportunities to achieve significant, positive change.

JAMAICA

A business and cultural hub with ties to neighboring communities and JFK airport

It's 2040, and after years of development, Jamaica is a thriving regional downtown with bustling, multicultural neighborhoods that have maintained affordability while expanding the economy in sync with the growth of nearby John F. Kennedy International Airport.

As a regional downtown, Jamaica has much to offer. It is a cultural hub with theaters and dining options as well as shopping that attracts residents and visitors from both the region and around the world. Traveling on the Long Island Rail Road (LIRR) from Jamaica to downtown Brooklyn is fast and easy with a new regional rail service that helps many city employees get to work. New hotels attract international travelers from JFK, who prefer Jamaica's reasonable rates to those of the more expensive Manhattan. During the day, local restaurants serve food from all over the globe to the many people who work nearby, including airport workers and employees of light-manufacturing businesses.

Intensify downtown Far Rockaway

Strenthen the airport support district

Designate green corridors inland

Restore Jamaica Bay

Build new runways at JFK

Revitalize downtown Jamaica

Redesign Van Wyck corridor

Promote logistics/production at Aqueduct

Image: ORG Permanent Modernity for the Fourth Regional Plan

New terminals and runways at JFK allow the facility to handle nearly twice as many people—59 million passengers in 2016—and more goods than ever before coming through the airport. Thousands of back-office airline jobs, concessions, and other aviation-related or -dependent workers have offices in Jamaica, a short walk from Social Security Administration offices and civil courts in the area. There has been redevelopment in industrial areas outside the airport perimeter, and the former Aqueduct Racetrack has been redeveloped as a state-of-the-art goods-distribution hub with light industry, leveraging JFK's role as a global gateway. A new park—the Queensway—runs on a former abandoned rail line from Rego Park to just north of Atlantic Avenue. Redesigned downtown streets have bike lanes and pedestrian greenways, while new pedestrian connections and activities link the north and south sides of the Long Island viaduct. Jamaica has maintained its diversity and social cohesion through anti-displacement measures, and its affordability by focusing larger-scale developments around the train station and selected major streets, with smaller, residential buildings on local streets.

The community remains largely nonwhite, and truly mixed-income, with new employment offering local residents additional job opportunities.

Why it happened

Jamaica has always had a number of advantages. It is located at the nexus of rich rail transportation infrastructure and the New York region's largest airport, as well as long-term anchor institutions like York College. Strong community-development organizations, arts-related festivals and performances, and the multicultural Jamaica Market add to the unique character and street life of the area.

But for years, downtown Jamaica lagged with respect to key equity indicators. There was a need to lift the overall quality of life by creating better jobs for its residents, increasing the availability of affordable housing, and improving traffic and congestion.

How it happened

Reversing years of limited growth, Jamaica started to see an uptick in development at the turn of the century. By 2017, more than $1 billion in public and private investments had been made. Led by the Greater Jamaica Development Corporation and partners, a mix of city and state agencies and non-profit planning groups dedicated resources to help revitalize the area. These included the Jamaica NOW Action Plan, Regional Plan Association's Downtown Jamaica: Gateway to the New York Region, and New York State's $10 million economic development investment in 2016. Anti-displacement protections, including anti-harassment protections for residents and small businesses put in place soon after, protected the most vulnerable lower-income households, while more mixed-income housing was constructed.

New offices and hotels opened, and then complemented by a wide range of retail establishments and restaurants, primarily located along Jamaica Avenue and Sutphin Boulevard, and above the subway stations. The area near the AirTrain station started to become a thriving mixed commercial and office district, and more airport-related office jobs came to buildings nearby. An extension of the LaGuardia Airtrain from Flushing Meadows down the Van Wyck to Jamaica was considered, in order to connect it to the new airport-related hub as well as provide a direct link between the two airports. The 165th Street bus terminal was redesigned as a modern mixed-use multimodal facility with subterranean connections to the E, F, J, and Z subway lines. Downtown Jamaica built on its strong cultural foundation as home to the Jamaica Center for Arts and Learning, King Manor Museum, the Central Library of the Queens Library system, and the Jamaica YMCA to attract new arts-related festivals and events.

The MTA's transformation of its commuter rail lines into a more integrated and affordable regional rail system greatly improved access between Jamaica and all major employment centers and communities in southeast Queens. The opening of East Side Access provided a direct connection to Grand Central Terminal via commuter rail, and new one-seat ride transit service connected JFK to downtown Brooklyn and all major destinations in Manhattan. This new service, the Trans-Regional Express, made JFK accessible from all corners of the region. The hotel at the TWA Terminal became popular with New Yorkers and visitors alike, providing conference and event space. The airport was hardened to address sea-level rise and storm surges, just as other airports in the region addressed the effects of climate change.

How the recommendations of the Fourth Regional Plan helped

Regional downtowns in the tri-state area can be developed until they thrive, provide good jobs and affordable communities with policies that promote mixed-use development near transit services, maintain neighborhood diversity, and improve the overall quality of life with safe streets and green spaces. An inclusive planning process takes time, but helps craft a vision that has strong local and regional support. New regional rail networks can create better connections to more job opportunities, and areas around airports can help support airport growth while serving as destinations themselves.

RELEVANT PLAN RECOMMENDATIONS

19. Combine three commuter rail systems into one network

21. Modernize and refurbish New York City's subway stations

23. On city streets, prioritize people over cars

28. Expand and redesign Kennedy and Newark airports

46. Protect low-income residents from displacement and homelessness

50. Build affordable housing in all communities across the region

54. Restore regional job centers

THE FAR WEST SIDE

A new anchor for the region's core

It's 2040, and Manhattan's Far West Side is a dynamic commercial and residential district stretching from Midtown to the Hudson River, and anchored by a revitalized Penn Station complex.

This once remote industrial frontier of the city has been transformed. A modern mixed-use development around Penn Station provides commercial office space and amenities for workers and residents, all reachable by pedestrian walkways seamlessly integrated into Midtown. In nearby Hudson Yards, which features vibrant contemporary architecture, residents can take advantage of riverfront activities and access to all the city offers. Through preservation efforts and strict design guidelines, a diverse mix of building types and original housing stock was maintained, adding to the area's distinctive character even with the addition of thousands of new jobs and residents. The Far West Side is not only a transportation hub, but also an integrated city landscape that serves many purposes for residents and visitors alike.

Improve the Northeast Corridor

Extend Gateway to Sunnyside Yards

Create new parks and development around a new Penn Station

Promote mixed-use production in the Garment District

Designate new corridors to a resilient waterfront park

Build a second bus terminal below smaller Javits Center

Image: ORG Permanent Modernity for the Fourth Regional Plan

Why it happened

For more than half a century ago, city planners struggled to formulate a cohesive vision for the Far West Side. Important investments were made, including new offices and homes over Hudson Yards and the extension of the #7 subway line. But a fundamental obstacle remained: the larger district was composed of oversized "superblocks," and the area was disconnected from the rest of the city. Penn Station, a critical transit link for the city and the region, was aging and dysfunctional and surrounded by equally unappealing streets. The Port Authority bus terminal was deteriorating and well over capacity. Just to the north was the Garment District, home to a legacy industry but which struggled with rising rents and a changing marketplace that resulted in 1.7 million square feet of vacant floor space.

How It happened

The district's failing infrastructure was either removed or redesigned, including the elevated ramps to the Port Authority Bus Terminal and the cuts for the Lincoln Tunnel approaches. A new bus terminal beneath the Javits Convention Center consolidated intercity bus service into Manhattan and reduced bus overflow onto streets, while also shortening the commute for office workers in the growing Hudson Yards district.

With bus traffic reduced by nearly 30 percent, the old Port Authority Bus Terminal was refurbished with more commuter bus gates on the ground level, providing better access to subway lines and streets that were cleared of overhead ramps.

A new district also took root around Penn Station. Madison Square Garden, once located above Penn Station, was relocated, with its circular steel frame repurposed to enable light and air to stream down into the station. The platforms had been freed of hundreds of columns that used to support the arena. To make the area more conducive for shopping, dining, and entertainment, many streets around the station were closed off to become pedestrian walkways, and a lively public space was created along Seventh Avenue. This is also the grand entrance to the station, which in 2040, serves some one million daily riders. New escalators and widened stairs allow commuters and travelers to easily access the station from the sidewalk. And travellers are able to make through-running trips by connecting to Amtrak's new High-Speed Rail or a Regional Express train.

Riders are now able to use new through-running service to reach destinations beyond Manhattan. A professor from Cornell Technion is in the completed Moynihan Station waiting room about to board a High-Speed Rail Amtrak train to Boston; a commuter from Queens is staying on a Regional Express train to a new job in Paterson; and a car enthusiast is sitting on a train headed for Sunnyside Yards, where the relocated Javits Convention Center is hosting the annual Zero-Carbon Driverless Car Expo. These new through-running trips are possible because of Gateway East, two new East River tubes to Sunnyside Yards, and connecting tunnels along 31st Street, which were built after the new Gateway Tunnels, as part of the Penn South project.

The Garment Center was remade into a 21st century production district. The city funded the consolidation of garment manufacturing into permanently reserved space in the lower floors of the old loft factories, which now house manufacturing activities of all kinds, while start-ups and design firms have offices on the upper floors, along with residents.

All across the Far West Side, neighborhoods and signature open spaces—the High Line, Hudson Yards, new plazas around Penn Station, and pocket parks over the Lincoln Tunnel access roads—were connected by walkable and bikeable streets. Cross streets that once blocked the Convention Center were extended to a new waterfront park, which was widened from a narrow strip of greenway to a rolling landscape that holds back the raised waters of the Hudson. At the new water's edge are wetlands, new walls, and piers for ferry terminals and recreational activities.

How the recommendations of the Fourth Regional Plan helped

This transformation of the Far West Side was only possible because the agencies responsible for infrastructure and development began to collaborate, and recognized they shared a common goal of bringing prosperity and resilience to the area. A special-purpose authority delivered the new Penn Station and rail tunnels on time and on budget. Restructuring at both the Port Authority and the MTA enabled both trains and buses to operate reliably even as major construction was underway, and facilitated coordination between New York City, New York State, and New Jersey.

The creation of the Far West Side showed that New York City remained committed to housing affordability and economic opportunity. It preserved existing apartment buildings and encouraged a diverse economy of manufacturing and office employers in the Garment District, while commercial office space and residential towers were built near Penn Station. New transit connections supported a reciprocal and mutually beneficial relationship between New York City and the constellation of other cities in the region, which became centers of prosperity in their own right. At the same time, the city met the challenge of climate change on the vulnerable Far West Side by building new kinds of parks and public spaces at the water's edge, protected from sea-level rise.

RELEVANT PLAN RECOMMENDATIONS

16. Build a second bus terminal under the Javits Convention Center

18. Expand, overhaul, and unify the Penn Station Complex

23. On city streets, prioritize people over cars

40. Upgrade infrastructure to high standards of resilience

48. Remove barriers to transit-oriented and mixed-use development

53. Maintain a globally competitive regional business district

61. Expand and improve public space in the urban core

TRIBORO LINE

A new transit link
for the boroughs

It's 2040, and New York City's Triboro Line—24 miles of once abandoned railway tracks stretching from Sunset Park in Brooklyn to Co-op City in the Bronx—has become a vital part of the urban transit system for 100,000 daily riders, a catalyst for economic growth, and a place for recreational activities.

Once hidden below street level and behind trees, the rail lines of the Triboro now efficiently link people and goods moving between Brooklyn, Queens, and the Bronx—all without going through Manhattan. Travel times along the route have been reduced, with service every five to 15 minutes, enabling a passenger from Parkchester, in the Bronx, to get to her housekeeping job in Astoria and home in time to pick up her child at daycare. New manufacturing businesses are thriving in Ridgewood Queens, and freight deliveries arrive on time from a Hunts Point food distributor to a customer in East New York, a delivery that previously went by truck. All along the route, cyclists and pedestrians enjoy a car-free greenway and new parks, while the elderly and disabled easily access trains.

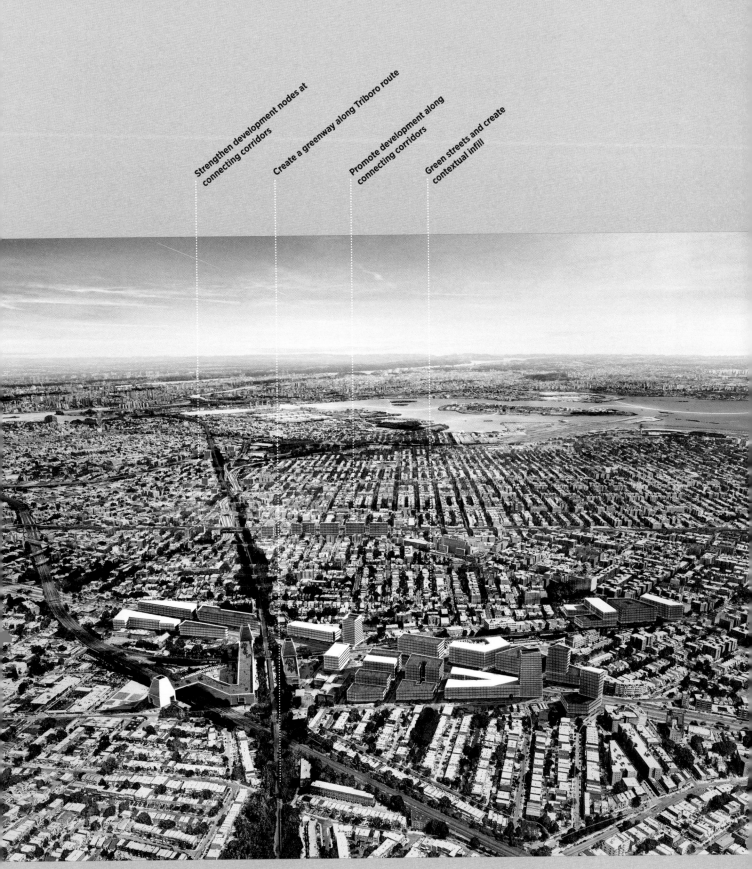

Strengthen development nodes at connecting corridors

Create a greenway along Triboro route

Promote development along connecting corridors

Green streets and create contextual infill

Image: ORG Permanent Modernity for the Fourth Regional Plan

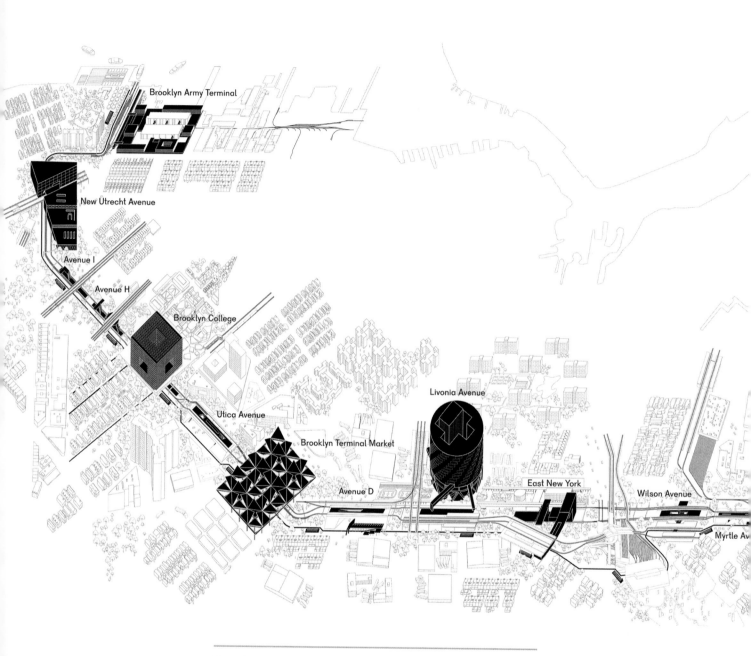

Brooklyn Army Terminal

New Utrecht Avenue

Avenue I

Avenue H

Brooklyn College

Utica Avenue

Livonia Avenue

Brooklyn Terminal Market

Avenue D

East New York

Wilson Avenue

Myrtle Av

Running 24 miles from Co-op City in the Bronx to Bay Ridge in Brooklyn, the Triboro Line would act as the wheel connecting the various spokes of the subway system branching from Manhattan. It would also act as a catalyst for the communities along the line. Only If and One Architecture, working with RPA, envisioned new programs for equitable development to facilitate intermodal links and generate positive impacts in Brooklyn, Queens, and the Bronx.

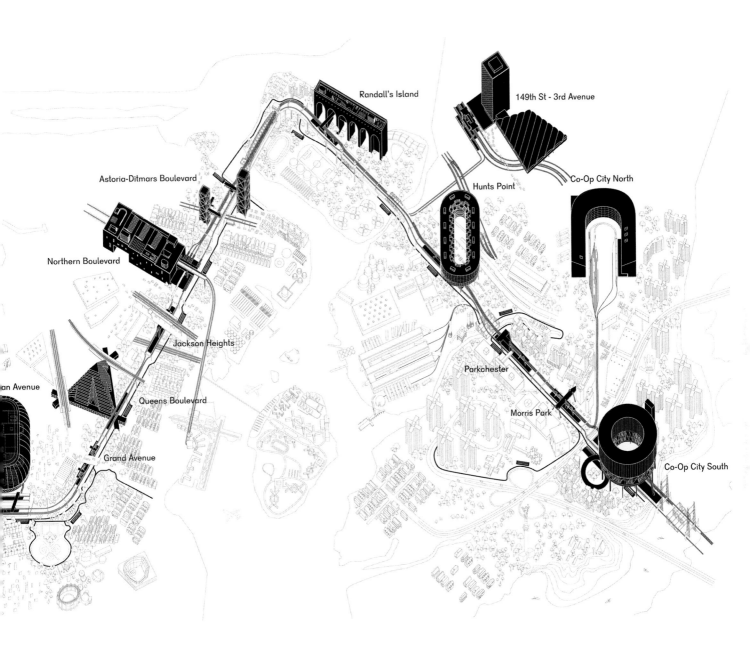

Astoria-Ditmars Boulevard

Randall's Island

149th St - 3rd Avenue

Northern Boulevard

Hunts Point

Co-Op City North

Jackson Heights

Parkchester

an Avenue

Queens Boulevard

Morris Park

Grand Avenue

Co-Op City South

Why it happened

The Triboro Line was a valuable asset waiting to be developed. It covers 80 square miles in area with a population of 2.6 million people, one of the most diverse communities in the city, and a large aging population. It intersects with 17 subway lines and four commuter trains. Before the Triboro, commute times were often long, and access to reliable transportation inconvenient, especially for those who didn't commute to Manhattan. When it was built, nearly 60 percent of households in the Bronx and Brooklyn, and 36 percent in Queens, did not own cars, making the Triboro a critical link to get to work or school, and for recreation.

These challenges will only grow as NYC jobs grow. Fifty percent of NYC's job growth has occurred outside of Manhattan in the last 15 years, and that's only projected to continue.

How it happened

The Triboro Line took some time to build, but cost less than $2 billion, less than other projects like the Second Avenue subway. New signals and track were added, and a few new substations, as well as a complementary network of urban greenways and open spaces. The existing track was either raised, sunken, or decked, and connecting bridges and tunnels were built to improve access to stations. The rail right-of-way is now intact and fully grade-separated, which required structural improvements.

The line was built in a way that protected existing residents and businesses. Legal protections against displacement started in East New York, and extended throughout the corridor, enabling many families to remain in their homes. New stations were designed around centers of activity: a revitalized industrial district in Sunset Park, an expanded college campus above the line near Brooklyn College, an expanded mixed-income neighborhood in East New York, a new intermodal mixed-use node near Queens Boulevard, and a regional goods-distribution hub in Hunts Point. Most of this development was incremental and carried out with close community cooperation, rather than large development proposals that transformed large areas at once.

Some 9,000 acres of government-owned land were redeveloped as open spaces, and new businesses funded vocational training programs linked directly to small-scale manufacturing.

As in other major cities (see Chicago Metra example), the Triboro Line was built to accommodate both passengers and freight. The movement of food into NYC followed projections, and increased 61 percent by 2035, following a dramatic rise in population growth. With the Triboro freight connection, congestion and truck traffic in Hunts Point has been reduced and the cleaner air has led to lower asthma rates.

How the recommendations of the Fourth Regional Plan helped

The Triboro did more than just improve regional mobility. It also addressed inequities in the transit system, gave more people access to jobs, created opportunities for affordable housing, improved public health in an area with high rates of obesity and asthma, and made the transportation network more resilient to storms, flooding, and other disruptions. The Triboro Line brought workplaces closer to the workforce, particularly for economic sectors not traditionally centered in Manhattan, such as education, health care, logistics, manufacturing, and food. Designed for an older and more diverse population, the new transit option has shown how a city can meet a citizenry's evolving needs and capitalize on its existing assets.

RELEVANT PLAN RECOMMENDATIONS

24. Improve bus service, and introduce new light rail and streetcar lines

39. Create a tri-state trail network

46. Protect low-income residents from displacement

47. Strengthen and enforce fair housing laws

48. Remove barriers to transit-oriented and mixed-use development

60. Expand healthy, affordable food access in the region

Image: ORG Permanent Modernity for the Fourth Regional Plan

The proposed Triboro Line would connect 17 subway lines and four commuter trains in Brooklyn, Queens, and the Bronx, significantly cutting down on borough-to-borough travel times.

BRIDGEPORT

A green and healthy city along the Northeast Corridor

It's 2040, and the city of Bridgeport is flourishing again as the center of a new green economy in Connecticut.

This coastal city is alive with entrepreneurial activity. At the Lake Success eco-business park, innovative urban agriculture is producing food for school cafeterias and downtown restaurants. A long-time resident of the South End who lives in a permanently affordable home has a job with a living wage at the University of Bridgeport. A doctor from a nearby town travels by train to the new Barnum Station to work at Bridgeport Hospital. Across the city, residents enjoy clean air and abundant parks, paths along Long Island Sound, and the Tri-State Trail Network, which connects the city to transit, nature, and neighboring towns. Young families have access to quality childcare and schools, and older residents are connected to services that let them age in place.

Build an eco-industrial park

Promote Bridgeport University as an anchor institution

Create a resilient park edge

Revitalize South End neighborhoods

Revitalize downtown

Provide continuous waterfront access

Create a transit-oriented development node at new Barnum Station

Complete the Seaview Avenue Connector

Image: ORG Permanent Modernity for the Fourth Regional Plan

Why it happened

Bridgeport had a strong legacy as a center of commerce and industry, but like so many similar cities across the country, languished in the post-industrial era. From the late 19ᵗʰ century through World War II, Bridgeport produced machinery, garments, and munitions and was the headquarters for many national corporations including Dupont, General Electric, Remington Arms, and Remington Shaver. After World War II, the jobs that powered Bridgeport's economy disappeared as production declined.

In the middle of last century, Bridgeport lost jobs and people as those who were able to leave for the suburbs—primarily the city's White population—abandoned the city. This exodus, fueled by the GI Bill, excluded Black residents who were refused loans for mortgages and were not allowed to purchase homes in nearby suburban towns through redlining and steering practices. The resulting racial segregation, loss of jobs and tax revenue, and brownfield contamination left little remaining economic opportunity for Bridgeport residents. The city struggled to find its footing, and as property values declined, property taxes soared.

How it happened

The tide turned for Bridgeport early in the 21ˢᵗ century with land reclamation. Many hazardous sites—including the infamous landfill dubbed "Mt. Trashmore"—were cleaned up. Pleasure Beach was reopened to residents and visitors, and a $500 million federal grant supported resilient infrastructure investments in the South End to help control flooding. Coal-powered electricity was converted to gas, and the red and white smokestacks standing beside I-95 no longer polluted the air.

As redevelopment continued over the next few decades, Bridgeport actively worked to correct environmental injustice and pursue sustainability. East Bridgeport, once dominated by brownfields and vacant lots, became a regional employment center with the new "Barnum" rail station along the Northeast Corridor, a thriving Bridgeport Hos-

pital, and an innovation hub for biotech companies. The Echo Technology Park, developed on reclaimed industrial land in the West End, grew into Connecticut's premier location for sustainable industrial practices, including district heating and cooling. Commuting times to New York City and Hartford by rail were substantially reduced with efficient regional rail service. Highway commuting times also decreased with congestion pricing on I-95 and more people using faster and more reliable train and bus service.

The transformation of Bridgeport wasn't easy. Over time, the City of Bridgeport became a strong partner with its residents, businesses owners and community development organizations, and working together they moved the city forward. Visionary and diverse local leaders became more actively engaged in planning and decision-making alongside long-time community advocates. Bridgeport's higher education and healthcare institutions became stronger neighborhood anchors through training and hiring local residents, helping to create and support local purchasing supply chains and investing in affordable housing and neighborhood infrastructure.

With state reforms and incentives for inter-municipal collaboration and shared services, property taxes in the city started to decline and are now on par with neighboring suburban towns. The region is less segregated by race, ethnicity and income and the achievement gap between low income and affluent students has narrowed. School performance in Bridgeport is now high and strong partnerships between anchor institutions and local companies are providing easily accessible career pathways to students. Substandard, unhealthy housing has been replaced with new, affordable homes in walkable, mixed-income, and diverse neighborhoods. Downtown is a vibrant, walkable, live/work hub for the region's creative entrepreneurs who take advantage of fast, reliable, local train and bus service. Old and new residents in Bridgeport are able to live comfortably without owning a car. Steelpointe Harbor has evolved into a mixed-use waterfront, attracting residents and visitors from throughout the region, and the Seaview Avenue connector is a thriving complete street corridor linking the Bridgeport waterfront and I-95 to the Naugatuck Valley.

How the recommendations of the Fourth Regional Plan helped

Bridgeport is a model for how to transform once struggling small industrial cities in the tri-state area. Investment in redevelopment and sound urban policies allowed Bridgeport, and other cities like it in the region, to become centers of economic growth with a talented workforce and attractive properties—just as New York City became too expensive. This urban resurgence took place without the displacement of longtime residents. The exact formula was different in each place, taking advantage of unique assets and circumstances. But the elements were similar: committed, sustained leadership from government, business, and civic groups and anchor institutions; a strong partnership with local residents and meaningful community engagement in planning and development decision-making; collaboration with the state and neighboring towns; catalytic investments in transportation and resilient infrastructure; property tax reforms that reduced reliance on local property taxes to fund local services; and resources and incentives that encouraged school district consolidation and integration.

RELEVANT PLAN RECOMMENDATIONS

9. Reduce reliance on local property taxes

10. Create regional school districts and services

12. Make the planning and development process more inclusive, predictable, and efficient

19. Combine three commuter rail systems into one network

40. Upgrade infrastructure to high standards of resilience

46. Protect low-income residents from displacement

54. Restore regional job centers

56. Promote partnerships between anchor institutions and local communities

CENTRAL
NASSAU

New transit links for a diverse suburb

It's 2040, and central Nassau County has become a model suburb with affordable housing, good schools, and a strong sense of community.

New rail connections link the Long Island Rail Road's Oyster Bay and West Hempstead Branch Lines, and the once separated North Shore and South Shores are connected via a quieter rapid transit service that replaced noisy rail lines. Improved transportation and streetscapes enliven the new mixed-use downtowns along the route, while residential neighborhoods are quieter and safer for walkers and bikers.

Create connections to nature reserves

Provide new rapid transit line from Mineola to West Hempstead

Create mixed-income transit-oriented development

Extend rapid transit to the completed Nassau Hub

Restore job center in downtown Hempstead

Convert heavy rail to quieter rapid transit

Link open spaces and create new green corridors

Image: ORG Permanent Modernity for the Fourth Regional Plan

Image: ORG Permanent Modernity for the Fourth Regional Plan

Shared, on-demand, and driverless vehicles can extend the reach of the commuter rail system into the suburbs, making it easier for people to commute without having to drive and park at the train station. And the acres of parking that surround stations can be transformed into walkable neighborhoods with new apartments, shops, and offices.

This new connectivity and economic development supports what is now a true center for Nassau County, including a major office, research, entertainment and government hub from Mineola to West Hempstead. More people use shared, on-demand and autonomous vehicles, as well as shared parking and bikes, and the streets are safer and more pedestrian friendly. Previously segregated areas on Long Island are now a collection of neighborhoods with high quality, affordable housing and schools available for everyone, regardless of race, age or income.

Why it happened

In the first part of the 21st century Long Island was a typical American suburb, dependent on cars using congested highways to commute. At the geographical center of Nassau County, the Village of Hempstead, was a significant employment center and directly north of Hempstead, downtown Garden City was the center of Nassau County's government offices and courthouses.

Both of these business districts were heavily car-oriented and lacked good transit connections, and surface parking accounting for almost a quarter of these downtowns, including public streets. Another area, the Roosevelt-Mitchell Fields east of Hempstead (known as the Nassau Hub) with universities, museums, and the Nassau Coliseum, also could not reach its full potential due to poor transit options.

Like many other parts of the region, Central Nassau was sharply divided by race and income. For example, the Garden City and Hempstead's school districts, despite being in direct proximity, were among the most segregated in the region, a reflection of the segregated housing of the time. Hempstead public schools were 96 percent Black and Hispanic; Garden City public schools, 90 percent White.

Most public transportation consisted of either slow and unreliable local buses, or infrequent heavy rail access via the LIRR to New York City, which was noisy and ran almost exclusively through residential neighborhoods. Traveling even a short distance between north and south by public transit was very difficult: From the West Hempstead LIRR station to the Garden City LIRR station directly to its north took only five minutes by car; yet public transportation required either two buses and a ten minute walk, or a rail transfer through Queens.

How it happened

Change began when Nassau County, the Town of Hempstead and the Long Island Rail Road agreed on a plan to develop the Hub to provide affordable housing, commercial office space, and entertainment options, as well as a new transit link that built on decades of analysis by local planners.

The planning process was made easier through greater public engagement and an effort by officials to address concerns about traffic and schools. Leaders committed to focus on schools, adding art, after-school, science and language programs that provided more options for a more diverse student body at each school. Performance was closely monitored to ensure all schools continually improved. Spurred by state incentives, school districts began to collaborate with shared transportation, academic programs and magnet schools. This eventually led school district to merge into larger ones, resulting in more integrated, high-performance schools.

The area had many transportation assets, but they were underutilized. The two least-used branches of the Long Island Rail, the West Hempstead and Oyster Bay branches, were reconfigured as a north/south rapid transit line, connecting through Hempstead and Garden City but retaining their frequent links to Manhattan. An extension to the Nassau Hub was added by utilizing a disused rail right-of-way for part of the route. Communities on the north and south shores now had easy access to the jobs, services, universities and entertainment in Downtown Hempstead, Garden City, and the Nassau Hub. Residents of central Nassau and the south shore were able to easily visit Oyster Bay, the Nassau Museum of Art and two nature preserves on the Oyster Bay line. In addition to better transportation options, the surrounding communities saw a major quality-of-life improvement as the conversion from heavy rail to quieter and low-emitting rapid transit significantly reduced noise.

This transit connection also helped downtown Hempstead and Garden City become a vibrant, walkable corridor with new shops, restaurants, and pedestrian and streetscape improvements including better lighting, more trees, and safer crossings. More walkable areas opened up 22 percent of the land area formerly used for surface parking for new homes, shops, offices, parks, and public facilities such as libraries, schools, and senior centers.

Another benefit was social integration. In addition to the regional school districts, mixed-use, mixed-income development helped provide affordable homes and more shops and restaurants throughout the corridor from Mineola through Garden City, to Hempstead and West Hempstead. Affordable homes attracted young families, which in turn brought new businesses and investment. And because the new development focused not only on housing but also on expanding civic and commercial space, the area's anchor institution—museums, universities and hospitals—were able to grow as well and contribute more to the larger community.

How the recommendations of the Fourth Regional Plan helped

New rapid transit lines gave more people easier access to jobs, nature, and educational, cultural, and recreational opportunities, and the reduced noise and pollution improved life in the surrounding residential neighborhoods. Better streetscapes improved safety and made walking more enjoyable. Transitioning to regional school districts saved money and improved education. The improved transit connections, access to affordable housing, and mixed-income development allowed people of all ages and backgrounds to live in an attractive suburb with complete neighborhoods and a strong sense of community.

RELEVANT PLAN RECOMMENDATIONS

10. Create regional school districts and services

13. Increase participation in local government

24. Improve bus service, and introduce new light rail and streetcar lines

25. Expand suburban transit options with affordable, on-demand service

48. Remove barriers to transit-oriented and mixed-use development

50. Build affordable housing in all communities across the region

NEWBURGH

A model for equitable and sustainable development in the Hudson Valley

It's 2040, and the former industrial city of Newburgh is an equitable, healthy, and sustainable city with thriving businesses and culture, and a majestic gateway to the Highlands and the Hudson Valley.

Newburgh has succeeded in building on its many strengths: diversity and affordability, location on the Hudson River with ferry access to the Metro North railroad in Beacon, historic urban fabric, proximity to freight and highway infrastructure, and the proximity of anchor institutions including Mount Saint Mary College and Saint Luke's Cornwall Hospital. A now vibrant downtown features affordable housing, live-work artist spaces, tech start-ups, and light-industrial manufacturing. On sunny days, families stroll along green streets linking city parks with surrounding natural areas, including the Quassaick Creek blue/green corridor. Safe, walkable neighborhoods feature dedicated bike lanes, while reliable local bus service allows residents of Newburgh and nearby Beacon to spend evenings in the other city.

Link neighborhoods to the waterfront with green corridors

Reduce urban heat and manage stormwater with green streets

Redevelop corridor from downtown to Stewart Airport

Promote transit-oriented development at the ferry to Beacon

Build more mixed-use and affordable housing in downtown

Create a resilient waterfront park, greenway, and development

Contain development at a well-designed green edge

Image: ORG Permanent Modernity for the Fourth Regional Plan

Why it happened

Like other former industrial cities that peaked in the mid-20th century, Newburgh experienced decline and then forged its own renewal in the 21st century. The city's revitalization had benefits for the whole region—development in the city reduced sprawl, helped bring people out of poverty, and allowed greater access to economic opportunity.

How it happened

Unable to rely on the strength of Manhattan's central business district, the city built its own by improving the digital infrastructure—seeded with state and local government support—that allows newer, smaller businesses to flourish. Municipal partnerships with Mount Saint Mary College and Saint Luke's Cornwall Hospital included collaboration on workforce development, a "buy local" strategy, and reciprocal capital and economic investments. Bus rapid transit has greatly eased congestion on Route 17 and interstate 84, while connecting Newburgh's downtown with an expanded Stewart Airport and the Metro North rail station at Beacon.

Upgraded neighborhood housing stock, anti-displacement measures, strong rent regulations, and providing legal counsel to low-income residents who faced eviction allowed residents to stay in the city as the economy strengthened. The Newburgh Land Bank, formed in 2014, played a critical role in rehabilitating hundreds of formerly blighted properties and supporting infill mixed-use development of vacant lots. Houses were made available to low- and moderate-income first-time homebuyers, and many apartment buildings were turned into affordable cooperatives or community land trusts with permanently affordable units.

The city built contextual, mixed-income, mixed-use developments that include community-owned affordable housing, as well as artist and commercial spaces. Newburgh entered into intermunicipal-transfer-of-development-rights agreements, which played an essential role in bringing positive development to the city while stopping the sprawl that had been threatening to destroy the farming communities and natural areas of the Hudson Valley. The city planned inclusively, listening to its diverse communities and organizations in the planning process before making land-use decisions. And, many local organizations engaged in a collective impact strategy to ensure existing residents benefit-

ted from changes in their community. As a result, Newburgh is still home to people from many races, ethnic groups, and income levels.

To improve the city's access to nature, there is a network of open spaces connecting neighborhood parks to Snake Hill, Quassaick Creek, and a Hudson river waterfront greenway that also links to a mixed-use waterfront at the downtown to natural edges to the north and south. The former consolidated iron site was transformed from a city-owned superfund parcel into a great public park on the Hudson River.

State-of-the-art green infrastructure technologies including rain gardens, bioretention areas, swales, green roofs, cool and permeable pavement, tree plantings, and storm-water planters reduce dependence on the city's sewer system and protect the region's water quality. Distributed generation provide affordable energy alternatives to local residents and businesses (link to Envt-13).These improvements have also contributed to the restoration of Lake Washington, and made summers more bearable for residents by mitigating urban heat island effects.

How the recommendations of the Fourth Regional Plan helped

Newburgh's economic development has focused on reducing poverty and inequality by providing state support for a collaborative city-town-county strategy. This allowed for the sharing of property tax revenues to support worker cooperatives, urban markets that collaborate with surrounding agriculture, and local artists and cultural organizations, all connected with high-speed internet. In addition, revenue sharing also drastically improved the quality of area schools.

Newburgh also capitalized on a broader regional push toward compact urban living by playing to its greatest strengths: diversity and affordability, a beautiful historic urban fabric, proximity to freight and highway infrastructure, and its proximity to nature and open spaces. Newburgh even partnered with surrounding municipalities in Orange County to ensure development was concentrated in the city through transfer of development-right agreements that conserved land outside. These agreements facilitated much broader cooperation, from revenue sharing between school districts to agreements on cooperative businesses, including agricultural businesses.

RELEVANT PLAN RECOMMENDATIONS

9. Reduce reliance on local property taxes

14. Expand affordable internet access across the region

37. Cool our communities

39. Create a tri-state trail network

42. Modernize the electric grid

46. Protect low-income residents from displacement

54. Restore our regional job centers

59. Support and expand community-centered arts and culture

60. Expand healthy, affordable food access in the region

MEADOWLANDS

A national park for the region

It's 2040, and a signature national park has been created in the Meadowlands, once a largely underappreciated industrial landscape and transit crossroads.

The Meadowlands has embraced its identity as a new kind of park that is not a pristine landscape, but a compelling demonstration of how vital natural systems services—habitat, flood control, clean water—can be reconciled with the infrastructure that is essential to the region's prosperity. Through a balanced approach of protection and retreat, Meadowlands communities are thriving, healthy, mixed-use centers of activity, protected from storm surges and sea-level rise flooding, and connected to the restored beauty and biodiversity of a new model of national park that grows as the climate continues to change. Places like Secaucus are protected from rising waters, while smaller communities, like Teterboro and its airport, are returned to nature where floodwaters can be absorbed.

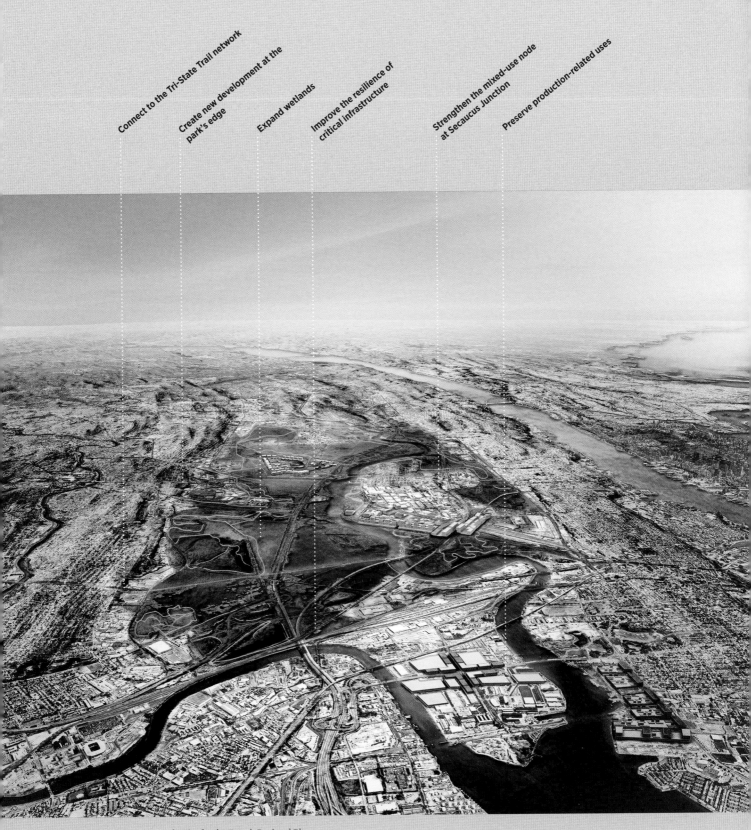

Connect to the Tri-State Trail network

Create new development at the park's edge

Expand wetlands

Improve the resilience of critical infrastructure

Strengthen the mixed-use node at Secaucus Junction

Preserve production-related uses

Image: ORG Permanent Modernity for the Fourth Regional Plan

At-risk infrastructure and population in the Meadowlands
Sea-level rise threatens to inundate or regularly flood
hundreds of contaminated sites, miles of rail track, and other
critical pieces of energy and water infrastructure. Thousands
of residents and jobs will be either displaced or disrupted by
sea-level rise or more frequent flooding events.

Source: RPA

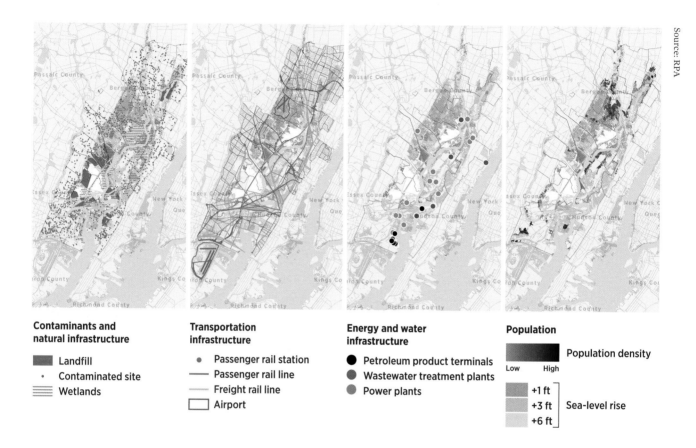

Contaminants and natural infrastructure
- ▨ Landfill
- · Contaminated site
- ≡ Wetlands

Transportation infrastructure
- ● Passenger rail station
- — Passenger rail line
- — Freight rail line
- ▭ Airport

Energy and water infrastructure
- ● Petroleum product terminals
- ● Wastewater treatment plants
- ● Power plants

Population

Population density
Low → High

+1 ft
+3 ft   Sea-level rise
+6 ft

Communities on the edge of the Meadowlands, on higher
ground, are more dense with a greater mix of uses. The
region's job-rich warehousing and distribution centers are
reconfigured and consolidated, becoming more vertical and
aligning along a regional industrial corridor of roadways and
rail lines. Vital infrastructure, including major roadways, rail
lines, and wastewater and energy facilities is protected and
elevated where necessary, ensuring this critical juncture
keeps the region moving and thriving.

Why it happened

Over the past century, the New Jersey Meadowlands has
been a distributed mix of communities and employment centers located in a significant, though compromised, estuarine
system. The Meadowlands was also burdened with freight,

commuter, and inter-city rail lines; and roads, power lines,
refineries, and distribution and warehousing facilities that
kept the northeast megaregion thriving. It was also home to
some of the greatest concentrations of contaminated sites
in the country.

Of all of the places in the region at risk of increased flooding from climate change, the Meadowlands presented perhaps the greatest challenge of all. In addition to threatening
the infrastructure and natural systems described above, permanent flooding from sea-level rise was becoming a real risk
for up to 36,000 residents and up to 51,000 jobs, while periodic flooding from increased precipitation and storm surges
had threatened to disrupt the lives of 40,000 residents.

As the consequences of climate change (greater precipitation, more frequent and intense storms, sea-level rise, and
extreme heat) began to accelerate, natural and human communities as well as vital infrastructure began facing greater
risks, with few plans for addressing them.

How it happened

Transforming the Meadowlands into the climate-proof, natural, and economic amenity has taken vision, cooperation, and significant investments. First, the concept of a new model for a national park—where park boundaries expand as the sea level rises and communities recede from the water's edge—was tested and applied. An initial 10,000 acres of parks, protected wetlands, vacant land, and landfills were transferred from state, local, and land-trust ownership to the federal government. The 872-acre Teterboro Airport site was abandoned by the Port Authority and engineered into a natural flood storage site. A robust buyout program was created for the Meadowlands and vulnerable residents took advantage, selling their homes ahead of the coming flood and adding acreage to the growing park. At the same time, federal and state investments into cleanups of contaminated sites quickened, along with restoration efforts, and these former hotspots became educational features of the new park.

On the periphery of the Meadowlands, on higher ground, nearby towns saw the opportunity presented by the buyout program and national park and rezoned areas of communities for increased densities and mixes of uses. These border towns have become thriving, mixed-use suburbs with direct access to an environmental and recreational amenity.

The region's Adaptation Trust Fund was tapped to invest in protective measures for those places with the greatest concentrations of population, employment, and critical infrastructure to guard against sea-level rise, storm surges, and heavy precipitation flooding. The town of Secaucus sits at the center of such an area, with the highest population of any single town in the Meadowlands, and is now a thriving suburban center. A new master plan for the area around Giants Stadium includes investments into flood protection and the phasing in of mixed uses. New Jersey Transit, the Port Authority, CSX, and the New Jersey Turnpike Authority have begun the complicated process of elevating rail- and roadways.

Private warehousing and distribution companies, and their tens of thousands of jobs—aided by federal and state economic development grants—joined together to relocate into concentrated, protected areas with good access to road and rail. These new vertical facilities represent a new model for the industry.

How the recommendations of the Fourth Regional Plan helped

The dramatic changes taking place in the Meadowlands were only possible because of strong and forward-looking leadership provided by a Regional Coastal Commission, focused solely on the issue of adaptation. Members of the commission from all three states recognized the critical regional link the Meadowlands provides for roads, railways, and energy infrastructure, and could reach agreement on funding from each state's Adaptation Trust Fund to ensure the region remains connected and thriving.

At the same time, the concept of a new model of National Park captured the imagination of residents and regional stakeholders, who were able to galvanize support at all levels and push through the formal state and federal processes. Municipalities at the greatest risk of permanent flooding were able to develop a timeline and begin participating in an innovative buy-out program to justly transition development away from the flood zones, knowing their former home would be part of a new park and natural habitat.

Communities surrounding the park were well-prepared to capture the economic and other benefits of this new amenity. Development around the edges of the park increased dramatically, due to transit and road connections. The Meadowlands was also able to maintain its role as a distribution and warehouse employment center by consolidating industrial uses into modern and resilient facilities.

RELEVANT PLAN RECOMMENDATIONS

31. Protect densely populated communities along the coast from storms and flooding

32. Transition away from places that can't be protected

33. Establish a national park in the Meadowlands

36. Restore the region's harbor and estuaries

40. Upgrade infrastructure to high standards of resilience

55. Make room for the next generation of industry

PATERSON

Connecting a former factory town to the region's economy

It's 2040, and Paterson is a vibrant regional center with new rail connections and a growing economy and tourism sector.

With new rail connections linking Paterson with Newark and New York City, as well as stations in Passaic and Essex counties, it is now possible to commute from Paterson to Manhattan in about 30 minutes without transferring, roughly half of what it was in 2000. A new light-rail service utilizes the formerly dormant Erie Railroad Main Line, and has reinforced Clifton, Nutley, Belleville, and other places it passes as viable communities, with direct connections to the Newark subway and Newark Penn Station.

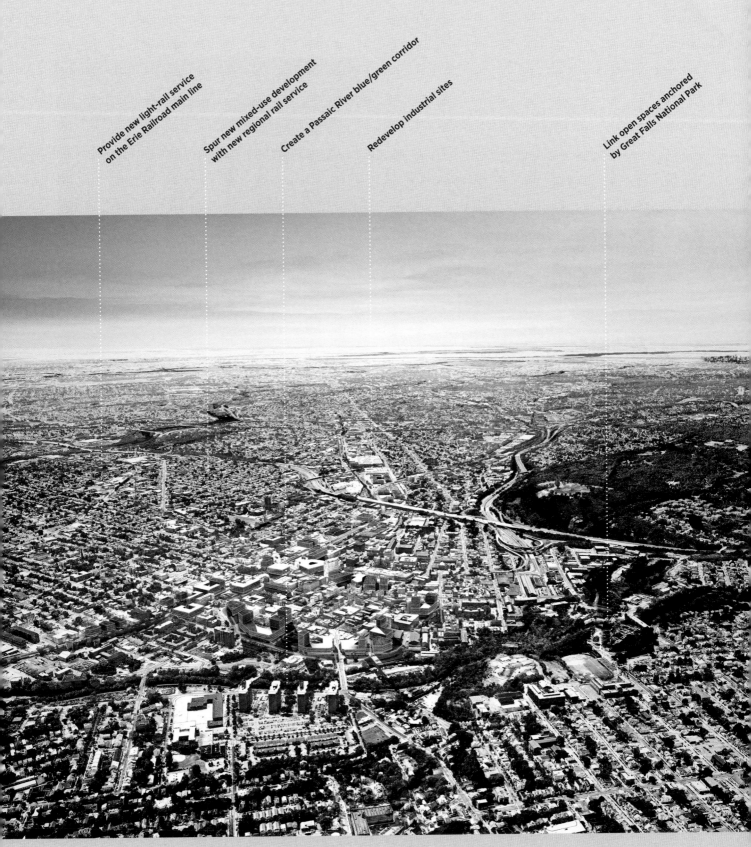

Provide new light-rail service
on the Erie Railroad main line

Spur new mixed-use development
with new regional rail service

Create a Passaic River blue/green corridor

Redevelop industrial sites

Link open spaces anchored
by Great Falls National Park

Image: ORG Permanent Modernity for the Fourth Regional Plan

Faster commutes to New York City have spurred the building of new homes and apartments around the rail station. But Paterson, the third largest city in New Jersey, is also a destination: visitors can easily access Great Falls in Paterson's National Historic Park, which has dramatically increased visitor numbers. Paterson is also an important downtown destination for restaurants with international cuisine, which provide jobs for local residents.

By maintaining and upgrading its existing housing stock and balancing historic preservation with new development, Paterson has been able to remain an affordable and diverse community. It has also drawn creative and food sector companies from all over the region to relocate or start businesses, providing jobs and economic growth.

The industrial areas north and south of the downtown have been consolidated and reconfigured to accommodate a new generation of environmentally friendly, small-scale manufacturing and companies, many of them part of the "maker movement" or focusing on food. New enterprises occupy formerly vacant warehouses clustered along the Passaic River, which are served both by light rail stations and a bikeway that follows a green belt from the National Historic Park.

Development has allowed residents to remain in Paterson and thrive while stimulating a broader, more economically diverse workforce to move there seeking new opportunities.

Photo: Rich Mitchell

A new Master Plan was initiated in 2014, giving local Community Development Corporations more resources to take action. The light rail line was built over three years, benefiting from an inclusive planning process and faster construction timelines. The Master Plan also changed zoning regulations, making it easier to convert one-family homes to two- or three-family homes; construct new recreational facilities: and redevelop the Hinchliffe Stadium. There was more activity in the downtown area, while the government addressed crime and safety concerns. As this change took place, Paterson was able to remain the most ethnically diverse city in New Jersey.

Why it happened

Paterson, once the home of a thriving silk manufacturing industry struggled for many decades with a loss of industrial jobs, and as a result, experienced an increase in crime.

Yet things started to change in 2009 when Congress authorized the established of Great Falls as National Park, boosting tourism. The popularity of the Broadway musical Hamilton encouraged visitors to explore Alexander Hamilton's role in the area's history, while Paterson rapper Fetty Wap drew attention to the city.

How it happened

New transit links and adapting vacant industrial buildings for creative purposes were crucial to redevelopment and revitalization. Community-based organizations and youth groups played a vital role in the transformation, which was carried out using state tax credits. Placing New Jersey's first municipal internet network in Paterson was crucial for artists using new digital technologies. New rail lines were built in record time, funding by increased revenues from highway tolls. An inclusive planning process allowed communities to express concerns as the project was designed.

Image: ORG Permanent Modernity for the Fourth Regional Plan

How the recommendations of the Fourth Regional Plan helped

The revitalization of Paterson demonstrated how new transit options can connect people to more opportunity, and bring residents and visitors to jobs and cultural and recreational destinations throughout the region. New transit connections also encouraged development in centers most in need, and helped channel investments. Clean industries, using modern production techniques, were able to flourish in the former factory town.

RELEVANT PLAN RECOMMENDATIONS

24. Improve bus service, and introduce new light rail and streetcar lines

39. Create a tri-state trail network

51. Make all housing healthy housing

54. Restore our regional job centers

55. Make room for the next generation of industry

59. Support and expand community-centered arts and culture

THE INNER LONG ISLAND SOUND

Industry, nature, and neighborhoods in harmony

It's 2040, and the Inner Long Island Sound has been transformed from one of New York City's worst-polluted areas into a healthy place to live and work.

From the Whitestone Bridge to the Triboro Bridge, the waterfront is finally open and accessible, with protections against sea-level rise and storm surges. An urban park ranger gives a tour on the newly opened North Brother Island, explaining how pollution was reduced; wildlife restored to the water, land, and air; and asthma and other respiratory illnesses in the nearby neighborhoods virtually eliminated. A Bronx woman takes the new Triboro line to her good-paying industrial job, a 45-minute commute reduced to ten. On Rikers Island, the notorious detention center, now provides jobs instead of jails, with state-of-the-art energy generation, education, and environmental facilities.

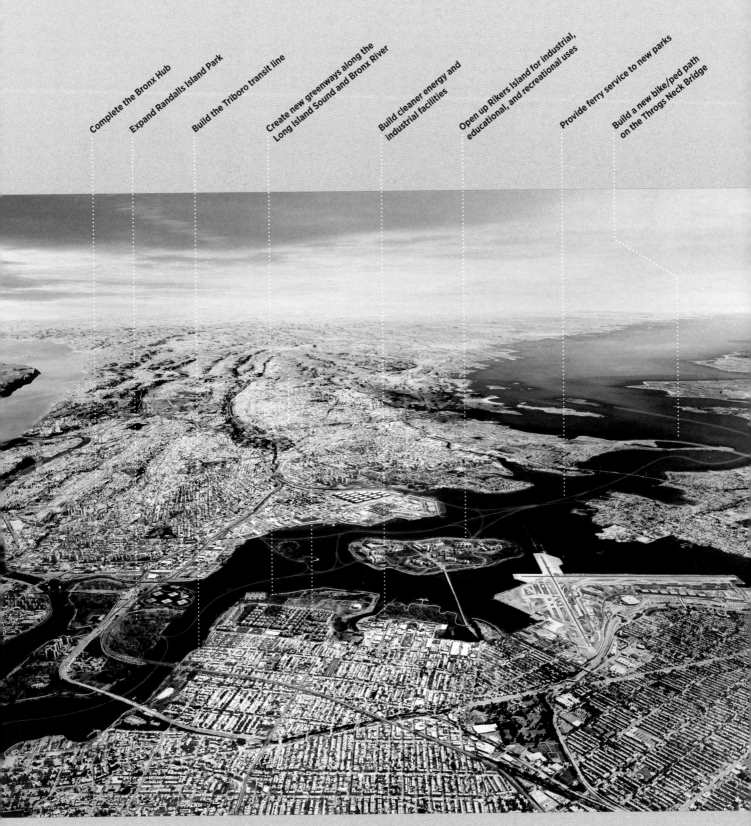

Complete the Bronx Hub

Expand Randalls Island Park

Build the Triboro transit line

Create new greenways along the
Long Island Sound and Bronx River

Build cleaner energy and
industrial facilities

Open up Rikers Island for industrial,
educational, and recreational uses

Provide ferry service to new parks

Build a new bike/ped path
on the Throgs Neck Bridge

Image: ORG Permanent Modernity for the Fourth Regional Plan

Image: ORG Permanent Modernity for the Fourth Regional Plan

Replacing older, dirty power plants as they are retired with smaller, more efficient facilities can free up valuable space for parks and other community amenities.

Why it happened

For decades, the Inner Sound area was one of the most inequitably treated places in the region, with multiple wastewater-treatment facilities, power plants, jails, noxious industries, combined sewer overflow, and waste-transfer stations. Pollution was commonplace in the surrounding mostly low-income communities, with subsequent health problems. Asthma rates in Mott Haven were the worst in the city, and children in Hunts Point were more likely to live within walking distance of a waste-transfer station than a park.

Along the seven miles of South Bronx shore, the inaccessible industrial waterfront contained only two small parks totaling less than 1,000 feet of shoreline. On the North Shore of Queens, there were nearly nine miles of inaccessible industrial and airport waterfront from Astoria to East Elmhurst. At the center of this was the 413-acre Rikers Island, a violence-prone and isolated jail where 79 percent of those incarcerated were never convicted of a crime and were simply unable to make bail.

Yet the Inner Sound also was home to badly needed blue-collar jobs and protected islands. Instead of eliminating them, the city found ways to integrate the natural amenities with industry and residents in an environmentally friendly way.

How it happened

Much of the transformed area was owned by the city, including all of the islands in the harbor (Rikers Island, North and South Brother islands, and Randall's Island), four waste-treatment plants, the Hunts Point Cooperative Market, and several other large parcels of land. Utility companies and other quasi-public entities owned other large parcels of land. This provided an opportunity for implementation of a comprehensive vision for the entire area.

The first step was closing the Rikers Island jail complex and transitioning to smaller borough-based jails, as recommended by The Independent Commission on New York City Criminal Justice and Incarceration Reform, and supported by the City Council and Mayor de Blasio. This approach not only reduced incarceration rates throughout the city but also opened up Rikers for industrial, educational, and recreational uses. These include a composting center, wastewater-treatment plant, waste-to-energy facility, related education and job training facilities, a public greenway, and a memorial to Rikers's notorious past. As a result, wastewater-treatment plants and truck-to-truck waste-transfer facilities were eliminated in the surrounding neighborhoods, reducing air and water pollution and allowing the creation of clean industry along the waterfront. A new Triboro rail line provided a new transportation link for Northern Queens and the South Bronx, including access to open space on Randall's Island.

The future of the Inner Sound was determined to a large extent through a comprehensive community planning process, which included neighborhood residents, community groups, public agencies, and large local employers and institutions such as Con Edison and the Hunts Point Food Co-op. This built on previous, smaller planning efforts in these neighborhoods.

New parks and recreation areas could be developed quickly, because much of the unused or lightly used land in the area was already owned by the city, utilities, or public

agencies. As more land gradually became available through decommissioning, the plan was further refined and implemented. And as technology improved, new energy-efficient and environmentally friendly industrial facilities—including power generation, wastewater transfer, and food delivery—were added, improving the health of surrounding communities as well.

How the recommendations of the Fourth Regional Plan helped

Building a new waste treatment station on Rikers Island and eliminating combined sewer overflows drastically reduced pollution, restored natural environments, and improved health. Opening access to the waterfront, creating more parks, and reducing truck traffic and noxious uses in residential neighborhoods helped address environmental and social injustices of the past. Preserving industrial land and brought more good-paying jobs, and a new transit option in the Triboro line has enable more access to them. It has also provided a national model for other cities throughout the country, illustrating how technology can allow modern infrastructure and recreation to coexist on the waterfront.

RELEVANT PLAN RECOMMENDATIONS

35. End the discharge of raw sewage and other pollutants into waterways

36. Restore the region's harbor and estuaries

39. Create a tri-state trail network

55. Make room for the next generation of industry

58. Turn environmentally burdened neighborhoods into healthy communities

New York City

Sustain and broaden prosperity

In the past two decades, New York City has experienced a remarkable turnaround. The city's dynamic economy, robust transit system, walkable neighborhoods, cultural diversity, and global connections have restored its leadership position both nationally and internationally. Nearly nine out of ten jobs added in the region from 2005 to 2015 were in the five boroughs, after decades of being outpaced by suburban neighbors.

While the city benefited from global urbanization trends, the resurgence would not have been possible without intentional policy choices. Large capital investment programs dating back to the 1980s restored much of the city's housing stock and returned public transportation infrastructure to working order. Public safety improvements starting in the 1990s made New York one of the safest big cities in America. And over the last 15 years, renewed focus on public health, education, and public spaces has improved the well-being of city residents.

But this success remains fragile and incomplete. Poverty remains high, incomes haven't risen for the majority of households, and increased demand for living in the city has resulted in skyrocketing housing costs. Neighborhoods that were once bastions of affordable housing have become too expensive for long-time poor and working-class residents, forcing many to move, with fewer and fewer options of places to go.

The city's wide disparities in race and socioeconomic status are perhaps most pronounced in the areas of health and longevity. Residents of the more affluent Upper East Side live, on average, ten years longer than residents of Harlem, who are primarily Black, Hispanic, and less wealthy, and are more likely to have less access to stable housing, a good job, and a healthy environment.[108]

More than 360,000 more people call New York City home today than in 2010, and 610,000 more people work here. Yet investment in the city's infrastructure has not kept pace, leaving many systems in disrepair. Subways are overcrowded and frequently delayed—and more serious disruptions occur with alarming regularity. Streets are more congested than ever before, costing billions in lost economic productivity. Bus service is slow and ridership has dropped dramatically, due in part to passengers switching to faster and more reliable to on-demand services. Two of the city's major transit hubs—Penn Station and the Port Authority Bus Terminal—cannot handle current passenger loads, and rail services are prone to frequent failures.

The impacts of climate change will add to these challenges. Many of the areas most susceptible to sea-level rise and storm surge are densely populated neighborhoods with lower-income residents, or residents of color. These include communities in the Rockaways, Jamaica Bay, Coney Island, and the East Shore of Staten Island. Much of the city's critical infrastructure is also located in the floodplain, such as power plants, rail yards, public housing, and hospitals.

Addressing these challenges will require reforming many of New York City's public agencies and authorities, and reforming their regulatory structures to enable faster decision-making and unlock new funding sources. And because these challenges are regional in nature, addressing them will also require greater collaboration with neighboring cities and towns outside the city's borders, as well as with state government.

Fortunately, New York City has a strong track record dealing with crises. Whether reducing crime or improving transit, the city's civic, business, and political leadership have usually come together to make things happen.

The Fourth Regional Plan recommends actions that would build on the city's successes to sustain and broaden its prosperity.

Modernizing the subway system to increase capacity and improve service is a priority. The plan proposes a Subway Reconstruction Public Benefit Corporation to oversee overhauling the entire system within 15 years, and providing fast and reliable service, clean and accessible stations, and better customer service. The subway system would also be extended to underserved neighborhoods.

Another transit priority for New York City is to significantly improve commuter rail service across the Hudson River by building and extending the Gateway tunnels to Sunnyside Queens, allowing through service at a renovated and expanded Penn Station, renovating the Port Authority bus terminal at 42nd Street, and building a second bus terminal under the Javits Center.

Image: ORG Permanent Modernity for the Fourth Regional Plan

Longer term, the region's three commuter rail systems should be unified into a comprehensive regional rail network that would provide a second rapid transit service for city residents, with frequent service and affordable fares. High-speed train service to Washington, D.C., and Boston, better transit connections to all three New York airports, and increased capacity at Kennedy and Newark would ensure New York remains connected to other cities.

Charging drivers to enter the Manhattan commercial core is an important strategy to reduce traffic and raise revenue for the transportation system. City streets should also be redesigned to prioritize walking, biking, and transit, with wider sidewalks, more bike and bus lanes, and new streetcar and light-rail lines. As on-demand, and ultimately, driverless vehicles become commonplace, the city must take steps to prevent additional traffic while taking advantage of the benefits these vehicles provide, such as reduced demand for parking and more efficient travel. Parking spaces should be converted to rain gardens, bus or bike lanes, or sidewalk space.

The plan includes many recommendations to relieve the city's housing crisis. Tens of thousand of homes could be added with new construction by encouraging more vacant units to be put on the market, and more two- and three-family homes out of existing single-family homes. Zoning regulations should be reformed to lift arbitrary density caps in Manhattan and allow for denser development near train stations in higher-income as well as lower-income neighborhoods. Inclusionary zoning should be applied not just citywide, but throughout the region.

The city must preserve the affordable housing that already exists, and invest in the public, shared-ownership, and supportive housing systems that can help end homelessness and build wealth in low-income neighborhoods. The city should also provide stronger legal protections for low-income tenants, and proactively inspect rental units to identify and address unhealthy living conditions. Many of these policies could be paid for by redirecting existing housing subsidy programs.

The city can support sustained, diversified job growth by expanding mixed-income districts near the Manhattan Central Business District and promoting job centers in places such as Jamaica and the Bronx Hub. A diversified job market also requires that the city limit the conversion or redevelopment of older commercial buildings and industrial land so that different building types can accommodate a variety of businesses.

Adapting to climate change will require major investments in both green and grey infrastructure citywide. Green roofs, rain gardens, more trees, and permeable pavement would reduce heat, storm-water runoff, and contaminated water released into the harbor and other waterways. These features would also create healthier and more livable neighborhoods.

Many projects are already underway to protect the Lower East Side, Lower Manhattan, Edgemere and other communities from coastal storms and sea-level rise. These projects should be fully funded and completed. But in the longer term, the city must make difficult decisions about coastal adaptation. In some neighborhoods, the best strategy may be to protect against rising sea level and storms, while a managed transition in other neighborhoods would be a better solution if there is greater risk or the densities don't justify the cost of protection. In those cases, the transition will need to be led by local communities and supported with effective buyout programs and assistance to low-income renters and other socially vulnerable people. The proposed Regional Coastal Commission and state adaptation trust funds, capitalized with surcharges on homeowner insurance, could help coordinate strategies and fund these investments.

Long Island City

Since Long Island City (LIC) was rezoned in 2001, the desolate manufacturing hub has become the fastest-growing residential and cultural district in New York City. In the last decade alone, nearly 10,000 apartments have been built, and more than 20,000 are planned or under construction. LIC is also a thriving arts community, with large institutions such as MoMA PS1 and dozens of smaller galleries and artist spaces.

Just a stone's throw from Midtown Manhattan, LIC is served by six subway lines, 15 bus lines, the Long Island Rail Road (LIRR), and ferries. The Queensboro Bridge and Queens-Midtown Tunnel also give LIC direct access to Manhattan by car.

LIC residents love the neighborhood's convenient location, excellent transit, attractive waterfront, and lively cultural amenities. But many residents are also concerned about rising housing costs, overcrowded schools, and lack of affordable housing.

And more change is coming. The opening of Cornell Tech on Roosevelt Island, a major engine of New York City's tech ecosystem, gives LIC the opportunity to add more commercial development to its solid residential base.

The MTA's East Side Access project, to be completed by 2023, will bring a new intermodal LIRR station to LIC, and the proposed Brooklyn-Queens Connector, a light rail line running along the East River waterfront, would provide easy access up to Astoria, Queens, down to Sunset Park, Brooklyn. The Fourth Regional Plan calls for extending the proposed Gateway project from its current planned terminus at Penn Station through Manhattan to connect to LIRR in LIC.

With these transportation improvements, the development of Sunnyside Yards—a site of almost 200 acres—could finally materialize. Redevelopment of the yards could bring new homes, businesses, convention and exhibition spaces, and parks, and help tie together Astoria, Sunnyside, Hunters Point, and LIC.

New investments in Long Island City could increase pressures on rents. The fourth plan recommends strategies to protect existing residents from displacement, while their neighborhoods transition to denser, more mixed-use areas. Residents, businesses, and cultural institutions should be involved in planning for the future of their communities, supported by city and state policies to better target housing subsidies, protect existing residents and businesses from displacement, create more homeownership opportunities, and preserve land for industrial uses.

Long Island City's future is bright, and with the right investments and policies, will become home to thousands more residents and workers that contribute to the vibrancy of New York City.

Flushing

The Flushing area already has the makings of a real regional hub, with its diverse international population and bustling streets. The busiest subway station outside Manhattan is Flushing's Main Street station on the #7 line, with weekday ridership on par with Rockefeller Center and 42nd Street–Bryant Park. The intersection of Main Street and Roosevelt Avenue is the third busiest intersection in the city, after Times Square and Herald Square.

With more than 30,000 residents born in China, Flushing is one of the biggest and fastest-growing Chinatowns in the world. Indeed, 70 percent of its residents are of Asian descent, including large numbers from China, Taiwan, South Korea, Pakistan, Afghanistan, Bangladesh, India, and Sri Lanka. It is a major cultural center and the fourth largest central business district in New York City.

Yet, many residents are concerned about Flushing's ability to grow. The #7 line is near capacity, school overcrowding is beginning to be a major concern, affordability for residents and businesses is a challenge, and there aren't enough parks in the neighborhood.

The Fourth Regional Plan includes many recommendations to help Flushing achieve its vision of becoming an even stronger cultural and economic hub, and still remain a livable, affordable neighborhood with a cohesive identity and character for residents with a wide range of incomes.

The plan recommends strategies to protect existing residents from displacement while their neighborhoods transition to denser, more mixed-use areas. City and state policies should better target housing subsidies and create more home ownership opportunities.

Furthermore, neighborhood-led planning processes could help local arts and cultural institutions partner with residents and businesses to make downtown Flushing even more walkable and active, supported by Flushing's strong cultural identity.

Neighborhood stakeholders are already eager to achieve the remediation of Flushing

Creek, which is overwhelmed with untreated sewage and storm water when there is as little as half an inch of rain. Cleaning up the creek would create healthy recreation opportunities for area residents.

Finally, the additional transit capacity needed to sustain more job and population growth could be achieved by repurposing the nearby Long Island Rail Road Flushing Main Street station, which is currently underutilized. By integrating the LIRR into a regional rail system, residents of Flushing could gain new express transit service for the same price as a subway fare—and Flushing-based companies could draw from a larger pool of employees throughout the city and the region. Locally, land preserved for industrial uses would support Flushing's manufacturing jobs, and complement its retail.

East Bronx

The population and economy of the Bronx is growing faster than the rest of New York City, and will receive another boost when four new Metro-North stations open in 2022 in the East Bronx (at Hunts Point, Parkchester, Morris Park, and Co-op City). Annexed to the city 20 years after the West Bronx, the East Bronx is much less dense than the rest of the borough. With the exception of the lower-income and more industrial areas to the South, the East Bronx is home to residents with a wide range of incomes. Many residents depend on the #5 and #6 subway lines to get to work in Manhattan, while others rely on local and express buses, or take their car.

The new Metro-North stations will dramatically improve the commute to Midtown Manhattan, especially for the residents of Co-op City heading to the Far West Side. Those stations and the Triboro Line proposed in the Fourth Regional Plan would also give East Bronx residents easier access to Queens, Brooklyn, and Connecticut.

The fourth plan recommends creating more safe streets that prioritize pedestrians, bicycles, buses, and goods movement over private automobiles, which would reduce traffic and make it easier for people to reach the new transit services. The plan also recommends transforming the Sheridan Expressway, one of the Bronx's many highways, into an urban boulevard with fewer lanes, additional crosswalks, traffic signals, and trees to better serve the community. A highway interchange at Oak Point instead of Edgewater Road would better connect the surrounding communities to the Hunts Point market and waterfront.

As East Bronx neighborhoods gain better transportation access, it will be essential to both preserve and build new affordable housing for a range of household incomes and protect residents from displacement. Community-driven planning processes would help neighborhoods navigate future planning efforts to allow the creation of more homes, either in new buildings or by allowing more units within existing buildings.

The fourth plan outlines ways to create more parks and green infrastructure in the East Bronx, which would reduce the urban heat island effect, mitigate flooding, clean the air, enable easier access to the Long Island Sound, and protect waterfront communities from sea-level rise and storm surge.

Bronx Hub

The Bronx Hub is the civic and cultural center of the South Bronx, centered at the intersection of East 149th Street and Third Avenue. In the 1970s and 1980s, the communities of the South Bronx suffered more than any other area of New York City from white flight and the abandonment, crime, and arson that resulted. Yet since then these neighborhoods of the South Bronx have undergone a dramatic community-led transformation: between 2005 and 2015, the Bronx outpaced the city as a whole in both job and population growth.

Maintaining this momentum, however, is not guaranteed, and many residents are also questioning if they will benefit from the changes. The area's excellent transit access and high concentration of low-income households has made it particularly vulnerable to gentrification, and therefore displacement of existing residents. In fact, Bronxites face the highest risk of housing displacement of any county in the New York region.

The fourth plan's recommendations would enable the Bronx Hub to protect existing residents by strengthening tenant protections, preventing tenant harassment, and directing scarce housing subsidy dollars to the lowest-income families. The plan also outlines strategies for promoting community wealth through land trusts and other shared equity structures, and recommendations to enable local anchor institutions such as Hostos Community College, Lincoln Hospital, Metropolitan College of New York, and Bronxworks to be more engaged with the surrounding communities, thereby building small business capacity and increasing economic opportunity for residents. The area's cultural richness would be protected in part by targeted investments in a naturally occurring arts district anchored by the Bronx Museum and Pregones Theater.

The plan includes additional strategies to increase economic opportunity and job access for Hub residents. The plan identified the BX6, BX15, and BX19 bus routes for significant service improvements, as well as the introduction of streetcar service. The proposed Triboro line would start on Third Avenue at 149th sSreet, and take passengers to Queens and Brooklyn. The Second Avenue Subway would be extended from its current terminus at 96th Street to the Grand Concourse line (at 149th and Grand Concourse), connecting with the 2 and 5 subway lines. Longer term, the plan's proposed regional rail service (T-REX) would provide rapid transit to other commercial centers while expanding access to the underserved Third Avenue corridor.

Better management of the Hub's bustling streets would prioritize pedestrians, buses, and goods movements, reducing pollution that contributes to asthma. The plan also proposes improving healthy food options and adding more trees, green roofs, and other green infrastructure to improve health and well-being. The construction of each of these projects would lead to better paying jobs for Bronx residents in the Hub, and link residents to more opportunities in more business centers.

New Jersey

Create a sustainable economic powerhouse connected to New York and points south

The most densely populated state in the nation, New Jersey, is a "corridor state" located between two major metropolitan regions: New York and Philadelphia. Benjamin Franklin famously referred to it as a keg tapped at both ends. It has prospered from this unique position, and in the 20ᵗʰ century it invested in highways, a global airport, and a seaport, and attracted companies to suburban office parks. In the 1980s and 1990s, with strong public leadership, New Jersey revitalized mass transit and made major investments in farmland and woodland preservation. It was a national leader both in growth management, and in affordable housing policies to address the state's history of housing discrimination and segregation.

For many decades, this was a formula for success: a pro-business climate, excellent infrastructure, improved transit connections to New York City, higher rates of affordable housing production, and bountiful natural resources—from the farms of Sussex County to the Jersey Shore. Although an expensive state with high property taxes and housing and labor costs, for many, it was worth it to live and work there.

In the last decade, however, New Jersey's economy has faltered, while neighboring New York City has surged. New Jersey incomes have stagnated, while housing costs have escalated.

Lack of investment in new and expanded transportation capacity to New York City has failed to keep pace with growing demand, leaving New Jersey's commuter-rail and bus riders frustrated and angry. Penn Station and the Port Authority Bus Terminal, which together account for more than 600,000 daily trans-Hudson trips—more than half of all commuters entering New York City every day—are over capacity and prone to frequent delays. Major repairs are needed to prevent a catastrophe and protect this vulnerable infrastructure from climate change.

While New Jersey has preserved almost one million acres of open space in the Highlands, and a similar amount in the south Jersey Pinelands, there are always efforts to weaken or dismantle these protections. Superstorm Sandy exposed the state's vulnerability to violent storms and sea-level rise caused by climate change, but little has been done beyond rebuilding in place.

Regulations and incentives to promote affordable housing—especially in walkable downtowns and near train stations—were also dismantled over the last decade. Court orders have reaffirmed the state's commitment to enforcing fair-share housing laws, but the Christie administration did little to support those provisions.

Cities and walkable downtowns are now capturing most new economic activity in the tri-state region and across the country—and globally as well. The Fourth Regional Plan outlines strategies for New Jersey to take advantage of this development by investing in its cities and downtowns, and capitalizing on its proximity to New York City on NJ Transit.

First and foremost, New Jersey must solve its transportation crisis by building a new commuter rail tunnel under the Hudson River and a second bus terminal in Manhattan, in cooperation with New York State and City. Yet even these major investments would only provide enough capacity for a few decades, requiring further rail connections before mid-century. With a third pair of tunnels under the Hudson River to Midtown Manhattan, both the West Shore Railroad and New York, Susquehanna and Western Railway lines could be reactivated, giving Bergen and Passaic counties a one-seat commuter rail connection to New York City. In the meantime, PATH and the Hudson-Bergen Light Rail should both be extended to underserved communities, and investments should be made to increase their carrying capacity. A redesigned and expanded Newark Airport would reduce travel delays and generate more local jobs.

New Jersey should invest in its major cities, including Newark, Elizabeth, Jersey City, Paterson, and Trenton. But as these cities gain new jobs and more housing, existing residents should be protected from rising costs and displacement. Redesigning streets to be pedestrian- and bus-friendly would help improve neighborhoods and provide better transit options. As on-demand and ultimately driverless vehicles become commonplace, cities must take measures to ensure they don't dominate streets and roads and cause congestion. More intentional street management could improve the benefits of these technology-enabled vehicles, such as less need for parking and more efficient movements. These actions would lead to healthier environments for communities with high rates of asthma, diabetes, and other chronic diseases.

New Jersey's commercial corridors, office parks, and shopping centers can also become more walkable, transit-friendly places with new highway-design guidelines, model land-use codes, investments in rapid buses and other transit, and state incentives for inter-municipal collaboration.

The state should also re-assert its national leadership in housing policy, reviving and strengthening its affordable housing laws with a statewide inclusionary zoning policy to ensure all new multifamily housing includes low- and moderate-income homes.

A new national park in the Meadowlands would join New Jersey's well-known natural attractions such as the Highlands, Jersey Shore, and Great Swamp, and help mitigate the impact of climate change on neighboring communities.

At the same time, a comprehensive strategy for New Jersey's coastal communities, coordinated by a regional coastal commission and funded by a state trust fund, would reduce the risks to both residents and the economy posed by climate change.

New Jersey should also regain its leadership position in energy and environmental policy, rejoining the Regional Greenhouse Gas Initiative (RGGI), and working to broaden its carbon pricing into a comprehensive market for greenhouse gases.

Newark

With the help of strong leadership, as well as committed anchor institutions, businesses, and community organizations, the city is attracting new ventures and restoring abandoned factories and other buildings as hubs for education, innovation, and even urban farms.

The new Riverfront Park is reconnecting the city with the Passaic River. Teachers Village, a mixed-use redevelopment project, is nearly complete, attracting educators and new residents to downtown, and serving as a model for similar mixed-use, mixed-income projects. Newark Fiber, the product of an innovative public-private partnership, has brought very high-speed internet service to Newark, and positioned the city to become a hub for tech start-ups. The former Hahne's Building is now an arts incubator and education hub. New plans for a PATH train extension to Newark Airport could open up further job opportunities for residents in some of the city's lowest income neighborhoods.

Newark's revitalization should continue by leveraging the city's unique cultural, transportation, and historic assets. These include Newark's unique transportation assets (NJ Transit, Amtrak, the Newark subway, and the PATH train), its cultural institutions (the New Jersey Performing Arts Center and Newark Museum), and its colleges and universities (Rutgers University, Seton Hall University of Law, the New Jersey Institute of Technology, and Essex County Community College).

Many Newarkers are excited about the changes, but they also want to ensure benefits reach existing residents in addition to newcomers, and to forestall displacement as development accelerates. To address these concerns, Newark took a historic step in 2017 by passing an inclusionary housing policy that requires 20 percent of all new housing construction to be set aside for low- and moderate-income families.

The Fourth Regional Plan urges the three states to focus efforts and investments in "legacy" cities like Newark. It features strategies that would help Newark achieve inclusive prosperity by protecting current residents from displacement, and suggests incentives for new housing that would help the city retain and attract residents of different income levels. The plan recommends transportation infrastructure projects such as the Gateway project, the PATH extension, and a new light rail connection to Paterson that would increase economic opportunities for Newarkers. The plan also suggests greening urban landscapes to improve the health and well-being of all residents.

Trenton

New Jersey's capital, Trenton, has an opportunity to connect its neighborhoods, historic downtown, and waterfront, and become a vibrant midpoint between New York and Philadelphia. The city's master plan, Trenton250, envisions becoming both a bigger city, with more residents and jobs, and a more equitable city, with a better quality of life for all.

The master plan outlines ways to strengthen Trenton's residential, retail, and cultural sectors with a diverse local economy, supported by investments in education and the arts. The plan promotes universal access to the internet to enhance innovation and expand opportunity. Trenton250 also aspires to create a more healthy, safe, and walkable city. One specific proposal, long on the books but still not approved, entails transforming Route 29 into an urban boulevard and reclaiming park space along the Delaware River waterfront. The plan also includes the construction of new homes, offices, and retail, a new public square, and the expansion of the historic William Trent House Museum.

The recommendations of the Fourth Regional Plan would help the city of Trenton realize its vision by calling for state and municipal collaboration for building housing downtown, attracting new businesses, and creating cultural and arts attractions. In particular, the fourth plan calls for more state resources to help cities transform limited-access highways into urban boulevards. Strategies to create universal high-speed internet access and develop partnerships with anchor institutions such as hospitals and universities are particularly relevant for Trenton. And improvements that would result in faster, more reliable rail service between Trenton, northern New Jersey, and New York City would make the city more attractive to residents and businesses alike.

Route 23

Like many highway corridors in the tri-state region, Route 23 in northern New Jersey has evolved over decades without any singular plan or coherent vision. From Cedar Grove to Riverdale, Route 23 passes through single-family neighborhoods, shopping centers, strip malls, and largely undeveloped areas. At times, it is a two-lane suburban street; at others, a six-lane divided highway. Drivers rely on Route 23 for local trips or to connect to other highways, such as Route

Photo: J. Stephen Conn

202, US 46, and I-80. In 2008, NJ Transit opened a Transit Center in Wayne, NJ on Route 23, allowing commuters to park and take a train or a bus to New York, Newark, Paterson, and other destinations.

Route 23 could become a model for how to retrofit a suburban highway into a better connected, pedestrian-friendly corridor than benefits the communities along it. The road already supports some level of transit, but with the right kind of growth and investment, it could become an essential component of northern New Jersey's transit network. Recommendations in the Fourth Regional Plan include changing local zoning to enable new nodes of mixed-use development where there are already concentrations of activity near transit stops. At these nodes, new design standards for the highway would reduce accidents and create the conditions to promote walking and biking. With more people on public transportation, walking, and biking; with better management of highways through pricing; and ultimately, with the advent of shared, driverless vehicles, parking lots could be reclaimed for green infrastructure or new development.

Long Island

Renew the promise of America's first suburb

In the mid-20th century, Long Island emerged as the nation's first modern suburban landscape, with a potent combination of attractive amenities such as affordable homes, strong public schools, access to nature, good highways, and proximity to New York City. Long Island grew rapidly eastward. Incomes rose, houses got bigger, and the one-car family became the two-, three-, and four-car families of today.

By the beginning of the 21st century, however, it was clear this growth model was no longer working. Open space was dwindling, encroached on by new subdivisions. Residents had to drive longer distances for employment or services, choking major highways and local roads in traffic. The scarcity of affordable rental housing made it difficult for young adults to find their own homes on the island. Segregated communities and school districts prevented the growing Hispanic and Black populations from accessing good schools, housing, and jobs. Property taxes soared as economic growth slowed.

In 2012, Superstorm Sandy caused widespread destruction on Long Island and brought home the reality of the threat posed by climate change. With over 1,000 miles of coastline, the island is particularly vulnerable. By 2050, more than 90,000 Long Island homes could be vulnerable to flooding from more frequent and intense storms, up from around 60,000 today.

Long Island has already begun a transformation in response to these challenges. Villages including Patchogue and Westbury have revitalized their downtown areas and shown that walkable communities with affordable multi-family housing can improve suburban living. Amityville, Glen Cove, and other places are undergoing similar change. Many coastal communities such as Long Beach and Mastic Beach have begun integrating resilience measures into local planning.

Still, the pace of change is slow. Zoning codes, for example, still prohibit or greatly restrict multifamily housing in too many downtowns and around too many train stations. Towns and villages need more help to prepare for climate change, and have barely begun coordinating even though the most effective solutions often require cross-municipal collaboration. Few attempts are being made to use new technologies to address traffic congestion and parking.

Transportation projects already underway will strengthen Long Island's economy by promoting more growth around train stations. Long Island Rail Road's East Side Access project will allow riders to travel directly to Grand Central Terminal, saving as much as 40 minutes a day and boosting property values near stations. A third track on LIRR's Main Line will improve reliability and service into job centers like Mineola and Hicksville. And a second track from Farmingdale to Ronkonkoma will improve service between Long Island's largest concentration of jobs along Route 110, and Suffolk County's busiest rail station and airport. Together, these projects should lead to the creation of many more jobs, homes, stores, and services around LIRR stations.

While these transportation projects are sorely needed, they won't solve all of Long Island's transportation problems. North-south transit links will still be scarce, and traveling the "last mile" from the train station to home or work will still be challenging without a car. And as service improves and ridership grows, additional train capacity will be needed through Queens and into Penn Station.

The Fourth Regional Plan's recommendations build on Long Island's recent successes and enable it to become the model for a sustainable and equitable 21st century suburb.

Connecting and expanding the region's three commuter rails into one regional rail system would increase the frequency of trains, and allow riders to travel directly to destinations throughout the region. Integrating affordable, on-demand services into last-mile transportation strategies, along with improved bus service and better north-south rail links, would expand travel options and reduce the need for parking.

Diverting car trips to transit, strategically upgrading components of the highway network, and using tolling based on time of day and traffic levels would reduce congestion on the island's overcrowded highways and also reduce air pollution.

Shifting more of the responsibility for education funding from local school districts to the state and encouraging school district consolidation would relieve local property tax burdens and improve educational outcomes in low-performing schools.

Allowing multifamily housing such as townhouses and garden apartments near every train station, and requiring all new housing projects to include low and moderate-income homes would make housing more affordable for people of different incomes.

A new Regional Coastal Commission, backed by a state adaptation trust fund, would help Long Island towns and villages coordinate and implement strategies to deal with the impacts of climate change across municipal boundaries. In the longer term, some communities will need to be supported in their efforts to transition away from the areas at very high risk of sea-level rise and storm surge—with more effective buyout programs, for example, and assistance to socially vulnerable residents.

Connecting more Long Island neighborhoods to coastal areas and parks with a network of accessible walking and biking trails would improve recreation options, make residents healthier, and support the island's tourist economy.

Ronkonkoma

Ronkonkoma is home to the second busiest Long Island Rail Road station outside of New York City as well as MacArthur Airport. These two critical components of the region's transportation network provide the central Suffolk County hamlet the opportunity to become a focal point of a growing Long Island economy.

The completion of a third track on the Long Island Rail Road's main line and a second track from Farmingdale to Ronkonkoma will also make it possible to support more homes, offices, retail, and entertainment in the area. Already, a new walkable, mixed-use community of 1,400 new homes and more than 500,000 square feet of commercial space has been approved by the town of Brookhaven. Planning is also underway by the town of Islip and Suffolk County, in consultation with the Ronkonkoma community, to expand this hub, improving connections to MacArthur Airport and other activity centers in the community.

The recommendations of the Fourth Regional Plan would enable Ronkonkoma to sustainably support this growth while improving local conditions for existing residents. Policies to promote the use of shared, on-demand vehicles to improve access to the Ronkonkoma station should be linked with efforts to transform station-area parking into mixed-use developments, community amenities, and park space. Affordable housing and fair housing policies should be emphasized to make Ronkonkoma work for everyone.

Route 110

In just a 15-mile stretch, Route 110 is home to 30 percent of all jobs in Suffolk County. From Amityville on the South Shore to Huntington on the North Shore, Route 110 takes in a varied suburban landscape of commercial strips and shopping centers, walkable main streets, gritty industrial districts, tidy office parks, townhouses, and neighborhoods with single-family homes.

Like other intensely developed highway corridors across the region, there is significant potential for transit-oriented growth along Route 110. In addition to the three Long Island Rail Road lines that cross the corridor, there is also the potential for new Bus Rapid Transit (BRT) along Route 110 (a study by Suffolk County, in collaboration with the Towns of Babylon and Huntington, is underway). RPA analysis found that an additional 4.8 million square feet of office space, 1.3 million square feet of retail space, 800,000 square feet of industrial space could be built around transit in the corridor, as well as new residential development.

Recommendations in the fourth plan would help advance the transformation of Route 110 by identifying ways to reform land-use regulations and design guidelines to promote building walkable, transit-oriented communities, particularly in places like the Huntington Quadrangle and the four corners at Conklin. New York State and Suffolk County departments of transportation must adopt and implement design standards for "complete streets" to better connect the corridor to adjacent neighborhoods and other nearby destinations such as Republic Airport and Farmingdale State College.

The fourth plan's recommendations would support the redevelopment of Route 110 into a transit-oriented corridor with calls for new state highway design guidelines and increased focus on transit-oriented development by regional transportation agencies. The plan also includes "combined mobility" strategies to seamlessly link different modes of transportation, including car and bike sharing, on-demand car services, and shuttles. Highway recommendations would reduce congestion on Route 110 and other major highways. If the progress already underway continues, Route 110 could become a model for similar transit, economic, and residential corridors throughout the region.

Hicksville

Hicksville, where the Ronkonkoma and the Port Jefferson LIRR lines converge into the Main Line, is the busiest rail hub on Long Island, and also one of its largest centers for bus travel. By the early 2020s, three new infrastructure projects that will further increase Hicksville's potential to become a major employment center will be completed: East Side Access, which will connect the LIRR to East Midtown in Manhattan; a third track on the Main Line, which will enable more reverse and intra-island commutes; and a second track to Ronkonkoma, which will improve capacity and reliability on the LIRR's most crowded line. A $121 million dollar renovation of the Hicksville Station is already underway.

With ample room to add new development on parking lots and underutilized properties near its multimodal train and bus stations, Hicksville is poised for growth. Community-based revitalization plans for more commercial space, new homes, parks, and community services in downtown Hicksville look promising.

Proposals in the Fourth Regional Plan would help Hicksville build on these plans. Statewide inclusionary zoning, for example, would ensure Hicksville's new homes support a mix of families. Recommendations about street redesign could make Hicksville more walkable, green, and healthy as the area is redeveloped. Large commuter parking lots could be converted to stores, offices, homes, and parks, and integrated into Hicksville's downtown if the city is able to take advantage of technology-enabled shared car services and driverless cars instead of being overwhelmed by the traffic they could bring. With its central location and access to research facilities, technology companies and workers from throughout Nassau, Suffolk, and New York City, Hicksville could become the hub of an innovation economy on Long Island.

Connecticut

Transition to a dynamic and diverse economy

Southwestern Connecticut's proximity to New York City, and its historic cities and villages, coastline, and natural beauty have long attracted people and businesses. During the late 20th century, Connecticut became the headquarters of many large corporations, and was renowned for its excellent suburban schools, strong industrial base, and high quality of life. While cities like New Haven and Bridgeport lost jobs and population, the state's suburban municipalities prospered with the highest per-capita income in the nation.

But over the last decade, many of the forces that propelled Connecticut's economy now pose challenges to its future success. Fortune 500 companies are no longer clamoring for space in auto-dependent suburban office parks, preferring vibrant cities instead. While some Connecticut cities such as Stamford are attracting new businesses and talented workers, others continue to struggle after decades of disinvestment and industrial downsizing. Meanwhile, public schools are suffering due to insufficient resources. In many prosperous suburban areas with good schools, residents are resisting multifamily or affordable housing. Some are resistant to any commercial activities.

Connecticut relies heavily on its roadway infrastructure, much of which is congested and in poor condition. Yet it is the only state in the region without highway tolls. Metro-North is chronically underfunded, and service is deteriorating. Coastal communities are vulnerable to storms, flooding, and sea-level rise due to climate change. And while significant investments are being made to increase resilience, municipal efforts to plan and adapt remain uncoordinated.

Connecticut has been slow to capitalize on the increased demand for walkable downtowns and neighborhoods by allowing for more multifamily homes and mixed-use development. Aligning local land-use and statewide economic development strategies is difficult. And without county-level government or strong state-level planning capacity, cross-jurisdictional coordination is weak. The state has also invested relatively little in new infrastructure.

The Fourth Regional Plan proposes actions that would help Connecticut build more affordable housing in all communities, capitalize on mixed-use, mixed-income downtowns, and invest in a reliable transportation system. The recommendations in the fourth plan would help mitigate the impact of a changing climate, improve health by reducing pollution and promoting physical activity, and reduce long-standing racial and economic inequality.

Proposed investments in Metro-North's New Haven Line would improve inter-city service, reduce travel travel time between regional hubs in Connecticut, and provide a direct connection to New York City. Connecting commuter rail into an integrated regional rail system would give Connecticut cities better access to destinations throughout the tri-state area.

More inclusive local planning would create dynamic communities with greater housing choice and economic opportunities. State incentives would foster more walkable communities, and bring work and recreational opportunities closer to where people live. On a state and regional level, investments and zoning changes would increase rental and affordable housing options, reduce housing costs, and encourage economic growth.

The plan encourages partnerships between municipalities, local residents, and anchor institutions, such as hospitals and universities, to increase capital and human resource investments. These institutions are often a community's largest employer, and partnerships with local government and neighborhoods can create added value through local hiring and purchasing, as well as housing and infrastructure investments.

Curbing an overreliance on property taxes to fund local services would reduce inequities between rich and poor communities, enhance housing production, and reduce sprawl. This can be achieved if the state government assumes a larger share of local school budgets, increases incentives for shared services, and encourages municipalities to diversify sources of revenue (with income taxes or sales taxes) or more innovative property tax structures.

Providing resources, incentives, and guidelines for school districts to consolidate and share programs and services would reduce costs, as well as disparities between urban and suburban school districts that undermine equal opportunity and access to workforce skills..

A regional coastal commission and state adaptation fund would help communities prepare for rising seas and more intense storms more effectively, and promote green infrastructure in cities.

Stamford

Stamford holds a strong position in the region's economy. Just 47 minutes from Grand Central Terminal on Metro-North's New Haven Line, the city is an attractive and affordable urban center for people and companies looking for a dynamic, smaller-scale city within easy reach of Manhattan. Over the last 15 years, Stamford has been a national model for mixed-use and mixed-income districts. The city's 2002 Master Plan laid the foundation for nearly $6 billion in new development within a half-mile of the Stamford Transportation Center, the busiest train station on the New Haven line. This has been a key element of the "Work, Live, Play, Learn" environment created in Stamford's downtown and South End.

Over the past decade, Stamford has expanded its growth strategy to attract a wider variety of businesses such as technology companies, smaller entrepreneurs, and maker industries. To do this, the city has focused on the built environment, adding new housing in the South End and downtown, and enhancing pedestrian and transit connections within and between these areas. Since 2010, more than 2,500 new apartments and 450,000 square feet of commercial space have been built in the South End, with an additional 1,580 apartments downtown. Plus, the University of Connecticut recently opened a dormitory for 300 students on its downtown campus.

Several recommendations in the Fourth Regional Plan would benefit Stamford, including significant infrastructure upgrades to the New Haven line, and proposals to provide better transit service. The Stamford Transportation Center needs to be renovated and reimagined as a gateway to the city, welcoming people and connecting downtown to the South End, both visually and functionally. Streets should be redesigned to emphasize walking, biking, and bus use. As shared, on-demand, and ultimately, driverless vehicles become more common, and as more people walk and bike, Stamford should repurpose parking spaces (on- and off-street) for new development and green infrastructure. Stamford also needs to continue building affordable housing as prosperity drives increases in property values. With an extremely low retail vacancy rate, Stamford should prioritize maintaining affordable ground-floor retail space in downtown and the South End.

Norwalk

Downtown Norwalk's pedestrian scale, historic buildings, diverse housing stock, and strategic location at the crossroads of Connecticut's highway and rail networks have helped position it to become a regional employment hub. The city's walkable and lively neighborhoods have attracted start-ups and entrepreneurs looking for a lively and diverse urban environment to incubate ideas and grow companies. In particular, the areas around the city's South Norwalk and Merritt 7 train stations, as well as the West Avenue and Wall Street neighborhoods, have seen substantial investment and job growth over the last decade.

Merritt 7 has become a flagship corporate office park for regional and national tech companies. Since the Norwalk Maritime Aquarium opened in the late 1980s, 500 new apartments have been built in the South Norwalk neighborhood. A recent grant from the U.S. Department of Housing and Urban Development will leverage $414 million in public and private funds to transform the Washington Village public housing site into a mixed-income community. In the West Avenue-Wall Street neighborhood, anchored by Matthews Park and Stepping Stones Museum for Children, more than 775 new apartment units have been built since 2010. On Wall Street, the historic Globe Theater is expected to become the anchor for a growing arts community with shared workspaces and housing for a diverse mix of residents.

Implementation of the recommendations of the Fourth Regional Plan would help Norwalk further capitalize on these assets. High-speed broadband would help attract more businesses in the creative and technology sectors and close the digital divide between high- and low-income households. Improved commuter rail service, affordable on-demand car service, and proactive planning for autonomous vehicles would strengthen Norwalk's position in the region as an accessible and attractive place to live, work, and play. Support for community-centered arts and culture would leverage Norwalk's role as a hub of creative industries and improve community cohesion. Streets designed for people emphasizing walking, biking, public transit, and green infrastructure would enhance residents' well-being and improve stormwater management and resiliency.

New Haven

One of the keys to New Haven's future is better transit access both within the city and to other parts of the region. The city has major plans to invest in Union Station—renovating the historic station building, providing better passenger amenities, and creating parking facilities that better fit a downtown railway station. The station will also be better connected to both the Hill and downtown with more active, pedestrian-friendly streets and better bus access. Also underway are an ambitious development plan for 3,400 homes and 3,000 jobs, a new Union Square Park, and the transformation of Route 34, a major highway bisecting the city, into a boulevard with more space for apartment and office buildings.

The recommendations in the Fourth Regional Plan would accelerate New Haven's role as a major transit hub for the state and the region with upgraded commuter, regional, and high-speed rail service along the New Haven Line. Improved services would allow for faster regional travel between New Haven and New York City; more frequent commuter service and increased capacity between New Haven and other Connecticut cities, including Stamford and Bridgeport; and higher-speed service between New York City and Boston.

The fourth plan's recommendations also detail how cities should plan to take advantage of ride-hailing services and ultimately, shared, driverless vehicles. With the right regulatory structures, these services could improve access to Union Station and the station area itself, as demand for nearby parking declines and more space becomes available for homes, restaurants, offices, and parks.

New Haven should continue to develop more complete, mixed-income neighborhoods to promote equitable job access and economic growth. New development should incorporate green infrastructure to mitigate rising temperatures and reduce flooding caused by climate change. A state adaptation fund overseen by a Regional Coastal Commission could help accelerate these and other climate-adaptation projects and help provide financing.

Route 8

Route 8, in the Naugatuck Valley, is the main artery of a growth corridor anchored by two important regional centers: Bridgeport to the south and Waterbury to the north. Route 8 also links several other downtowns including Derby and Naugatuck.

The landscape along Route 8 varies enormously. It includes open space reserves such as the Naugatuck State Forest, low- and medium-density single-family neighborhoods, shopping centers, and, significantly, industrial parks with advanced-manufacturing firms. Because the Naugatuck Valley is more affordable than other places in Connecticut, population has grown significantly over the last 25 years. The valley has also become more racially and ethnically diverse.

The Waterbury branch of the Metro-North Railroad runs parallel to Route 8. The Fourth Regional Plan's recommendations for a unified and expanded regional rail network—including electrification and/or the addition of a second track, among other improvements—would reduce travel time to Manhattan and improve reverse-commute access to employment centers along the Route 8 corridor.

Because Route 8 is a limited-access highway, it could also become a Bus Rapid Transit (BRT) corridor, modeled on the success of the New Britain/Hartford CT Fastrak line. These investments in transit—whether BRT or train—would support more compact, mixed-use development, create new employment opportunities, and provide more affordable housing. Other recommendations in the fourth plan pertaining to redesigning roads to be more pedestrian- and transit-friendly, reforming zoning to encourage more mixed-use downtowns, and consolidating services would help the Route 8 corridor thrive and grow.

Mid-Hudson

Build on the Hudson Valley's urban and natural heritage

The Mid-Hudson Valley is one of the the most geographically diverse parts of the tri-state region, with the Catskill peaks, rural landscapes, villages and hamlets, and cities from Yonkers to Kingston. The seven-county area includes both very affluent suburban towns and much poorer communities, in both urban and rural settings. While some places in the Mid-Hudson Valley are losing population, others are expanding with new tracts of single-family homes.

The Mid-Hudson Valley is connected by an extraordinary river estuary renowned for its natural beauty, protected watersheds, and productive farmland. Yet development continues to overtake open space, threatening the environment of the entire region as well as the agricultural and recreation jobs that are critical to the Hudson Valley economy.

This landscape is essential to the region's ecology, as it protects much of the drinking water supply and absorbs heat-producing greenhouse gases—which are particularly important functions in the era of climate change. Sea-level rise (which affects the Hudson River), Intense storms, and rising temperatures threaten the passenger and freight railroad lines that run along either side of the river, agriculture, and the tourist-based economy.

Over the last decade, the Mid-Hudson Valley economy has slowed dramatically. From 1996–2006, the area added 108,000 jobs—a 14 percent increase, and a faster rate of growth than any other part of the tri-state region. But in the following decade, the area gained only 25,000 jobs, or just 3 percent. (By comparison, jobs grew by 18 percent in New York City and 6 percent on Long Island in that same period.) The manufacturing that drove much of Mid-hudson Valley economy in previous decades has largely gone, replaced by industries such as healthcare, education, tourism, and goods distribution.

The future of the Mid-Hudson Valley depends on linking its many natural, human, and historical assets to a new technology-driven economy. The Fourth Regional Plan recommends ways to allow these communities to capitalize on their high quality of life, relative affordability, and access to rail transportation to take advantage of changing demographics, changing work patterns (such as flexible hours and working remotely), and shared transportation services to connect to New York City and other job centers.

The plan supports Metro-North's initiative to connect the New Haven Line to Penn Station. It also includes a proposal to build new rail tunnels under the Hudson River to allow for reactivation of passenger rail service in Rockland and Orange counties.

Express bus service across the Mario Cuomo (Tappan Zee) Bridge would connect job centers, residential communities, and commuter rail lines in Westchester and Rockland counties. Highway congestion would be reduced by using technology to remove bottlenecks and manage traffic, and tolling that would vary by time of day and level of traffic.

Connecting communities in the Mid-Hudson with affordable, high-speed internet service is key to ensuring that they are tied to jobs throughout the region, and opening up new opportunities for isolated, low-income communities.

Even with these improvements, achieving a strong and equitable economy won't be possible without expanding housing choices for low-, moderate-, and middle-income residents, and ensuring everyone has access to affordable homes close to good schools and jobs.

Recommendations in the fourth plan would support stronger state assistance and requirements for all municipalities to permit affordable, multifamily housing near transit, and encourage two- and three-family homes in areas where environmental conditions don't permit greater densities. Strengthening fair-housing laws and protecting residents from displacement would benefit all residents.

Proposals in the Fourth Regional Plan build on both long-standing and recent efforts by local residents, organizations, and public sector leaders to preserve and enhance its natural assets—forests, farmland, wetlands, and waterways—for tourism, agriculture, and resilience. Funding for open-space preservation should be increased and also used more strategically, with a focus on the places that can best mitigate the effects of climate change, support local economies, and strengthen the food-supply chain that stretches from Hudson Valley farms to New York City green markets.

The proposed 1,620-mile regional trail network would build on existing and planned trails in the Mid-Hudson

Photo: Axel Drainville

Valley, including the Appalachian Trail, the Empire State Trail, and the Long Path, putting far more of the region's residents within walking or transit distance of these natural landscapes.

New Rochelle, Yonkers, and Mount Vernon

Plans are underway for the southern Westchester County cities of New Rochelle, Yonkers and Mount Vernon to accelerate population and economic growth, while expanding opportunity and improving affordability for their residents. By taking advantage of their walkable downtowns, diverse populations and neighborhoods, and close proximity to New York City, these cities can provide Westchester and the larger region with room for the economy to expand in places that are both accessible and energy efficient.

New Rochelle's ambitious redevelopment plan calls for nearly 12 million square feet of new mixed-use development near the train station, including more than 6,000 new homes. This plan is backed by a community benefits policy that allows developers additional building height in exchange for such things as historic building preservation, affordable housing, educational facilities, parks, or pedestrian passageways.

Mount Vernon has plans to build hundreds of new rental apartments, with both market-rate units and units that are affordable for households making between 60 and 80 percent of the median income in the area. Yonkers is also encouraging development in its downtown and near the train station, having just broken ground on 600 new rental apartments on the waterfront.

This type of transit-oriented, equitable growth in the region's downtowns is very much in line with the Fourth Regional Plan. The plan aims to support these efforts by calling for the three states to provide more resources and flexibility to municipalities seeking to create mixed-use, mixed-income downtowns and neighborhoods. The plan encourages local governments to partner with anchor institutions such as hospitals and colleges to benefit both the institutions and the surrounding neighborhoods. These partnerships could help push, for example, for creating more complete streets that balance all users in these transit-oriented downtowns.

Recommendations in the fourth plan include ways to increase participation in local government, which would give the diverse populations of these three cities a stronger voice in development planning. Improving broadband services and adopting better data policies would help cities going through this type of major transformation, giving them the tools they need to analyze and optimize growth.

Westchester-Rockland I-287 Corridor

The I-287 and Mario Cuomo (Tappan Zee) Bridge corridor in Rockland and Westchester counties is a key artery that should, in the future, support faster transit and more equitable and sustainable growth in the Lower Hudson Valley.

Unlike the old Tappan Zee Bridge, the new Mario Cuomo Bridge includes a walking and cycling path, and was designed to accommodate the region's first Bus Rapid Transit (BRT) service. With 200,000 daily trips between Rockland and Westchester counties, there is already enough demand for new BRT service in the corridor. And demand is certain to increase in coming years as Westchester County and Rockland County grow in population and jobs—seven new buildings are under construction in White Plains alone.

The Fourth Regional Plan supports this type of dense, transit-oriented, equitable growth in the region's downtowns. It includes recommendations to revise road design standards and promote collaborative planning for highway corridors to improve the type of transit services the I-287 Corridor needs. Siting new bus (and ultimately, BRT) stations near housing and jobs would both provide alternatives to traveling by car, and promote pedestrian-friendly development in vacant or underutilized properties, such as the parking lots at the Nanuet and Palisades malls.

Managing highway congestion through pricing and demand management, as the plan proposes, would make travel by car or bus faster and more reliable in the corridor. State resources and incentives to support mixed-use, multi-family development would help revitalization efforts already underway in downtown centers such as Suffern, Tarrytown, White Plains, and Port Chester. The fourth plan's proposed regional rail service (T-REX) would promote job growth in the corridor by dramatically improving rail access in the morning peak hours.

Poughkeepsie

In the 18th and 19th centuries, Poughkeepsie's strategic location on the Hudson River, halfway between New York City and Albany, made the city an important economic and political hub. That history can be seen today in Poughkeepsie's architecture, from its quaint downtown to opulent mansions and dramatic bridges. To this day, the city continues to be a major cultural center in the Hudson Valley, with important art, music, and educational institutions.

Yet like many other 19h-century industrial centers, Poughkeepsie experienced significant declines in population and economic activity since 1950 and continues its struggle to rebound. A quarter of all households live below the poverty level (three times the county rate), while graduation and career-readiness rates are low. More than half of all households pay 30 percent of their income on housing, and nearly a quarter of all residents receive food assistance benefits.

There are some indications that a turnaround may be underway. The number of higher-income residents has grown, efforts to renew the downtown seem to be gaining traction, and the city is taking advantage of its reputation as a cultural center.

City leaders are hopeful that the high residential vacancy rate is an opportunity to grow without displacement. Local leaders are hoping for an economic turnaround that is inclusive of the city's Black and Hispanic population.

The recommendations in the Fourth Regional Plan would help Poughkeepsie become an engine for economic and equitable growth in the Hudson Valley. The plan recommends state incentives to build and preserve market-rate and affordable homes, and promote healthier living conditions in the city's historic, but often poorly maintained, housing stock. Strengthened local transit service would provide more reliable connections for residents to job centers and other essential services withi n the city. As Poughkeepsie grows, green infrastructure should be included in all new development to protect the city's combined sewer system.

Partnerships with Poughkeepsie's many anchor institutions—such as Vassar College, Marist College, Dutchess Community College, St. Francis Hospital, and Vassar Brothers Medical Center—would bring jobs and economic opportunities to surrounding e communities and help revitalize Main Street as a downtown retail and entertainment hub.

The fourth plan includes many recommendations to better connect Poughkeepsie's economy to New York City's and the region's. The plan's regional rail proposal would provide residents and businesses with faster and easier transit access to a number of destinations in the tri-state area. Also critical is greater investment in high-speed and affordable internet service, as identified in Poughkeepsie's Main Street Economic Development Strategy.

Poughkeepsie's Waterfront Redevelopment Strategy includes a single, connected waterfront, which would be part of the proposed tri-state regional trail network connecting the city with rural areas throughout the Hudson Valley, the Catskills, and beyond

Northeast Corridor

A megaregion of national and international significance

Photo: Amtrak

The tri-state area is located in the heart of the Northeast megaregion, an agglomeration stretching from Portland, ME, to Richmond, VA, and encompassing parts of 13 states and the District of Columbia. The engines of the Northeast's $3.8 trillion economy are its five big metro regions: Boston, New York, Philadelphia, Baltimore, and Washington, D.C. The Northeast Corridor is one of the most productive areas of the country, accounting for 20 percent of GDP but only 2 percent of its land area.

The region is one of 11 megaregions analyzed by the Regional Plan Association in its America 2050 initiative. Megaregions like the Northeast are characterized by interlocking economic systems, shared natural resources and ecosystems, and common transportation systems. Megaregions have captured most of the nation's economic growth in the latter half of the last century and are expected to power growth in the 21st century. Economies of scale make these megaregions competitive with similarly sized "global integration zones" of Europe and Southeast Asia, which have invested tens of billions of dollars in high-speed rail and goods-movement systems to support a highly mobile global workforce.

The Northeast faces serious challenges despite its immense wealth, productivity, and concentration of highly skilled knowledge sectors. In many ways, these challenges reflect the problems of the New York metropolitan region: high housing costs, uneven economic growth, sharp disparities in incomes, highway congestion, unreliable railroads and overcrowded airports, and coastal regions that must adapt to climate change.

Many of the issues surrounding infrastructure and natural systems addressed in the Fourth Regional Plan are also of concern to the entire Northeast, and therefore to the rest of the country. These include the Northeast Corridor train line, I-95 highway corridor, the Appalachian Highlands, and the Atlantic coastline along the Eastern Seaboard. Many critical components of these systems are located in the tri-state region: Penn Station, bridges and tunnels across the Hudson River, and the New York Harbor. When there are delays at New York's airports, disruptions to its power grid, or changes in its greenhouse gas emissions, the impacts ripple across the Northeast and the nation.

The Fourth Regional Plan advances many of the key strategies needed to maintain a strong megaregional network stretching from Washington, D.C., to Boston, with New York City at its center. Implementing the fourth plan will address a number of the leading economic, transportation and environmental challenges of the megaregion, and provide a foundation for a larger megaregion strategy.

One priority is building new rail passenger tunnels under the Hudson River while allowing traffic to continue in the existing tunnels—a vital connection. Extending the proposed Gateway project to Sunnyside Yards, and creating through-running services at an overhauled Penn Station complex, would significantly expand capacity throughout the entire Northeast Corridor. It would allow high-speed rail service that cuts the travel time between New York and Washington, D.C., by 90 minutes, to 1.5 hours, and between New York and Boston by 60 minutes, to 2.5 hours.

Expanding capacity at Kennedy and Newark airports would bolster the economy of the megaregion and help relieve delays at other airports throughout the Northeast and the rest of the country. Investments in the region's seaports and rail freight systems would reduce truck traffic and the costs of moving goods throughout the megaregion.

Reducing highway congestion with more extensive use of tolls would accelerate the movement of people and goods throughout the Northeast.

Modernizing the electric grid in the tri-state region to handle increased demand and the need for a cleaner, more flexible system would improve reliability elsewhere in the Northeast, but require collaboration with providers and regulators in the megaregion. In a similar way, upgrading broadband infrastructure to provide high-speed internet in the metropolitan region would improve connections in other locations.

One of the fourth plan recommendations that would require the most cooperation is the expansion of the Regional Greenhouse Gas Initiative (RGGI) carbon market to include all greenhouse gases from all sources. This would greatly reduce emissions throughout the Northeast while providing increased revenue to invest in an energy-efficient, equitable economy.

The landscapes and water systems that would be protected and improved as part of the Fourth Regional Plan are integral to natural ecosystems and to the health and well-being of all Northeast residents. The national park proposed for the New Jersey Meadowlands would adapt a habitat that is critical to species along the East Coast and would be a model for other regions. The proposed Regional Coastal Commission could connect with similar commissions in bordering states, and the proposed regional trail network would connect to systems and landscapes well beyond the boundaries of the tri-state region.

4C/Design

In an effort to drive Fourth Regional Plan policy with good design, RPA collaborated with some of the region's most talented designers to illustrate challenges, develop proposals, and project fantastic visions of the future for four different corridors in the metropolitan region: the Highlands, the Coast, the City, and the Suburbs.

In collaboration with Paul Lewis and Guy Nordenson of Princeton University, and Catherine Seavitt of City College of New York, RPA called on architects, landscape architects, designers, and urban planners to visually demonstrate how policy changes, new investments, and innovative thinking proposed in the Fourth Regional Plan could reshape the four different corridors, and prepare them for the next 25 years.

Thanks to the corridors' unique needs and opportunities, and to the designers' different approaches to design and representation, the 4C initiative created a heterogeneous set of design materials—an essential asset in the context of a regional plan with an extensive scope of issues, enormous geography, and most challenging of all, a time horizon to mid-century and beyond.

Design challenges

The settlement patterns in the large, mature region that is the New York-New Jersey-Connecticut Region are complex —the result of several hundred years of development and change.

Much of the region's legacy may be regrettable, such as low-density auto-dependent sprawl, development in floodplains and other environmentally sensitive places, and housing development patterns that foster and exacerbate segregation. But this is the region we have inherited, and now must grapple with. The work of the 4C design teams was more about accommodating and improving these legacies than about imposing altogether new "ideal" realities from above.

The 4C design teams also had to deal with the fact that this is a region characterized by a variety of conditions that defy the tidy categories of urban, suburban, and rural. In the "Highlands," rather than open-space preservation versus development, PORT +Range suggested a new model wherein development responds to natural systems, and natural areas are conserved by monetizing their productive value as sources of food, water, clean air, and recreation. Rather than wet versus dry along the hard edge of a protected "Coast," Rafi Segal + DLAND Studio imagined a semiwet zone that over time can be wet or dry as sea levels rise. In the "Suburbs," WORKac explored how to use green in the ways we associate with the suburbs, but mix uses at densities in ways we associate with cities. And in the "City," Only If + One Architecture called for a synergistic mix of both large-scale, transformative public-private projects and new ways for communities to benefit from neighborhood-scale development.

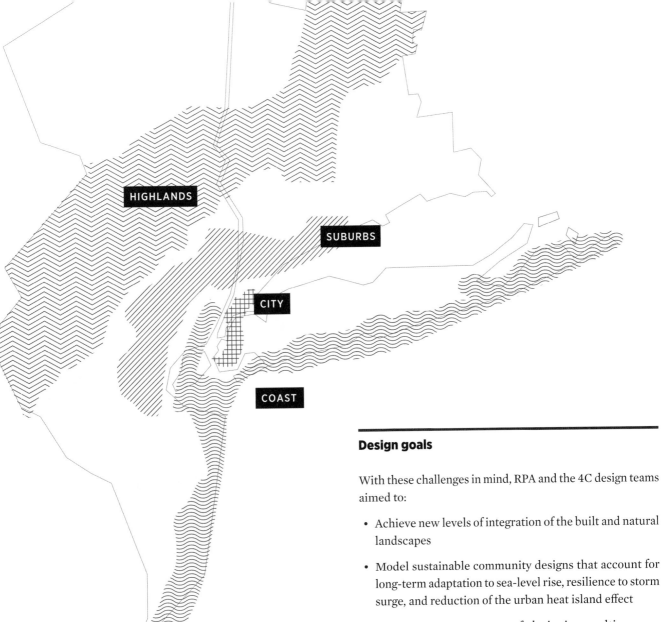

HIGHLANDS

SUBURBS

CITY

COAST

Design goals

With these challenges in mind, RPA and the 4C design teams aimed to:

- Achieve new levels of integration of the built and natural landscapes

- Model sustainable community designs that account for long-term adaptation to sea-level rise, resilience to storm surge, and reduction of the urban heat island effect

- Demonstrate new ways of designing multipurpose infrastructure, such as utility corridors that function as greenways

- Retrofit and reinvent a range of suburban typologies that are now underutilized, including office and industrial parks, shopping centers, commercial strips, and institutional campuses

Highlands

The Highlands Corridor extends from the Delaware River in New Jersey to northern Connecticut, a nearly continuous swath of green open space. The Highlands are our "green belt," dividing the region between its coastal and upstate areas and creating places for the region's residents to visit and discover nature. The Highlands also provide an opportunity to link open and protected park spaces, and pathways for wildlife and species that may need to migrate northward as a result of climate change.

By harnessing the character of the Highlands that stretch across New York, New Jersey, and Connecticut, PORT + Range's designs create communities and promote natural ecosystems. The team imagined waterways and trails that would not only improve water quality and supply, but also reduce flooding and provide open space. Through their design solutions, PORT + Range sought to support environmental well-being, increase access to public space, and better educate the community about environmental stewardship and farming-ecosystem services.

A distributed system of floodways, carbon sink forests, and water treatment basins upstream can mitigate the need for massive flood works and filtration plants downstream.

PORT + Range

Team members
Christopher Marcinkoski
Ellen Neises
Megan Born
Nick McClintock
Yelena Zolotorevskaya
Claire Hoch
Ao Zhang
Naeem Shahrestani
Qi Wang

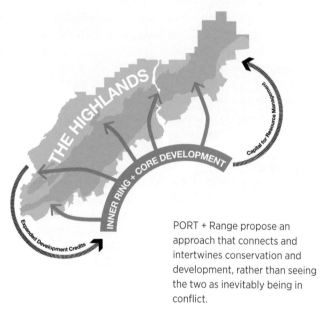

PORT + Range propose an approach that connects and intertwines conservation and development, rather than seeing the two as inevitably being in conflict.

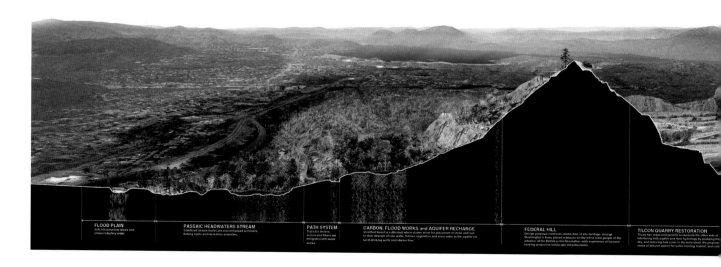

 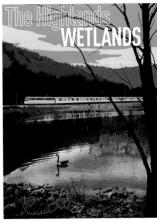 

Campaign for the Highlands
In the Highlands, humans and nature can coexist in harmony. Land is a resource to be exploited, and also cultivated and conserved.

Lowland Front View
Large-scale soft infrastructure (flood fingers) provides unique landscape character and community open space for new moderate-density development in the Lowland Front.

The Great Valley
With its well-drained soil and flat land, the Great Valley is a target for low-density real estate development. New incentives to keep the land as farm- and forestland could create watershed-scale landscape infrastructure for flood management.

Suburbs

WORKac

Team members
Amale Andraos
Dan Wood
Jonah Coe-Scharff
Efe (Ronald Ramirez)
Bryan Hardin
Zahid N. Ajam
Chije Kang

A surge of interest in urban living has breathed new life into Manhattan and the communities that directly surround it. But beyond Brooklyn, Jersey City, and New Rochelle, there are dozens of small cities and large towns—such as Port Chester, White Plains, Paterson, Montclair, Rahway, and Perth Amboy—that have tremendous potential for creating new jobs, increasing the availability of affordable housing, and improving public transportation options. These inner-ring suburbs are a critical component of the region's future: growing communities using innovative design strategies.

WORKac designed solutions for the network of inner suburbs that ring New York City, stretching from Port Chester, New York down to Perth Amboy, New Jersey. The firm focused on transforming the region's "corridor downtowns"—stretches of strip malls, parking lots, and office parks—into an exurban ribbon of density and diversity. WORKac proposed transforming parking lots and underused spaces into mixed-use residential complexes, with a focus on integrating those spaces with nature.

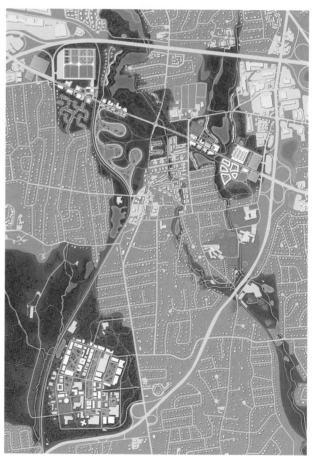

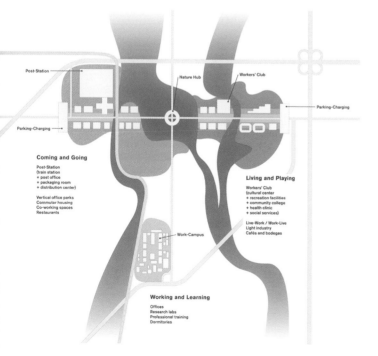

Changing patterns of work, shop, and play create the opportunity to reimagine the built environment in the suburbs.

As commercial strips are reinvented into community downtowns, new developments can be organized around restored natural systems.

Reintroducing nature to the suburban landscape

City

The City Corridor envisions the transformation of an existing freight rail linking the Bronx, Queens, and Brooklyn, and creating a Triboro line for freight and passengers. This circumferential line would connect 17 subway and commuter train lines, dramatically improving travel times between the boroughs. Each station along the Triboro line also presents opportunities for new housing, office, retail, and institutional spaces directly around the stations. The City Corridor has the potential to link many neighborhoods with new employment, cultural, and open-space opportunities.

How different would the Bronx, Brooklyn, and Queens look if they were linked by the Triboro line—a proposed 24-mile passenger train line first proposed by RPA in the Third Regional Plan? Designers at New York's Only If and the Dutch spatial-planning firm One Architecture used the existing right-of-way and adjacent spaces to create a linear park and greenway along the proposed line to improve community health; created a bike "superhighway" for commuter and recreational use; introduced new models for economic growth and job generation; managed stormwater runoff through sustainable features such as a reduction in asphalt; and devised development strategies for large catalytic projects and small-scale development that manage neighborhood growth and maintain local values.

Only If + One Architecture

Team members
Adam Frampton
Matthijs Bouw
Karolina Czeczek
Travis Bunt
Dalia Munenzon
Lindsay Woodson
Pierre de Brun
Kutay Biberoglu
Angelina Andriani Putri
James Schrader
Arianna Armelli
Rebecca Book
Jieru Hedy He
Jesse McCormick
Mat Staudt
Despo Thoma
Tim Tsang

Using existing rights-of-way and adjacent spaces, the Triboro line can also become a 24-mile linear park and bikeway, providing new public space for nearby residents.

Brownsville

Livonia Avenue

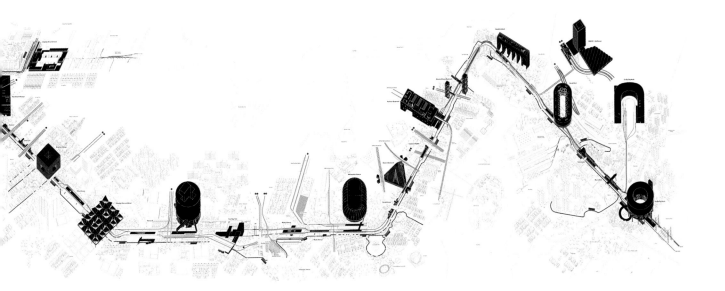

Coast

**Rafi Segal A+U +
DLAND Studio**

Team members
Rafi Segal
Susannah Drake
Sarah Williams
Greg Lindsay
Brent Ryan
Benjamin Albrecht
Mary Lynch-Lloyd
Chaewon Ahn
Jan Casimir
Mary Hohlt
Erin Wythoff
Charles Huang
Dennis Harvey
Zach Postone
Ellen Shakespear
Xinhui Li

From Atlantic City to Montauk, our coastal communities are threatened by climate change and sea-level rise. Though Superstorm Sandy sounded the alarm and put into motion several initiatives to improve resilience and protection, these efforts have largely been location-specific. The New York-New Jersey Bight Corridor develops strategies that can be applied to a range of communities along the coasts, paying special attention to those with socially vulnerable populations.

How could the coastline of the region transform to meet the reality of rising sea levels? Rafi Segal + DLAND Studio developed designs that would create an environmental buffer to help ease the tension between vulnerable coastal communities and nature's unstoppable forces. As envisioned, the buffer would relieve the stress on the coastline and communities by creating a space for land and water to co-mingle while providing space to live, conserve, work, and play. The buffer would do this by attracting new residents at higher densities, protecting low-lying areas using the absorptive capacity of the buffer, and adapting to a more amphibious lifestyle in the zone. This would transform the coastline into a new urban frontier. Using this approach, Rafi Segal + DLAND hope to educate coastal communities about a new reality through the development of homes, neighborhoods, and cities built to withstand water and succeed in the era of climate change.

In Sea Bright, NJ, a small community on a vanishing barrier island, residents welcome the "flood life," choosing to elevate homes and travel by boat.

From Line to Zone

Thousands of homes in Mastic Beach, NY, will be permanently underwater in the next 25 years, and many will need to be rebuilt on high, dry ground. But between low and high ground, some homes could remain in wet or partially wet areas as they evolve into new elevated neighborhoods built along docks.

Mastic Beach

About

For nearly 100 years, Regional Plan Association has been an indispensable source of ideas and plans for policy-makers and opinion shapers across the tri-state region, and RPA's three previous regional plans have fundamentally shaped the growth of the tri-state area. The Fourth Regional Plan was developed over the course of five years leading up to 2017. It is the product of in-depth research and extensive public engagement with a wide range of policy experts, advocates, and community members.

About Regional Plan Association

Since its inception nearly a century ago, RPA has conducted groundbreaking research on issues of land use, transportation, the environment, economic development, and opportunity. It has also led advocacy campaigns to foster a thriving, diverse, and environmentally sustainable region, helping local communities address their most pressing challenges.

RPA staff includes policy experts, urban planners, analysts, writers, and advocates. RPA collaborates with partners across sectors to find the best ideas to meet the challenges facing our region today and in the future.

RPA's work is informed by these partnerships as well as by our board of directors and our New York, New Jersey, and Connecticut committees.

RPA's Regional Plans

Since the 1920s, RPA has developed groundbreaking long-range plans to guide the growth of the New York-New Jersey-Connecticut metropolitan area.

These efforts have shaped and improved the region's economic health, environmental sustainability, and quality of life. Ideas and recommendations put forth in these plans have led to the establishment of some of the tri-state region's most significant infrastructure, open space, and economic development projects, including new bridges and roadways, improvements to our transit network, the preservation of vital open space, and a renewed emphasis on creating sustainable communities centered around jobs and transit.

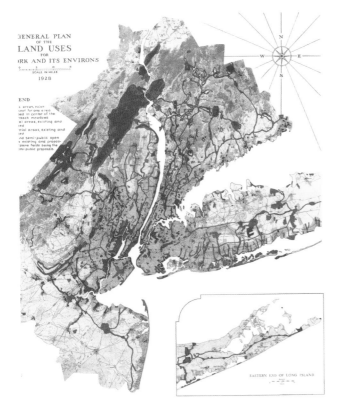

Regional Plan of New York and Its Environs, 1929

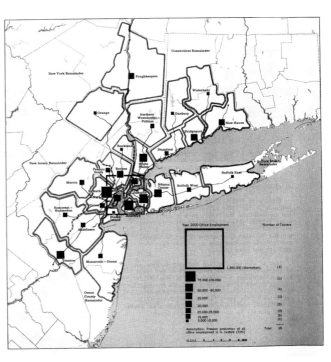

Second Regional Plan, 1968

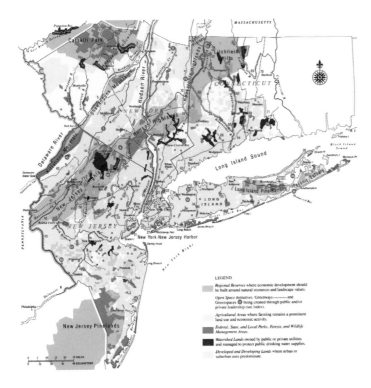

Third Regional Plan, 1996

Fourth Regional Plan, 2017

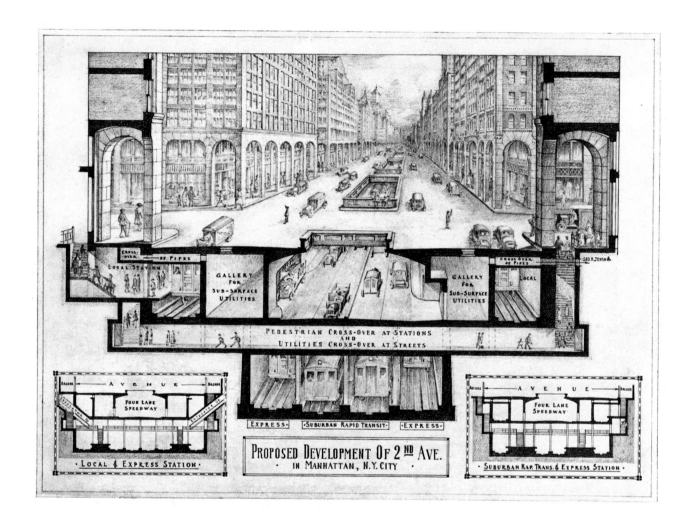

Proposed Development of 2nd Ave. in Manhattan, N.Y. City

Regional Plan of New York and Its Environs, 1929

RPA's first plan provided the blueprint for the transportation and open space networks we take for granted today.

The Regional Plan produced the first definitive regional map of New York, documenting existing conditions block by block. It collected and analyzed extensive quantitative data about demographics, population distribution, economic conditions, land utilization, transportation, natural features, and other characteristics of the greater region, at a time when such data were difficult to come by.

Many proposals from the first plan were implemented in the 1930s and 1940s. When Franklin Delano Roosevelt, first as New York governor and then as president, needed construction programs to put unemployed workers back to work in New York, he turned to RPA's plan. Later, as Robert Moses, Austin Tobin, and John D. Rockefeller set out to shape New York into a modern city, they also relied on RPA's proposals.

By the middle of the 20th century, the majority of the first plan's key urban and infrastructure recommendations had been implemented. The plan inspired hundreds of billions of dollars in infrastructure and city-building projects that enabled New York to become the leading global city in the middle of the 20th century.

Major recommendations that shape the region today include:

- A more connected region with better railroads, highways, and parks. The goal was to provide access to more of the region and give options for living beyond the overcrowded core. The fundamental concept of metropolitan development driven by transit and limited-access highways, pioneered in the first plan, created a precedent for every modern 20th century metropolis.

- The proposed network of highways led to the relocation of the planned George Washington Bridge from 57th Street to 178th Street. RPA understood the bridge would primarily be used for traveling through the region, and should therefore avoid the congestion of Midtown. The construction of the Verrazano-Narrows Bridge in the early 1960s effectively completed the regional highway system proposed in RPA's first plan.

- The first plan's call for preserving large swaths of natural areas, as well as the identification of the most critical areas to be preserved, persuaded several public agencies to purchase and preserve land. Acquisitions in Nassau, Suffolk, Putnam, and Dutchess counties, and in Flushing Meadows, Orchard Beach Park, and the Palisades, doubled the region's park space.

- RPA helped local governments establish planning boards, including New York's City Planning Commission, to advise local elected officials on development decisions. From 1929 to 1939, the number of planning boards in the region increased from 61 to 204. Today, they are an essential component of local land-use and budget planning in the region.

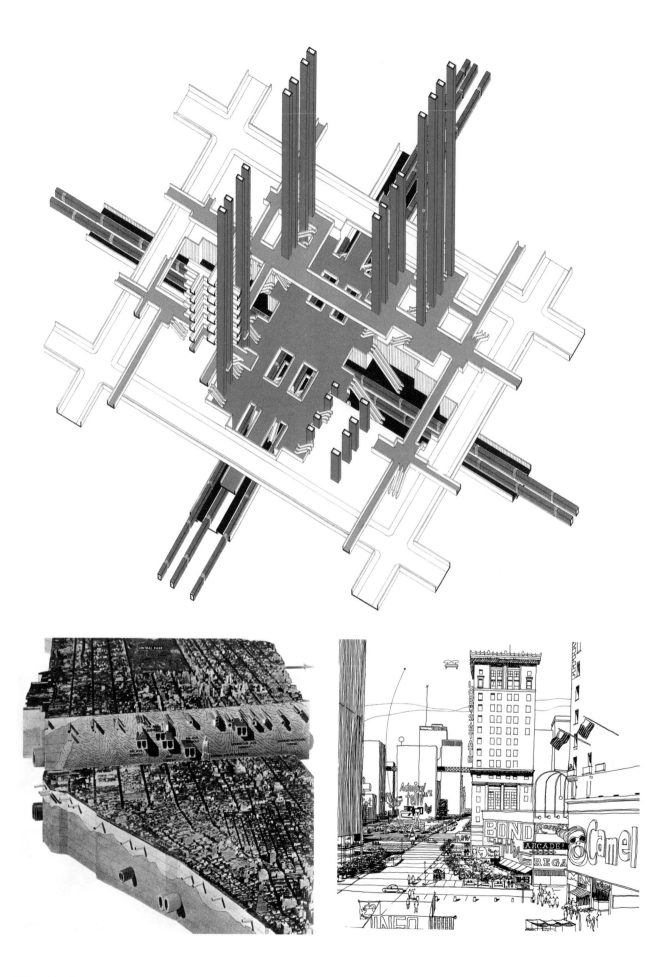

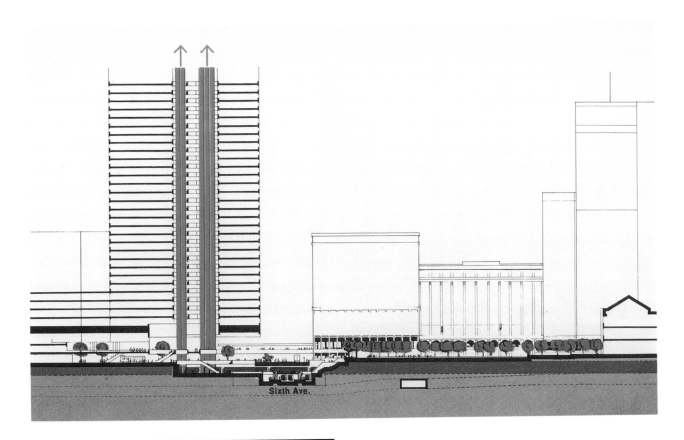

Sixth Ave.

Second Regional Plan, 1968

The Second Regional Plan envisioned a regional network of economic centers connected by robust and federally funded mass transit.

At a time when wealthier white residents were fleeing the city for the suburbs, RPA's Second Regional Plan focused on the need to invest in regional centers and transit, and to reign in sprawl.

RPA successfully pushed the federal government to fund public transit like it funded highways. The second plan's focus on federal funding of mass transit paved the way for the formation of Metropolitan Transit Authority, the recovery of the subway system, and the creation of New Jersey Transit.

As employers began to leave Manhattan in favor of suburban campuses, the second plan advocated for creating dense subregional centers of employment in cities such as Stamford, New Brunswick, and White Plains. The plan also introduced the need for mixed-income, mixed-use neighborhoods in regional centers as well as high-rise apartments in the center of metropolitan communities.

Lastly, the second plan called for the preservation of the region's natural resources, which led to the permanent preservation of thousands of square miles of open space.

Major recommendations of the second plan that shape the region today include:

- The federal Urban Mass Transportation Act adopted RPA's principle of federal support for capital costs for urban mass transit. By ensuring adequate funding, the region's transit agencies were able to plan for the long term. RPA supported the formation of the Metropolitan Transportation Authority, which brought together the subway, bus, commuter rail, and many bridge-and-tunnel toll facilities under one roof.

- The second plan identified the potential for revitalizing the Lower Hudson River area with better infrastructure, housing, and public parks. Its vision for Manhattan, Hoboken, and Jersey City has largely become reality, with better transit, an attractive waterfront, and mixed-use development.

- RPA called for the revival of regional centers in Jamaica, Queens, Downtown Brooklyn, Newark, and Stamford.

- RPA introduced the concept that the supply of undeveloped natural spaces was limited and called for an aggressive program to acquire, protect, and permanently preserve natural landscapes for future generations. RPA led the effort to create Gateway National Recreation Center, which in 1972 became the first major federal recreation area in an urban setting.

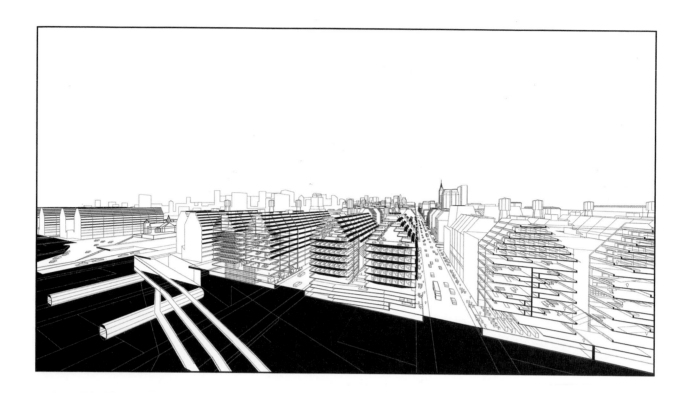

Third Regional Plan, 1996

A cornerstone of RPA's Third Regional Plan was the recognition that the region's continued prosperity and global standing were no longer guaranteed.

The plan warned that, without major new investments in New York City, as well as the region's infra-structure and the environment, the tri-state region would be at risk of a slow and painful recovery from the economic downturn of the early 1990s.

It laid out a vision for the Far West Side that included a mixed-use expansion of the Midtown business district. Today's Hudson Yards community closely resembles RPA's proposal for the site.

The plan also emphasized the importance of having a transportation network that could support growth. RPA worked closely with public sector leaders to identify the route and service for several key transit expansions, and called for charging drivers to enter Manhattan to pay for it.

The third plan also set in motion steps for the permanent conservation of several region-shaping open spaces, including Governors Island and post-industrial waterfronts throughout the region.

Major recommendations of the third plan built or in progress include:

- The redevelopment of the Far West Side to expand the Midtown business district helped shape RPA's alternative development scenario for the Hudson Yards when city leaders proposed building a football stadium on the site. The plan ultimately adopted by the city and developers closely resembled RPA's proposal.

- The third plan proposed a new rail system to connect existing commuter rail lines and optimize the transit system as a whole, including a Second Avenue Subway, a connection for Long Island Rail Road into Grand Central known as East Side Access, the extension of the #7 subway line to the Far West Side, AirTrain to JFK Airport, and the Fulton Street Transit Center.

- The third plan set in motion steps that led to the permanent conservation of several region-shaping open spaces, including Governors Island, the New Jersey Highlands, the Central Pine Barrens, the Brooklyn Waterfront Greenway, and the large, underutilized urban waterfronts of the New York-New Jersey Harbor and Long Island Sound.

Current

Business as usual

Preferred

The planning process

RPA began work on the Fourth Regional Plan by speaking with residents and experts, and aggregating data. RPA's report "Fragile Success," published in 2014, assessed and documented the region's challenges: affordability, climate change, infrastructure, and governance.

During the subsequent five years, RPA staff analyzed gigabytes of data; read hundreds of strategic plans and policy reports; held working sessions with more than a thousand partners; hosted dozens of community meetings with thousands of local leaders, residents, and business owners; and collaborated with five talented design teams.

RPA integrated analytical research and outside input into a cohesive plan that is ambitious but practical, and presents both a long-range view of the region and recommendations that can be implemented right away.

Supporting these recommendations are substantive white papers, infographics, charts, and tables to make our data easily understandable, along with images to better visualize the challenges and opportunities.

Each of RPA's three previous regional plans was a product of its time, in both content and process. There are certainly some aspects of today's planning process that RPA planners a half-century ago would recognize. The fourth plan was based on rigorous analysis of data and trends, poring over spreadsheets and creating maps, just as the last three plans were decades ago.

Yet today, the availability of fine-grain data, and the computing power to analyze and visualize it, meant staff could delve much deeper into housing and travel patterns, economic trends, and environmental impacts.

For example, staff used data from a dozen different sources, at a half-mile-square level, to document the region's built form, quantify past population and employment trends, and with that information extrapolate future growth.

RPA's transportation team used data to estimate future travel demand, and then determine which transportation investments would most improve access to jobs and a higher standard of living.

RPA's environment and energy group tracked where rising sea levels were likely to have the greatest impact, and where the region has invested the most in terms of infrastructure, housing, and jobs in order to identify a range of resilience solutions tailored to particular places.

RPA's community planning experts estimated the region's current and future housing shortage, and documented which communities were most at risk of displacement, in order to understand how to increase the number of homes and protect residents from rapid change.

But RPA staff didn't just sit in front of a computer for the past five years. RPA also spoke with thousands of people across the region: industry experts, agency leaders, community organizers, elected officials, civic partners, business owners, and neighborhood groups. Each person we spoke with generously shared their knowledge and advice, and RPA is deeply grateful for their time and the trust they placed in the process.

In fact, if there is one thing that sets the fourth plan apart from previous RPA plans it's the effort we made to reach deep into communities, particularly those that have been excluded for so long from the planning process. Thanks to community organizations around the region, RPA staff was able to hear a wide range of perspectives on affordability, jobs, transportation, and environmental justice—and tailor our research accordingly. It is in part these exchanges that led us to intentionally infuse the important values of heath and equity throughout the plan—and also into who we are as an organization.

The Committee on the Fourth Regional Plan and its associated working groups, as well as RPA's board and committees, were also instrumental advisors, sharing their insights, deepening our understanding of the work they were doing, and most pragmatically, reviewing drafts of the report.

The committee began with three cochairs: Rit Aggarwala, Tony Shorris, and Paul Francis. Along the way, two had to step down for happy reasons. Tony was tapped by Mayor Bill de Blasio to be his first deputy mayor, and Paul was tapped by Governor Andrew Cuomo to become New York State's deputy secretary for Health and Human Services. Rit Aggarwala, a veteran of Mayor Michael Bloomberg's administration, remained throughout. We are honored to have had such a thoughtful and experienced team of people leading this process, and are especially grateful to Rit for spending countless hours guiding us with his rigorous analytical approach and creative ideas.

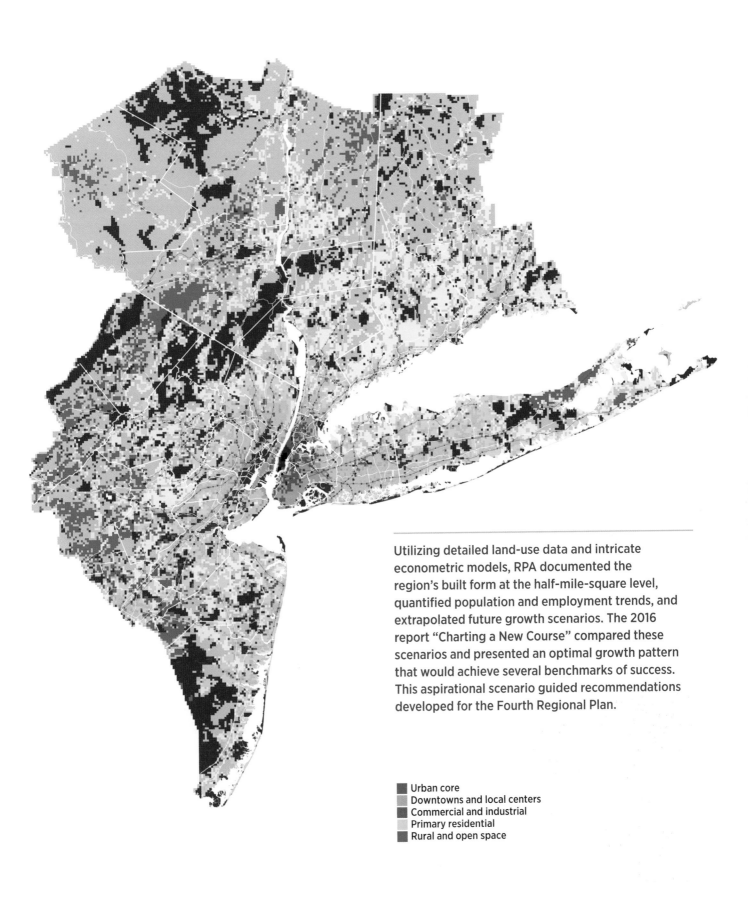

Utilizing detailed land-use data and intricate econometric models, RPA documented the region's built form at the half-mile-square level, quantified population and employment trends, and extrapolated future growth scenarios. The 2016 report "Charting a New Course" compared these scenarios and presented an optimal growth pattern that would achieve several benchmarks of success. This aspirational scenario guided recommendations developed for the Fourth Regional Plan.

- Urban core
- Downtowns and local centers
- Commercial and industrial
- Primary residential
- Rural and open space

Community engagement

To ensure that that the fourth plan's recommendations reflected the needs and priorities of all residents of the region, RPA collaborated with organizations representing low-income individuals and communities of color, as well as other constituencies that have traditionally not been included in planning processes. Make the Road New York, Make the Road Connecticut, Community Voices Heard, Housing and Community Development Network of New Jersey, Partnership for Strong Communities, and Right to the City Alliance—together representing more than 50,000 residents—helped RPA staff stay connected at the grassroots level—no easy task in a region with 23 million residents.

Partners held dozens of workshops and focus groups, and surveyed more than 1,500 individuals, to learn that low-income residents in the region are feeling a growing sense of instability from job insecurity, unsafe housing conditions, capricious evictions, ever-increasing costs of living, racial discrimination, and a lack of access to quality food, health care and other services. The lived experience of these individuals shaped the plan.

In a second phase, community leaders and partner organizations discussed RPA's preliminary proposals on community development, resilience, and infrastructure. At workshops around the region, participants critiqued proposed policies and projects to revitalize communities, protect against displacement, address rising sea levels, and connect less-dense areas. The process strengthened plan proposals in their early stages.

Ultimately, this community engagement helped the plan prioritize recommendations that most strongly support low-income residents in the tri-state region: building local capacity for underrepresented constituencies to advocate for more inclusive land use and planning, allowing for the construction of more affordable housing, promoting better connectivity, and increasing environmental resilience. RPA and partners jointly wrote an Equity Agenda for the New York Region, committing to continue collaborating in the future in order to promote the equitable implementation of the Fourth Regional Plan.

Community Voices Heard: a member-led multi-racial organization, principally women of color and low-income families in New York State, that builds power to secure social, economic and racial justice for all. CVH accomplishes its mission through grassroots organizing, leadership development, policy changes, and creating new models of direct democracy.

Partnership for Strong Communities: a statewide nonprofit policy and advocacy organization dedicated to ending homelessness, expanding the creation of affordable housing, and building strong communities in Connecticut.

Housing and Community Development Network: a statewide association of over 250-non-profit housing and community development corporations, individuals, professional organizations, and prominent New Jersey corporations that support the creation of housing choices and economic opportunities for low- and moderate-income community residents.

Make the Road Connecticut: an organization that builds membership with low-income and working class Latinos living in Bridgeport, CT and has become a powerful voice on immigrant rights, worker rights, public schools, LGBTQ justice, and more.

Make the Road New York: a statewide nonprofit that builds the power of Latino and working class communities to achieve dignity and justice through organizing, policy innovation, transformative education, and survival services.

New York Communities for Change: multi-racial membership based organization of working families fighting against economic and racial oppression. NYCC members are agents of change, building movements and campaigns from the ground up and fighting corporate power at its core.

Right to the City Alliance: a national alliance of racial, economic and environmental justice organizations building a national movement for racial justice, urban justice, human rights, and democracy. RTC seeks to create regional and national impacts in the fields of housing, human rights, urban land, com-munity development, civic engagement, criminal justice, environmental justice, and more.

Hester Street Collaborative: an urban planning, design, and development nonprofit that works to ensure that neighborhoods are shaped by the people who live in them. HSC offers technical and capacity-building assistance to community-based organizations, private firms and government agencies on land use processes, neighborhood planning and design, and public and private community development projects. We strive for more vibrant, equitable, sustain-able and resilient neighborhoods.

Alliance for a Greater New York: a longstanding alliance of labor and community organizations united for a just and sustainable New York. ALIGN works at the intersection of economy, environment, and equity to make change and build movement. Our model addresses the root causes of economic injustice by forging strategic coalitions, shaping the public debate through strategic communications, and developing policy solutions that make an impact.

Fourth Regional Plan Reports

Over the course of five years, RPA released a number of reports to support the Fourth Regional Plan.

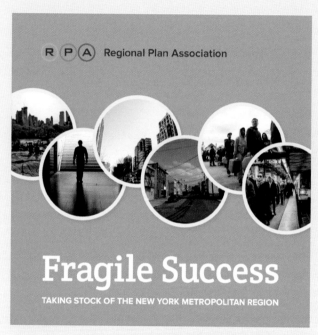

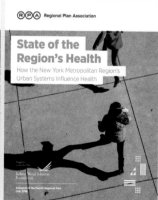

April 2014: Fragile Success documented some of the region's most critical urban planning challenges: uneven distribution of wealth, skyrocketing housing prices, systematic underinvestment in transportation infrastructure, climate change and sea-level rise, and finally, a disheartening loss of faith in public institutions.

June 2016: Charting a New Course described RPA's vision for a successful region: a place that fulfills its promise of equal opportunity; a coastal region that shows the rest of the world how to adapt and prosper in an age of rising seas and temperatures; and a global hub that harnesses its immense resources and innovative talent to make this fast-paced, expensive metropolis an easier, healthier and more affordable place to live and work.

Early 2017: State of the Region's Health, Pushed Out, and Under Water provided more detailed analysis of the region's challenges.

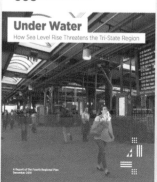

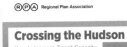

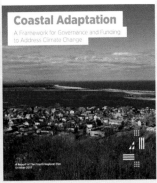

Crossing the Hudson
How to Increase Transit Capacity and Improve Commutes

Accessing Nature
Recommendations for a Tri-State Trail Network

Coastal Adaptation
A Framework for Governance and Funding to Address Climate Change

Regional Resilience Trust Funds
An Exploratory Analysis for the New York Metropolitan Region

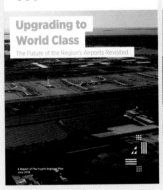

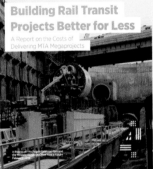

New Mobility
Autonomous Vehicles and the Region

Untapped Potential
Opportunities for affordable homes and neighborhoods near transit

Building Rail Transit Projects Better for Less
A Report on the Costs of Delivering MTA Megaprojects

Creating more affordable housing in New York City's high-rise areas
The case for lifting the FAR cap

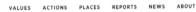

Upgrading to World Class
The Future of the Region's Airports Revisited

Trans-Regional Express (T-REX)
Transforming the New York Region's Commuter Rail System into an Integrated Regional Rail Network

Save Our Subways
A Plan to Transform New York City's Rapid Transit System

Summer 2017 to early 2018: A series of reports provided more detailed data and analysis for some of the Fourth Regional Plan's most critical recommendations.

The Fourth Regional Plan

VALUES   ACTIONS   PLACES   REPORTS   NEWS   ABOUT

The Fourth Regional Plan

Making the Region Work for All of Us

READ THE EXECUTIVE SUMMARY   ORDER YOUR COPY OF THE PLAN

November 2017: The Fourth Regional Plan was released online, complete with 61 recommendations to create a region of equity, health, prosperity and sustainability.

Endnotes

1 RPA, "Spatial Planning and Inequality," 2015

2 Springer Link, "Income inequality and economic growth: a panel VAR approach," 2015

3 PolicyLink, "The Equity Profile of Long Island," 2017

4 NAACP, "Criminal Justice Fact Sheet," 2016

5 PolicyLink, "Full Employment for All: The Social and Economic Benefits of Race and Gender Equity in Employment," 2015

6 Riders Alliance, "Community Service Society, Riders Alliance Launch 'Fair Fares' Campaign for Reduced-Fare MetroCards for Lowest-Income New Yorkers," 2016

7 RPA, "State of the Region's Health," 2016

8 Regional Plan Association, "Spatial Planning and Inequality," 2015

9 American Journal of Public Health, "Regional Planning in Relation to Public Health," 1926

10 World Commission on Environment and Development, "Our Common Future: Report of the World Commission On Environment and Development," 1987

11 New Jersey For Transit, "Stuck at the Station 15 Years of Declining Investment Has Harmed New Jersey's Ability to Deliver High-Quality Transit Service," 2016

12 Acadia Center, "Outpacing the Nation: RGGI's environmental and economic success," 2017

13 Georgetown Climate Center, "Reducing Greenhouse Gas Emissions from the Transportation Sector: Opportunities in the Northeast and Mid-Atlantic," 2015

14 RGGI, "Market Monitor Report for Auction 37," 2017

15 RGGI, "The Investment of RGGI Proceeds in 2015," 2015

16 Center for Climate and Energy Solutions, "Analysis of California Air Resources Board 2017 Climate Change Scoping Plan Update," 2017

17 Center for Climate and Energy Solutions, "Analysis of California cap-and-trade program," 2017

18 Georgetown Climate Center, "Reducing Greenhouse Gas Emissions from Transportation: Opportunities in the Northeast and Mid-Atlantic," 2015

19 U.S. Department of Agriculture, Forest Service, Climate Change Resource Center, "Forests and Carbon Storage," 2012

20 Keenan, J.M., "Regional Resilience Trust Funds: An Exploratory Analysis for Leveraging Insurance Surcharges. Environment Systems and Decisions," 2017

21 Keenan, J.M., "Regional Resilience Trust Funds: An Exploratory Analysis for Leveraging Insurance Surcharges. Environment Systems and Decisions," 2017

22 Tax-Rates.org, "Income Tax Rates by State," 2017

23 U.S. Bureau of the Census, "2015 Public Elementary-Secondary Education Finance Data," 2015

24 Long Island Index, "A Tale of Two Suburbs," 2007

25 Lincoln Institute of Land Policy, "The Effects of the Two-Rate Property Tax," 2014

26 National Center for Education Statistics, "Monitoring School Quality," 2000

27 The National Coalition on School Diversity, "School Integration and K-12 Education Outcomes, Brief No. 5," 2011

28 The Century Foundation, "Hartford Public Schools," 2016

29 Center for American Progress, "Size Matters: A Look at School-District Consolidation," 2013

30 Civil Rights Project, UCLA, "Brown at 62: School Segregation by Race, Poverty and State," 2016

31 Long Island Index, Rauch Foundation, "Inter-District and Intra-District Segregation on Long Island," 2012

32 The Fund for New Jersey, "Persistent Racial Segregation in Schools," 2017

33 The Fund for New Jersey, "Persistent Racial Segregation in Schools: Policy Issues and Opportunities to Address Unequal Education Across New Jersey's Public Schools," 2017

34 ibid

35 ibid

36 State Environmental Quality Review (SEQR for jurisdictions outside NYC) and City Environmental Quality Review (CEQR) for development applications within the five boroughs.

37 Environmental impact assessment is mandated by law in New York State through the State Environmental Quality Review Act (SEQR). New York City has its own specific requirements for environmental review through CEQR. In Connecticut and New Jersey, environmental impacts are evaluated through environmental permitting processes and by individual municipalities through local land use regulations.

38 Seattle Neighborhood Greenways, "Safe Routes to Health," 2014

39 County Health Rankings & Roadmaps, "Walking School Buses," 2015

40 Child In The City Foundation, "Incorporating play into pedestrian walkways," 2016

41 ChangeLab Solutions, "Fair Play: Advancing Health Equity through Shared Use," 2015

42 American Planning Association, "Quenching Community Thirst: Planning for More Access to Drinking Water in Public Places," 2013

43 Next Century Cities, "'One Touch' Make-Ready Policies: The 'Dig Once' of Pole Attachments," 2016

44 Wired Magazine, "It's Time to Take Mesh Networks Seriously (and not Just for the Reasons You Think)," 2014

45 Columbia University, "Hollerith 1890 Census Tabulator," 2011

46 RPA, "Surface Transit: Upgrading local mobility for the region," 2017

47 TransitCenter, "A Bid for Better Transit," 2017

48 RPA, "Untapped Potential: Opportunities for affordable homes and neighborhoods near transit," 2017

49 "An Integrated Perspective on the Future of Mobility." McKinsey & Company and Bloomberg New Energy Finance, October 2016.

50 "An Integrated Perspective on the Future of Mobility." McKinsey & Company and Bloomberg New Energy Finance (2016).

51 Bertoncello, Michele, and Dominik Wee. "Ten Ways Autonomous Driving Could Redefine the Automotive World." McKinsey & Company, June 2015.

52 RPA, "Under Water: How Sea Level Rise Threatens the Tri-State Region," 2017

53 RPA, "Buy-In for Buyouts," 2016

54 RPA, "Under Water: How Sea Level Rise Threatens the Tri-State Region," 2016

55 Riverkeeper, "Combined Sewage Overflows (CSOs)," 20010

56 RPA Lab, "Mapping the Region's Vanishing Wetlands," 2016

57 RPA, "Doris Duke Grant Proposal," 2017 (unpublished)

58 New York City Department of Health and Mental Hygiene, "Epi Data Brief," 2014

59 The National Resources Defense Council, "Killer Summer Heat," 2012

60 The National Resources Defense Council, "Health and Climate Change: Accounting for Costs," 2011

61 Centers for Disease Control and Prevention, "Climate Change and Extreme Heat Events," 2016

62 Public Health Institute and Center for Climate Change and Health, "Extreme Heat, Climate Change and Health," 2016

63 Madrigano, Jaime et al., "A Case-Only Study of Vulnerability to Heat Wave-Related Mortality in New York City (2000–2011)," Environmental Health Perspectives, 2015

64 Friends of the Earth Europe, Nature for Health and Equity, 2017

65 Hudson River Valley Greenway

66 U.S. Renewables Portfolio Standards: 2017 Annual Status Report, Lawrence Berkeley National Laboratory

67 NYSERDA, "Commercial Property Assessed Clean Energy (PACE) Financing Guidelines," 2017

68 RPA, "Pushed Out: Housing Displacement in an Unaffordable Region," 2017

69 Glynn, Chris, and Fox, Emily, "Dynamics of homelessness in urban America," 2017

70 Dwyer, Lee Allen, "Mapping Impact: An Analysis of the Dudley Street Neighborhood Initiative Land Trust," 2015

71 Curbed New York, "De Blasio signs into law sweeping protections against tenant harassment," 2017

72 City of New York, "Mayor de Blasio Signs Three New Laws Protecting Tenants From Harassment," 2015

73 Coalition for the Homelessness, "Basic Facts About Homelessness: New York City," 2017

74 Monarch Housing Associates, "New Jersey's 2015 Point-In-Time Count of the Homeless," 2015

75 New York City Department of Health and Mental Hygiene, "New York/New York III Supportive Housing Evaluation," 2011

76 New York Magazine, "A Cash-strapped New York City Public Housing Authority Faces a Cut in Federal Funds," 2017

77 New York City Housing Authority, "Report on the 2015–2019 Operating and Capital Budget & the Fiscal 2015 Preliminary Mayor's Management Report," 2015

78 Stout Risius Ross, "Pro Bono and Legal Services Committee of the New York City Bar Association," 2016

79 RPA, "Spatial Planning and Inequality," 2015

80 New York-Connecticut Sustainable Communities Consortium, "Implementation Plan for Sustainable Development in the New York-Connecticut Metropolitan Region," 2014

81 RPA, "Spatial Planning and Inequality," 2015

82 RPA, "Untapped Potential: Opportunities for affordable homes and neighborhoods near transit," 2017

83 RPA, "Charting a New Course," 2016

84 Elsie Gould, "Childhood Lead Poisoning: Conservative Estimates of the Social and Economic Benefits of Lead Hazard Control," 2009

85 Center on Budget and Policy Priorities, "Major Study: Housing Vouchers Most Effective Tool to End Family Homelessness," 2015

86 RPA, "Charting a New Course," 2016

87 Lincoln Institute of Land Policy, "Revitalizing America's Smaller Legacy Cities," 2017

88 Center for Real Estate and Urban Analysis, George Washington University, "Walk Up Wake Up Call New York," 2017

89 The New School, "Does Gentrification Increase Employment Opportunities in Low-Income Neighborhoods?" 2015

90 RPA, "Charting a New Course," 2016

91 Center for Real Estate and Urban Analysis, The George Washington School of Business, "The WalkUP Wake-Up Call: New York," 2017

92 RPA, "Route 110 Corridor Opportunity Analysis," 2015

93 People living within the equivalent of 500 meters to over 1,000 vehicles on major roads

94 NYC Health, "The Public Health Impacts of PM2.5 from Traffic Air Pollution," 2017

95 State of New Jersey Department of Health, "Asthma in New Jersey," 2017

96 RPA, "Charting A New Course," 2016

97 People living within the equivalent of one mile from at least one hazardous site. For the purposes of this analysis, hazardous sites are defined as superfund sites, major direct dischargers, treatment storage and disposal facilities and sites that require a risk management plan by the EPA.

98 Devos Institute, "Diversity In The Arts: The Past, Present, and Future of African American and Latino Museums, Dance Companies, and Theater Companies," 2015

99 University of Pennsylvania Social Impact of the Arts Project, "The Social Wellbeing of New York City's Neighborhoods: The Contribution of Culture and the Arts," 2017

100 The New York City Council, "Participatory Budgeting," 2017

101 The City of Seattle, "The CAP Report," 2017

102 New York's Naturally Occurring Cultural Districts Council, "Creative Placemaking From the Community Up," 2017

103 National Endowment for the Arts, "How to do Creative Placemaking: An Action Oriented Guide to Arts in Community Development," 2017

104 National Endowment for the Arts, "Creative Placemaking," 2010

105 The Food Trust, "Access to Healthy Food and Why It Matters: A Review of the Research," 2013

106 Fiscal Policy Institute, "Immigrant Small Business Owners: A Significant and Growing Part of the Economy," 2012

107 USDA, "Community Food Systems," 2017

108 New York City Department of Health, "New York City Community Health Profiles Atlas," 2015

Acknowledgments

The Fourth Regional Plan is the product of dozens of RPA staff members, hundreds of close collaborators, and thousands of community members and other experts who shared their knowledge and ideas with us. We are grateful for all the support.

RPA SUPPORT

We thank all our donors for their generous support of RPA and the Fourth Regional Plan.

Major grant support from

Ford Foundation
The JPB Foundation
Robert Wood Johnson Foundation
Rockefeller Foundation

Additional grants from

Albert W. & Katharine E. Merck
    Charitable Fund
Anonymous
Doris Duke Charitable Foundation
Durst Organization
Edison Properties
Fairfield County's Community Foundation
Fund for the City of New York
The Oram Foundation: Fund for the
    Environment & Urban Life
Google
Howard & Abby Milstein Foundation
J. M. Kaplan Fund
Leon Lowenstein Foundation
Lily Auchincloss Foundation
Lincoln Institute of Land Policy
The New York Community Trust
Rauch Foundation
Siemens USA
Stavros Niarchos Foundation
TransitCenter
Verizon Communications
Volvo Research & Educational Foundations

Major organizational support from members of our patron program

Jeff Blau
Anthony Borelli
Helena Durst

Andrew Mathias
Scott Rechler
Denise Richardson

Frank Cohen
Suzanne Heidelberger
Anaita Kasad
Richard Oram

Michael Regan
John Santora
Sharon Taylor

Rohit Aggarwala
David Armour
Charles Avolio
Giacomo Barbieri
Elizabeth Belfer
Charles Bendit
William Best
Robert Blumenthal
Mark Blumkin
Kevin Corbett
James Fitzgerald
Timur Galen
Jonathan Goldstick
Richard Haray
Carol Joseph
Sabrina Kanner

Gregory Kelly
Hope Knight
Mitchell Korbey
Judith Lagano
Christopher LaTuso
Trent Lethco
Mark Marcucci
Douglas McCoach
Jan Nicholson
Kevin Pearson
Tom Prendergast
Marc Ricks
Janette Sadik-Khan
Monica Slater Stokes
Michael Sweeney
Hon. Darryl Towns

Marcia Bateson
Stephen Beckwith
Robert Billingsley
Eugenie Birch
Tonio Burgos
Vishaan Chakrabarti
Hon. Jun Choi
Frank Cicero
Michael Critelli
Thomas Patrick Dore, Jr.
Luke Fichthorn
Doreen Frasca
Maxine Griffith

Dylan Hixon
David Huntington
Paul Josephson
Matthew Kissner
Jill Lerner
Gregg Rechler
Gary Rose
Samuel Schwartz
James Simpson
Kent Swig
Marilyn Taylor
Richard Thigpen
Jane Veron

THANK YOU

Regional Plan Association staff wishes to express our heartfelt gratitude to the hundreds of thought leaders who participated in the creation of the Fourth Regional Plan. The plan is stronger thanks to their deep expertise and commitment to the region. RPA staff would like to particularly acknowledge Rohit T. Aggarwala, as chair of the Committee on the Fourth Regional Plan.

Zak Accuardi
Ignacio Acevedo**
Douglas Adams**
Lena Afridi
Reena Agarwal
Rohit Aggarwala*
Mark Ahasic
Chaewon Ahn
Jennifer Akchin
Benjamin Albrecht
Eric Alexander
Sol Marie
    Alfonso-Jones**
Allison Allbee
Eva Alligood
Sharon Alpert
Joel Alvarez
Richard Anderson
Scott Anderson**
Sean Anderson**
Amale Andraos**
Roland Anglin**
James Ariola**
Kenneth Armellino**
David Armour*
Regina Armstrong**
Kate Ascher**
Hiro Aso
Caron Atlas
Afua Atta-Mensah**
Charles Avolio*
Victor Bach**
Ellen Baer**
Richard Bagger**
Jessica Bailey**
Linda Bailey
Vivian Baker
Zoe Baldwin**
Nisha Baliga**
Hillary Ballon
Ana Baptista**
Linda Baran**

Mary Barber**
Giacomo Barbieri*
Joseph Barile
Eve Baron
Jordan Barowitz
MarySue Barrett
Tarika Barrett**
Walter Barrientos**
Richard Bass
Rene Baston**
Andrew Bata**
Marcia Bateson*
Quantel Bazemore**
Philip Beachem**
Eric Beaton
Ernest Beck
Stephen Beckwith*
Alyson Beha
Ron Beit**
Elizabeth Belfer
Charles Bendit**
Gerald Benjamin
Jamie Bennet
Josh Benson
Barry Bergdoll**
Staci Berger**
Christine Berthet
Richard Besser
William Best**
Peter Bienstock
Robert Billingsley*
Eugenie Birch*
Richard Bivone
Betsy Blair
Roger Blakeley**
Edward Blakely
Jeff Blau
Ralph Blessing**
Robert Blumenthal*
Mark Blumkin*
Stephanie Boarden
Jerry Bogacz

Erin Boggs**
Dennis Bone**
J. Tedrowe Bonner**
Andrew Boraine**
Anthony Borelli*
Megan Born
Judi Boswirth
Jo Ivey Boufford*
Dana Bourland**
Patricia Bourne
Matthijs Bouw**
Eli Bovarnick
Jonathan Bowles**
Andrew Bowman**
David Bragdon**
Noam Bramson**
Quentin Brathwaite**
Josh Breitbart**
Gale Brewer
James Brinkerhoff*
Ben Britton**
Zachary Broat
Fred Brody**
Bennett Brooks
Michael Brotchner
Karen Brown**
Clarke Bruno**
Miguel Bucalem**
Travis Bunt
Tonio Burgos*
Ross Burkhardt**
Karen Burnaska**
Jamie Bussel
Kuan Butts
Tom Byrne**
Joan Byron**
Greta Byrum**
Marcia Bystryn**
Michael Cacace*
Peter Cafiero
Amy Cairns
Helene Caloir**

Juan Camilo Osorio**
Steven Caputo
Joseph Carbone**
Armando Carbonell**
Greg Carey**
Francesca Carlow
Angie Carpenter
Joan Carty**
Jan Casimir
Colin Cathcart**
Peter Cavallaro
Peter Cavaluzzi
Jean Celender
Vishaan Chakrabarti*
Manju Chandrasekhar
Art Chang**
Jason Chapin**
Susan
    Chapman-Hughes
Sarah Charlop-Powers
Nupur Chaudhury
Kevin Chavers*
Don Chen
John Chen
Terrance Cheng**
Amy Chester**
Lionel Chitty
Jun Choi*
Donald Christian
Rory Christian
David Church**
Frank Cicero*
Greg Clark
Patty Clark
Patty Clarke
Jonah Coe-Scharff
Arnold Cohen**
Frank Cohen*
Nevin Cohen**
Jeremy
    Colangelo-Bryan
Henry Coleman**

Louis Coletti
Bret Collazzi
Lorraine Collins
Sheena Collum
April Condon**
Bill Conis
Kevin Corbett*
Felipe Correa**
Anthony Coscia*
Linda Cox**
Carter Craft
Jeremy Creelan**
Jennifer Cribbs**
Rebecca Gilman
    Crimmins
Michael Critelli*
Deborah
    Cullen-Morales**
Jeorge Cymon
Karolina Czeczek
Haya Daawi
Christopher Daggett*
Dorian Dale
Emmett Daly**
Candace Damon**
George Davidson
Peter Davidson
Lee Davis
Pierre de Brun
Michelle de la Uz**
Xavier de Souza
    Briggs**
Jack Dean
Tabitha Decker
Joshua DeFlorio
Joseph Della Fave**
Alfred DelliBovi
Steven Demichele
Stephen DeNardo**
Barry Diggs
Stephen Dilts**
David Dinkins**
Daniel D'Oca**

Shaun Donovan**

Thomas Patrick Dore, Jr. *

William E. Dornbos**

Brendan Dougher

Nancy Douzinas

Ruth Douzinas

Susannah Drake

Jonathan Drapkin**

Frances Dunwell

Douglas Durst*

Eva Lauren Durst*

Helena Durst

Projjal Dutta**

Susannah Dyen**

Roxanne Earley

Ralph Eckstrand

Caroline Ehrlich**

Peter Elkowitz**

Christopher (Kim) Elliman

Logan Emser

Carlos Encarnacion**

Amy Engel**

Joel Ettinger

Antalovsky Eugen**

Ann Fangmann**

Irene Fanos Barth**

Ed Fare

Rachel Fee**

Thomas Fehn

Alexander Felson**

Leo Fernandez**

Fernando Ferrer

Jeffrey Ferzoco**

Luke Fichthorn*

Marianna Fierro

Barbara Fife*

David Fink

Adam Finkin

Joseph Fiordaliso**

James Fitzgerald*

Steve Flax

Fiona Fletcher-Smith**

James Florio*

Michael Flynn

Jeanne Fox**

Patrick Foye

Adam Frampton

Paul Francis

Barbara Franco

Michael Francois**

Emil Frankel

Doreen Frasca*

Adam Freed**

Michael Freedman-Schnapp

John Freeman**

Lance Freeman**

Omar Freilla**

Amy Freitag

Ben Fried

Adam Friedman**

Mike Frumin

Ester Fuchs**

Pete Fuller

Kim Gaddy**

Margarita Gagliardi**

Timur Galen*

Jim Gallagher**

Bill Galligan

Emily Gallo

Drew Galloway

Mario Gandelsonas

Margo Garant

Ana Garcia**

Carmelo Garcia

Arturo Garcia-Costas**

Sargent Gardiner**

Samuel Gardner**

Dan Garodnick

David Garten

Marianne Garvin**

Nicole Gelinas**

Rosalie Genevro**

Lourdes German

Sean Ghio**

Mary Ann Gilmartin

Peter Glus**

Jennifer Godenzo

Dara Goldberg

William Golden**

Robert Goldsmith**

Elizabeth Goldstein

Jonathan Goldstick**

Ann Golob**

Daisy Gonzalez**

Edward Goodell**

Kirk Goodrich**

Emily Gordon**

Mark Gorton

Jerome Gottesman

Ingrid Gould Ellen**

David Green

David Greenbaum

Amber Greene**

Toni Griffin

Maxine Griffith*

John Griswold

Elaine Gross**

Dennis Grossman

Nick Grossman**

Eric Guerra

Ashok Gupta**

Javier Guzman**

Rosanne Haggerty**

Yoav Hagler

Lynn Haig**

Veronique "Ronnie" Hakim

Elizabeth Hamby**

Emily Hamilton

Richard Haray*

Jordan Hare

Fletcher Harper**

Britt Harter**

Molly Hartman

Robert Harvey**

Ryan Harvey**

April Hawkins

Tracey Heaton

Suzanne Heidelberger*

Bill Heinzen

Jeanne Henry

Jeanne Herb**

Peter Herman*

Daniel Hernandez**

Mateu Hernández**

Andrew Herz**

Alexandra Herzan

Laura Jo Hess

Tony Hiss**

Dylan Hixon*

Claire Hoch

Deborah Hoffman**

Douglas Horne

Lois Howes

Kerry Hughes*

Carri Hulet

David Huntington*

Hiroo Ichikawa**

Arthur Imperatore

Arthur Imperatore, Jr.**

Adam Isles*

Kenneth Jackson*

Klaus Jacob

Marc Jahr**

Kiki Jamieson

Patricia Jenny**

Curt Johnson**

Nathan Johnson

Dennis Jones

Mary Jones**

Alexander Jonlin

Melissa Jorgensen

Marc Joseph

Paul Josephson*

Abha Joshi-Ghani**

Amy Kacala**

Melissa Kane**

Sabrina Kanner*

Dave Kapell**

Daniel Kaplan**

Marjorie Kaplan**

Richard Kaplan

Peter Kasabach**

Anaita Kasad*

Barbara Kauffman**

Sarah Kaufman

Madeline Kaye

Jesse Keenan**

Marcia Keizs

Carol Kellermann**

Gregory Kelly*

Sue Kelly**

Tara Kelly

David Kennedy

Kelly Kennedy**

Zia Khan

Iyad Kheirbek

Nathaniel Kimball

Michael Kimmelman

Kleo King**

Inbar Kishoni

Matthew Kissner*

Alex Klatskin**

James Klauder

Michael Klein

Naomi Klein

Linda Kleinbaum**

Steven Kleppin**

Nathaniel Klipper

Robert Knapp**

Hope Knight*

Anna Knoell

Alex Knopp**

Kim Knowlton**

Kenneth Knuckles**

Fran Kohler

Charles Komanoff

Peter Koo

David Kooris**

Pamela Koprowski**

Mitchell Korbey*

James Korein**

Seth Kramer**

Alisa Kreynes**

Jay Kriegel

Matthew Kroll

Philip Kuchma**

Nils Kuehn

John Kukral*

Charles Kuperus

Susannah Kyen

Craig Lader

Rachel LaForest**

Judith Lagano*

Naveen Lamba**

Brad Lander**

Joshua Landes**

Philip Langdon**

Justin Lapatine**

Jessica Lappin**

Christopher LaTuso*

Kevin Law**

Paul Lecroart**

Susan Lederman**

Karen Lee

Matt Lee

Jill Lerner*

Mark Lesko**

Trent Lethco*

Christopher Levendos

Mark Levine

Juanita Lewis**

Neal Lewis**

Paul Lewis**

Roland Lewis**

Kimberly Libman**

Kay LiCausi**

Robert Lieber**

Laurie Lieberman

Jackie Lightfield

James Lima**

Greg Lindsay

Megan Linkin**

Britt Liotta

Ya-Ting Liu

Peter Lobo

Kayleigh Lombardi**

Dave Lombino

Dina Long

Raymond Long**

Måns Lönnroth

Julio López Varona**

Brian Loughlin**

Gina Lovasi

Luis Luna**

Jason Lynch

Mary Lynch-Lloyd

Andrew Lynn

Betsy MacLean**

Nicole Maher**

Sergej Mahnovski**

Charles Maikish

Alan Maiman
Jerry Maldonado**
Matthew Maldonado
Nadine Maleh
Alan Mallach**
Shambhavi Manglik**
Raju Mann
Debbie Mans**
Andrew Manshel**
Joseph Maraziti**
Kristin Marcell
Anthony Marchetta**
Tom Marchwinski
Christopher Marcinkoski
Mark Marcucci*
Marvin Markus
Ariella Maron**
Michael Marrella
Theresa Marshall**
Ron Martere
Jorge Martinez
Andrew Mathias*
Marc Matsil**
Charlotte Matthews**
Alex Matthiessen
David Mayer
David McCarthy**
George McCarthy
Nick McClintock
Douglas McCoach*
Paul McConnell
Kevin McDonald**
Debra McDowell
Fawn McGee
Joseph McGee**
E. Phillip McKain**
Dan McPhee
Linda Mead**
Carolyn Grossman Meagher
Christopher Meberg
Manasvi Menon**
Petra Messick
Gabe Metcalf
Melanie Meyers**
Alana Miller**
Dawn Miller
Donna Milrod
Howard Milstein
Peter Miscovich**
Sanjay Mody**
Jeffrey Moerdler**
Josh Mohrer
T. Niklas Moran

Thomas Moran
Tom Morgan
Armando Moritz-Chapelliquen
Patrick Morrissy**
Leah Moskowitz
Britta Mulderrig**
Dalia Munenzon
Elizabeth Murphy**
J. Andrew Murphy
Andrew Murray
Mark Muyskens Swier**
Regina Myer**
Nathan Myers
Aaron Naparstek
Ellen Neises**
Matthew Nemerson**
Lois New
Kristina Newman-Scott
Foster Nichols**
Jan Nicholson*
Suzanne Nienaber
Karima Nigmatulina**
John Nolon**
Guy Nordenson**
Alyssa Norwood**
Joseph Oates
Michael O'Boyle
Nelson Obus
Raymond Ocasio**
Mark O'Luck**
Doug O'Malley**
Michael Oppenheimer**
Richard Oram*
Jack Orchulli**
Jon Orcutt
Kate Orff**
Patricia Ornst**
Larisa Ortiz**
Ty Osbaugh
Henk Ovink**
Shauneequa Owusu
Robert Paaswell**
Peter Paden**
Norma Padron**
Sotiris Pagdadis
Mitchell Pally**
Stephen Palmese**
Chris Pangilinan**
James Parrott**
Charles Patton**
Kristen Pawling
Kevin Pearson*
Deroy Peraza
Jerilyn Perine**

Lee Perlman
Anthony Perno**
Alexis Perrotta
Frank Petrone
Dawn Phillips**
Elisa Picca
Barbara Picower
Seth Pinsky*
Rob Pirani**
Michael Piscitelli**
Philip Pitruzzello**
Clint Plummer**
Marianne Pollak**
Richard Polton**
Merrill Pond**
Paul Ponteiri
Todd Poole**
John Porcari
Amale Port
Jason Post*
Matt Powers**
Neysa Pranger**
Thomas Prendergast*
Michael Preston**
David Pringle**
Milton Puryear*
Andri Putri
Jim Quinn**
Michael Rabinowitz
Douglas Rae**
Isella Ramirez**
John Raskin
Richard Ravitch*
Cathe Reams
Gregg Rechler*
Scott Rechler*
Jason Redd**
James Redeker
Ingrid Reed**
Michael Regan*
Terry Reilly**
Peter Reinhart**
Michael Replogle
Erin Reuss-Hannafin**
Antonio Reynoso
Damon Rich**
Donovan Richards
Denise Richardson*
Todd Richman*
Anna Ricklin
Marc Ricks*
Alle Ries-Mendoza**
Lisa Rivers
Rich Robbins**
Stephen Roberson**

Christopher Roberts
Richard Roberts**
Martin Robins**
Carrie Rocha**
Judith Rodin
Arlene Rodriguez**
Matt Roe
Sharon Roerty**
Elizabeth Rogers
Ed Romaine
Steve Romalewski
Ambika Roos
Richard Roper**
Gary Rose*
Steve Rosenberg**
Scott Rosenstein
Eric Rothman
Wendy Rowden**
Mary Rowe**
Christina Rubenstein**
Scott Russell
Gene Russianoff**
Ryan Russo
Kobi Ruthenberg
Brent Ryan
Sruthi Sadhujan
Janette Sadik-Khan*
Lynne Sagalyn*
KC Sahl
Sean Sallie
Joe Salvo
Andrew Salzberg
Lucas Sánchez**
Elliot Sander*
Eric Sanderson**
Thomas Santiago
Anthony Santino
John Santora*
Robert Santy**
Laura Schaefer
Rich Schaffer
Joshua Schank**
Oliver Schaper
Matthew Schatz**
Jay Schneiderman
Jonathan Schrag**
Samuel Schwartz*
Elliott Sclar**
Ralph Scordino
Catherine Seavitt**
Paula Segal
Rafi Segal**
Kathryn Shafer**
Rajiv Shah
John Shapiro**

Chad Shearer
Nicky Sheats**
Bill Sheehan**
Peggy Shepard*
Stuart Shinske
Tokumbo Shobowale**
Anthony Shorris
H. Claude Shostal*
Risa Shoup
Valarie Shultz-Wilson**
Nick Sifuentes
Camilla Siggaard Andersen**
Steve Sigmund
James Simpson*
David Siscovick**
Monica Slater Stokes*
Howard Slatkin
Michael Slattery**
Stephen Jacob Smith
Jeremy Soffin**
Irma Solis
Darius Sollohub**
Randall Solomon**
Susan Solomon*
Julia Solow**
Alex Sommer
Xavier de Souza Briggs**
Sacha Spector
Maura Spery
Reggie Spinello
Jamie Springer
Thomas Stanton**
Robert Steel*
Paul Steely White**
Rodney Stiles
Scott Stonbely**
Jessie Stratton**
Scrott Strauss
Carter Strickland**
Elizabeth Strojan
Robert Stromsted*
David Strong**
Chris Sturm**
Aaron Sugiura
Richard Sun
Gail Sussman
Erika Svendsen**
Eileen Swan**
Pat Swann**
Michael Sweeney*
Mark Swier**
Kent Swig*
Nava Tabak
Warren Tackenberg

Luther Tai
Debra Tantleff**
Lacey Tauber
Jordan Taylor**
Marilyn Taylor*
Sharon Taylor
Matt Tepper
Kellie Terry-Sepulveda**
Richard Thigpen*
Ron Thomas**
Tupper Thomas**
William Thompson**
Ahmed Tigani
Paul Timpanelli**
Leanne Tintori Wells
KT Tobin
Elizabeth Torres**
Ritchie Torres
Timothy Touhey**
Darryl Towns*
Anthony Townsend**
Brian Trelstad**
Polly Trottenberg
Shin-pei Tsay
Vincent Tufo**
Barbara Turk
Edward Ubiera
Barbara Udell**
Seth Ullman
Radhika Unnikrishnan
Javier Valdes**
Midori Valdivia
David Van Zandt
Veronica Vanterpool**
Leonardo Vazquez
Lou Venech
Jim Venturi
Jane Veron*
Paul Victor**
RuthAnne Visnauskas
Jon Vogel**
James Von Klemperer
David Waggonner
Karen Wagner
Seth Wainer
Donna Walcavage**
Jay Walder
Peter Waldt**
Jed Walentas

Darren Walker
Sean Walter
Christopher Walters
Eric Wang
Qi Wang
Christopher Ward**
Natalie Ward**
Theresa Ward
Alexandros Washburn**
Matthew Washington**
Orson Watson
Celia Weaver**
Kevin Webb
David Weinberger
Ben Wellington**
Gregory Wessner
Jonathan Westin**
William Wheeler
Sean Jeffrey White
A. Dennis White
Peter White**
Rachel Wieder
Kevin Willens
Barika Williams**
Marlon Williams
Sarah Williams**
Tim Williams**
Michael Willig**
Craig Willingham
Richard Windram
Randy Wissel
Daniel Wood**
Alicia Woodsby**
Joelle Woodson
Lindsay Woodson
Cortney Worrall**
Lyle Wray**
Kathy Wylde
William M. Yaro
Sondra Youdelman**
Michelle Young
Brian Yudewitz
Dan Zarrilli
Audrey Zibelman**
Yelena Zolotorevskaya
John Zuccotti

We are grateful for the intellectual input provided via the Milstein Forums on New York's Future.

Rohit Aggarwala
David Armour
Richard Bagger
Larry Belinsky
Anthony Borelli
Tonio Burgos
Armando Carbonell
Anthony Coscia
Andrew Farkas
Michael Fascitelli
Patrick Foye
Jerry Gottesman
Gary Hack
Leo Hindery
David Klinges
Jay Kriegel
Tom Madison
Marvin Markus
Howard Milstein
Angela Pinsky
Seth Pinsky
John Porcari
Richard Ravitch
Scott Rechler
Ed Rendell
Lucius Riccio
Denise Richardson
Marc Ricks
Stephen Ross
Lynne Sagalyn
Elliot Sander
Rob Schiffer
Samuel Schwartz
Jim Simpson
Jeffrey Stewart
Marilyn Jordan Taylor
Bill Thompson
Julia Vitullo-Martin
Thomas Wright
Bob Yaro

*RPA Board of Directors

**Members of the RPA State & Program Committees, Fourth Regional Plan Committee, Working Groups, and Community Partners

PARTNER ORGANIZATIONS

A special thanks to our nonprofit and academic partners who work with us to create a more equitable and sustainable tri-state region.

Alliance for Downtown New York
American Littoral Society
Association for a Better New York
Association for Neighborhood Housing & Development
Bike Tarrytown
Bridgeport Neighborhood Trust
Bronx River Alliance
Brooklyn Greenway Initiative
Business Council of Fairfield County
Center for an Urban Future
Citizens Budget Commission
Columbia University Graduate School of Architecture, Planning & Preservation
Community Service Society of New York
Community Voices Heard
East Coast Greenway Alliance
Rutgers University Edward J. Bloustein School of Planning & Public Policy
Enterprise Community Partners
Environmental Defense Fund
ERASE Racism
Fair Housing Justice Center
Friends of Hudson River Park
Greater Jamaica Development Corporation
Hester Street Collaborative
Housing & Community Development Network of New Jersey
Hudson River Waterfront Conservancy
Hudson Valley Rail Trail
Ironbound Community Corporation
La Casa de Don Pedro
Lincoln Institute of Land Policy
Long Island Housing Partnership
Make the Road Connecticut
Make the Road New York
Merritt Parkway Trail Alliance
Motor Parkway East
Municipal Art Society
National Association of City Transportation Officials
Natural Areas Conservancy
Natural Resources Defense Council
New Jersey Bike & Walk Coalition
New Jersey Board of Public Utilities
New Jersey Future
New Jersey Highlands Council

New Jersey Institute of Technology
New York-New Jersey Trail Conference
New York Academy of Medicine
New York Building Congress
New York Communities for Change
New York Housing Conference
New York League of Conservation Voters
New York University Furman Center for Real Estate & Urban Policy
New York University Rudin Center for Transportation Policy & Management
Newark Alliance
Newark Regional Business Partnership
NYPIRG Straphangers Campaign
Open House New York
Open Space Institute
Orange County Land Trust
Pace University Land Use Law Center
Partnership for New York City
Partnership for Strong Communities
Pattern for Progress
People Friendly Stamford
PlaceWorks
Pratt Center for Community Development
Project for Public Spaces
Riders Alliance
Right to the City
Scenic Hudson
Science & Resilience Institute at Jamaica Bay
Shawangunk Valley Conservancy
SUNY New Paltz
The Harbor Ring
The Nature Conservancy (New York)
The New School Tishman Environment & Design Center
Time of Day Media
TransitCenter
Transportation Alternatives
Tri-State Transportation Campaign
Trust for Public Land
Upper Manhattan Empowerment Zone
Urban Justice Center
Vision Long Island
WE ACT for Environmental Justice
World Bank

STAFF & INTERNS

Creating this plan would not have been possible without the incredible dedication and passion of the RPA team over the last five years.

Staff

Tessa Andrew
Ana Baptista
Richard Barone
Vanessa Barrios
Alex Belensz
Maya Borgenicht
Dare Brawley
Ellis Calvin
Lilly Chin
Jane Cooke
Chasity Cooper
Brian Dennis
Jim Finch
Robert Freudenberg
Moses Gates
Ricardo Gotla
Allison Henry
Christine Hsu
Rossana Ivanova
Doneliza Joaquin
Christopher Jones
Melissa Kaplan-Macey
Christina Kata
Amanda Kennedy
Amie Kershbaum
David Kooris
Emily Korman
Kyle Kozar
Robert Lane
David Lee
Sharai Lewis-Gruss
Mark Lohbauer
Alex Marshall
Sarabrent McCoy
Courtenay Mercer

Juliette Michaelson
Lucrecia Montemayor
Ben Oldenburg
Howard Permut
Corey Piasecki
Alyssa Pichardo
Robert Pirani
Wendy Pollack
Emily Roach
Nicolas Ronderos
David Sabatino
Steven Salzgeber
Pierina Sanchez
Daniel Schned
Mandu Sen
Sarah Serpas
Sanjay Seth
Melat Seyoum
Janani Shankaran
Dani Simons
Kate Slevin
Roma Tejada
Emily Thenhaus
Petra Todorovich-Messick
Laura Tolkoff
Karen Trella
Julia Vitullo-Martin
Jackson Whitmore
Thomas Wright
Robert Yankana
Robert D. Yaro
Zachary Zeilman
Fiona Zhu
Jeffrey Zupan

Interns

Ahmad Abu-Khalaf
David Andrew
Kellan Cantrell
Corey Chao
Alex Chohlas-Wood
Dustin Fry
Noni Ghani
Crystal Godina
Dennis Harvey
Shahneez Haseeb
Adia Klein
Taylor LaFave
Zoe Linder-Baptie
Mariana Llano
Reva Marathe
Claire Mardian
Alexandra Moscovitz
Anna Oursler
David Perlmutter
Michael Phillips
Rebecca Ramsey
Ann Regan
David Young Shin
Samudyatha Subbarama
Eline Toes
Renae Widdison
Xinyun Wu
Xu Yuan

Regional Plan Association

New York
One Whitehall St, 16th Floor
New York, NY 10004

New Jersey
179 Nassau St, 3rd Floor
Princeton, NJ 08542

Connecticut
Two Landmark Sq, Suite 108
Stamford, CT 06901

rpa.org
fourthplan.org